D1551553

PRAISE FOR *WHEN WOMEN STOOD*

"A fascinating account of how, throughout history, women in sports took the lead—and continue to lead—in the journey to equality with the other half of the population."—**Sandy Rosenthal**, author of *Words Whispered in Water: Why the Levees Broke in Hurricane Katrina*

"Alexandra Allred tells the stories of the unknown, the unheard, and the unpopular truth of women in sports."—**Chenell Brooks**, "Coach SoHo," defensive coordinator and football Hall of Famer

"Cascading through centuries of time, this book quickly engages the reader as it highlights the rarely told stories of women sport icons, from centuries past to the well-known game changers of today. The author's research and historical insights in this eye-opener delve into the tumultuous plight of women in sports and the dysfunctional social norms they continually face . . . and break."—**Andrea Harkins**, author, speaker, and world champion martial artist

"A respectful tribute to remarkable women influencers and the historical contributions they made throughout sport and society. An inspiration to all."—**Jill Bakken Linder**, U.S. Olympic bobsledder

"This book took me on a journey to realizing the fundamental truth I had been missing: For women, sports represent freedom—the freedom to control their own bodies and their own destiny. For a history buff, it's a feast. For someone studying women's history, it's essential."—**Lissa Bryan**, history enthusiast and author of *The End of All Things*

"An original, important, and timely contribution to women's history. Focusing on the struggle for equality in sports, Allred vividly illuminates how this affects every other aspect of the ongoing fight by women for our rightful place in the world. Thoroughly researched, the book is also compelling and highly readable."—**Jean Kilbourne**, award-winning documentary filmmaker (*Killing Us Softly*), public speaker, writer, and activist

"*When Women Stood* inspired me. The strong and courageous women profiled have paved the way for so many girls to have opportunities that their grandmothers would not have dreamed of. I'm reaching for my gym bag now."—**Holly Kondras**, president of Wish Publishing, the first women's sports publisher

When Women Stood

*The Untold History of Females
Who Changed Sports and the World*

Alexandra Allred

ROWMAN & LITTLEFIELD
Lanham • Boulder • New York • London

Published by Rowman & Littlefield
An imprint of The Rowman & Littlefield Publishing Group, Inc.
4501 Forbes Boulevard, Suite 200, Lanham, Maryland 20706
www.rowman.com

86-90 Paul Street, London EC2A 4NE, United Kingdom

British Library Cataloguing in Publication Information Available

Library of Congress Cataloging-in-Publication Data
Names: Allred, Alexandra Powe, 1965– author.
Title: When women stood : the untold history of females who changed sports and the world / Alexandra Allred.
Description: Lanham, Maryland : Rowman & Littlefield Publishing Group, [2023] | Includes bibliographical references and index. | Summary: "When Women Stood is an unapologetically new sport and social history that unveils the often-overlooked chronicle of women and their fight for equality. From early Amazons and suffragists to modern-day athletes and social influencers, this is an eye-opening history of women told through the always-influential world of sports"—Provided by publisher.
Identifiers: LCCN 2022025379 (print) | LCCN 2022025380 (ebook) | ISBN 9781538171349 (cloth) | ISBN 9781538171356 (epub)
Subjects: LCSH: Women athletes—History. | Women athletes—United States—History. | Sports for women—History. | Sports for women—United States—History. | Sex discrimination in sports—History. | Sex discrimination in sports—United States—History.
Classification: LCC GV709 .A43 2023 (print) | LCC GV709 (ebook) | DDC 796.082—dc23/eng/20220708
LC record available at https://lccn.loc.gov/2022025379
LC ebook record available at https://lccn.loc.gov/2022025380

To Ella and Harper,
as well as
every girl and boy who deserves the joys
of sport and self-discovery

#BeFearlessButBeKind

Contents

Merely an Introduction: To the Most Complicated and
Brilliant History of Women in Sport and Society . . .   ix

Chapter 1   Early Women Warriors to Domesticity   1

Chapter 2   The Media Image of Women of Enlightenment   9

Chapter 3   White Women in Sport   19

Chapter 4   The Women's Suffrage Movement : A Step Up
             to First Base   27

Chapter 5   Women of Color and Their Place in the
             Women's Movement   39

Chapter 6   The Importance of Race, Sports, and the
             Polite Society   53

Chapter 7   Women, War, and Their Entry into Sport   63

Chapter 8   A League of Their Own   77

Chapter 9   The Real History behind Title IX and the
             Battle of the Sexes   95

Chapter 10   Media Relations and the Second-Wave Woman   105

Chapter 11   The Third Wave and the Women of the 1980s
             and 1990s   119

Chapter 12   Exploitation of the Female Image   137

Chapter 13   Modern Medicine for the Modern Woman   151

Chapter 14   The (Recognized) Entry of Lesbians in Sport   171

Chapter 15   The Closing of the Twentieth Century   179

Chapter 16   Sports and Abuse   195

Chapter 17   The Fourth Wave in Sports and Society   205

Chapter 18   Transgender Female Athletes in Sport   219

Chapter 19   Title IX in the New Millennium   237

Chapter 20   Game Changers   249

Chapter 21   Where to Go from Here?   267

Postscript   281

Notes   287

Acknowledgments   329

Index   331

About the Author   351

Merely an Introduction

To the Most Complicated and Brilliant History of Women in Sport and Society . . .

But for brief moments in time, women have rarely held positions of power in patriarchal societies. Instead, the rights of women have been heavily controlled so that specific groups could wield power. The standard of beauty was set for women by these patriarchal cultures as was the manner of women's dress, where they could go, and with whom they could travel. The right to vote, to voice an opinion, and even to marry was never a woman's choice. Her value was tied exclusively to domestic chores, childbearing, and appearance. Even what and how she ate was linked to femininity.

Early literature, from fairy tales and historical accounts, portrayed women as one-dimensional characters who, while present, were inconsequential to important events. Well into the twentieth century, the perfect female was quiet, obedient, and in need of saving. And so it was that when a wayward female hoped to fly a plane, ride a bicycle, enter a race, or put on a pair of pants, repercussions were swift and often harsh.

Today, the idea that a woman wearing trousers could threaten societal values is hard to imagine, yet even in 2020, girls were forbidden from wearing pants or shorts to school, even in the United States. A charter school in North Carolina, for example, was taken to court for its demand that girls uphold "traditional values" by wearing skirts.[1] Long is the history that women, through fashion, uphold patriarchal systems.

In 1938, when a woman appeared in court to testify as a witness to a burglary case, she shocked the courtroom by appearing in slacks. The judge admonished Helen Hulick (1908–1989), also a renowned educator and pioneer in audio-verbal therapy, and sent her home to change her clothing before she could testify. True to female pant-wearing behavior, she returned on two separate occasions wearing her trousers. She was given a five-day jail sentence.[2]

It was well into the 1960s when younger women began wearing pantsuits to their place of work, which were scornfully viewed by men;

however, in France, it was not until 2012 that a two-hundred-year ban on women wearing pants was lifted.

Women had so little to aspire to and had so little control in their own lives that fashion became their leverage. While they also fought for fashion equality, many more succumbed to societal demands. Women of centuries past aspired to have sixteen- to twenty-inch waists, collapsed under unimaginably heavy petticoats, and stunted and deformed their own bodies to fit horrific ideals at the detriment of their own health.

As women fought for their rights (and health), it was sport—again and again—that promised independence, strength, and happiness. While early physicians declared women too frail for such endeavors, women knew better. By the 1800s, softball became popular with women, but they would be restricted from play for well over one hundred years. With Title IX, the sport evolved, rapidly becoming one of the most popular recreational, high school, and collegiate sports in the world.

By 2012, an estimated 40 million Americans, males and females, played at least one game a year with more than 65 million playing worldwide,[3] yet without warning, the International Olympic Committee (IOC) removed both baseball and softball from the Olympic Games, which ruined "the lives of millions, actually billions of women" who had used the sport for athletic scholarships, higher education, and a place in sport, according to U.S. softball legend and Olympian Lisa Fernandez (1971–).[4]

Lisa Fernandez. *Reuters/Alamy Stock Photo*

Long had been the argument that female athletes were not as exciting or competitive as men. In reality, women have been warriors, adventurers, and champions since the beginning of time.

Ronda Rousey (1987–), an Olympic bronze medalist in judo, became known to the world as a mixed martial arts (MMA) fighter who repeatedly choked out opponents within mere seconds, setting records in and out of the ring. The 2015 Rousey vs. Holly Holm (1981–) bout broke records when it sold out a seventy-thousand-seat stadium with premium seats at $468 and corporate box and VIP seats at ringside for $18,000 in mere minutes. Rousey broke another record within this same fight that would ultimately last only fifty-nine seconds into the second round.

In addition to the stadium tickets, the Rousey vs. Holm fight netted $1.1 million pay-per-view purchases. It was the first time a fight—male or female—exceeded both a million pay-per-view purchases and more than fifty-thousand fans in attendance.[5] Inside the ring, Rousey dominated. She was strong, quick, and ruthless. She was beautiful, boasted of promiscuity, sported tattoos, and cursed unapologetically. In all manner, she was a true female warrior who lived up to the history of Amazons in antiquity.

When the world got those rare glimpses of just how exciting female actors in sports, activism, and politics are, there was cause for celebration. Understanding the contributions of the other half of the world's population that has otherwise been omitted from the record books provides a much greater picture of the entirety of humanity and its history. As historian Linda Grant de Pauw wrote, "Women have always and everywhere been inextricably involved in war, but hidden from history. During wars, women are ubiquitous and highly visible; when the wars are over and war songs are sung, women disappear."[6]

In the history of women in sport, however, she would never disappear but continued to reemerge again and again. Despite the unsurmountable odds, restrictive laws, negligent medical care, and even violence levied against her, the true spirit of the female warrior could never be restrained. This is women in sport and society.

ONE

Early Women Warriors to Domesticity

Most of us have been taught that early women were the gatherers while men were the hunters, that women were bound to domestic roles because of childbearing while men roamed in battle and conquest. In reality, nomadic tribes of men and women rode and fought together, and shared parental duties and leadership positions. Couples usually lived with the woman's mother[1] and children retained the clan name of their mothers. It was not until the advent of agriculture and homesteading that inequality among sexes emerged. As more societies abandoned the nomadic lifestyle for settlements, population growth led to emerging and specialized occupation, which led to a new hierarchy based on status and wealth. What followed was "patrilocal residence," where women were expected to live with their husband's family and all land, laws, rights, and record keeping fell under the male name.[2]

Patriarchal societies are not and have never been the natural state of human behavior, but ones contrived to support male social structures. Once established, the oppression of women expanded to include racism, slavery, even sizeism and homophobia—all to give power to male landowners (and, thus subordinating and stratifying populations).

Arguably, most patriarchal systems today no longer consciously impose these antiquated ideals, but *the system* is so deeply rooted in all aspects of life that people have come to believe that patriarchy is nature's way with humans.

The women of ancient Greece, Asia, and Africa, however, lived very different lives.

THE FIRST RECORDED GAMES

Long before the first modern Olympic Games in 1896, there were others. Like today's Olympics, the ancient Greek Olympic Games were held every four years. The event was both a religious festival to honor the god Zeus

1

and a show of military prowess. Because a Greek male could be called at any time to serve in the military, it was essential that he keep himself in top physical condition at all times. Slaves, non-Greeks, and women were prohibited from attending the Games in Athens with the exceptions of young "maidens" and prostitutes. Ancient Athenian women, considered second-class citizens, were allowed to exercise only minimally.

In Sparta, however, laws were more liberal for women. By the seventh century BC, Sparta was a highly disciplined and collective society that focused on military strength and procreation. For these reasons, Spartan girls and women were expected to exercise for the greater good. They were seen as the vehicle by which Sparta could grow and dominate because, it was believed, strong women would reproduce more, making stronger babies and, thus, stronger Spartan men.

This belief in exercise allowed for a Spartan woman to become the first recorded female Olympian. In 396 BC, a woman named Kyniska (or Cyniska) entered and won the four-horse chariot race against men. As the daughter of King Archidamus II and sister to King Agesilaus, she had privileges that other women did not have, including land and horses. Because women traditionally did not and could not afford such things, there were no written rules regarding women entering the tethrippon—an extremely dangerous and prestigious nine-mile chariot race in which the owner/master of the horses could enter based solely on status and ownership. Owners did not have to race, selecting slaves instead, but there were those occasional daring owner-athletes who drove the horses. Like Kyniska.

Kyniska not only entered and drove the horses but won in the Olympic Games of 396 BC. Ill prepared for such an anomaly, no one thought to rewrite the rules and Kyniska entered the following 392 BC Games and, again, won. While denied access to the ceremony to claim her winnings, she was allowed to place her trophy in Zeus's sanctuary, a custom among tethrippon winners. True to her warrior spirit, she had her statue inscribed: "I declare myself the only woman in all Hellas to have won this crown."[3]

Indeed, hers remains a historic feat and the beginning of the female athlete's journey in sport.

HERAEAN GAMES

In the sixth century BC, the Heraean Games, dedicated to the goddess Hera, queen of Olympian gods and wife of Zeus, were the first official female competition and were held in the Olympic stadium. Unmarried young women participated in footraces (married women could watch but not participate) and the winners' names were inscribed on the columns of Hera's temple. There may also have been other events such as javelin, pentathlon, wrestling, and equestrian. However, very little is known about the Games, except that competitors wore knee-length tunics that left one shoulder and breast bare, similar to tunics working men wore. The only known recorded champion is Chloris, the mythical granddaughter of Zeus.

WOMEN'S PLACE

Because traditional ancient Greek women were considered of so little value in society, most record keepers and historians failed to document information about their day-to-day lives, including who the early female competitors were and how the Games impacted their lives. We only know more about the Spartan women because their behaviors were seen as unseemly and distasteful to rest of ancient Greece. Ancient Greek philosopher Aristotle (384–322 BC) held little respect for women, arguing in his book *Politics* that "the male is by nature better suited to leadership than the female." But he held particular disdain for the women of Sparta, whose strength and liberties he considered "contrary to nature."

Aristotle's disgust for the appearance and independence of Spartan women was a win for historians, anthropologists, and archeologists who have used his descriptions as well as those found in art, pottery, and poems to piece together a historical picture of ancient Greek women, including the lives and culture of Athenian and Spartan women. Yet his treatise on male superiority over women was also devastating for women, according to Edith Hall, a scholar of classics who specializes in ancient Greek literature and cultural history, and a professor in the Department of Classics at King's College in London. "No passage in ancient Greek or Roman literature has exerted more influence on subsequent justifications of patriarchy. Its impact can be traced from the Church Fathers and Thomas Aquinas to Hegel, Schopenhauer, and Nietzsche."[4]

Though Aristotle wrote only to disparage Spartan women, their history and contributions cannot be overstated. Spartan women could own businesses and property, partake in local politics, and speak publicly. In short, Spartan women enjoyed a much different experience than the rest of their Greek sisters.

As girls, Spartan females trained alongside boys, and sometimes men, as they sprinted, wrestled, and learned the arts of weaponry throughout puberty and into womanhood, always with emphasis on becoming strong for childbirth. This is significant as weak or sickly babies were not acceptable to the state and had to be thrown off cliffs or sent away to become slaves. It was the responsibility of strong mothers to bear, rear, and create strong male warriors.

Although these liberties for Spartan women were simply a way for the city-state to ensure strong male babies, Spartan women must be celebrated for their strength, athletic achievements, and participation in local politics. Sparta showed the world that women could and did manage property and work alongside men. While Spartan women did not share the same egalitarian and communal rights and liberties as the nomadic Scythian and Amazonian tribes that dominated the Pontic steppe from seventh to the third century BC, Spartan women sat on the precipice of equality and social change.

THE AMAZONS AND ANCIENT GREECE

In literature, Amazons existed in deference to Greek gods and heroes. In Greek mythology, Amazons were a race of warrior women—the daughters of Ares, the god of war—who famously battled against Hercules, Theseus, and Bellerophon. While they lost each time (often being raped or seduced into submission), the tale of mighty women warring against these Greek heroes captivated ancient Greece. Scenes from these epic battles appeared in Greek art, on pottery, and even on sculptures that decorated such buildings as the Parthenon of Athens and other government buildings. Their strength and fierce fighting skill set were legendary.

According to legends, they were man haters; they were highly sexualized; they were lesbians; they were heterosexual; they were an all-female tribe who took on lovers only to give birth to and rear girls for another generation of Amazons, killing any male children born; they were nomads; they lived on the edge of civilization—both literally and figuratively; they were so savage that they cut off their left breasts so that they might have greater precision with bow and arrow.

Most of what was written about them was myth, such as the story of the one-breasted warrior woman. In 490 BC, a Greek historian searching to explain the name "Amazon" deduced that "mazon" sounded much like the Greek word for "breast," and "a" meant "without." From there, he surmised that Amazon could only mean these fierce women removed a breast so they could draw back their bow in war. However, the word "Amazon" is not Greek but borrowed from another ancient culture, possibly ancient Iranian, and means "warrior."

The first written record of Amazons appeared in the eighth century BC, in Homer's *Iliad*. The ancient Greek poem tells of the Trojan War and talks of Amazons or *antianeira*, which translates to "antagonists of men" or "the equal of men."[5] Although the Greeks defeated the Amazons in the *Iliad*, these antagonists of or equals to men were so mighty that feats against them lent more credibility to the victor.

Some historians of ancient Greece believe that the portrayal of Amazons as *man haters* was used to scare Athenian women into adhering to appropriate feminine behaviors. Spartan women, however, may have been encouraged, as Amazons were symbols of strength.

THE AMAZONS AND EXTINCTION

Despite dismissals of mythology, legends, and lore, Amazons did exist.

Amazons were nomads who traveled far and wide. However, most of their graves have been found in the steppes (flatlands) of Scythia (which spread from modern Ukraine; southern Russia; Central Asia, including Iran; and northern Africa).

Recovered Amazonian battle-scarred skeletons revealed that these nomadic women rode horseback for days at a time, so much so that their legs were often bowed. They were skilled archers, preferring the bow and arrow, and are credited with inventing the recurve bow. The recurve bow generates tremendous power from a small bow, thus equalizing strength differences between male and female warriors.[6] They also fought with swords, spears, and battle-axes, a favored weapon among many.

In fact, in the 1990s, German archeologist Renate Rolle (1941–) and American archeologist Jeannine Davis-Kimball (1929–2017) both made significant discoveries (independent of one another) of warrior women in southern Russia and Ukraine. Davis-Kimball, who specialized in gender studies and women of antiquity, became best known for the Amazon tombs of Scythian women who had been buried with weapons and armor. She traveled to Central Asia, where she lived for an extended period to study nomads, and, in 1994, she collaborated on archaeological excavations in Kazakhstan using DNA to identify warriors once assumed males to be early Amazons.

Amazons had their own sense of style. They were noted to wear tall, pointed hats, and wore tunics and trousers, or leggings. In fact, Amazons have been credited with inventing pants, with the earliest preserved trousers dating back to 1200–900 BC from burial sites of horsemen and women found in the Tarim Basin.[7] Archeologists have found over a thousand images of warrior women clad in trousers on Greek vase paintings, offering a greater perspective on the traditional Amazon warrior as well as differentiating her from traditional Greek women.

While proper Greek women were permitted to attend only certain religious functions, Amazons gathered with men and women for festivals, feasts, funerals, even athletic contests. The Scythian lifestyle demanded that all members of the community be proficient in hunting and gathering, and skilled in combat. Unlike the Greek women who had no legal rights, including the right to choose who they would marry, Amazons chose their partners.

The women of Scythian societies that coexisted with ancient Greeks rode, fought, hunted, and lived equal to men. They were advanced in not only military strategy and warfare, but also surgical procedures and the preservation of bodies.

"I had no idea that these women existed," Davis-Kimball said. In her previous studies she had found "no indication that women have any particular state. In fact, women are sort of invisible."[8] When she found "living proof of the Amazons," she reportedly found a genetic link between the female warriors entombed in Kazakhstan and the present nomad tribe of Kazakhs in western Mongolia.

No one knew these women existed because their freedom and strengths were deeply despised by leaders who, through art, philosophy, legend, and law, did everything to defile and later eradicate their images. As Professor Hall at the King's College of London asserts, the continued references to defeated Amazons being raped into submission demonstrates the male need for strong women "to have settled down into 'natural' patriarchal relationships."[9]

In truth, Scythian women (Amazons) were not an anomaly in women's history but true representations of who and what women were meant to be before ideologies of "appropriate behaviors." Amazons engineered women's first sportswear, created their own laws, and served as scouts, leaders, herbalists, and medicine women. In too short of time, however, they were literally written out of history.

FROM WARRIOR TO DOMESTICITY

Amazons were also forced to assimilate into societies as the world changed. When the Hun Empire collapsed in 459 BC, the nomadic people (including Amazons) who lived in Central Asia, the Caucuses, and Eastern Europe assimilated out of necessity into the civilizations they had once terrorized. It was during this period that Hua Mulan, now most recognized as the Disney version of Mulan, once fought as a warrior. The Goths, who appeared in the third century, were born of nomadic tribes and, like the Huns, were vicious, efficient warriors, both male and female. Serving as both friend and foe to the Roman Empire, the Goths would travel, fight, and travel again, plundering and looting as they went. By the sixth century, however, they were destroyed by the Eastern Roman Empire and assimilated into Roman society.

The Vikings were Scandinavian seafaring pirates and traders (mostly from Denmark, Norway, and Sweden) who raided and settled in many parts of Northwestern Europe in the eighth through eleventh centuries. Both men and women fought in battles, acted as chieftains, and took to the open seas. They used their swift boats and fierce fighting skills to strike and plunder and conquer. But, by 1066, the Viking Age came to an end. With the spread of Christianity throughout Europe, what remained of the pagan Viking "culture" assimilated. Just as the Amazons, Scythians, Huns, and Goths were demonized by historically biased cultures (most prominently from the Roman and Chinese Empires), so too were the Vikings, forever changed in history and popular culture to depict large, blond white men wearing horned helmets conquering lands with nary a female in sight unless she was to be raped and then taken as a slave.

But all of these female warriors were real. Shieldmaidens lived and fought before political and religious leaders began their active eradication of strong women from history during the Middle Ages and the rewriting of a new submissive female history through oppressive and restrictive laws.

Yet, at least one female warrior depiction in modern movies remained true. Perhaps the most realistic portrayal of female warriors is that of the Dora Milaje, the all-female special forces unit in the movie *Black Panther*. In the movie, the Amazons are called the Dora Milaje, a fictional group of warriors, a nod to the historical connection to the very real all-female military force of Dahomey, West Africa (now Benin), who the French called "Dahomey Amazon warriors." The kingdom of Dahomey and its Amazons are known to have existed from 1624 to 1894. Dahomey had been called the "Black Sparta" of its time, a fiercely militaristic society, of which the Dora Milaje were an important part, that battled neighboring tribes and fought off invading European advances during the growing slave trade.

Unlike the early Amazons from over two thousand years ago, the Dahomey Amazons date back just four centuries. As was the case with ancient Athenians and Spartans, slavery was very much a part of the Dahomey culture, and the Dahomey were active in the transatlantic slave trade until 1893.[10] As warriors, they both conquered and enslaved but also fell to slavery if captured. Yet, as European nations began invading and occupying in the "scramble for Africa," many of the military forces of these nations were met by the Dahomey Amazons.

While historians attribute the disappearance of these warriors to their nomadic lifestyle and oral history that left no real record of geographical and/or territorial change, the Dahomey warrior lived on through witness accounts. By the 1940s, it was believed the last of the warriors had died, but a Beninese scholar reportedly met "the only Amazon still alive" in the village of Kinta in 1978. Her name was Nawi.

Nawi told stories of fighting the French in 1892, destroying her enemies while fighting alongside her sisters. Nawi died in late 1979, well over one hundred years old, not as a warrior but a woman reduced to domestic duties following one of the few but final defeats the Dahomey warriors ever knew. When the French ultimately conquered the Dahomey in 1892, they quickly passed a decree prohibiting women from any further service in the military or bearings arms.[11]

Of that last battle, it was said that of the 434 Amazons who held their ground against the encroaching French battalion, only 17 women survived. By the nineteenth century, many oral traditions became written accounts, yet questions persist: How many more female warriors fought on the vast, often unforgiving African continent? What impact had they made in their territories? Whatever the questions, one answer is most evident: The Amazons did exist.

Two

The Media Image of Women of Enlightenment

The image of women through the "rise of the Western civilization" (sixteenth century) and the Age of Enlightenment (eighteenth century)—considered a period of intellectual, social, and political ferment—was intensely focused on the hegemonic feminine ideal. How a woman looked, dressed, behaved, married, prayed, and lived was directly tied to her father's and husband's social standing and to those around him. The image was classically white, frail, and submissive. It was also quite unrealistic.

Throughout the sixteenth and seventeenth centuries, the activities of women are known to historians mostly through church record keeping and literature. The Roman Catholic Church was the single most powerful church in Western Europe, meticulous in its record keeping and rooted in control of its people, and highly critical in its portrayal of women. All women lived with daily reminders of their inadequacies. The Bible, church officials preached, told of how women were to be controlled. The idea that women could be athletes, warriors, landowners, or, in any fashion, independent, was an affront to the teachings of the Church and to man. Or so it was taught.

It is important to understand how the female was portrayed in both literature and the church throughout history as these sweeping idealisms fought to undermine any women who entered the world of sport. Aristotle argued that women were ruled by their reproductive systems. While the male was reportedly able to control his sexual urges, the woman, he said, could not, and throughout history women have been portrayed as whores and corrupt and lustful beings, all the while living under strict patriarchal systems that denied them freedom, education, travel, financial security, ownership, and independence.

By the eighteenth century, however, the Church had created an ideal of femininity for women of wealth or higher economic standing. The image of the ideal female was now of the chaste virgin, the innocent, the subservient and desirable.[1] Newer and greater emphasis was placed upon the upper classes to ensure that their women were creatures of leisure to emphasize the position of her man in society. Throughout the eighteenth century, the characterization of women paralleled society. When females were pure, virginal, and delicate, only then could society be strong. Strong women, however, could jeopardize societal structure.

This was, of course, problematic, as the Industrial Revolution relied upon all of its working-class citizens to remain unchanged. Society could not afford—literally—for those women to become women of leisure. What remained a constant for all women, no matter their socio-economic standing, was the patriarchal system. Female insubordination—independent thought or economic standing—could not be tolerated within the family any more than it could be accepted in society.

THE ESSENTIAL AND NONESSENTIAL FEMALE

Throughout the early centuries, moving into the early fifteenth and six-teenth centuries, it is absurd to think of women, nonroyal women, as anything but nose-to-the-grindstone warrior women fighting for food and survival against disease, famine, and the relentless assaults of war and territorial encroachment upon their people and their own persons. This is who women were and who they had to be to survive. However, the image of the helpless, frail feminine was important.

By the Victorian and Industrial Revolution eras, the typical working-class woman worked long, laborious hours for diminished pay compared to her male counterparts only to endure the sole responsibilities of child care and domestic work. A woman's work was never done.[2] Quite liter-ally, the lives of these nineteenth-century working women were centered on family and factory while men of any status were afforded leisure time.

Despite the need for most women to work, women who tilled the fields, worked as dressmakers or domestics, and toiled in factories or mines were not always accurately or legally recorded or paid as employees. Historians have found that women's work was often not included in of-ficial records, thereby distorting the census returns from the early nine-teenth century but also distorting how history portrayed women in the workforce. Historians note how early census returns during this period show blank spaces under the occupation column despite women's names entered into work documents.[3] Ironically, these women who helped stabi-lize the economy were considered *"nonessential"* for the record books and in society. This was the case around the world.

While there was not enough time in the day for working women, middle- and upper-class women had too much time on their hands. These were the *essential* women. Even those middle-class women who needed to be productive citizens for financial reasons could only undertake positions that were considered "respectable" for their status, such as governess or caregiver. These positions often were unpaid (but offered housing and shelter), since they were giving these "lucky" women life training skills for their true callings as mothers and homemakers.

For women of leisure, it was also socially acceptable to participate in a few sports, such as tennis or golf, but both their clothing attire and allowable time to move—lest they be too physically taxed—were limited. For the adolescent daughters of both the working-class and upper-class women, the preview of their own futures must have been bleak.

Into the late 1700s, archery and croquet were allowable sports for upper-class women in England, with clubs having a more social aspect than competitive. To be competitive and perspire was considered lowbrow, imitating something closer to manual labor, and was, therefore, unacceptable. But there were women who stood out—both in history and among the upper class in their physical endeavors.

In 1767, a Frenchwoman, believed to be Louise-Bonne Bunel (1728–?), made headlines when it was reported that she had been in training for an upcoming tennis match against a man, Mr. Tomkins, "for a considerable Sum of Money."[4] What made the story so extraordinary was not just that Mr. Tomkins was named as "the greatest player in England," or that Bunel had previously beaten another man, "Monseigneur le Prince de Condé" (Louis François de Bourbon, Prince of Conti), when she "threw herself into the game like a grasshopper,"[5] in 1763, but the 1767 write-up of Bunel's training was the first official record of such activity by a female athlete.

When the game took place in early 1768 before a large crowd that largely included members of the upper class and nobility, Bunel's defeat of Tomkins was upsetting to the men in attendance. Those who bet a significant amount of money demanded a rematch, unable to accept that Tomkins had lost. Eleven days later, Bunel won again by an even bigger margin. It had long been held (even taught) that women were incapable of strategic play, physical exertion, and hand-eye coordination. It had also been unnerving that Bunel had not only demonstrated the courage to play in public but had soundly beaten a male player, demonstrating a physical superiority.

Exclusive to women in sport, not only was this match the first such recorded activity, but also it would be the first coverage of a female athlete in which her appearance and fashion style were also reported upon, as she wore "a short skirt and an easy jacket, which placed no restraint upon the activity with which she flew from side to side of the Court."[6]

But it was Elizabeth Wilkinson (ca. early 1700s–?), the "Mother of Boxing," who challenged social conventions and fought a local woman in 1722 in what is believed to be the first women's boxing match. Angry that the woman had testified in court against her husband, a known criminal, Wilkinson wrote a challenge that ran in the press:

"I, Elizabeth Wilkinson, of Clerkenwell, having some words with Hannah Hyfield, and requiring satisfaction, do invite her to meet me on the stage and box with me for three guineas, each woman holding half-a-crown in each hand, and the first woman that drops her money to lose the battle."[7]

So began a prolific career in boxing during the 1720s and '30s in which Wilkinson fought bare-knuckles or with weapons, and is believed to be the first known MMA fighter. If money was involved, Wilkinson came to fight. She fought both women and men. She fought where rules stipulated the winner was the fighter who gave the most cuts with a sword,[8] continued to use the media to insult and berate opponents, and is believed to have remained undefeated. A celebrity in her own right, she enjoyed an allegiance of fans who were both commoners and aristocrats, all of whom delighted in her witty, brash, public invitations of or responses to open challenges.[9]

But it was women like Ann Glanville (1796–1880) of Cornwall, United Kingdom, who stood as not the exception but the exceptional norm. Married at a very young age, she bore fourteen children and when her husband, John Glanville, became an invalid following a prolonged illness, she took over his job as a waterman, who rowed people and cargo across the River Tamar, rowing ten-mile stretches while also running the ferry.

Noted for her large and muscular stature, Glanville always dressed in the traditional white cap and long dresses. When, however, she noted regattas (a series of races in a rowing competition) offered prize money, Glanville organized a crew of female rowers, which began more than a fifteen-year winning streak in women's racing, including the defeat of many men's teams. Local merchants sponsored Glanville for, presumably, advertisements for boats and steamship services, but also more exciting and lucrative betting opportunities.

One such bet was placed in Portsmouth in 1842, when officers of the Thirty-Sixth Regiment were to race Glanville's team. After watching her team race, however, they withdrew from the race. Again in Le Havre, a French male crew also withdrew, citing chivalry as the reason. At age sixty, she was able to retire on her winnings and became a popular figure in her country, telling stories of her time with Queen Victoria, the Prince of Wales, and the Duke of Edinburgh.[10]

When women stood against the norms, they were typically punished. Particularly in sport, only those who enjoyed a wealthy, elitist status could afford such bold actions. However, women such as Wilkinson and Glanville, uneducated and without a man, could be given a pass; but it helped immensely that many of their fans were royalty.

In the case of baseball's Dolly Vardens, the first women's professional sports team that was established in 1867, they were (temporarily) permissible because they were Black and too few cared. To date, little is known about this groundbreaking history in women's sports because the press rarely covered such events. What little information has been gleaned offers more information about what they wore (corsets, long skirts, high-button shoes) than how they played. When, in 1883, the *New York Times* did a feature on the team, great detail was given to the players' red jockey caps and different colored dresses.[11]

While women have fought for footing in the world of sport, for strength, for a sense of well-being and belonging, this has also posed a direct threat to the patriarchal system designed to keep women in place.

THE HYSTERICAL WOMEN

Hysteria, as we know it today, is defined as an uncontrollable outburst of emotion, but during the Victorian era, hysteria was considered a physical illness of females, so much so that hysteria and fainting were often linked together, as it was believed upper-class Victorian women were more prone to both. Though more myth than reality, the terms "fainting couch" and "fainting rooms" are attributed to this time period most reasonably for two reasons: tight-lacing and Sigmund Freud.

From the sixteenth to the early nineteenth centuries, corsets were used by both men and women, believed to help posture, ease back pain, and help, if not cure, scoliosis. Both men and women also used corsets as fashion, which, by 1828, introduced the ability of tight-lacing. Metal eyelets enabled lacing to be pulled so tightly that there were recorded measurements of sixteen-inch waists for the popular hourglass female figure. While those measurements became an ideal for women, particularly women of leisure, it was not uncommon for the laces to be so tight that women fainted, had trouble breathing, and, over time, developed digestive issues, internal organ damage, and deformation to the rib cage and back. Dating back as early as 1793, physicians began writing opinion pieces to alert the public of the dangers of tight-lacing.[12]

In the eighteenth and nineteenth centuries, at the height of corset popularity, "women wore corsets to shape their bodies away from nature and toward a more 'civilized' ideal form," Rebecca Gibson of American University explained. Not only that, "a woman would wear her corset for almost her entire life." Interested in the long-term effects of corseting, Gibson studied skeletal remains dating from 1700 to 1900 at the Musée de l'Homme and the Museum National d'Histoire Naturelle in Paris and at the Centre for Human Bioarchaeology at the Museum of

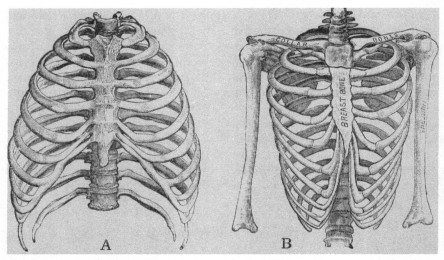

The dangers of tight-lacing. *Roger Sherman Tracy, 1889*

London. She measured the widths of rib cages and found that, over time, corseted women's rib cages had become deformed.[13] Though Victorians would come to view corset usage as vain and improper, the damage for many was already done and the notion of hysterical women and fainting couches was implanted.

Corseting and the damage it did to women was not unlike one of the first documented cultural practices that maimed and disabled females— foot binding, which was very popular in China (and Japan) in the tenth century and was a status symbol among the elite. The process typically began when a girl was four to nine years old; the foot was soaked for an extended period of time, making it soft and easier to manipulate. Then, the last four toes were bent beneath the sole of the foot with "great force," and binding cloth was used to press and hold the toes in place against the undersole or pad of the foot. Later, breaking the toes and arch with force allowed for reenforced, tighter binding to, essentially, cripple the female.[14] The desired result was a three-inch foot, which became so valued that social status and even marriage proposals hinged on the size of a woman's foot.

It stands as a reminder of how very prevalent and important it was for a patriarchal culture to physically bind its females socially, sexually, economically, and politically. It remains yet another graphic example of the treatment females endured for simply being female.[15]

Before tight-lacing, however, the *hysterical* woman already existed. The ancient Egyptians and Greeks long held that the woman's uterus was a free-floating organ that put pressure on other organs in the body, causing a kind of hysteria in the body. Philosopher and physician Galen (AD 130–210) taught that the retention of the "female seed" (free-floating uterus) within the womb created anxiety, insomnia, depression, fainting, as well as any other ailment a female might suffer. So began a problematic history in which experts, who had no working knowledge of the female anatomy, simply made up diagnoses for and of women. By the seventeenth century, male physicians decided that male semen was a healing property to the agitated uterus. If a female could not achieve an orgasm from male penetration, manual stimulation to the female genitals was prescribed, particularly to young or unmarried women, widows, even nuns, stimulation that male physicians could helpfully provide.

French neurologist and professor of anatomical pathology Jean-Martin Charcot (1825–1893) attributed female hysteria to internal injury that affected the nervous system, but it was his student and the founder of psychoanalysis, Sigmund Freud (1856–1939), who theorized that female hysteria stemmed from a woman's realization that she did not have a penis.[16]

Freud's theories, combined with his use of a fainting couch, became synonymous with the hysterical female, as that fainting couch was where his patient would lie as she received a pelvic massage from a midwife to quell the hysteria. Though, arguably, Freud made great contributions to modern science regarding data collection and man's inner thoughts, he was negligent in the way of women's health. Rather than better understand and study women, he denounced women as inconsequential other than for giving birth.

SEX, THE DRESS, AND THE MOVEMENT

In the 1880s, when women began to ride bicycles, the response was outrage. Suddenly, women were able to escape their homes for brief but exciting moments, experiencing the sensation of speed, even coasting, and, many times, seeing their own neighborhoods in ways they never had before. Their social circles grew as they moved about without chaperones.

There was, however, much harassment from the press, local and state leaders, and members of their own families. Female cyclists were perceived as "loose" as physicians warned that the female rider received sexually stimulating vibrations from the cycle itself. Once again, as throughout history, when women were empowered or free in any way, they must be "loose."

While manufacturers, enjoying the surplus of new consumers, busied themselves creating a sexual-stimulation-free bicycle seat, the Rational Dress League was founded in 1898 for the purpose of creating clothing for women that allowed them to, at last, move more freely.

In 1851, some thirty years prior, Amelia Bloomer (1818–1894) debuted the women's pantaloons (or "bloomers" as they were later called on behalf of the inventor) in London. Though the bloomers initially sold well in Britain, the vast majority of women wore the bloomers beneath their long dresses to stay in line with societal norms.

The reality was riding in heavy petticoats was dangerous, and it was for this reason that the original Rational Dress Society was founded in London in 1881, following the lead of Amelia Bloomer. It was the contention of the Rational Dress Society that no woman should have to wear more than seven pounds of underwear. In the 1850s, the "gathered" cotton and wool flannel undergarments beneath the dress often weighed up to fourteen pounds.[17]

As was so often the case, it would have to be a woman of privilege, who was above reproach from most men in Britain, a viscountess, who would argue against the sheer weight of undergarment and for a "rational" alternative. Lady Florence Harberton (1843–1911) proposed that women wear a divided skirt worn under a long coat that would be practical but also modest and respectful. As more and more women of privilege adopted this style in 1895, so, too, did the press and fashion industries.

By 1890, women in the United States were also wearing looser, split skirts with baggy bloomers as undergarments; and, like their British counterparts, female riders found themselves scrutinized as sexually aggressive, immoral, and reckless. American press and physicians suggested that bicycle riding could make women sterile, cause depression, heighten anxiety, and produce "bicycle face."

Using the threat of beauty to frighten women from cycling, physicians warned against a "medical" condition that could irreversibly change a woman's face by strain and exhaustion, causing deep wrinkles, pursed lips, and a furrowed brow. It was claimed that overexertion, the upright position on the wheel, and the effort to maintain one's balance tended to produce a wearied "bicycle face."[18]

The patriarchal system was cracking. At least, this was how many Victorians viewed it, and at its roots, the bicycle was taking its women much farther than its two wheels allowed. Female cyclists, it was feared, were moving toward independence. An editorial in the 1896 *Munsey's Magazine* stated: "To men, the bicycle . . . was merely a new toy. . . . To women, it was a step upon which they rode into a new world."[19]

In 1891, a writer for the *Sunday Herald* wrote in "The Woman on a Bicycle" that, "I think the most vicious thing I ever saw in all my life is a woman on a bicycle—and Washington is full of them. I had thought that cigarette smoking was the worst thing a woman could do, but I have changed my mind."[20]

For such alarmists, the words of Susan B. Anthony (1820–1906), a social reformer and women's rights activist, must have been terrifying when, in 1895, she said, "I think [bicycling] has done more to emancipate women than anything else in the world. It gives women a feeling of freedom and self-reliance. I stand and rejoice every time I see a woman ride by on a wheel." Were this not enough, her friend and fellow suffragist Elizabeth Cady Stanton (1815–1902) added to Anthony's sentiment, saying that "the bicycle will inspire women with more courage, self-respect, self-reliance," predicting that the bicycle would transform the lives of women as well as cultural and political norms and become an emblem of women's rights.[21]

Cultural norms were being transformed. In 1902, British figure skater Madge Syers (1881–1917) noted that while ice-skating was a male-only sport, the rule book did not specify that women could not enter. She entered and earned a silver medal, skating in a long, heavy dress that extended to her skates. The gold medalist, Swedish skater Ulrich Salchow, repeatedly tried to give his medal to Syers, saying he believed she had actually won the competition.[22]

Immediately following the event, the World Figure Skating Championship (WFSC) barred women from skating in the World Championships, citing "concern" that long skirts prevented judges from properly watching the competitor's feet. Syers fought to have skirts raised to midcalf,[23] but future skaters would then frequently be penalized for indecency if the skirt briefly flew up to the knees.

THE HISTORY OF CLOTHES AND CONTROLLER OF WOMEN

Women and fashion have inextricably been entwined throughout history, not by choice but by force. How a woman presented herself had great bearing on the status of her father, then husband, and his station in society. Her appearance helped guide male nonrelatives to understand how to address the woman, a second-class citizen.

These double standards first appeared in ancient Sparta, Athens, and other Greek city-states when appointed magistrates, called γυναικονόμοι or "controllers of women," monitored how women presented themselves in the fourth century BC. Such power was given to the controllers of women that they could determine if a woman wore too much gold, spent too much money on her clothing, or dressed in a manner offensive to others, which then allowed the controllers of women to take the women's fineries, impose punishments, and even rip the clothing from the women's bodies.

The controllers of women also took care to make sure a woman's fabric coincided with her status. The stola, for example, a long tunic that only married women or widows could wear, alerted males that the wearer should be granted deference. It also offered greater protection to females and so it was not unusual that other women attempted to wear the stola as self-protection. If caught, the woman would be severely punished as she had *tricked* males.

Conversely, if a man assaulted a woman dressed as a slave girl or prostitute, punishment was far less as the female had less importance in society. It was the historical beginning of the argument "that how a woman dresses might invite a sexual assault upon her."[24]

While the magistrates were no longer called *controllers of women* through time, that same system that monitored how women dressed continued as a means of establishing control over the feminine ideal. As will be discussed, even into the year 2022, the uniforms of female athletes were designed for visual appeal for fans while uniforms for male athletes have always been designed for functionality.

THREE

White Women in Sport

It was not all women but women of leisure who first engaged in (light) sport, and while systematically unfair, it was these women who then pushed the boundaries to show what the female body could do. But even before the first women of privilege took to the tennis courts and golf courses, it had to be a woman with great communal standing to be the first. It had to be a queen.

Mary, Queen of Scots (1542–1587)—who ruled Scotland from 1542 (at the age of six days old) until 1567, at which time she was imprisoned for the suspicious death of her husband—is regarded as the "Mother of Golf." It was Mary, in fact, who coined the term "caddie," derived from the "cadets" who assisted her.[1] Incidentally, it was partially golf that lent to Mary's imprisonment, as Mary played a round of golf just days after her husband's murder.

It would take another two hundred years before it was permissible for women to publicly participate in an organized tournament. The first known women's golf tournament was held at Musselburgh Golf Club in Scotland, which was extraordinary for two reasons. At the beginning of the nineteenth century, women were relegated to specific roles, according to social and economic status. Women who were allowed to "play" anything were both rare and limited in what they could actually do, but to do so in public was relatively unheard of. It would be another fifty-six years before the first ladies golf club would be established in St. Andrew's in Scotland, and, by 1886, it had just over five hundred members.

Little is known about that first golf tournament other than it was held in the town of Musselburgh, East Lothian, Scotland on January 9, 1811, when the wives of the town's fishermen and the neighboring village of Fisherrow teed off. It was not a full round—it began at the eighteenth-hole pitch and putt course—but it did mark a "first" in women's golf.

EDUCATION, IMMIGRATION, AND "RACE SUICIDE"

The 1830s brought about even more change with rapid industrialization. Just as Britain began aggressive hiring for wage labor, the United States was in the same sudden and demanding economic turmoil that created more social changes. Within the United States, a great number of immigrants from southern and Eastern Europe, Germany, and the British Isles, as well as those from East Asia and alongside Anglo-Americans, gravitated to these new jobs located in the midwestern and northern states. There were two immediate results: a seemingly new emergence of immigrants (the reality is the *wave* of immigration was not new but relocating for employment was) and a shift in the American family structure.

Still some thirty years away from the abolition of slavery, the movement of non-Anglos across the nation alarmed white slavery advocates and those who subscribed to the superiority of the white race. At the same time, the structure of American families was changing. With the need for unskilled labor, young women considered new opportunities they had never had or held before. As urban America grew, more families moved into the cities and the practicality and practice of having six or seven children changed with more families having just two to four children. By the turn of the century, the idea that immigrants were having more children than Anglo-Americans was a terrifying consideration for many, including Theodore Roosevelt, who, in 1905, publicly called upon white women to have more children and chastised patriarchs for committing "race suicide" by allowing their daughters to attend college.[2]

This rising paranoia and Roosevelt's calls for the "fittest" race emboldened many to adopt the Spartan philosophy that stronger women could ensure better, healthier pregnancies to be able to endure the labors of childbirth, as well as rigors of motherhood and domesticity.

Throughout the United States and Europe, it was also reasoned that by providing a modicum of education for women, there was greater chance of having more intelligent children—specifically, sons.

By the late 1880s, physical education became part of central component of education for girls in the public schools, and, by 1890, some competitive sports and games made their first appearance and began to emerge in the United States as well. In 1866, Vassar College in New York became the first college to have two baseball teams, "the blondes," and "the brunettes," although it would be a near decade (September 11, 1875) before the teams would be allowed to play publicly. Three years later, the Amateur Athletic Union (AAU) was formed for men and women to establish a standard of rules and regulations within amateur sports. In 1882, the YMCA (Young Men's Christian Association) in Boston opened competitive games to women and, in 1892, after a full decade of observation, concurred that "women need physical strength and endurance, dismissing the popular idea that women were too weak to exercise," in its journal *Physical Education.*[3]

More often than not, however, women were not given such chances. More progressive than their European counterparts, the French, by 1789, had instituted equal physical education for boys and girls, but more than twenty years later, Napoleon reversed the decision, allowing only boys to exercise for decades to come. While other nations did allow women of nobility some "play" time, competition was not allowed and the sports were restricted to archery, horseback riding, swimming, tennis, and golf.

Again, despite an early history in golf, by the end of the nineteenth century, there was much opposition to their participation. It was not until 2017 that Scotland's historic Muirfield club made international headlines when it announced female members would be allowed into the private Edinburgh course for the first time in its then-273-year-old history.

Blondes vs. Brunettes. *Archives and Special Collections, Vassar College Library, Archives 8.17*

THE FIRST MODERN-DAY FEMALE OLYMPIANS (1900–1912)

The first modern Olympic Games were held in Athens, Greece, in 1896. Like the ancient Olympics, there were no female competitors. Four years later in 1900, however, twenty-two women (out of 997 athletes) competed in five sports: tennis, sailing, croquet, equestrianism, and golf. Hélène de Pourtalès (1868–1945), a member of the Swiss sailing team, became the first female champion of the modern Olympic Games. England's Charlotte Cooper (1870–1966), a tennis player, was the first individual female Olympic champion at the same Games, also winning gold in the mixed doubles.

The first-ever mother–daughter competitors from the United States made their debut in golf in which Margaret Abbott (1878–1955) won, becoming the first-ever American to win a gold although she never received the medal for her achievement. As a strong indicator as to just how minimally the women were treated, Abbott never knew she was actually participating in the Olympic Games, believing only that she had been invited to a golf tournament while the Olympics were being played. Rather than receiving a gold medal, she was awarded a gilded porcelain bowl. Her mother, Mary Abbott (1857–1904), a novelist, also competed not understanding that she was an Olympian, and finished in a joint seventh place.

The 1904 Games in St. Louis were a regression in sport for women. Of nearly one hundred sports showcased at these Games, women were only allowed to participate in archery with just six contestants and five of the six competing from the same archery club. However, female boxers appeared as an exhibition. The reaction to women fighting, however, was so distasteful to fans, the media, and officials that it would be another 108 years before women could fight in the Games.

Officially speaking, women were never actually approved to participate in the 1900 and 1904 Olympic Games while the IOC underwent internal structural issues. It was not until 1908 that the Games were formally structured, although it was not by the IOC but the British Olympic Committee (BOC). At those London Games, thirty-seven female athletes participated in the sports of archery, tennis, and figure skating. This includes Queenie Newall (1854–1929) who won gold in archery at the age of fifty-three years and 275 days. Today, Newall remains the oldest female gold medalist Olympian in history. The 1908 Games also featured demonstration in women's gymnastics and aquatics.

In sports history, the 1908 Games are best known for the decision of British race officials to extend the length of the marathon so participants would cross the finish line in front of King Edward VII as a tribute to the monarchy. Women's marathon would not become an Olympic event for another seventy-six years, although it is written that Stamata Revithi

(1866–?), a poor Greek woman, ran unofficially at the first modern Olympics of 1896. Further confusion regarding Revithi came with reports that *two* women actually ran at the race. The name "Melpomene" (the Greek muse of Tragedy) was initially the only name documented until more detailed accounts of Revithi, who was said to have run the day after the official race, appeared in numerous publications. Yet it was not until 1993 that Swiss writer and runner Noël Tamini published "Women Always Win in the Race," in *Olympic Review* magazine, also supported by the International Society of Olympic Historians[4] and the Olympic Studies Centre,[5] that a second female participant was identified. Still, because women were so very rarely documented, this historic event was no different. Given the reports that appeared in Greek, French, German, and Austrian publications, it would appear two women did the unthinkable; but soon enough, "Melpomene" and/or Revithi were forgotten from history.

Back to the 1908 Games, it was the Danish gymnasts from the Kvindelig Idraetsforening (the Female Sports Association) who captivated audiences and the media. As one paper wrote, "The Danish ladies have taken the town by storm."[6]

Throughout the eighteenth and nineteenth centuries, gymnastics was used for military training and was associated with citizenship and patriotism. In particular to Pierre de Coubertin (1863–1937), the founder of the IOC, it was also exclusively a male sport. Women in gymnastics, he surmised, would emasculate the sport, but audiences said otherwise. While at least one Danish gymnast was noted to be an "amazon" for her beauty and strength, the media reassured audiences about the Danish gymnasts, the only female team at the Games, on the day of the opening ceremony in which the *Daily Mail* wrote, "In their physique there was nothing of the Amazonian. . . . No one of their number could have established even the remotest pretensions of 'massiveness.'"[7]

It was these Danish gymnasts who would reappear for the 1912 and 1920 Games for more demonstrations and assurances that female athletes could keep the feminine ideal intact, but when de Coubertin gained full control of the IOC by 1912, he worked doggedly to remove female athletes from competition. The 1912 Stockholm Games featured forty-seven female athletes, adding swimming and diving, but figure skating and archery were removed. Further, information about these female Olympians remains sparse as no records were kept of the entrants.[8]

THE ECONOMICS OF SPORTING ATTIRE

Just as bicycle manufacturers saw the value in female consumers (and benefited mightily), swimming clubs, seaside and lake resorts, swimming

pools, and private clubs ignored societal values of modesty and morality as *mixed bathing* became more commonplace. Husbands and wives,
families, and even "ladies only" competitions brought in greater revenue
and publicity. When the Duke and Duchess of Connaught presented a
silver trophy for the women's open sea championship of the Portsmouth
Swimming Club, it was even more scandalous to publicly question the
duke and duchess. With more and more influential members of society
condoning mixed bathing and increased memberships in various sports
clubs, even the bathing suit industry began to change.

In 1907, Australian swimmer Annette Kellerman (1886–1975) visited
the United States wearing her formfitting one-piece tank suit (which
would later inspire female swimmers at the 1912 Olympic Games in
Stockholm) to perform as an "underwater ballerina" but was instead arrested for indecent exposure in Boston.

For a woman to show her arms, legs, and neck was considered shocking and wildly inappropriate. To accommodate her U.S. audience, Kellerman added legs, arms, and a collar to the suit (but it remained formfitting) while also marketing her own line of one-piece suits as the Annette
Kellerman Collection. Although the United States would not adopt this
style until later, the Kellerman suit was highly popular in parts of Europe
by the 1910s.

By the 1912 Olympic Games, the Kellerman suit was back to its original
form—arms and legs at midthigh were exposed with a receding neckline
that scooped down to the top of the bosom line. Beyond the daring look,
the suit was far more practical. Previously, popular belief held that females were inferior swimmers, a theory supported by the unusually high
number of female drownings, when, in reality, not only were women not
taught to swim but their heavy, ankle-length wool dresses weighed them
down. Worse, some women even sewed weights into the hemlines of
their dresses (which already weighed up to thirty pounds when wet) to
keep them from floating up and exposing their legs.[9]

At the Games, athletes from nine of the seventeen attending countries
wore swimsuits by or similar to Kellerman's style. It was a particularly
exciting time as women were dictating a change in their own style. Three
years later, Jantzen Knitting Mills, a sweater manufacturer, created the
name "swim suit," and launched the brand name Red Diving Girl.[10] This
marked the first time such an attire expected women to actually swim or
be active in the "bathing suit."

As women entered into more sports and new sporting attire, a new
threat against female athletes arose with the entrance of cricket, hockey,
and lacrosse. Participants in these sports brought about the first known
"identified, categorized, and defined lesbianism as a form of sexual de-
viance," which was believed to be found in the woman who was lean,

muscular, and "now inextricably linked with mannish lesbianism."[11] It is, perhaps, an early explanation as to why women continue to wear skirts in the sport of lacrosse well into the twenty-first century.

Bicycle face and lesbianism, however, mattered not for the women of the early twentieth century as team sports opened a world of possibilities. The new women found companionship, a new appreciation and understanding of their own bodies, and a sense of freedom that they had not ever known. Their entrance into sport and recreation also created change. Whether they knew it or not, it was the beginning of the women's suffrage movement.

THE ECONOMICS OF SPORT

Imagine headlines today proclaiming that college female athletes are at most risk to no longer want or be able to have children. Yet in 1904, the president of the Royal College of Surgeons in Ireland, Sir Lambert H. Ormsby (1850–1923), worried that higher education for women would cause them to "cease to breed altogether."[12] It was a popular opinion, backed up by another notable physician, the famous "Father of Pathology," Dr. Rudolf Virchow (1821–1902), who said, "Woman is a pair of ovaries with a human being attached, whereas man is a human being furnished with a pair of testicles."[13]

To be clear, these threats came to women who simply wanted education. That a female might want to engage in sport was unthinkable. In the mid-nineteenth century, however, women fought against all social norms and medical advice to do what felt right—engage in both education and sport. When basketball was introduced at Smith College in 1892, it was an instant success with the first women's intercollegiate games played between the University of California, Berkeley vs. Stanford and the University of Washington vs. Ellenburg Normal School in 1896.[14] At the close of the century, schools around the nation had women's basketball programs, but there was a prerequisite. To ensure that female athletes did not overexert themselves, basketball was taught with modified rules. Senda Berenson Abbott (1868–1954), the "Mother of Women's Basketball" and director of physical education at Smith College, developed the rule book for women's college basketball and refereed the first official women's basketball game in 1893.

It was truly those women who secured a place in higher learning and sport who defied the notion that a woman's only function in life was to have children and serve a husband. But women also understood that as fun as sports were, until women got the right to vote, a woman would never have control of her own life.

FOUR

The Women's Suffrage Movement

A Step Up to First Base

At the turn of the century, it was still a white man's—and white woman's—world. It would be improper to detail the following events in any other way.

"DO EVERYTHING"

In 1879, when Frances Willard coined the phrase "Do everything," she meant to inspire women to become socially active and lobby for greater rights in politics, education, social reform, medicine, and pay. In both her personal and professional life, Willard saw rampant discrimination and abuse against women. She encouraged women to abandon the idea that women were weaker and less deserving; she believed that in empowering women, all people were empowered. "Politics," she said, "is the place for woman."[1] Her strongest council to women was to remind them that women were deserving of a place in society.

She was one of the first female presidents of Evanston College for Ladies in 1871 and became its dean of women in 1873 when it was renamed the Woman's College of Northwestern University. Ironically, Willard is also one of the first known recorded cases of sexual harassment at the workplace when the university president, Charles Henry Fowler, her former fiancé (with whom Willard broke off the engagement), then accused Willard of mismanagement of the Woman's College.[2] Willard, however, went on to become president of the Woman's Christian Temperance Union (WCTU) where she served until her death. It was there that she came up with the "do everything" campaign. Willard heeded her own advice, publishing books, traveling across the country to speak on the subjects of women's rights and temperance, and becoming a savvy lobbyist.

But Willard was also a woman of privilege—and a racist. While she traveled the United States and Europe speaking on temperance and women's rights, ever the lobbyist, Willard promoted the threat of drunken Black men assaulting and raping white women in her argument against alcohol while also actively shutting Black women out of the conversation of equality. Even within the liberal movement of equality and justice, politicians and activists were not above degrading Blacks or any nonwhites, who were very much in the fight with them, for their own personal gain.

While it can be argued that the prevalent thinking of the time was that the rights of Black women were very different than those rights of white women, it is difficult to conceptualize how Willard (and others) could have accepted this. But Willard continuously marginalized others with the goal of uplifting the rights of (white) women.

"FREE SPEECH"

Not everyone was impressed with Willard. During a speaking tour in Britain in 1893, the progressive Black abolitionist, antilynching newspaper publisher, and fearless journalist Ida B. Wells publicly challenged Willard, who was also on the speaking tour, for her silence on the issue of lynching in the United States. Although Willard repeatedly denied this, calling the act of lynching "barbaric" and insisted that the WCTU had routinely denounced it, Willard was also hard pressed to explain her earlier accusations in an 1890 interview she gave to the *New York Voice*, disparaging Black people, proclaiming the dangers of their voting power, and condoning the terrorist acts of lynching.[3]

Under pressure by Wells, Willard and the WCTU eventually publicly opposed lynching and recruited Black women as members, though Wells also continued to press the WCTU and Willard to oppose segregation. Wells was a force in a time when speaking out was far more dangerous for a Black woman than any white woman.

Seventy-one years before Rosa Parks refused to give up her seat on a public bus in Montgomery, Alabama, twenty-two-year-old Ida B. Wells was ordered to give up her first-class seat in the ladies car (a ticket she had purchased) with the Chesapeake & Ohio Railroad and move to the overcrowded smoking car in Memphis, Tennessee. The year prior, in 1883, the U.S. Supreme Court had ruled against the Civil Rights Act of 1875, which banned racial discrimination in public accommodations, allowing the railroad to essentially take Wells's ticket from her. When she refused, she was dragged out of the car. Wells decided to take the case to court and won, but when the Tennessee Supreme Court quickly overturned the lower court's ruling, Wells was forced to pay court costs.

Though Wells had been employed as an elementary school teacher, these experiences only ignited her passion for writing and truth telling. Offered an editorial position for a paper in Washington, D.C., Wells began writing weeklies under the pen name "Lola" and became an outspoken activist regarding Jim Crow policies, antilynching, and discrimination. She became the editor and co-owner with J. L. Fleming of the *Free Speech and Headlight*, a Black-owned newspaper in Memphis in 1889, then befriended and joined forces with Belle Squire (1870–1939), a white suffragist, author, and prominent critic of paying taxes when women were not given the right to vote, to organize the Alpha Suffrage Club based in Chicago in 1913.

In regard to Squire, she was the perfect companion for the outspoken Wells as Squire argued that expecting women to pay taxes while disenfranchised was a form of "taxation without representation"[4] and, while never married, insisted upon being referred to in the media as "Mrs.," out of principle. "They say it's confusing. They will not know then whether we are single or married. I don't think it is anyone's business what we are. Why should we be obliged to print our marital relations on our business cards? Men don't."[5]

Squire fully supported Wells's mission to educate Black women how to, as Willard had once said, "do everything," from petitioning and protesting, to lobbying and working to elect Black leaders.

On March 3, 1913, the day before Woodrow Wilson's inauguration, the National American Woman Suffrage Association (NAWSA) planned to march in Washington, D.C. Women from across the nation were expected to walk for universal suffrage, including Wells and Squire's delegation from Chicago, who had been told that they must walk in the back of the parade in a "colored delegation" as NAWSA's organizer, Alice Paul (1885–1977), wanted to keep the delegation "entirely white." It is a moment that has never received the appreciation much less the fanfare it deserved when Wells instead waited alongside spectators until the white Illinois delegation walked by, then stepped out and led the Illinois suffragists for the rest of the parade procession.[6]

Ida B. Wells was a champion in her own right. Born into slavery in Holly Spring, Mississippi, she was freed along with her family during the Civil War only to lose her parents and brother during the 1878 yellow fever epidemic, yet she never pitied herself or her position and instead fought for change.

Posthumously, numerous awards have been created in her honor, including the Ida B. Wells Memorial Foundation and the Ida B. Wells Museum. In 1988, she was inducted into the National Women's Hall of Fame, awarded a Pulitzer Prize special citation posthumously in 2020,[7] and in 2022, Mattel introduced the Ida B. Wells Barbie doll.

While Wells's stand was notable, American racism was on the rise as nonwhite communities struggled under renewed oppression and regression. Susan B. Anthony would turn against Frederick Douglass (1818–

1895), and the gap between double standards, briefly bridged by hope, was vanishing. For the women (and men) of the early twentieth century, yet another change was coming—political and social reform through sport.

WOMEN MAKING HISTORY

There was a movement, the undeniable intertwining of female sport enthusiasts and suffragists, taking hold throughout the United States, England, and Europe. In 1908, Muriel Matters (1877–1969), a suffragist and balloonist, flew over the British House of Parliament and dropped hundreds of leaflets urging "votes for women"; in 1909, Annie Smith Peck (1850–1935) became the first person—male or female—to climb twenty-one thousand feet, topping the highest peak in Peru on Mount Huascaran; while in 1910, the French Academy of Sports awarded Marie Marvingt (1875–1963) a medal "for all sports," as she was an extraordinary athlete in fencing, swimming, ski jumping, ice-skating, and mountain climbing. Of the latter, she was the first woman to climb most of the peaks of the French and Swiss Alps, and became the first woman to fly a balloon solo across the North Sea and English Channel from Europe to England.

In 1909, American Eleonora Sears (1881–1968) became the first woman on record to play polo on a men's team. Also a champion tennis and squash player, as well as an expert horsewoman, there seemed to be very little she could not do. In fact, she excelled in nineteen different sports, from from shooting rifles and ice skating to yacht racing. Although it was "well known" that Sears was a lesbian, a woman of her status (she was friends with the Roosevelts, danced with the Prince of Wales, and was the great-great-granddaughter of Thomas Jefferson) would never be identified as such by the media or those in her inner social circle. And to self-identify as such would also "collapse to" the societal norms and titles placed upon women, according to Sears.[8]

Instead, she continued to push back, engaged in all forms of sport, including golf, boxing, football, and long-distance running. She was named to numerous sporting Halls of Fame, founded new sporting associations, and was dubbed the "Universal Female Athlete." Perhaps what brought her the most media attention, however, was her determination to drive and fly. She was one of the first women to fly an airplane and drive a car. It was also in 1909 that she became the first woman on record to fight a speeding ticket and, the following year, intentionally got herself arrested for smoking a cigarette in the prestigious Copley Square Hotel in Boston as a show of passive resistance, as women were not permitted to smoke there. Sears was not a known smoker but always advocated for women. She was a woman of great privilege and, certainly, it can be argued that these opportunities were made available to her because of her wealth just as it can be easily argued that Sears continuously advocated for other women throughout her varied and expansive athletic career.

While open discussion on her sexuality appeared off limits, social commentators and sportswriters railed against Sears's pant-wearing ways. The more they attempted to publicly shame Sears, the more she adopted trousers as stylish daywear, and by the early twentieth century she had made the "best-dressed" women's lists. As a sportswoman, Sears helped in changing how women were viewed as athletes. She used her adventurous spirit and prestige to open the doors for others. While *Life* magazine named Sears as one of the "most remarkable American women" in the past two hundred years,[9] both her name and contributions only validated the need for Title IX, which would come four years after her death.

While many sports fans were ready to watch female athletes play, those in position of power fought against such progress. When the first-ever women's baseball game with the New York Female Giants took place on May 25, 1913, before a crowd of fifteen hundred, it was interrupted by police. Seventeen-year-old third baseman Helen Zenker (1896–?) was handed a citation to appear before court for selling programs on a Sunday. The attempt to permanently stop the game, however, was a failure.

Teams such as the Harlem "Bloomer Girls," named for their baggy Turkish-style trousers, and the New York Female Giants won over fans.[10] In particular, the outspoken captain and pitcher for the New York Female Giants, Ida Schnall (1888–1973), would bring the heat with her letter to the *New York Times* when she wrote on July 13, 1913:

> This is not from a suffragette standpoint, but a feeling which I had for a long time wished to express. I read in the newspapers wherein James E. Sullivans again objecting to girls competing with the boys in a swimming contest. He is always objecting, and never doing anything to help the cause along for a girls' A.A.U. [Amateur Athletic Union]. He has objected to my competing in diving at the Olympic games in Sweden, because I am a girl. He objects to a mild game of ball or any kind of athletics for girls. He objects to girls wearing a comfortable bathing suit. He objects to so many things that it gives me cause to think he must be very narrow minded and that we are in the last century. It's the athletic girl that takes the front seat to-day, and no one can deny it. I only wish that some of our rich sisters would consider the good they can do with only a small part of their wealth and start something like an A.A.U. for girls and bring out healthy girls that will make healthy mothers.[11]

As it happened, James E. Sullivan (1862–1914) was one of the founders of the Amateur Athletic Union (AAU) and a renowned sportswriter and publisher but also held significant influence with the International Olympic Committee. A known racist and misogynist, the athletic "czar" who fought to prove white male superiority during his career was particularly invested in excluding women from sport. When he could not stop the 1912 Olympic Games from allowing women to participate in swim and dive events, he influenced the U.S. Olympic Committee (USOC) to bar American women from participating.[12] Despite the fact that Ida Schnall was said to be the greatest female athlete of her time; held records in tennis, baseball, gymnastics, wrestling, bicycling, rowing, boxing, running, bowling, ice-skating, roller-skating, high jumping, broad jumping, bag punching, as well as swimming and diving; and believed to be a top contender for a medal, Sullivan ensured that no American female athlete competed.

Behind Sullivan, the U.S. Olympic Committee formally opposed athletic competition of women in the Games. It stated the only exception was the floor exercise in which women were expected to wear long skirts. So strong was Sullivan's hold over the USOC and AAU that it was not until his death in 1914 that the bans were lifted. With the cancellation of the 1916 Games because of World War I, it was not until 1920 that American female swimmers were allowed to compete.

Meanwhile, the Edmonton Grads, an all-woman's basketball team, began its reign of what would become the world's most successful basketball team—male or female—in history, winning seventeen world titles and dominating the sport for over twenty-five years, winning 95 percent of their games, frequently beating (soundly) men's teams as well as women's.[13]

With players like Noella "Babe" Belanger MacLean (1911–1999), at just 5'3" tall, who delighted fans with her speed, high jumps, and accuracy in shooting baskets and was called "one of the classiest little forwards ever seen in the game," the Grads offered great appeal to fans both on and off the court. Sisters Daisy Johnson (1902–1979), aka "Flash," and Dot Johnson Sherlock (1906–2003) were both respected leaders on the team who played with the Grads for over seven years before retiring, as well as Doris Neale Chapman (1911–1992), whose on-court reputation was such that in 1929, James Naismith, the inventor of basketball, traveled to watch the Grads play given their growing reputation for outstanding ability, leadership, and play.

The Grads, most of whom had started playing together in high school, became a sports dynasty, credited for shattering stereotypes about female athletes while encouraging more girls and women to play.

Though these amazing women and their stories of triumphs are but a handful of women at the turn of the century, the theme is constant. Despite the norms of society, they defied all the rulings of proper feminine behaviors and clothing, as well as the *concerns* of inferiority.

While Baron Pierre de Coubertin remained steadfast in his beliefs that women had no place in sport and that the Olympic Games would continue to uphold a standard of culture and society through elitism, he was not prepared for the results of the 1920 Olympic Games and one woman, in particular.

ALICE MILLIAT

The 1920 Antwerp Games in Belgium had been a disaster. By the closing ceremonies, the local Olympic Organizing Committee was bankrupt and no official report of the Games was ever produced. In addition to the sufferings following war, there had also been bad weather, a flu epidemic, too little housing and food for the athletes with even fewer spectators. For de Coubertin, however, his undoing would be the Women's Olympic Games.

For Alice Milliat (1884–1957), an avid swimmer and hockey player whose true passion was rowing, the fight had begun in 1917. Professionally, Milliat, a Frenchwoman, was a translator, but her strong belief and insistence that women be included more fully and fairly into the Olympic Games turned her love of sport into activism. Milliat was an early suffragist who used sport as her platform for equality and had believed, beyond equality, that women could help to build a stronger Olympic Games.

In 1917, one year following what would have been the Berlin Games, Milliat was interested in the idea that more sports, including rowing, be available to female athletes at the 1920 Games. In talking to other athletes and coaches from numerous countries, Milliat had also taken notice of the growing number of magazine publications for women and media coverage of females partaking in hockey, cricket, and tennis matches, as well as cycling and competitive walking.

Walking had become part of the curriculum at Cambridge as early as 1878, but with increasing competition in the "running" sports of hockey, cricket, field hockey, and tennis,[14] it stood to reason that audiences were ready to see more women running in the Games. When Milliat broached the idea of women's track and field in the Olympics in 1919, however, "I came up against a solid wall of refusal, which led directly to the creation of the Women's Olympic Games."[15]

Milliat formed La Fédération Sportive Féminine Internationale (FSFI) to oversee international women's sporting events, and, two years later, the first "Women's Games" were held in Monaco. In 1922, thirty-eight countries from five continents were affiliated with the FSFI with hundreds of athletes and thousands of spectators. Milliat had been right about the public's interest in female athletes. During the FSFI's Paris Games in 1924, more than fifteen thousand spectators purchased tickets, as the FSFI and Milliat were credited for creating opportunity and promoting athletes far more than either the IOC or International Association of Athletics Federations (IAAF) had ever done.

For de Coubertin, it was particularly vexing when the press compared Milliat to de Coubertin and gave her higher marks. The successes of the FSFI pushed the IOC to include more women and sports. Between November 1926 and April 1927, the IOC exchanged eleven letters with Milliat as it negotiated with the FSFI in an attempt to regain some of the power, popularity, and even mystique the Olympic Games once—exclusively—held. Ultimately, when the French government reduced its funding to the FSFI in 1928 as the IOC also demanded that the FSFI stop using the word "Olympic" with its games, the IOC did regain its hold in the sports world but not before Milliat and the FSFI ensured that women's athletics had indeed arrived in the new century. By the 1928 Games in Amsterdam, Milliat had made her mark in sports history and for the women's suffrage movement.[16]

THE MEDIA AND THE MOVEMENT

Throughout the United Kingdom and the United States, opponents of the suffrage movement used the "threat" of the destruction of the family unit, lesbianism, and even economic crisis through cartoon images and newspaper reports. Politicians and religious and community leaders as well as the National Association Opposed to Woman Suffrage made threats of higher taxes, loss of jobs for men, and the masculinization of women. Most common cartoon depictions were those of "man-haters" or homely women who "couldn't get" a man.[17]

The campaign to discourage women from voting, with physicians and family counselors weighing in that the fight for "women's vote" must never outweigh children, instilled fear in countless women. It would be one of the most effective messaging campaigns geared for/against women in modern times. Family and child care were very much a part of who the twentieth-century woman was.

In-house fighting and divisions over strategy, media, and inclusiveness nearly dismantled the movement on numerous occasions. But women also began to learn how to use the media to their advantage. This would become even more clear into the Roaring Twenties when women, as a movement, began to show true independence and put their own wants and needs over the family—the patriarchal family unit. In the last decade of the 1800s and into the early 1900s, the image of the perfect female was named the *Gibson Girl*, with long hair piled on top of her head, waist cinched, wearing floor-length dresses that covered her legs at all times. The Gibson Girl image grew into a cultural standard that included limited activity but also a calm, sweet, and demure nature. The '20s, however, promised new beginnings for many women who had served in the military and worked in factories and businesses during World War I. They earned salaries and tasted a freedom they, their mothers, and their grandmothers had never known, and they were not ready to relinquish these positions when the men returned.

In July 1922, a small publisher introduced a magazine called the *Flapper* that celebrated the new modern and independent woman, with the tagline "not for old fogies."

The origin of flapper is unknown but is believed to mean *to take flight*, to be free, while others suggested it meant this new young woman was so reckless that she refused to fasten her galoshes, which then flapped as she walked. Regardless, this new woman wore knee-length dresses, makeup, and short hair. She drank alcohol, smoked in public, and danced into the night.

Flapper magazine cover. *International Newsreel*

It was a display that shocked societal norms. Institutional and patriarchal leaders warned of the end of the family unit and conventional society even as the November issue of the *Flapper* displayed a female football player on its cover. On the heels of the woman suffragists, never had the image of females been discussed so heavily in American media. To be clear, never had the image of a male or female ever been discussed so intensely. Still, to this day, the media image of the flapper continues to represent the 1920s.

WOMEN ON THE MOVE

For the first time, a disposable sanitary napkin was made available in a Woolworth's department store in Chicago in October 1919. It was the beginning for American women that would be a game changer, allowing women to discreetly dispose of pads and, more importantly, become more mobile. With Kotex, the first commercial sanitation pad, women could leave home, travel, even engage in physical activity with confidence. To overcome the stigma of such a highly personal female issue, drugstores implemented a system in which the female consumer could place money in a box, then retrieve a packet of Kotex pads without having to interact with the male store clerk.

Though they would never get credit for it, it was women who invented this disposable pad. During World War I, an American paper products company produced bandages for soldiers, made from a material called Cellucotton. The company, Kimberly-Clark, discovered that Cellucotton, made from wood pulp, was five times more absorbent than cotton and far less expensive. As the war came to a close, however, Kimberly-Clark executives hoped to find a new need for Cellucotton, and it came in the way of army nurses who had improvised their own sanitary pads while serving in the war by using the Cellucotton surgical dressings. So grateful were the nurses, who were then allowed to continue their work and care for soldiers, that many wrote letters of appreciation, presenting Kimberly-Clark their invention by way of thank-you letters—and the company pounced.

Kotex did not become commercialized and nationally distributed until 1921 when it had become so popular that the name "Kotex" was used interchangeably with "sanitary pad." Manufacturing the product almost never happened, however, as Kimberly-Clark was repeatedly told that producing such a product was "too personal and could never be advertised." It was aggressive advertising in women's publications that proved profit was far more powerful than traditional social norms.[18]

In particular to female athletes of the 1920s, the topic of menstruation was both private but also of grave concern to patriarchal leaders. At Purdue University, for example, female students were forbidden from participating in sport during their period. To ensure this, it was written in the university's constitution, mandating that any woman who violated this regulation "shall forfeit her place on said team or squad and . . . her points for the same," while those team(s), captains, and managers who "allow a menstruating woman to play basketball, soccer, or to swim will likewise be denied their points." The Kotex was more than a matter of convenience for millions of women; it allowed a new kind of freedom from oppressive eyes.[19]

The Kotex, the flapper movement, and the prospects of becoming legally equal to man in the U.S. Constitution brought about a new excitement for women and a new kind of athlete. In 1926, Gertrude Ederle (1905–2003) became the first woman to swim across the English Channel, swimming from France to England in fourteen hours and thirty-one minutes and breaking the men's record (only five men had swum the channel) by one hour and fifty-nine minutes.

In the span of just four years, Ederle held 29 U.S. and world records and won a gold and two bronze medals at the 1924 Olympic Games before turning professional in 1925, when she set her sights on becoming the first woman to swim the English Channel.

Her first attempt was disrupted when her coach, Jabez Wolffe, touched her—an instant disqualification. Wolffe, who had attempted but never succeeded in crossing the English Channel twenty-two different times, would later reveal he believed women were not capable of swimming the channel. Undaunted, Ederle set out again in 1926 without Wolffe. She shed previous fashion norms and wore a controversial two-piece suit, also smearing grease over her body as protection from jellyfish in the water. Her greatest decision (and design) was her own swim goggles (found today in the Smithsonian).[20]

Hers was not just a personal victory but one for all women. By the late 1920s, Ederle helped to fuel women around the world with the new anthem, "I just knew if it could be done, it had to be done."[21]

Still, for the oppressed woman of color at the turn of the nineteenth and twentieth centuries, more work was to be done.

FIVE

Women of Color and Their Place in the Women's Movement

The women's movement did not start at the historic Women's Rights Convention in Seneca Falls, New York, in 1848. It began at the 1840 Anti-Slavery Convention in London when abolitionists Elizabeth Cady Stanton and Lucretia Mott (1793–1880) met each other and began to organize the conference in Seneca Falls.

While in London, they had been denied entry to the convention floor, and so began the idea of founding a women's rights movement in the United States. Their eventual conference announcement was printed in the *Seneca County Courier* on July 14, 1848, capturing the attention of none other than author and abolitionist Frederick Douglass, a well-known and respected leader in the abolitionist movement and prominent author who had escaped slavery.

Douglass attended the conference and encouraged others that "it is the duty of the women of this country to secure to themselves their sacred right to the elective franchise."[1] Notably, no Black women spoke at the convention, although historians have theorized that they may have been in attendance.

Three years after this historic event, Susan B. Anthony was recruited by Stanton to join their cause. She and Stanton would later form the American Equal Rights Association (AERA), with the ultimate goal of achieving equality for "all American citizens, especially the right of suffrage, irrespective of race, color, or sex."

The same year that Stanton recruited Anthony to join the cause, Sojourner Truth (1797–1883) spoke at the Ohio Women's Rights Convention in Akron, stepping into the spotlight. Again.

Truth was born into slavery—bought and sold four times and subjected to harsh labor, sexual abuse, and violent punishments in New York. In 1827, she escaped with her infant daughter, Sophia, to the home of an abolitionist family. The Van Wageners bought Truth's freedom for $20. They also bought the freedom of her son, Peter, for another $5, but five-year-old Peter had already been illegally sold into slavery in Alabama. Truth sued for the return of her son and won, making her the first Black woman to win a court case against a white man in the United States.[2]

Unable to read or write, she dictated her autobiography, *The Narrative of Sojourner Truth: A Northern Slave*, to her friend Olive Gilbert. It was published in 1850, and the proceeds from sales served as her livelihood and brought her national recognition. She had already met Douglass and become an equal rights activist when she spoke at the Ohio Women's Rights Convention in 1851, asking, "Ain't I a woman?" In what is now recognized as one of the most famous abolitionist and women's rights speeches in American history, Sojourner Truth shined a light on the different treatment among women, particularly those of Black women even within the women's movement.

This would never be more evident than in 1869, when the AERA fractured. Stanton and Anthony had formed it in 1866 during the eleventh National Woman's Rights Convention, with that written, public goal of achieving equality for "all American citizens, especially the right of suffrage, irrespective of race, color, or sex." Yet when the Fifteenth Amendment was ratified in 1870, granting the right for Black males to vote, Stanton and Anthony were incensed. The reality was that as Stanton and Anthony (and so many other white women) had called for equality, they primarily meant equality for middle- to upper-class, educated women of prestige. Stanton believed that white women were above Black men. "I would not trust him with my rights; degraded, oppressed himself, he would be more despotic with the governing power than even our Saxon rulers are." If possible, her feelings toward Black women receiving the right to vote were even worse, with Stanton stating that "their emancipation is but another form of slavery." She believed that Black women's lives under the thumbs of white slaveholders were better because "it is better to be the slave of an educated white man, than of a degraded, ignorant black one."[3]

Stanton and Anthony left the AERA and founded the National Woman Suffrage Association (NWSA). Lucy Stone, who was a good friend of Sojourner Truth, cofounded the American Woman Suffrage Association (AWSA). Stone and the AWSA both championed the Fifteenth Amendment as abolitionists but also maintained that the AWSA would continue its fight for all women to gain the vote, sponsoring Truth, Mary McLeod Bethune (1875–1955), Ida B. Wells, Mary Church Terrell (1863–1954), and Alice Dunbar Nelson (1875–1935), among others, who spoke out and fought for women's rights and lobbied for new recruits in Black churches, women's groups, and educational institutions.

When the Atlanta Baptist Female Seminary (now known as Spelman College) was founded in 1881, becoming the first historically Black female institution of higher education (now also the oldest historically Black women's college), it was a great sign of progress and promise for Black women. Still, the reality of economics, racism, and a white patriarchal society would plague the rights of women of color for decades to come. Why Stanton and Anthony became the faces of the movement in spite of the tremendous efforts and honest intentions of more true equalitarian suffragists is a conundrum.

FREE SPEECH AT THE RISK OF FREEDOM

When Mary Ann Shadd Cary (1823–1893) began speaking out for equal rights as a Black woman, it could have meant slavery and/or death. Shadd Cary was an American Canadian antislavery activist who became the first Black female publisher in North America and the first to edit a weekly newspaper, the *Provincial Freeman*. She was the first woman to speak at a national African American convention and testified before the Judiciary Committee of the House of Representatives, alongside Anthony and Stanton. She became the first Black woman to cast a vote in a national election, and the second Black woman in the country to earn a law degree. She was a celebrated educator, abolitionist, editor, attorney, and feminist.[4]

When the Fugitive Slave Law of 1850 was imposed, Shadd Cary and her brother, Isaac Shadd, were forced to relocate to Canada as even free Blacks were illegally captured and sold into slavery under the guise that they were escaped slaves.[5] She encouraged other Blacks, free and escaped slaves, to travel to Canada. In 1853, Shadd Cary founded her antislavery paper and traveled throughout Canada and the United States to promote her cause. As she did so, her name and her work began to gain prominence and, with each appearance, she put her own life in danger. Still, when the Civil War broke out, Shadd Cary returned to the United States to help in the war effort, recruiting soldiers and encouraging Blacks to join the fight.

For Shadd Cary, speaking out against injustice and inequity came with great risk, but she was willing to take the risks for the greater good. She was not alone.

Born Araminta Ross, Harriet Tubman (?–1913) changed the trajectory of women, history, military warfare, and human rights. Called the "Great Emancipator," Tubman was the double threat to the Confederate army for as both "a Black and a woman, she became doubly invisible."[6]

Tubman became the first woman to lead a combat assault in the United States when, in 1863, using information she had gathered from enslaved people she had helped to escape, she secured Union riverboats in Confederate territory. She also worked as a nurse, cook, and spy for federal troops from 1862 to 1865, receiving three years of salary for combat pay and later applying for veteran's compensation. It took thirty-four years of fighting with the veteran's agency through the federal government but, with the intervention of President Lincoln's secretary of state, she secured her earned wages. Tubman invented medicinal solutions, saving countless lives as she discovered the cure for dysentery as well as treatments to relieve symptoms of chicken pox, cholera, and yellow fever, all with self-taught knowledge of local flora.[7]

Tubman's exact date of birth is unknown but is believed to be around 1820. She escaped slavery in 1849 and dedicated her life to helping others escape. She was so prominent in this role, she also became known as "Moses" and "the conductor" of the Underground Railroad, a system created in the eighteenth century by Black and white abolitionists. Tubman did the unthinkable: she learned all the different routes of the Underground Railroad and repeatedly returned to the Southern territories to guide those seeking freedom. She is credited with freeing over three hundred men, women, and children. As her reputation grew, slaveholders put up a $40,000 (the equivalent of more than $1 million today) reward for her capture. Tubman's heroic and historic contributions to the U.S. Army led to her induction in 2021 into the U.S. Army Intelligence Hall of Fame. (Details about her intelligence work can be found at the Military Intelligence Museum.)

Like Sojourner Truth, Tubman was illiterate (as it was illegal in the South to teach slaves to read and write), and she left no written record of her own. Despite her remarkable acts of courage, Tubman's initial contributions were deliberately omitted from history. One explanation may be provided in the introduction to the 1969 reissue of R. C. Smedley's 1883 *History of the Underground Railroad in Chester and the Neighboring Counties of Pennsylvania*, a region where Tubman operated as a conductor. Smedley was a white physician and perhaps the "first nonparticipant" to write about the Underground Railroad. According to editor William L. Katz, Smedley was "more concerned and aware of the selfless devotion of local whites, particularly those motivated by deep religious conviction" than he was with Black "participants" such as Tubman. In his four-hundred-plus-page book, "Smedley included only three paragraphs about a 'colored woman named Harriet Tubman' who was 'active in helping hundreds to escape.'"[8] Another explanation may be provided by Frederick Douglass who wrote this to Tubman:

The difference between us is very marked. Most that I have done and suffered in the service of our cause has been in public, and I have received much encouragement at every step of the way. You, on the other hand, have labored in a private way. I have wrought in the day—you in the night. I have had the applause of the crowd and the satisfaction that comes of being approved by the multitude, while the most that you have done has been witnessed by a few trembling, scarred, and foot-sore bondmen and women, whom you have led out of the house of bondage, and whose heartfelt "God bless you" has been your only reward. The midnight sky and the silent stars have been the witnesses of your devotion to freedom and of your heroism. Excepting John Brown—of sacred memory—I know of no one who has willingly encountered more perils and hardships to serve our enslaved people than you have. Much that you have done would seem improbable to those who do not know you as I know you.[9]

Although Tubman would never know she would one day be inducted into the U.S. Army Intelligence Center's Hall of Fame, one can argue that she may have found joy that she, Araminta Ross/Harriet Tubman, would one day take the place of President Andrew Jackson, a prominent slave-owner, to adorn the $20 currency bill for the United States.[10]

THE SILENT SENTINELS AND THE "MAMMIES" OF THE SOUTH

By the mid-1850s, Lucy Stone "vehemently distrusted that Stanton and Anthony would tell the suffragist story properly," regarding the Woman's Rights Convention.[11] Certainly, Stone understood that neither Stanton nor Anthony were true abolitionist/suffragists as they paired up with known racist George Francis Train (1829–1902) who, before a Leavenworth, Kansas, crowd in November 1867, declared, "Women first, and negro last."[12]

Stone and members of the AWSA dissolved the relationship with Anthony and Stanton, while Anthony and Stanton, along with Matilda Joslyn Gage (1826–1898) and Ida Husted Harper (1851–1931), coauthored and coedited *History of Woman Suffrage*, the six-volume history and biography of women's suffrage and Susan B. Anthony. Not surprisingly, when the Nineteenth Amendment was ratified on August 18, 1920, it was nicknamed the "Anthony Amendment" in honor of the woman who made sure her name got top billing.

By the turn of the century, the majority of the nation did not support women suffrage, so women suffragists, led by Alice Paul (1885–1977) and Lucy Burns (1879–1966), picketed outside the White House in November 1917. Given their status in society, these protesting white women would never have believed they would be arrested, much less beaten, but that is precisely what happened. Dubbed the Night of Terror, word of the women's treatment became common knowledge. Mainstream America could not tolerate the abuse of white women of leisure. The D.C. Court of Appeals ruled that the women had been illegally arrested and, by June 1919, both the Senate and House passed the Nineteenth Amendment. The "Silent Sentinels," the white suffragists, had won and quietly began to disband while the voices of Black women were entirely muted.

During the movement, many white suffragists distanced themselves from Black women as it was important for mainstream America to *see* the difference. For suffragists such as Lucy Stone, the terms were non-negotiable. The suffragist movement was for *all* women.

In the early 1920s, the United Daughters of the Confederacy (UDC) proposed that a statue tribute to the "Mammy of the South" be erected in Washington, D.C., mere blocks from the Lincoln Memorial. Incomprehensibly, the idea was pitched as a way to pay tribute. The idea that a mammy, an enslaved woman forced to care for her captors' children, was content in her position, that slaves were well treated, was propaganda used that both improved the UDC's cause but also distanced them from Black females.

In 1923, Hallie Quinn Brown (1845–1949), an educator and activist, promptly served a more historically accurate portrayal of the old South, writing that "slave women were brutalized, the victims of white man's caprice and lust. Often the babe torn from her arms was the child of her oppressor."[13] This dispelled the South's obscene image of the mammy but also highlighted the reality of what was happening to Black women. Brown, president of the National Association of Colored Women (NACW), an organization that was founded in 1896, understood that not only Black women but society as a whole could not afford to allow the building of "Monument of the Faithful Colored Mammies of the South." Instead, more organizations such as NACW and the National Association for the Advancement of Colored People (NAACP), founded in 1909, were needed. The goals of the NAACP were simple: "To ensure the political, educational, social, and economic equality of rights of all persons and to eliminate race-based discrimination."[14]

But, in surviving both slavery and the Jim Crow era, Black women had learned that eliminating race- and gender-based discrimination was easier said than done. Fear of repercussions against Black women and those they loved was very real. One of the first steps in combating systematic silence was for the Black woman "to be able to tell 'her story.'"[15] Many Black women did begin to find their voices in more public and dangerous formats, but it was the NACW's sixth president, Mary Morris Burnett Talbert (1866–1923), who publicly challenged white suffragists about their obligations toward *all* women. Talbert believed that equality among all men and women could only come about through communal cooperation breaking the systemic silence. However, it would be another four decades before minority women truly had the vote.

In 1926, Black women were beaten by elected officials in Birmingham, Alabama, when they attempted to register to vote. There was no national outcry. In fact, well into the 1960s, state officials (most particularly, in the South) used voting taxes, literacy tests, and violent intimidation to prevent Black voters (along with Asian, Indian, Indigenous, nonwhite, and Hispanic populations) from registering to vote, triggering a new movement—Freedom Summer, in which thousands of civil rights workers of all races and backgrounds traveled to the South to help Blacks officially register to vote.

BLACK MEDIA IMAGES OF FEMALE ATHLETES

When pioneers such as Shadd Cary and Ida B. Wells created newspapers for their own communities, it was not only to get information out but also to preserve history that had otherwise been lost. In the world of sport, male nonwhite athletes were very rarely mentioned in local, white-owned newspapers, and for Black female athletes, events were largely ignored. As just one example, too little is known about Alma English Byrd, who won an Arkansas state basketball championship in 1939, despite having never played on a wood floor before the tournament. "We didn't know anything about how the ball would bounce off the floor." Having only ever played basketball on dirt, her team had to adjust to how the ball reacted on wooden floors while playing.[16]

For historians, gathering information on nonwhite, particularly Black female athletes in the nineteenth and early twentieth centuries is extremely challenging. According to Professor Amira Rose Davis, a professor of women's and African American studies at Penn State, "you have to get creative," finding information about Black athletes in scrapbooks, yearbooks or letters. "Black newspapers are the real treasure trove," as they covered local and state events, including those of female athletes.[17]

It was those stories and media images that encouraged colleges and universities to invest in Black female athletes and offer scholarships. According to Davis, by the 1920s, "college-aged Black women were saying, 'give us competitive sports. We want a place to compete.'"[18]

In that same time period, education and sport had opened up to middle-class white women, and as more and more were earning athletic scholarships, Black and nonwhite women saw opportunities slip away. The nation's obsession with the hegemonic feminine ideal also impacted how nonwhite athletes might be portrayed. It was Black-owned media and sports that allowed Black women, in particular, to challenge the current ideologies of beauty and race. While recurring images of these same athletes challenged what womanhood looked like, "sports was a way to refute our supposed inferiority," Davis said.[19]

THE RIGHT TO VOTE AMONG INDIGENOUS PEOPLE

Despite the history (and ownership) of the Indigenous to this land, they had become invisible. In particular to their rights, Indigenous people were used and/or discarded as a matter of convenience to the laws that served new property owners, thereby creating a false narrative. In April 2021, former U.S. senator Rick Santorum (1958–) spoke before the Young America's Foundation, telling the youth, "We [pre-Colonialists] came here and . . . birthed a nation from nothing," later adding that "there isn't much Native American culture in American culture."[20]

Actively ignoring the varied cultures of Indigenous people who occupied what is now North America, Santorum diminished not only their social and political structures and varied history, but also their inventions such as medical syringes, anesthetics, topical pain relievers, mouthwash, oral contraceptive, baby bottles, raised-bed agriculture, and even cable-suspension bridges, to name a few.[21] This would also include vast contributions to sport as we know it today, including the rubber ball, nets, and sticks for such sports as lacrosse, prehockey, and field hockey games; kayaks, snowshoeing, snow goggles; and a series of games that involved foot races, horseback riding, spear and bow/arrow events; and all had rules and regulations. Those precolonial and colonial migrants Santorum spoke of actually learned how to hunt, track, forage, and develop agriculture in a new land from hospitable Indigenous people.[22]

The history of Indigenous cultures, including the history of female warriors, is indeed rich with powerful women who changed the landscape. Likewise, the real history of what was done to the original inhabitants of North America is both shocking and deserving of more coverage in the pages of history books.

Initially, the laws of 1868 and 1870 granted former slaves their citizenship and the Fifteenth Amendment stipulated that the vote could not be denied because of race, but soon individual states began to enact a measure of taxes and literacy tests as ways of blocking specific groups of people from voting, also using intimidation and violence against them. In reality, it was not until the Snyder Act of 1924 (over five decades later) that Native Americans/Indigenous people born in the United States could be given full citizenship. Despite the fact that the Fifteenth Amendment granted such rights to all (male) citizens, Native Americans would have to wait until the Snyder Act.[23]

By 1876, courts ruled that (as defined by the Fourteenth Amendment) Indigenous people were not citizens of their land and therefore could not vote. The Dawes Act, passed in 1887, was supposed to grant Indigenous people land and citizenship but only if they gave up their tribal affiliations. There was, however, a catch that many did not know about—

giving up tribal affiliation did not mean automatic citizenship. Instead, what happened was a weakening of tribes' traditional cultures and social structures, and the loss of as much as two-thirds of tribal land.

In 1897, the state of Montana was able to disenfranchise those living on Indian reservations, citing that the reservations were not legally a part of the state. Two years later, Idaho followed Montana's lead and excluded Native American/Indigenous people "who were not taxed, who had not severed their tribal relations and who had not adopted the 'habits of civilization'" from the right to vote.[24]

In 1906, an earthquake in San Francisco destroyed all the municipal records, and many Chinese immigrants then claimed to have been born in the United States and were allowed citizenship, including for their wives and children. Indigenous tribes of this land could not make such claims, and their rights continued to be pulled away from them. Only after it was taken to court were Indigenous people not living on a reservation given the right to vote in California.

In 1922, the Supreme Court ruled that those of Japanese heritage were ineligible to become naturalized citizens, including "Asian Indians." Then, in 1924, the Citizenship for Native Americans secured universal citizenship through the Citizenship Act; but, like the Dawes Act, there was a caveat—the act did not ensure that all Indigenous people were eligible to vote and only about 125,000 people got their promised citizenship. Throughout the United States during the 1920s to 1950s regarding Indigenous people, the arguments of living on reservations, tribal affiliations, and their own culture/language were weapons of ineligibility for the right to vote and/or become a U.S. citizen.

Even after the 1965 Voting Rights Act, intimidation tactics and complaints about residency vs. reservations would plague Indigenous voters. Up until 1982, specific states attempted to block the votes of those who resided on reservations.

INDIGENOUS WOMEN

For centuries, religious leaders had used their platform to determine who had the right to vote, often citing women as intellectually and physically inferior, but, in 1887, while interviewing Indigenous women, Alice Fletcher (1838–1923), an ethnologist, anthropologist, and suffragist, made a startling discovery. She learned that women, under Indigenous assimilation laws, lost rights in society that the civilized women of Western patriarchy never had. Fletcher recounted how Indigenous women had told her, "As an Indian woman I was free. I owned my own home, my person, the work of my own hands, and my children could never forget me. I was better as an Indian woman than under white law."[25]

At the 1888 International Council of Women, the first meeting of its kind in the United States, Fletcher addressed the congregation, sharing her discoveries, and stating, "The popular impression concerning Indian women is that they are slaves, possessing neither place, property, nor respect in the tribe." In reality, Fletcher explained how a woman never gave up her name upon marriage but, rather, "bears her birthright to her grave," while non-Indigenous women most often went into the afterlife as "'the wife of [husband's name]' or 'Mrs. . . .'"[26]

The tribe offered equal protection to all its members. Fletcher detailed how Indigenous women were free to choose their own husbands, leave an abusive union, work alongside her tribe, own property, and participate in community decisions. "The women had their voice."[27]

Fletcher warned that it was patriarchal law that was stripping women's rights from the Indigenous, saying that even the Indigenous men said, "Your laws show how little your men care for their women." Fletcher further expressed sorrow for the Indigenous woman who had once had rights but now faced the same plight as the *civilized* woman. "I crave for my Indian sisters . . . to hasten the day when the laws of all the land shall know neither male nor female, but grant to all equal rights and equal justice."[28]

THE POLITICAL VOICE OF INDIGENOUS WOMEN

The early history of the Indigenous tribes of America and the political/social experiences of their women is vastly similar to those of the Amazons of ancient Greece. Prior to white colonists arriving in America, Native American women were highly respected and admired within their own tribes. Women hunted, fished, and rode alongside their male companions. Like the Amazons, they battled in war, raised their children, chose when or if they wanted a divorce, and held leadership positions within their own tribes. They served as shamans, midwives, and herbalists but also voted in tribal affairs and, in the case of the Iroquois, chose the forty-nine chiefs sitting on the Five Nation Iroquois Confederacy, which consisted of five separate nations—the Mohawk, the Cayuga, the Onondaga, the Oneida, and the Seneca. The Tuscarora were included in 1722.[29]

The Iroquois women also distributed food and sat on councils of both war and peace. And so it was that when colonists began to arrive, particularly in the northeastern tribes, Indigenous women were used as guides and interpreters. As relationships with Europeans developed, the women even married the newcomers. They held valuable positions in the fur trade from the mid-1600s to the late 1800s in the United States and Canada. They wielded what historians determined was "significant, traceable power" within the fur trade.[30] These women were credited for their multicultural, economic, and political roles but also endured abuse and abandonment, when many white fur traders returned to Europe, leaving wives and children behind, or were "traded" like property to another trapper.

The story of Sacagawea (1788 or 1789–1812), a Shoshone woman who accompanied the Lewis and Clark Expedition in 1805 to 1806 from the northern plains through the Rocky Mountains to the Pacific Ocean, is legend in traditional U.S. history classes. Sacagawea was initially used as a translator, but her vast knowledge of the dangerous and rough terrain, her skills as a food gatherer, and her naturally calming nature brought success to the expedition. She acted as ambassador among presumably hostile Indigenous tribes and helped Lewis and Clark plot the course that would allow them to find a Northwest Passage (connecting the Atlantic and Pacific Oceans) that President Jefferson had hoped for after the Louisiana Purchase in 1803. Both Lewis and Clark had been tasked with surveying the landscape; it was Sacagawea who helped make that possible. From rescuing irreplaceable land survey notes from a sinking boat to teaching members of the expedition how to identify roots, plants, and berries for edible or medicinal purposes, Sacagawea also bartered with the Shoshone for horses that would make passage through the Rockies possible.

What is not taught is how she had been kidnapped by the Hidatsa tribe and sold to a Canadian trapper, Toussaint Charbonneau, who forced her into a nonconsensual polygamous marriage. She was pregnant and gave birth while serving as a translator and guide to the Lewis and Clark Expedition, having survived extreme weather and perilous situations. Her husband was paid $500.33 and received 320 acres of land while Sacagawea received no compensation.[31] This, despite the fact that Lewis himself wrote that Charbonneau was "a man of no particular merit" (two years prior to joining the Lewis and Clark Expedition, he had been stabbed while raping a girl) and offered little in the way of translation.[32]

The National American Woman Suffrage Association (NAWSA) adopted Sacagawea as a symbol of women's worth and independence. Similarly, when in 1893, Matilda Joslyn Gage, a women's suffragist, Native American rights activist, and abolitionist, was arrested for trying to vote in a local election in New York, the Wolf Clan of the Mohawk Nation of the Iroquois made her an honorary member. In allowing Gage to join the Council of Matrons, Gage would have a vote in Iroquois politics. Because women were considered life givers, it was believed they should also have a voice and vote in the political, economic, and social aspects of the tribe.

While early colonial historians recorded "savage and inhumane" behaviors of the Indigenous people of the new world, the Iroquois civilization is credited as being one of the most advanced and progressive. The Iroquois had an elaborate political system that included a two-house (or party) legislature, like the modern U.S. Congress. This complex political system was unknown in Europe at the time and may, in fact, be "the oldest living participatory democracy on earth." It certainly planted the seeds for the formation of the United States as a representative democracy.[33] The history of Indigenous women is as long as it is noble, following matriarchal and matrilineal societies for thousands of years, with women holding political, economic, and social prestige. Early colonists were surprised that Native American males would empower their women, not understanding that the "power" was for all within a cooperative society.

This would become most evident in 2016 when LaDonna Tamakawastewin Brave Bull Allard (1956–2021) put out a call to all Indigenous tribes to stop the Dakota Access Pipeline (DAPL). A noted historian and matriarch of the water protector movement, Allard called for the protection of the Standing Rock Indian Reservation and its ancient burial grounds, historic sites, and the area's water. Their ancestors now had no voice, but the youth of the Great Sioux Nation had Twitter.

The hashtag #NoDAPL trended quickly, garnering thousands of supporters of cultural preservation and the defense of Indigenous sovereignty. Still, protestors were met with attack dogs, tear gas, freezing cold water, rubber bullets, and threats of legal action.[34]

One of those protestors was athlete/activist Temryss Xeli'tia Lane (1982–), who became a face of this battle. Lane called the protest a historic moment of solidarity that "inspired the largest gathering of tribal peoples across North America for the first time in storied memory."

Like so many warriors before her, Lane's power came with and from sport. And it was sport that allowed her to connect to her culture. As a professional soccer player, Lane was a defender—a position, she came to realize, that transcended sport. She, of the Lummi Nation, was a defender and protector of the water, her environment, her people. "I finally understood that being a defender is innately who and what we are. Not just me but all of those who advocated for land protections before me." #WaterIsLife

Because of her time on the athletic field, as a defender, learning all that comes from competitive sport, Lane said she felt more prepared to become a water protector, a warrior for the environment, to stand up against men literally armed with weapons and readied to shoot, prepared by her "lifelong teachings in spaces of football 'battle' where sanctioned violence is a regulated and facilitated part of the game." When confronted with armed men, those leadership skills derived from being a highly competitive defender, as well as her fearlessness and strength, allowing her to sing in peaceful protest instead of engage in battle. Lane is credited for de-escalating a contentious situation while standing for her people.

Although LaDonna Tamakawastewin Brave Bull Allard did not live to see the pipeline shut down in 2021, Lane was there to carry on the legacy. "I choose to stand on the frontline as my grandmother did before me."

Six

The Importance of Race, Sports, and the Polite Society

In the 1920s, as a few liberties (not many) were granted to minorities, the terrorist organization the Ku Klux Klan (KKK) saw these liberties as a threat to their way of life and how they were seen as men. Sports played a huge role in this mindset. Data from the first five Olympic Games had verified to them what they had always believed—the white race was superior in strength, endurance, and character. The United States had rigorously segregated its sporting institutions, severely limiting opportunities for anyone nonwhite and female. White people of European/Nordic descent had dominated the Olympic Games—never mind that most nations participating in the Olympic Games were European and Nordic—so it must be true.

This racism, already ensconced in the educational, legal, political, and social arenas, was brought to the 1904 St. Louis Olympic Games in the way of an anthropologic experiment. St. Louis was also hosting the Louisiana Purchase Exposition, known as the St. Louis World's Fair, and members of Indigenous tribes from around the world were attending. Organizers randomly pulled fairgoers with no known athletic abilities or training and no knowledge of specific sports or their rules and had them compete in boxing, freestyle wrestling, track and field, swimming, and cycling against trained athletes.[1] Not surprisingly, Aboriginal Japanese, Native Americans/Indigenous, Igorot people from the Philippines, as well as people from South American and South African and other "uncivilized tribes," did not fare well, allowing the trained American and European athletes to declare victory as the scientists concluded racial and genetic superiority in what they called the "Tribal Games."[2]

This *scientific evidence* would allow for a greater distinction even among racists. The KKK was considered "lowbrow" and of lower class among the educated white men who argued that their superiority came not only from athletic brawn but academic brain and a hierarchy in genealogy. In short, this made the KKK's cause more vital than ever; they had to believe they were better than someone else. Racial purification became a national obsession. So much so that by the mid-1920s to early 1930s, the eugenics movement, a set of beliefs and practices aimed at improving the genetic quality of a people, had turned race based. The term "eugenics" was developed by Francis Galton (1822–1911) in the late 1800s in England, derived from the Greek roots "good" and "origin," and the concept was to create a stronger, healthier human race. However, as he began to analyze characteristics, Galton, a member of England's upper class, became interested in the idea of superior intelligence; he concluded that heredity and intellect (i.e., education) produced more superior humans.[3]

While sportswriters often refer to the 1920s as the *golden decade* or the *golden age of sports*, it was a very exclusive club. Because there were little to no extracurricular activities for minorities and no economic and political policies to support them, it remains unknown just how many organized teams of nonwhite males played and what those statistics might have revealed.

NONWHITE WOMEN FIND A FOOTHOLD

Excluded from national competitions, Black female athletes (if not all minority women) had their own contests—within local YMCAs, gyms, churches, and recreation programs. Track and basketball were inexpensive and offered fairly easy-to-find/easy-to-use venues.

Dorothy Cure, a high jumper from Lynchburg, Virginia, was such an athlete. She was the first Black woman to set a national record in 1914 for the running broad jump. Although she cleared 15 feet and 1½ inches in the jump but never made the sport's history records, as track meets began to open up to include all athletes, the press had a difficult time ignoring half of the competitors, particularly when they were winning titles.[4]

In communities in which Black and white girls raced in school meets, "race girls" brought pride to their neighborhoods by defeating white teams in track meets and basketball games. Women sports researcher and author Susan Cahn wrote that "when given the chance in fair competition, African Americans could equal or surpass white achievements," and it was news. From the "Roamer Girls," a women's basketball team of Chicago's South Side that would eventually reach international status, to high school track meets when "black and white women went head-to-head in physical competition . . . , crowds gathered to watch an athletic battle that symbolized the larger possibility of a black challenge to white power."[5]

Formed in 1921, the Roamer Girls had something beyond raw talent—they had 6'7" Helen "Streamline" Smith, who captured such write-ups as being a "pride" of the team, the "chocolate lassy who is seven feet tall.

That's more altitude than any male basketball player Missoula ever had," and Isadore "Izzy" Channels (1900–1959), reputably Chicago's "first trash-talker," who was known to pass and score with ease while joking with opponents. In 1926, the *Chicago Defender* reported of Channels, "She played a game far above the head of her opponents and far in advance of her colleagues," while also known for her "famous long shots from near the center" that demonstrated that "girls can charge and play as hard at basketball as boys."[6]

Sponsored by both their community and Black newspapers, it did not take long for such claims that "the world's champions colored girls' basketball team" could defeat almost any male (white) team to line up games. The Roamer Girls traveled extensively, logging more than ten thousand miles per year, as audiences wanted to see Streamline Smith but also "the fastest girl in the world," none other than Tidye Pickett, who briefly played for the Roamer Girls.[7]

When, in 1926, sixteen-year-old Ernestine Gloster (1909–2003) won five medals at a predominately white track meet, the *Pittsburgh Courier* headlined "Race Girl Is Star in Press Meet," noting her feats went beyond a race. In fact, Ernestine Gloster Parks went on to become a "respectable civic leader in the black community," who instilled self-esteem among young Black women. In 1940, she organized the "Outdoor Girls," which promoted community projects and communal responsibilities. While Gloster Parks never made the Olympics, the rewards of that 1926 race embody what sport represents to all people, how sport impacts women politically, socially, educationally, and economically. For so many, sports provided an opportunity to challenge social norms.

Like the Roamer Girls, the successes of the "race girls," highlighted by local media, began a movement that would change sports and, again, how society viewed its women.

"POLITE SOCIETY" AND EARLY LATINA PIONEERS

Courage to play follows when girls and women see those who first had to courage to stand. While the Latina history is full of such women, two in particular stood up against institutions deeply rooted in racism and violence.

The United States was not alone in its interests in nationalism or national eugenics. When the *Secretaría de Educación Pública* (Department of Education) was established in 1920 in Mexico, one of its first priorities was "to emulate how Western Europe and the United States had incorporated physical education within its systems to enhance the whole person.

No longer was the discussion if a girl should play sport but what sport would be most appropriate for a female."[8]

Mexico felt "the challenge of raising up its aristocratic classes vs. the expectations of the common citizens," which was essential in keeping with the Latina hegemonic feminine ideal. Males were dominant, active, and strong while females were to be quiet and feminine.[9] But Latina women found themselves bound by more complicated cultural feminine ideals that promoted thin but buxom, demure but hypersexualized, strong but submissive. The culture in which Latina women lived is described as "marianismo," incorporating cultural and Catholic values and revering both positive and negative aspects of traditional femininity, including submissiveness, chastity, "hyper-femininity" with absolute acceptance of the machismo attitudes of males.[10]

In short, women were to be seen, not heard. Most certainly, they were not expected to stand up against the establishment or, in the case of the following heroines, the Texas Rangers and the U.S.–Mexico Border Health Commission. The Rangers were initially a loosely organized military force tasked with protecting early settlers in Texas from Indigenous attacks, and, in 1935, the Rangers merged with the state highway patrol. But since its inception in 1830, the organization was steeped in racism and activities that ran afoul of both state and federal law.

Jovita Idar Juarez (1885–1946) had been well aware of who the Texas Rangers were. Having lived on the Texas-Mexico border, she witnessed many acts of aggression against women and both men and women of Mexican heritage. Idar Juarez realized her talents would be better served as a journalist rather than a teacher to elicit change, so she joined her family's newspaper, *La Cronica*, in 1910 to write about the injustices she saw. Her brothers and fathers used their own names but, as was so common for female writers, Idar Juarez used pen names: Ave Negra (black bird) and Astraea (Greek goddess of justice and innocence). Following the brutal murder in 1911 of a fourteen-year-old boy in Thorndale, Texas, Idar Juarez and her family formed El Primer Congreso Mexicanista, the First Mexican Congress, which would begin the first Mexican American civil rights movement. Shortly thereafter, Idar Juarez formed Liga Femenil Mexicanista (the League of Mexican Women) and was nominated to serve as its first president.[11]

Idar Juarez understood the dangers of her activism since racial segregation, unlawful discrimination, and violence also impacted Mexican Americans in the South. Referred to as the "Juan Crow" laws by scholars, it had become common practice for members of the KKK as well as police and election officials to beat, lynch, and drag ethnic Mexicans behind horses as a form of intimidation to dissuade Mexican Americans from voting or finding a voice for justice. Still, Idar Juarez refused to be intimidated when she literally challenged the Texas Rangers who had arrived at *El Progreso* to dismantle the newspaper. Sent by the Texas governor following the paper's critical editorial of United States troops intervening in the Mexican Revolution, Idar Juarez physically blocked the Rangers from entering the newsroom, refusing to let them infringe upon her First Amendment rights as a member of the free press.[12] The Rangers would return at a later date to destroy the printing press when Idar Juarez was not there.

Another brave Latina who stood up against racism and violence was Carmelita Torres (1900–?), who fought against inhumane treatment of Mexican workers by U.S. border and health personnel.

The conception that Hispanics were "dirty" supported a morally degrading and extremely dangerous practice on the Mexico–U.S. border: American health authorities were given permission to fumigate Mexican citizens who crossed the border daily for work by making them bathe in gasoline and other toxic chemicals. The purported purpose was to kill any lice, which carry typhus, that might then be transported into the United States, but the reality reflects the undeniable likeness between the U.S. Customs disinfection facility and the *Desinfektionskammern*, disinfection chambers in Nazi Germany.[13]

The Mexican migrant workers were forced to strip down to be deloused and their clothing sprayed with toxic chemicals (following their gasoline baths) in buildings called "the gas chambers." Several died. In 1938, a German scientific journal specifically praised these methods of fumigating the Mexican workers, and Nazi Germany later used these same tactics on Jewish prisoners, then going further to kill millions of Jews in gas chambers at "extermination camps."

On January 28, 1917, at the Santa Fe International Bridge between Juarez, Mexico, and El Paso, Texas, one seventeen-year-old girl had had enough. Having heard that U.S. health personnel were also photographing female workers in the nude and posting their pictures in a local cantina,[14] Carmelita Torres refused to take the gasoline bath. Not only that, the "auburn-haired Amazon" convinced thirty other women to join her protest of this degrading and humiliating process. Within hours, thousands had joined in what became known as the Bath Riots, shutting down the border, El Paso, and work. U.S. employers were forced, initially, to accept medical certificates of proof of health, although—in truth—the delousing process continued for years.

Still, it was the beginning of resistance to injustice, and Torres (who was arrested during the protest) became known as the "Latina Rosa Parks"—although Torres's act of civil disobedience predated that of Parks by thirty-eight years.

LATINA WOMEN COME TO PLAY

Unlike Black female athletes, sports and athletics were not withheld from Central or South American women due to race, but rather social standards. Like much of the rest of the world, Mexico moved slowly and cautiously with its female citizens; but, by the 1930s, Mexican women were playing (and winning in) basketball, golf, tennis, and track. Women of the upper classes were held to the feminine ideal, but women of lower socioeconomical standing broke into nontraditional sports.

One such woman was Margarita "La Maya" Montes (1913–2007), who played baseball but also participated in bullfighting and, in 1930, became Mexico's first boxer. During her illustrious career, she fought twenty-eight men and five women, losing only five of her thirty-three bouts, knocking out most of her opponents, and was named the Pacific Coast champion before retiring in 1936.[15]

Today, the most traditional female sport, escaramuza charra, is steeped in social, political, and military history. *La Adelita*, the female soldadera who contributed to the Mexican Revolution, became a complicated figure—empowered feminist and the hypersexualized woman with long, flowing hair; red lipstick; and seductive smile. This complicated image lives on in sport.

In rodeo (the official sport of Mexico), women compete in breakaway calf roping, tie-down calf roping, team roping, as well as the popular barrel racing. All-women's rodeos also offer female bull riding. In *charreria*, the most classic rodeo event in the country, female competitors or *escaramuzas* (who have the same abilities as male competitors or charros) are only allowed to compete in the *Escaramuza* ("skirmish") *charra*, which was introduced in 1992. Competitors ride sidesaddle while wearing a dress. Described as "ballet on horseback," given the precision and grace of the athletes (both horse and rider), this belies the danger, the speed, and the need for pinpoint accuracy as twelve-hundred-pound animals, in full gallop, narrowly miss one another. The sport is about strength, agility, camaraderie, and trust. It is a highly specialized sport that requires an extraordinary amount of balance and power as the athletes travel at incredible speeds, sitting sideways (more difficult than sitting astride), with the practiced expectations that all eight horses and eight horsewomen (there are sixteen athletes to a team with only eight competing in the arena) remain synchronized.

Beyond this, Latina girls and women have enjoyed a wide range of sports for decades but, in comparison to Black and white cultures, the push for athletics has remained much lower. By the 1940s, post–World War II, as more male Latinos migrated to the United States for work, attitudes about sports began to change and began to be seen as a way to assimilate (as Americans associated sports with patriotism), a way to connect with other migrants while also honoring their own heritage and country of origin.

For the most part, the entrance of Hispanic, Indigenous, and nonwhites into the sports world was ignored. During the early part of the twentieth century, they were never fully segregated as Black athletes had been, yet never fully accepted by white audiences and the media. In what researchers have termed "racially in-between,"[16] this in-between conundrum led to extensive misinformation and disinformation about Hispanic athletes, male or female. With cultural differences, language barriers, and feelings of isolation from their nation of origin, this in-between was particularly challenging for Latina athletes who had no real previous female role models.

Beyond Mexico, Brazil stands as an excellent example of the long-term ramifications of withholding sport from women. Brazilian female athletes were allowed to compete in some sports and, by 1932, they were competing in the Olympic Games with Maria Lenk (1915–2007) becoming the first female to represent her nation in swimming. Women participated in diving, tennis, and track and had begun to explore greater opportunities—until 1941, when the National Sports Council decreed women could no longer engage in organized sport because "the practice of sports [was] incompatible with the conditions of their nature."[17] Everything stopped.

By the mid-1970s, as Brazil's political landscape shifted, a renewed feminist movement fought to lift the ban and, in 1979, women won the right to participate in sports again.[18] No female athletes would medal until 2004. Without athletics or the visibility of female athletes to represent their nation, little attention and even less funding had been given to women's sports.

For Maria Esther Bueno (1939–2018), a four-time world tennis champion and the first South American to win Wimbledon, the law did not stop her. But without other female role models to look to, Bueno truly was her own country when competing abroad. Since the dawn of athletics, men have always had an unspoken and unbroken chain of support. They wanted to compete . . . and so they did. Women, however, had to prove not only that they could play but that they deserved to be there.

Perhaps no female sports team has suffered more indignation by its own country than the Brazilian women's soccer team. In 1999, when the world celebrated the U.S. women's soccer team victory, while China's team had become a medal contender and the Scandinavian nations were becoming powerhouses in the sport, "Latinos . . . were strangely absent" during the 1999 Women's World Cup.[19]

Soccer was still considered a male domain, and females were heavily discouraged from play. When soccer had first arrived in Brazil, it was widely believed that a woman's reproductive organs could be damaged, thereby negatively impacting the future population of Brazil. Even in the late twentieth century, there still was a standard of masculinity that could not be challenged by female athletes. According to Manolo Cevallos, a prominent sports radio commentator in Los Angeles, women were not "to step out of their feminine role—the home, children, housework—because it challenges the masculine role. The countries that performed the best [in the World Cup] are countries where women have a greater role in public life and society—and so, of course, in soccer."[20]

A case study on how Brazilian women were treated in the media found that in 2004, female athletes were still "subjected to gender-specific standards of behavior regarding their bodies and sexuality. Stereotypes are reinforced by the way the media often broadcast sports news covering women, not focusing on the talents and achievements of women athletes but, rather, focusing on perceived sensuality and beauty, and even in 'femininity.'"[21]

Known to the world as "Marta," Marta Vieira da Silva (1986–) of Brazil lived these standards. Considered the best female player in the world by many, she was the first—male or female—to score in five World Cups. In 2019, she outscored Cristiano Ronaldo (1985–) and the legendary Pele.[22] Yet she never saw herself as a role model or activist.

Fast, agile, and fierce on the field, she has dominated in positions as striker, midfielder, and wing but is also known for her leadership with her teams. Because so little attention had been given to female athletes, particular in the way of media, Marta believed she was "just" playing. In 2006, when she returned to her hometown of Dois Riachos (population eleven thousand) in northeast Brazil, she finally saw her impact:

> When I arrived there, it was nearly midnight and the whole town was out . . . people were waving and cheering for me in the streets. I couldn't believe that these were the same people who, only a few years earlier, called me names, . . . and told my mother she should forbid me from playing a sport that was made for men. That night, I realized the power held by women and girls in sport to change the world. . . .
>
> I was unaware that my own experience in fighting and overcoming endless gender barriers on my way forward was shaking up and reshaping gender norms for those around me. As a child, I was a lonely warrior who ended up demonstrating that girls could play as well as, or even better, than boys. . . . When I left my village at 14 years of age to play football professionally in Rio de Janeiro, I was sending the message that women and girls are courageous, independent, and can provide for themselves. . . . Because we build confidence and resilience through sport, we have greater opportunities

to break the cycle of gender-based violence and to help other women and girls to do the same. When female athletes get a chance to take the spotlight, the results are enormous.[23]

In addition to athletes, Marta pointed out that other female warriors have made a difference: "Female football players, coaches, referees and journalists challenged gender stereotypes in the media coverage, demonstrated respect for sexual diversity and, of course, fought for equal pay. These issues were raised in front of a massive audience and, as a result, gained momentum on the global agenda. Not only had they been transformed into action in the sports world, but also among a new generation who are demanding their rights."[24]

And that new generation will not back down from demanding their rights.

SEVEN

Women, War, and Their Entry into Sport

Even before World Wars I and II, before women were called upon to help in the war efforts, women had taken to the skies. While the bicycle had taken her down the street, the female aviator unwittingly changed militaristic strategies around the world.

EARLY FLYERS

Ruth Law (1887–1970) first earned her pilot's license in 1912 and began performing before crowds, including perfecting the aerobatic "loop the loop" and setting a world record for women, reaching an altitude of 11,200 feet. On November 19, 1916, she became the first American—male or female—to travel the distance of 884 miles in an outdated Curtiss pusher biplane. When Law first announced her plans, the media pounced, citing numerous *experts* who cautioned against a woman making such a challenging feat. When Law approached a manufacturer for a plane with a greater fuel capacity and engine, she was refused, told that the large plane would be "too much for a girl to handle."[1]

Despite this, Law found her plane and departed from Chicago to New York City in frigid weather. She was forced to stop in Binghamton, New York, when impending darkness made it impossible for her to read her compass, as well as other instruments. Without lights, Law landed, tied her plane to a tree, and asked local police to *watch* her plane. When she landed in New York City the following morning, she became a national hero. But she wanted more.

In 1917, she tried to enlist in the military but was turned away. The acting secretary of war had clearly stated, "We don't want women in the army," but Law persisted, eventually becoming the first woman allowed to wear a noncommissioned army officer's uniform when she piloted army recruiting trips. She continued to fly, breaking records, including becoming the first person to deliver air mail to the Philippines.[2] But Law, by no means, was alone. Harriet Quimby (1875–1912) became the first woman to earn her license in the United States and the first woman to fly across the English Channel.

In particular to these times, planes were unpredictable—engines stalled or stopped without warning, propeller blades and wings cracked or broke off midflight, and mechanical errors were constant. Still, women like Blanche Scott (1884–1970), believed to be the first American female aviator, took to the skies.

For Bessie Coleman (1892–1926), however, the need to fly was not for entertainment but born of something else. There were no opportunities for her as a Black and Indigenous female. Despite coming from a family of sharecroppers, Coleman earned her license from the Fédération Aéronautique Internationale in 1921, becoming the first black person, male or female, to earn an international pilot's license.

Though she died at age thirty-four while testing a new aircraft, she left behind a tremendous legacy. Nicknamed "Brave Bessie" for her stunts,

Bessie Coleman. *New York Public Library*

she was a crowd favorite who had hoped to one day open her own school for African American and Native American fliers, both men and women.

While their male counterparts had been called "daredevils," "adventurers of the sky," "aviators," and "heroes," the early women of the skies were either called "girl fliers," "tomboys of the sky," or "petticoat pilots," to name a few, or they were tagged with far less complimentary names. It was Amelia Earhart who stated simply, "We are still trying to get ourselves called just 'pilots.'"[3]

AMELIA EARHART

Like many great athletes before her and since, Amelia Earhart (1897–1937) may not have been the best, but she stood out. Hers was a career steeped in passion and dedication but also great timing and luck—until the end, all of which only added to her mystique. Born in 1897, she did not have her first pilot's lesson until 1921. By the next year, however, she broke the world's record for women pilots by reaching an altitude of fourteen thousand feet. It was with this record that Amelia's disapproving uncle reminded her of a proper lady's station in life when he said (in responses to the record) that there were only three times in a lady's life that it was appropriate to be in the news: her birth announcement, her wedding announcement, and her funeral.[4]

In 1928, she became the first female passenger to cross the Atlantic by airplane, and by 1932, she became the first woman to make a nonstop solo trip across the Atlantic. She joined the National Woman's Party and became an outspoken proponent for equal rights. She authored a book, was dubbed "Queen of the Air," and began endorsing sportswear, which, for the time, was an extraordinary step for women. She promoted women's clothing lines, becoming a favorite model while also becoming a competitive racer in 1929.

In that same year, the National Air Races allowed women to compete, flying across the country as an all-female competitive group, called the National Women's Air Derby. The press, however, termed it the *Powder Puff Derby*, ignoring both the danger and skill it took to compete. That same year, the women understood that if they were to endure negative press, persistent degrading names while fighting for equal air time, they all needed to come together. A mass invite was sent out to all the nation's licensed women and ninety-nine responded—thus naming their organization the Ninety-Nines (which still exists today).

In 1931, Earhart married publisher George Putnam, calling it a "partnership" with "dual control," and continued flying and setting seven new women's records in speed and distance. Determined to circumnavigate the globe, Earhart and her navigator Fred Noonan departed from Oakland, California, on June 1, 1937. On July 2, 1937, on the last legs of the incredible journey, they departed from Lae, New Guinea. Shortly thereafter, all contact was lost. They had approximately seven thousand more miles before reaching Oakland but were never seen again. The nation was in mourning, and theories on what had happened to Earhart and Noonan quickly emerged. While the U.S. Navy officially concluded that they had run out of fuel, crashed, and presumably drowned (Earhart and Noonan were declared legally dead in January 1939), others believed they had been taken prisoners by the Japanese, by Pacific Island Indigenous tribes, or that they were somehow still alive on an island awaiting rescue. She was, both on land and in the sky, larger than life.

THE SOVIET AMELIA EARHART

While the world had been watching Amelia Earhart, and women like her, setting records, another group of women had quietly been setting records of their own—the world's first fighter pilots. In 1925, Zinaida Kokorina (1899–?) became the first female to hold a military rank and serve as a military pilot. By the 1930s, the then Soviet Union was training its female citizens, by the thousands, in paramilitary organizations; teaching parachute jumping, weaponry, marksmanship, and tactical warfare. Of them, numerous became notable historical figures in both women's and military history only in recent years.

Marina Raskova (1912–1943), known as the "Soviet Amelia Earhart," petitioned dictator Joseph Stalin (1878–1953) to allow her to form an all-female fight squadron, after receiving letters from women from across the Soviet Union. Raskova was not only known to have been the first female navigator, but she had set a number of records in long-distance flights, most while she had served as a flight instructor at the air academy. What Earhart was to the Western world, Raskova was to Mother Russia.

In January 1943, while attempting to bring a three-ship formation to its new base outside Stalingrad, they were hit with extreme weather. The two other planes successfully crash-landed, but Raskova, as well as three others on board, died in the crash. Raskova's remains were interred at the Kremlin. She had been the *mother* of the movement, and her death had been a terrible blow to the women she trained.

Lt. Valeriia Khomiakova (1914–1942) became the first woman in the world to shoot down enemy aircraft at night, only to be killed herself two weeks later during a night takeoff. But it was Yekaterina Budanova (1916–1943) and Lydia Litvyak (1921–1943), also known as Lilya, who became the only two female fighter aces in the world. Budanova performed "solo hunting," an honor only given to aggressive ace pilots, while Litvyak held the record for greatest number of kills by a female fighter pilot.

Though Raskova was named the "Soviet Amelia Earhart," it was Litvyak who was most like Earhart, nicknamed the "White Rose of Stalingrad."[5] She was young, pretty, fearless, and calm under pressure. On August 1, 1943, during the Battle of Kursk, it is believed she was shot down by Nazi war planes. Like Earhart, Litvyak's body and plane were never found, and rumors circulated that she had defected to Germany while others insisted that she had been taken prisoner.

THE NIGHT WITCHES

Under Raskova, Stalin established three all-female air force units in 1941, making the Soviet Union the first nation in the world to deploy women in combat. Of the more than two thousand women who applied, Raskova chose four hundred and immediately began an intensive training program that demanded its students learn in three months what the male soldiers had been given in as many years. The women learned how to be pilots, navigators, ground crew, and airplane mechanics all while being given ill-fitting gear and uniforms, secondhand equipment and planes, many of which were unflyable until Raskova's crew made repairs. The women trained in 1920s crop dusters, made of wood, and offering no protection from the weather or gunfire. Steve Prowse, author of the screenplay *The Night Witches*, noted that simply touching the planes during Soviet winters could "rip off bare skin."[6]

In replace of parachutes, guns, radar, and radios (which the male aviators had), Raskova's women used stopwatches, rulers, and flashlights. And yet, with these planes they took to night flying. Despite the fact that the wooden planes, if hit, would instantly burn up, the women found they could maneuver, take off, and land more easily than the Germans. Because their planes could only carry two bombs at a time, Raskova's pilots began night formations, sending up as many as 40 two-woman crews each night, achieving more than thirty thousand missions. While British and American women were allowed to work performing ferrying duties (flying planes from factories to military bases and departure points, as well as towing targets for shooting practice for the ground and air gunners' airfields in their respective homelands), Soviet female pilots were in Germany, flying over enemy territory, temporarily idling engines so that they could glide in the darkness toward their intended target.

Using multiple planes for one mission, the first planes entered enemy territory to attract attention. Once German soldiers shined a spotlight on the planes, the navigator of the two-woman crew would drop a flare to "light up the intended target."[7] Though not all night flights were done by Raskova's pilots, their damage was extensive. Even if they missed their targets, the Night Witches caused distress among German troops as their reputation preceded them. Germans believed the women were criminals, sent to the front lines as punishment, and acted in suicide missions with nothing to lose, while others believed the Night Witches surely possessed some greater power beyond aviator. On May 4, 1945, the female pilots made their last flights, and just three days later, the Nazis officially surrendered. Maj. Valentin Markov, commander of the women's bomber regiment, commented on his time as their leader, saying, "During the war there was no difference between this regiment and any male regiments. We lived in dugouts, . . . flew on the same missions, no more or less dangerous. If I compare my experience of commanding male and female regiments, to some extend at the end of the war it was easier for me to command this female regiment. They had the strong spirit of a collective unit."[8]

In fact, there had been a significant difference between the male and female regiments. During all those estimated thirty thousand missions in wooden planes that flew at night without proper equipment, these women had had less than half the training time and never wore a parachute as none had ever been provided for them.

LIEUTENANT COLONEL NICHOLS

American Ruth Rowland Nichols (1901–1960) never knew battle, though she possessed the skills of her then-Soviet sisters. She, like her good friend Amelia Earhart, was an aviation pioneer. She beat Charles Lindbergh's record with a new cross-country flight time; set the women's world speed record of 210.7 miles per hour; set the women's world altitude record of 28,743 feet; set the women's distance record with 1,977 miles; and, in 1932, became the first woman to pilot a commercial passenger airline. After numerous plane crashes while attempting other records, including one where she suffered a broken back, Nichols was critically injured with broken bones and burns as a passenger in a plane crash that killed the pilot. Yet one year later, she was back to flying.

During the war, she headed Relief Wings, a civilian air service that performed emergency relief flights, and she assisted the Civil Air Patrol, eventually earning the rank of lieutenant colonel in the Civil Air Patrol. She continued with her humanitarian efforts, piloting around the world, but in 1958, at the age of fifty-seven, she copiloted the Air Force's TF-102A Delta Dagger, reaching a speed of one thousand miles per hour and an altitude of fifty-one thousand feet, setting a new record for women's speed and altitude, and the following year served as a guinea pig, of sorts, for NASA's Mercury program. To determine how isolation, weightlessness, and centrifuge would affect female astronauts, Nichols underwent the tests in hopes that her results would one day help a female astronaut enter into the space program.

As it would turn out, Nichols also had had her own personal battles and on September 25, 1960, committed suicide, succumbing to her depression but leaving behind a legacy that transcended her own personal feats.

THE WOMEN'S AIR DERBY

The story of the first and only official women-only air race in the United States in 1929 bears telling as the brave nineteen women who entered the race not only understood the dangers of early flying but also were targets of men who did not believe women should fly.

Severed wires, broken instruments, oil-filled gasoline tanks and/or tanks sabotaged by foreign objects, and punctured gas tanks were never reported as the women faced certain death from saboteurs. Many of the pilots were fortunate enough to have discovered someone had tampered with their planes before takeoff while others were forced to crash-land as they ran out of fuel, incurred engine failure, and even suffered carbon monoxide poisoning. So upsetting was the idea of female aviators that men were willing to kill a fellow American than watch her fly.

Amelia Earhart and Ruth Nichols were not the only big names or early pioneers to enter the derby. Besides Nichols and Earhart were Florence "Pancho" Barnes (1901–1975), who had divorced her first husband for her love of flying, transported bootleggers across the Mexican border, and never knew a challenge or cigar she would not accept, and Edith Foltz (1902–1956), who would later become a flight instructor during World War II and was recruited to join the British Royal Air Force. While serving, Foltz was chased by a Nazi pilot and later nearly a casualty of friendly fire. She escaped both times and was awarded the King's Medal for Courage in the Cause of Freedom.[9]

Other entrants included Mary Haizlip (1910–1997), who became the second-highest prizewinner of all male and female pilots in 1931; Opal Kunz (1894–1967), who became the first woman to race men in open competition; Blanche Noyles (1900–1981); Mary von Mach (1895–1980); Neva Paris (1883–1930); Margaret Perry (?–1951); Ruth Elder (1902–1977); and Vera Dawn Walker (1878–1978), all members of the Ninety-Nines who were aggressive recruiters for women in aviation and never gave up hope that women would one day find equal employment opportunities in aviation.

Another entrant was Phoebe Omlie (1902–1975), the first woman to receive her airplane mechanic's license as well as a licensed female transport pilot, but she was also another record setter in both aviation and parachute jumps, and was considered by First Lady Eleanor Roosevelt to be one of "eleven women" who transformed women in politics, society, and sport.

Two international pilots, Thea Rasche (1889–1971), Germany's first female aerobatics pilot, and Australian Jessie Miller (1902–1972), the first woman to fly solo from England to Australia, also joined Claire Mae Fahy (1899–1930), who made headlines early when she was forced to land and drop out of the derby due to wiring and extensive engine troubles. Fahy was one of the victims of sabotage that forced California's District Attorney's office to send out subpoenas to mechanics and race officials. By August 22, 1929, the *New York Times* reported insufficient evidence and no one was ever charged, but the damage had been done.[10]

Competitor Evelyn "Bobbi" Trout (1906–2003) was also forced out of the race due to an oil leak and extensive damage to her tank, while Rasche had had "foreign matter" in her gasoline tank. But it was Marvel Crosson (1900–1929) who paid the ultimate price. Crosson, who had become the first licensed pilot in Alaska and flown in the most extreme weather and terrain, was fearless but also seasoned. After her plane crashed just twenty minutes into the flight, her body was found tangled in a parachute some distance from the plane. She died on impact. In addition to suspected tampering to her engine, it was believed that she had actually suffered carbon monoxide poisoning, which led to the crash and her untimely death. Beyond grieving the death of their friend and dealing with criminal sabotage to their aircrafts, the competitors had their second-greatest fear quickly highlighted by headlines: "Women have conclusively proven they cannot fly."[11]

At the end of the race, however, Gladys O'Donnell, "the Flying Housewife" (1904–1973), would take second place with Amelia Earhart coming in third. It was Louise Thaden (1905–1979)—who set the women's altitude record, solo endurance record, and speed record during the 1920s, and cofounded the Ninety-Nines with longtime friend Amelia Earhart—who won. In fact, second only to Earhart, Thaden was the most recognized female American aviator whose own pilot's license was signed by Orville Wright. The outspoken Thaden also opined that it was women who were "innately better pilots than men."[12]

Despite negative press, the women had been a sensation with spectators lining up to see the women across the twenty-eight-hundred-mile stretch. It was an image that forever changed the perception of female aviators and, later, the war effort.

WAVES, WASPS, AND WACS

By the end of World War II, both the Army and Navy opened Nurse Corps, allowing women—the only women in uniform—to serve their nation. More than 350,000 women served, and though they never served in combat, 432 women were killed, with 88 becoming prisoners of war (POWs).

While women have served the U.S. Army as nurses since 1901, it was not until 1942 that Black nurses were inducted, and the 6888th Central Postal Directory Battalion, the only all-Black female unit, was created for the women to serve in Europe, sorting millions of letters for soldiers on the front line. In 1944, the Army and Navy nurses received commissions and full benefits, paving the way for others who would ultimately join the Army, Navy, Marine Corps, and Coast Guard. Always, of course, they were expected to wear a dress as it was imperative that they still "be a lady."[13]

The Women Accepted for Voluntary Emergency Services (WAVES), created by the U.S. Navy and Marine Corps, served in World War I. It was not until 1945 that WAVES were allowed to serve overseas and, until that time, only served in Alaska and Hawaii; but they did open to Black women in late 1944. Harriet Ida Pickens (1909–1970) and Frances Wills (1918–1998) would become the first Black women to serve as WAVES officers.[14]

The Women's Airforce Service Pilots (WASPs) were used primarily to free men of all noncombat roles so that they could be deployed; but they also became mechanics, air traffic controllers, drivers, parachute riggers, even instructors of aerial gunnery for servicemen, while learning how to fly the B-26 and B-29 bombers and every other type of aircraft as they served as test pilots.

Even as female pilots willingly gave their lives for the "war effort" and, more importantly, their men, they were blamed for mishaps at home and for sons/husbands being sent overseas. Known as the "Fly Girls" or, for those who trained at Avenger Field in Texas, the "Avenger Girls," their work was constantly downplayed. For women like Margaret Phelan Taylor (1923–2015), who was just 5'2", barely able to reach controls, and never wore a parachute as they "weren't fitted to us,"[15] or Mabel Rawlinson (1917–1943), too few understood the extreme sacrifices the women made (without compensation, benefits, or acknowledgment).

In the case of Rawlinson, who died in a crash when her cockpit hatch malfunctioned and she was unable to escape, it was her fellow WASPS who collected money to send her remains home to her family. Because she was not considered military, the Air Force refused to pay for her funeral. It was her family who draped an American flag on her casket and honored her as a fallen veteran.

In the summer of 1944, as flight programs shut down, male civilian instructors fearful of losing their jobs and being entered into the draft fought to replace the WASPs, citing the age-old argument that they were breadwinners and, as males, entitled to the positions. When the WASPs were unceremoniously dismissed—not even a thank-you letter from the government—many tried to find work as pilots in the public sector; but no major commercial airline would hire a woman, despite an outstanding resume. Some women found work as stewardesses while many more simply walked away from aviation; even so, most tried to stay in contact with one another. It was the Air Force's announcement in 1976, however, that ultimately united the WASPs.

The U.S. Air Force made a public statement regarding women's induction into its training program and service, saying, "It's the first time that the Air Force has allowed women to fly their aircraft,"[16] completely ignoring previous service of thousands of American women. Members of WASP fought for the official recognition they never received during the war; finally, in 1979, they could officially call themselves military veterans.

It was the Women's Army Corps (WAC), the original "skirted soldiers," however, who led the way and took much of the initial brunt against women in the Armed Forces. In a time when both men and women upheld the idealized notion that a woman's place was in the home, WACs were subjected to tremendous ridicule. In 1941, the Women's Army Auxiliary Corps (WAAC) was officially recognized.[17]

England had established its own Women's Army Auxiliary Corps, later to be renamed Queen Mary's Army Auxiliary Corps, in 1914, during World War I, and the Women's Royal Navy Service began in 1917 with the Women's Royal Air Force the following year. Women had already been working in the industrial workforce prior to the war, but, after 1915, women were also working in munitions manufacturing, including working with explosives. For morale among the women who had also been employed in factories, a women's football league was founded in 1917 but later banned in 1921. The first policewomen were also employed during World War I,[18] indicating that women could and should be used to serve their country.

American norms, however, were not quite ready. To counter the negative press, the Army (other branches would later follow) made sure all women in uniform wore makeup and nail polish, wore heels, and carried purses. Still, all too many Americans viewed women's participation in the war effort as a strike against the family unit. After the war, many women simply erased invaluable experience and patriotic contributions from their resume as many employers refused to hire "supposedly lascivious ex-WACs."[19]

ROSIE THE RIVETER AND THE MEDIA

The image of Rosie the Riveter is iconic; yet, for decades, no one knew who she was until a Westinghouse poster was discovered. For decades, it was long held that "Rosie" was a woman named Geraldine Hoff Doyle (1924–2010) who worked in a Navy machine shop during the war. More reasonably, others believed the real "Rosie" to be Rose Will Monroe

WACs in 1942. *National Archives*

(1920–1997) who worked at the Willow Run Bomber Plant outside Detroit. During the war, the three largest riveting manufacturing plants were Seattle, Baltimore, and Detroit. For many, it stood to reason that a "Rosie" would have been discovered at one of these plants. But the discovery of a 1942 photograph of Naomi Parker Fraley (1921–2018), working at the machine shop at the Naval Air Station in Alameda, California, wearing the famous polka-dotted bandana left no questions—this was the inspiration behind the iconic poster "We Can Do It."

Just what the poster actually meant, however, was a very different story. With the bombing of Pearl Harbor, everything changed in the American workforce. Livelihood and employment in the United States had already changed considerably since the Great Depression (August 1929–March 1933), but World War II made for even bigger changes for women. In the 1930s, only 10 percent of American women worked outside the home, but by 1941 an estimated 12 million women were employed, and by July of 1944, those numbers rose to 19 million. It was an era called the "Women of Steel." Women who had traditionally worked as teachers, nurses, and clerks became welders, machinists, and riveters.

The iconic poster has been a girl-power emblem for the feminist movement since its discovery in the 1980s. The reality is, however, when the

"We Can Do It" poster. *National Archives*

poster was created in 1943 by artist J. Howard Miller (1918–2004), who was employed by the Westinghouse Electric internal War Production advertising agency, it had little to do with women working in the war effort. Miller created forty-two posters with the idea that each poster would be displayed in the Westinghouse factories for two weeks, each with its own message to boost morale, reduce absenteeism, and lower unrest or any talk of factory strikes. The "We Can Do It" posters were initially only presented in the Pennsylvania and midwestern factories in 1943.

In studying the poster, the timeline, and Westinghouse's true motive for Rosie, scholars point out that despite the myths that Rosie the Riveter was a rally for women in the workplace or that it was a U.S. government propaganda for women's employment and the war effort, it was simply an in-house poster for Westinghouse employees.

Still, that image of Rosie evokes strong feelings among both men and women as it symbolizes strength and determination. It, by virtue of presenting a riveter, reminds us of not only the "Women of Steel," the WACs, the WAVES, the WASPs, the women of the air, but all women during World War II who worked in every way possible to help with the war effort.

For these pioneering women, it had felt as though the media had worked against them more than with them, despite their overwhelming and enthusiastic response when their nation called for help. Women who lost husbands and sons, who had to pick up extra work to feed their family, still ran the farms or the businesses, still put food on the table, found child care while working as welders, riveters, and construction workers also found themselves being shamed for not being "ladies." And they did so at half the pay.

Decades later, however, a renewed and empowered Rosie and the "We Can Do It" poster emerged in 1982, following a *Washington Post Magazine* article that featured the poster and, by 2015, the National Museum of American History reported it had become one of the most famous and popular icons (and top-selling poster) of World War II, as well as a symbol of empowerment for women.[20]

The reality is, Rosie did not go away after the war. There were hundreds of thousands of women in uniform, in pants, earning paychecks, and, for the first time, discovering a new kind of independence that would include sports and a new sense of empowerment.

EIGHT

A League of Their Own

In regard to women's sports, World War II also became an opportunity for female athletes, and, in 1992, actress/producer Penny Marshall (1943–2018) brought everlasting fame, if not only acknowledgment, with the film *A League of Their Own*. Although fiction, it is based on the real-life All-American Girls Professional Baseball League (AAGPBL). The movie centers around the Rockford Peaches catcher, Dottie Hinson, based on real-life Dorothy "Kammie" Kamenshek (1925–2010), who was actually a left-handed first baseman and outfielder. In the movie, Hinson and her sister, Kit, end up on different teams—Kit playing with the Racine Belles as a sometimes wild-throwing but all-star pitcher, resulting in a dramatic face-off in the AAGPBL championships. In reality, the Rockford Peaches never made the championships that first year in 1943. They would, however, become champions in 1945, 1948, 1949, and 1950. Kamenshek was considered the most fearsome batter in the league, and was called the "finest field first baseman" by Major League Baseball. In the movie, Kamenshek's character, Dottie, retires after just one season; but in real life, Kamenshek played for ten seasons and was a force on the field.[1] But Kamenshek and the AAGPBL were not the first.

"The brunettes vs. the blondes" was the first game recorded in 1866 while the first league of female players began in 1913. But when the war began to threaten the sport of baseball itself, Philip K. Wrigley (1894–1977) was moved to action.

Wrigley, along with several other business leaders, founded the AAGPBL in 1943, in hopes of saving the sport. While professional ballplayers were recruited into the Armed Forces for the war effort, the AAGPBL was designed to distract, entertain, and, they hoped, monetarily save baseball parks and the game until "the boys came home."

Twelve years prior to the AAGPBL, a seventeen-year-old pitcher named Virne Beatrice "Jackie" Mitchell (1913–1987), otherwise known as "the girl who struck out Babe Ruth," did just that on April 1, 1931. It was during an exhibition game between the New York Yankees and the

Chattanooga Lookouts, a minor-league baseball team, that made major headlines when Jackie Mitchell struck out not only Babe Ruth but the next batter as well—Lou Gehrig.[2]

Reporters and fans claimed that Gehrig and Ruth had "taken a dive."[3] Before four thousand fans, the media, and players, however, newsreel footage also showed that while Gehrig was gracious about the strikeout, Ruth was not as "he flung his bat away in high disdain and trudged to the bench, registering disgust with his shoulders and chin."[4]

Later, Ruth would tell the media, "I don't know what's going to happen if they begin to let women in baseball. Of course, they will never make good. Why? Because they are too delicate. It would kill them to play every day."[5]

Indeed, Mitchell's career had been short as she retired at the age of twenty, but not because of injury or delicacy but pride. Tired of being used as publicity stunts, she eventually left the sport.

Mary Elizabeth Murphy (1894–1964), "the Queen of Baseball," became the first woman to be signed to a professional team and played with all-men's teams for seventeen years as a first baseman. Not only did she play with the Traveling All-Stars, a semipro men's team, but she played in the women's league for the Bloomer Girls as well. In 1922, she became the first woman to play in the major leagues.[6] If there was a game, she would play.

The AAGPBL's obligatory skirt slide. *Florida Memory State Library and Archives of Florida*

There is no doubt that such publicity and talent demonstrated to Wrigley that a women's baseball league could be successful. Wrigley and his investors launched an aggressive public relations campaign depicting athletes who wore makeup and dresses (even when a slide into third or home base meant torn, ripped flesh and terrible bruising, what the players called "strawberries") and had the girl-next-door demeanor.

The hours were long, alcohol and smoking were strictly prohibited, and many nights were spent sleeping on buses, but for women of the 1940s, the opportunity to play ball, travel, and be paid was a dream come true.

Unlike any professional sport before it, the managers and owners of the AAGPBL had unique marketing issues from the start. Athletes got pregnant (Dottie Collins [1923–2008], who pitched with the Fort Wayne Daisies, played into her fifth month of pregnancy), women had their periods, and mothers traveled with children, while others received news of a husband killed in the war overseas. Management and owners were suddenly on an entirely new learning curve.

As much as fans loved to see a player lose her temper, there were far more waiting to use this behavior against the player, her team, and the entire league as evidence of sport vs. femininity. An example of this was when Pepper Paire Davis (1924–2013) hit the umpire for a call she did not like. As one fan had said, "You had to see it to believe it, and even then you didn't." It happened when Davis slid into second base. As Davis later recalled, "The ball beat me but I slid away from the tag and the girl missed me by about a foot. But I was blocking Lou [umpire] and the way he saw it, I was out. I was so mad, I jumped up and whirled around . . . my fist caught his jaw and I knocked him flat on his back. Both of us knew it was an accident but he said, 'I guess you know, Pepper, that I gotta throw you out of the game.' I said, 'Yeah, I know I'm out of the game, but I wasn't out at second base.'"[7]

Wrigley constantly defended virtues, femininity, and the ladylike qualities of his players. Babe Ruth had been a notorious womanizer and brawler yet remained one of the most popular athletes of his day while Wrigley, his managers, and his players routinely fought against labels such as "prostitutes" or "home-wreckers" as the women were not where they were "supposed" to be: in the home. But their talent could not be ignored and the fans couldn't stay away. The players and the plays were exciting. By the mid-1940s, there were fifteen teams in the league, and as the personalities of players were profiled, popularity grew. Many had nicknames, trading cards, and followers. By 1954, the women's league came to an end, and thirty-four years later, the AAGPBL was officially inducted into the Baseball Hall of Fame in Cooperstown, New York.

Throughout the AAGPBL's success, however, Black women were never allowed to play. In 1947, when Jackie Robinson was signed to Major League

Baseball, Black women were given no such opportunities. In 1949, how-ever, Marcenia Lyle "Toni" Stone (1921–1996) became the first woman to play in the Negro Leagues with the Indianapolis Clowns and would eventually go on to play with the Kansas City Monarchs. She played with Willie Mays (1931–) and Henry "Hank" Aaron (1934–). Sports historians have called Stone "the best baseball player you've never heard of" and "the female Jackie Robinson" (1919–1972), but, initially, she was used as a media ploy.[8]

Stone not only was a great athlete but stands as a reminder of how in-complete, if not inaccurate, sports records are. In just the sport of baseball alone, record keeping of rosters began with the first official game played in 1846. In 1901, the American League (AL) was established and its first World Series played in 1903. It was seventy-four years later, in 1920, when the Negro League was formed, but record keeping was informal.

As for Stone, she would only do things *her* way. When the Indianapolis Clowns' owner suggested she wear a dress with shorts (as the players with the AAGPBL did), Stone refused, saying, "I wasn't going to wear no shorts. This is professional baseball."[9] She traveled with her team on a bus as the only female, used the umpire's room at games to change, and managed to break the seemingly impenetrable line both the public and media drew when it came to female athletes.

She was known to be an outstanding second baseman, but she could play the entire field and pitch. She loved being rotated to different posi-tions, was known to be a power hitter and an equally impressive sprinter who crowds loved to watch. Moreover, that a female—a Black female—won the hearts of sports fans of the 1950s in an all-male league was significant. Had she been in the AL, what might her statistics look like against all other professional baseball players?

As for AAGPBL, producer Penny Marshall noted, "I didn't even know it [AAGPBL] existed."[10] When she pitched the idea about an all-girls professional baseball movie, studio executives were uncertain. Women's sports were still nearly a decade away from Brandi Chastain (1968–) rip-ping off her jersey and sliding across the field in a muscle-flex pose that would launch millions of posters. Sony had no idea how successful or not a movie about World War II female baseball players could be. In fact, it is not *Major League, Field of Dreams,* or *Moneyball* but *A League of Their Own* that stands atop as the most successful baseball movie of all time, grossing $107 million, with *Moneyball* coming in at second, earning ap-proximately $75 million.[11]

More importantly, the movie did not just portray how much the women endured just to play a sport they loved but also that it was their talent and passion that kept the sport alive during World War II and did so during times when they were not sure they would even be paid. Such is the story with so many pioneering female athletes who just wanted their turn to play. Joyce Hill Westerman (1925–2021), who played in the league for eight years, said it best: "We would have played in the league for nothing if it had come to that, and I think that was true because we loved it so much. It was a dream come true."[12]

BABE

Mildred Ella Didrikson Zaharias, known to the world as Babe (1911–1956), had earned the nickname, she told reporters, after Babe Ruth for her skills in baseball. She had also been an outstanding athlete in basketball, track and field, golf, swimming, skating, even billiards and football, as well as a member of the All-American basketball team. As her fame grew, Babe was invited to try out for the 1932 Olympic track team while playing for an amateur women's basketball team in Dallas.

Although rules stipulated women could not compete in more than three events at Olympic trials, as it was feared that the physical exertion could be too much on their delicate systems, Babe's coaches registered her as a team. Alone, Babe competed in shot put, javelin, baseball throw, long jump, and 80-meter hurdle. She set a world record in the hurdles and javelin, tied in the high jump, and finished fourth in discus. In total, she scored eight points higher than her nearest competition who, as a team, comprised twenty-two women.

At the 1932 Los Angeles Games, she won gold in the 80-meter hurdles and javelin but earned a silver in the high jump because she had used an unorthodox western roll and was docked. Although Babe was initially disappointed with the silver medal, she delighted in her overnight success. She was heralded "Wonder Girl" and "superathlete" in the press. Sports reporter Grantland Rice wrote of Babe: "She is an incredible human being. She is beyond all belief until you see her perform."[13] She was named Woman Athlete of the Year by the Associated Press in 1932—a distinction she would win five more times, which no other male or female athlete has ever achieved. By the early to mid-1930s, she was one of the most popular athletes—male or female—in the world. She met the president and aviator Amelia Earhart, and even appeared in an advertisement for Wheaties in 1935. In her career, she played professional basketball, softball, and golf but as a golfer won an unprecedented fourteen tournaments in a row—another feat no male or female athlete ever repeated, and won every major professional championship at least once in her career.

Despite another reporter's review that "it would be much better if she and her ilk stayed at home, got themselves prettied up and waited for the phone to ring,"[14] Babe had other plans. The 1932 Games made her an overnight sensation, but she was only getting started. By 1938, she became the first woman to compete in a men's golf tournament and, restored to amateur status again after playing as a professional, won the U.S. Women's Amateur tournament in 1946, the same year the first women's professional golf league was formed. In 1947, she won thirteen straight golf championships and became the first American to win the British Ladies Amateur. A professional once again, she then won the U.S. Women's Open in 1948.

Throughout much of her career, however, Babe was relentlessly attacked by one reporter, Paul Gallica (1897–1976). She would always be questioned about her femininity, even gender on a few occasions, by various members of the press and social conformists, but Gallica had been particularly vicious. It began during the 1932 Olympic Games and Gallica, known for his views on traditional gender roles, wrote his first article about Babe for *Vanity Fair*, titled "The Texas Babe." In the article, he repeatedly called Babe "boy," "strange . . . girl-boy child," and implied that she should use the men's locker room rather than the ladies'. As it turned out, reporter Grantland Rice had arranged for Babe and Gallica to play a game of golf that, as would only happen with Babe, resulted in a footrace challenge. Gallica's agreement was also his demise as his peers watched Babe easily beat Gallica and he would spend the remainder of his sports career insulting her.

Babe did not always help herself in the eyes of the public. She embellished stories for laughs, making implausible claims, and boldly announced not only a victory but how it would conclude. She would predict the route of a golf ball, the time in a race, the curve of a ball only to "delight the press and depress her opponents when her bravado proved true."[15] She was, perhaps, the first true female athlete to disparage and taunt her opponents (what is today's "trash-talk"). While she did, in fact, intimidate and infuriate opponents, she also promised great one-liners and headlines to the press. A reporter once asked Babe, "I'm told you also swim, shoot, ride, row, box, and play tennis, golf, basketball, football, polo and billiards. Is there anything at all you don't play?" to which she responded, "Yeah. Dolls."[16]

As early as the 1930s, Babe Didrikson understood *marketing* and *branding* in a way few others did. She transformed how women were seen as athletes but also how marketable female athletes could be. A 1947 interview with the *Saturday Evening Post* noted, "Not much has been made of the undeniable fact that the Babe has revolutionized the feminine approach of golf,"[17] while so many more historians have lauded her for challenging just what (and who) the female athlete is.

Unquestionably, Babe was one of the greatest female athletes of all time, but her talents were only contested against white women who upheld the hegemonic femininity ideal that even Babe herself could not. As her popularity grew, however, Didrikson Zaharias was forgiven for her brash behavior, boyish figure, and "masculine appearance." The media often referred to her as a "third sex,"[18] but because of her immense popularity the media's "oh, that's just Babe" attitude excused her many indiscretions, including the hegemonic feminine ideal.

THE UGLY TRUTH OF BLACK, WHITE, BABE, POLITICS, AND THE MEDIA

Later, when Babe was at the height of her golf game, she tried to play down racist comments she had made in the past, and the media obliged. Posthumously, it was repeatedly explained that by growing up in Beaumont, Texas, in the early 1900s, the "rallies and political rhetoric of the Klan did affect her growing up—she at times reiterated racist and anti-Semitic sentiments."[19] In reality, she did more than repeat words.

Babe's push to be better than everyone else, to the point of being a bad loser and possible cheater, was rooted in deep-seated insecurities. "She wasn't attractive, wasn't book smart or fashionable. She was a tomboy from a poor family who loved sports and fighting." Worse, there were stories of the "enjoyment" Babe is said to have derived from beating up "the Black kids in town."[20]

Over time, more stories from her youth revealed that same anti-Black sentiment. According to one of Babe's former grade school teachers, "She really did hate Blacks in those days. I think she went out of her way to antagonize them and, truly, to hurt them."[21]

Babe, herself, had been the victim of hateful rhetoric and behavior. Labeled as "deficient" in her gender, she had been described in a 1932 *Vanity Fair* article to have a "perpetually battled image of a creature not-quite-female."[22] Yet rather than identifying with what Tidye Pickett (1914–1986) and Louise Stokes (1913–1978), the first Black women to make an Olympic team, might have been going through, she antagonized and bullied them. She played cruel pranks on them and cared little that Pickett and Stokes had to sleep in quarters far away from the rest of their team. When Babe and her white teammates ate in the dining hall and met with the press, the Black teammates stayed in their room.

Yet for all three women, their backgrounds were remarkably similar. All three came from lower socioeconomic circumstances. All three were outstanding basketball players, each breaking and holding records in track and field from their hometowns. While Tidye Pickett made a name for herself as one of the sensational Roamer Girls (also billed as "the fastest girl in the world"), Stokes had tied the world's highest standing broad jump record of eight feet, five inches in 1931. But while Babe eventually got a sponsor, was allowed to train and compete in "whites only" clubs, was granted access to social clubs, and garnered media attention to further her quest for the Olympic Games, Pickett and Stokes remained invisible and had to enter every race they could to get noticed. Both Pickett and Stokes won every race they entered, but, unlike Babe, there was little fanfare. For the "many Black female athletes in this period, the starting point of their journey to the Olympics was crushing poverty, the result of institutionalized racism in the rural South and urban North."[23]

Together, Pickett and Stokes had hoped their entry into the Olympic Games and the media attention they would be assuredly given could help to change how Blacks were treated. In 1984, Pickett gave a rare interview about her experience with "that big girl from Texas," explaining that Babe Didrikson Zaharias "just plain didn't like me, didn't want me on the team . . . it was prejudice, pure and simple."[24]

Despite years of having to defend her gender to track officials and reporters, Didrikson was reportedly so offended by the presence of Stokes and Pickett that Didrikson broke into their room and poured a pitcher of ice water over their heads as they slept in their bunk beds.[25]

Shortly thereafter, Pickett and Stokes were removed from the team. Their times were better than their other teammates; there were no disciplinary issues regarding Pickett or Stokes, and, yet, they were unceremoniously replaced, creating "a pivotal point in Olympic history where politics and racial tensions" were in direct contrast to the Olympics creed.

By the 1930s, Black publications, leaders, and communities became more vocal about training opportunities for their athletes as the then very rigid, patriarchal press scrambled to explain how Black track athletes from the men's team dominated the Olympic Games. Prior to these Games, white press gleefully ran stories about white supremacy and its physical dominance.

As for Pickett, her position on the United States team for the 1936 Berlin Games officially placed her as the first Black female athlete to attend the Games.[26]

THE LONDON GAMES AND FANNY BLANKERS-KOEN

It was post–World War II when Babe was at the height of her golf game that the 1948 Olympics took place in the devastated city of London. For many, the idea of holding the Olympic Games (following the cancellation of the Winter and Summer Games of 1940 and 1944) was an irresponsible waste of money and resources but, in need of normalcy, the world pitched in.

As athletes from around the world arrived, their nations donated food, clothing, and equipment. Canada provided diving boards, Switzerland donated gymnastic equipment, and Finland offered timber for a basketball court, while more than one hundred tons of fruit and vegetables were sent from the Low Countries (Belgium, Netherlands, Luxembourg). Britain was nearly bankrupt, its buildings and roads in rubble, with a food shortage that resulted in many athletes relying on whale blubber for scarce protein.[27]

Fifty-nine countries participated with a record number of 4,100 athletes, of which 385 were women. Of the women, Dutch track legend Fanny Blankers-Koen (1918–2004) was poised to make history.

The 1948 Olympic Games were not her first. In fact, she had been in the 1936 Berlin Games, placing sixth in high jump while her relay team placed fifth overall, and had witnessed the great Jesse Owens (1913–1980). When the 1948 Games were announced and Blankers-Koen made the cut to represent her country, "I got very many bad letters," with people telling her she should stay home as a housewife, watch her children, and not be seen in "short trousers." But Blankers-Koen, like so many others, felt a need greater than sport to participate.

She would not just participate—she dominated. The oldest female competitor in the track and field events, Blankers-Koen won the 100-meter, the 80-meter hurdles, the 200-meter, and then the 400-meter relay as anchor. No woman had ever won four golds, and she was tied with a man she once cheered for—Jesse Owens.

Not only her nation but the world cheered "the Flying Housewife," who has been credited with transforming how women were viewed as athletes, dispelling myths about womanhood, motherhood, and stamina. Although Blankers-Koen is not a well-known name in sport, she remains the only female track athlete to have won four gold medals in a single Olympic Games. "I find it difficult to think of anybody who made a bigger contribution to the development of women's athletics," said Sebastian Coe, president of World Athletics, track's governing body. "Or who made a broader impact on societal change, particularly around gender equity and diversity, both on and off the track."[28]

For the United States, Alice Coachman (1923–2014) became the first Black woman from any nation to strike Olympic gold in track and field; her event was the high jump. Like Blankers-Koen and so many other athletes, Coachman was ready to compete in both the 1940 and 1944 Games but World War II prevented her from showcasing her gift of jumping. The 1948 Games, however, was her opportunity to perform. "I made a difference among the Blacks, being one of the leaders," Coachman said. "If I had gone to the Games and failed, there wouldn't be anyone to fol-

Fanny Blankers-Koen. *Archive PL/Alamy Stock Photo*

low in my footsteps. It encouraged the rest of the women to work harder and fight harder."[29]

In 1952, she became the first Black woman to endorse an international product when she signed as a spokesperson for Coca-Cola.[30] Coachman, like so many athletes before her, was denied access to proper training facilities and coaching based on her race, but she would not let that stop her. Her acceptance into the Tuskegee Preparatory School, which included an athletic scholarship, allowed her to shine. It was the first recorded athletic scholarship for a Black female athlete in 1939, at age 15. Following the treatment and groundless dismissal of Pickett and Stokes, Tuskegee and numerous other organizations responded, ensuring that standout Black female athletes had a place to study, train, and gain exposure.

Within the AAU Women's National Championships, not only did Coachman break college and national high jump records (while barefoot), but also she was a national champion in the 50-meter and 100-meter dash, as well as the 400-meter relay, and won three conference championships as a guard in basketball.

For very different reasons, Babe had once said, "Sports was a way to be equal." But, in 1948, as Coachman was awarded her gold medal—a first for all Black women in her sport—by King George VI, her sentiment was profound. How glorious must she have felt when she said, "We are all equal."

Upon her return to the United States, however, Coachman said in a 1997 interview that she was treated like a nonperson, having to use a side door of an auditorium where she was being honored. Once there, the mayor of her hometown of Albany, Georgia, refused to shake her hand. It was not only Coachman, but also all Black athletes who won gold medals for their nation, only to be demoralized on their home soil.

In particular to Black female athletes, they did not reap the same social standing and economic benefits as either the white female or Black male Olympians for decades to come. For Coachman, her struggle was more insulting than most had experienced as her gold medal was earned in a time when American society was not yet ready to acknowledge it. Because the media all but ignored Coachman's victory, it was believed (and printed) that when Wilma Rudolf (1940–1994) won gold in the 1960 Olympic Games, it was a first for Black women. "Go anyplace," Coachman said in an interview following the 1960 Games, "and people will tell you Wilma Rudolf was the first black woman to win a medal—that's not true."[31] In good spirit, Coachman attributed Rudolf's credit as "a first" to media.

A similar historical "first" happened for gymnast Luci Collins (1964–). Today, Dominique Dawes (1976–) or "Awesome Dawesome" has often been referred to as the first Black gymnast. In truth, it was Luci Collins who became the first Black female to make the U.S. gymnastics team for an Olympic team. When, however, the United States boycotted the 1980 Olympic Games in Moscow, Collins would never be seen.

Her contribution to sport remains invaluable as she broke down racial barriers and, ultimately, opened the door for Dianne Durham (1964–2021), then Dawes, who became the first Black athlete to win an individual Olympic medal in women's gymnastics, and is the first U.S. gymnast to be part of three separate medal-winning gymnastics teams.[32] Later, Gabby Douglas (1995–) became the "first woman of color of any nationality and the first Black-American gymnast to become the Individual All-Around Champion" and first American gymnast to win gold in both the gymnastic individual all-around and team competitions during the same Olympic Games.

At the 1948 Games, however, U.S. diver Vicki Manalo Draves (1924–2010) incurred particularly horrible treatment. Although she earned two gold medals in platform and springboard, becoming the first Asian American Olympic champion, she had not been wanted.

The daughter of an interracial marriage in a time that was still very disapproving of a Filipino man and an English [white] woman, sports offered a mostly safe refuge for Manalo Draves, who adopted her mother's maiden name at the insistence of her diving coach.

While out in public, her mother would tell Manalo Draves and her two sisters to keep their heads down. "You guys look down at the ground, don't look up." But this was far from the worst of her indignations. Despite her rising status as a diver, when she was done practicing or competing in a pool, the water would be drained the day after she used it. Manalo Draves's son, David, later reported, "This really hurt my mom. She would actually go to a pool and compete, and after she got done with the meet, they would empty the water out of the pool."[33]

As for the overall results of the 1948 Games, it was not only a politically and socially successful event, but an economic one as well, netting a profit of more than £29,000. It also showcased the highest number of female athletes in the Olympic Games with some of the most popular, talked-about performances of the time. Women were undeniably proving to be commercially lucrative spokeswomen as well as exciting to watch. An example of this would be the 1972 Munich Olympic Games when Fanny Blankers-Koen met Jesse Owens once again and said, "I still have your autograph. I'm Fanny Blankers-Koen," to which Owens said, "You don't have to tell me who you are. I know everything about you."[34]

Blankers-Koen would be voted "Athlete of the Twentieth Century" (despite enduring such write-ups during the Olympic coverage as, running "like she was chasing kids out of the pantry," and she "fled through her trial heats as though racing to the kitchen to rescue a batch of burning biscuits")[35] by World Athletics,[36] but her actual contribution to women and sport, to societal norms and modern medicine, came by way of a pair of brightly colored shorts and a secret. Blankers-Koen's bright orange shorts, cinched at the waist, were not just considered too eye catching but also entirely too short for many viewers. As she continued to dominate the field, however, her critics were silenced by the roars of approval. It is these small, seemingly unimportant strides that bring about long-term change. This would include her medical condition. As she won four gold medals, few knew she was also pregnant. This post-Games news debunked the dozens of myths about women and pregnancy that the medical community had promoted for centuries. Hers was a victory that belonged to all women.

THE RED SCARE AND THE TEXAS TORNADO

Once again, it was sport that changed the political and economic land-scape of the world. Following the 1948 Games, there had been a sense of global community, of peace and goodwill. The 1952 Olympic Games in Helsinki, Finland, changed that as it was the first appearance by Russia as a newly formed communist nation. The Soviets held that if they domi-nated the Games, took home the most medals, the world—especially the United States—would recognize and respect their power. At the end of the two weeks, the United States held the most medals, but not by much. The Soviet Union had come to send a message and it brought with it the big guns—little girls. Never mind new U.S. records by high jumper Walt Davis (1931–) or hurdler Charlie Moore (1929–2020); when three Soviet women took the gold, silver, and bronze in discus, it was headline news in Russia with no mention of American wins.

All media, however, reported the rising tension between the Soviet Union and the United States. Previously, the United States, along with many other Western nations, had marginalized the predominately *female* sports while the Eastern bloc nations recognized the value in training all athletes (not for gender equity but domination of all disciplines), and, for the first time, the world was seeing a nation and its dominance through sport. The term "Cold War" had always implied military prowess leading up to the 1952 Games, but the Soviet Union changed that and a new fear overcame Westerners. *What if we [physically] are not strong enough?*

The immense success of the Soviet Union's female athletes prompted Western nations, particularly the United States, to reevaluate their value on traditional femininity vs. strength. In the 1950s, it was not yet con-ceivable that one could hold both. In the face of the Cold War, still on the heels of World War II, the idea that even the Soviet Union's women were stronger than ours, that communism promoted greater strength and agility, that they threatened our global image of superiority was frightening as the world had witnessed these apparent truths through their own television sets.

New York Times columnist and sports reporter Arthur Daley (1904–1974), who was perhaps one of the more vocal writers of his time, condemned the Soviet women's participation, saying, "When those Amazons from the Russian steppes came muscling into Helsinki last summer to sweep virtually every available event in sight, they left an indelible imprint on the Games."[37] Daley petitioned hard for the International Olympic Committee (IOC) to remove the Soviet women from competition and further limit women's participation in sport.

In truth, Russian women were early benefactors of the inclusion of women in sport. At the turn of the twentieth century, prior to the Bolshevik Revolution in Russia, Vladimir Lenin (1870–1924) himself had said, "It is our urgent task to draw women into sport,"[38] understanding that when empowering, including, emboldening all members of society, they are stronger as a whole. Of course, the irony is that communist ideologies and human rights became two separate issues and the people of the USSR were anything but empowered, but the inclusion of women in sport (and the military) showed the world how very capable women are when given an equal platform.

Western countries were forced to recognize that their restrictive social ideologies had *weakened* them. Because social and cultural factors were rarely considered in sport, the sudden domination of the Soviet Union was all the more shocking. Daley argued that the Soviet women's successes emasculated their men. Rather than bolster the idea of training our own women, he simply wanted to see the Soviet women removed, citing the "Amazons as evidence of what would happen to society if female athletes were not stopped."[39]

But Russia was only warming up. It saw how well its female athletes had performed and pressured the IOC to expand the field of sports for women. President John F. Kennedy saw this as well and would later use sports as a political platform to speak to the people.

Years following what happened in the Helsinki Games, President Kennedy appealed to *Sports Illustrated* to speak to the American people about physical education and sport in the Cold War effort, noting the impact of the Soviet Union's "powerful and implacable" threat. As Kennedy reckoned that the United States had to "meet the challenge," this included females.[40]

The initial response by Western nations was anything but gracious. Before the Western nations' awakening to the benefits of gender equity, there was female-shaming that came from the press corps and public; specifically, regarding the definition of beauty, femininity, and image.

Suddenly, American women were no longer challenged as "mannish" or of being "boy-girl like" as attention shifted to the Soviet and East German female athletes. Nina Antonovna Bocharova (1924–2020), who won four gold medals in Helsinki but was also a pioneer in the first female gymnastic competitions in the Olympic Games, was a particular favorite target of Daley, next to Maria Gorokhovskaya (1921–2001), who remains the only woman to win seven medals at a single Games in any sport.[41]

By the late 1960s and into the early 1970s, this justification for name-calling would be made more difficult with the emergence of Olga Korbut (1955–), nicknamed "Sparrow from Minsk," a petite girl in pigtails, and the rising Romanian star Nadia Comaneci (1961–), all of 4'11" and eighty-six pounds. They were pixies; they were adorable; they were everything that sports reporters like Arthur Daley personified as female. But as the Soviet women's gymnastics team dominated gold in 1952, 1956, 1960, 1964, 1968, and 1972 (they would also go on to win gold in team competition in 1976, 1980, and 1988), it became clear that were it not "for the Soviet women competitors, the USSR would have lost the majority of matches."[42]

Kennedy understood this early on. The Olympics were not just sport; they were and are international relations and foreign policy; they were and are gender, racial, and cultural equity. Just one year after the Helsinki Games and Soviet domination, the 1953 Kraus-Weber report showed that American children were far less fit than European children.[43] Historically speaking, Western nations had always responded to war efforts with increased physical conditioning within their educational systems for male students, but the Helsinki Games, combined with the USSR's carefully crafted "superiority" propaganda, had hit upon something more primal.

THE IMPORTANCE OF MEDIA IMAGES

In 1956, under President Dwight D. Eisenhower (1890–1969), the President's Council on Youth Fitness for boys and girls between the ages of five and twelve was created. In 1961, under Kennedy, it was renamed as the President's Council on Physical Fitness to address all age groups.[44] There was, however, a more notable push to get girls into (still female-appropriate) athletics.

At long last, new sporting opportunities began to open up to women in the West. The story of Pam Sproule Murray (1949–), the "Tomboy Tornado," is a rare find in women's sports history, in that media very rarely covered girls' and women's sports unless it was the Olympics or the heroine of the story was a headliner, such as Babe, Althea Gibson, or Gertrude Ederle. But in 1959, a cinematic newsreel, a premovie clip that provided current affairs, information, and entertainment to millions of moviegoers around the nation, rolled a one-minute-and-twenty-three-second clip of the very unusual matchup between a boy and girl.

Billed as a "boy-vs.-girl exhibition battle" that ended in a draw, nine-year-old, fifty-eight-pound Ronal Bryant took on the likewise Sproule. It was Sproule who received the most commentary feed with, "Now meet a curly haired cyclone, Pam Sproule, nine, who thinks box fighting might as well be co-ed." As the commentator praised Sproule Murray for "packing a wallop," the "Tomboy Tornado" scored a victory for females everywhere.[45]

"My mother was getting phone calls from relatives" who had unexpectedly seen Pam in theaters around the country. Pam had dismissed her contribution to women's sports as "not a big deal," as she was "just doing what my older brothers did." Where they went so, too, did Pam, also playing baseball and football "any time they needed an extra player. I was there." However, the image of pint-sized female boxer in movie theaters around the nation was more powerful than she or her family could have ever recognized.

With the Cold War, the shock of the Helsinki Games, and fresh images of Russia's female Amazons, the American family found itself at the center of a new debate. Prior to the Helsinki Games, Americans had prided themselves on taking care of their women. While images of Soviet women revealed hard lives working in factories with little money and less hope, American celebrated the "happy" homemaker ideal. Media images crafted the working woman as selfish, "putting themselves first before the needs of their families,"[46] and the female athlete was inappropriate for a grown woman.

As U.S. politicians and patriarchal and community leaders wrestled with the feminine ideal vs. nationalism in the late '50s, the decade closed out with the 1959 national newsreel of the boy-vs.-girl boxing exhibition, no doubt spurring further conversation even as the commentator lamented, "Think of the lucky boy who gets Pam in a few years from now!"[47]

Instead, there was the larger-than-life image on the big screen of a girl fighting and fighting well. It wasn't just Blankers-Koen and Coachman who could change sports and social norms, it was little girls, too.

As was the history of the early Spartan and Athenian women, a symbiotic relationship would soon develop between the Soviet and Western women. As women from communist countries helped to develop programs for Western women in gymnastics, track and field, and rowing, for example, Western European and American women helped their Soviet sisters in soccer, marathon racing, and horse racing. By 1973, the USSR Sports Committee proclaimed specific (male-dominated) sports to be "harmful to a woman's organism," naming soccer as one. "Physical stress typical of soccer can cause harm to sexual functions, varicose veins, thrombophlebitis, etc.," was cited as their concern for women, yet they never addressed how soccer might impact male soccer players.[48]

From women of antiquity, well beyond Sproule Murray's boxing debut and the famous "battle of the sexes," to the twenty-first century, recurring themes prevailed. Unlike male athletes, female athletes continued their fight for every advancement, every game, and every match while their femininity, appearance, menstrual cycle, and the image of the "working woman" were publicly analyzed. Yet again and again, they showed up, ready to play, and forever changed sport.

NINE

The Real History behind Title IX and the Battle of the Sexes

In the United States, the social conscience of the country was changing during the 1950s and '60s. The Red Scare was still a threat to many, but even more threatening was a wave of activism among women and minorities. Title VII was a landmark civil rights and labor law that outlawed discrimination based on race, color, religion, sex, and national origin (later, sexual orientation would be added to the law) and prohibited any racial segregation in schools or public accommodations, in the workforce, or within the application process of and/or voting opportunities. And right in the middle of that, not quite four years after the implementation of Title VII but four years prior to Title IX, was a petite, quiet, but determined twenty-year-old college student named Kathrine Switzer (1947–) who ran a marathon and changed the world.

THE BEGINNING OF A MOVEMENT

Rosa Parks (1913–2005), best known as the woman who would not give up her seat to a white man on a public bus, had been sitting in the "colored" section of the bus on December 1, 1955, when she was arrested. Following her trial, the Black community protested the Montgomery bus transport (known as the Montgomery Bus Boycott) as a form of peaceful protest, devastating the city's transportation budget but also bringing Martin Luther King Jr. (1929–1968) into the national spotlight. King continued to use nonviolent tactics throughout the South in the early 1960s to bring about change. King's "I Have a Dream" speech on August 28, 1963, before a crowd of 250,000 across the National Mall in Washington, D.C., inspired John F. Kennedy to push for civil rights legislation in Congress.

The assassination of Kennedy less than three months later helped pass the Civil Rights Act in 1964, but the act lacked support in local, state, and even national arenas to enforce the new laws. However, following the assassination of Martin Luther King Jr. in 1968, riots broke out across the land. President Lyndon B. Johnson "seized upon the regrets over King's assassination" to push more legislation through a racist Congress.[1] With the Voting Rights Act already passed in 1965, Johnson pressured the House and Senate to pass the Fair Housing Act in 1968.

For the first time, the White House was truly invested in the idea of fair consumer rights, voting rights, Medicare, housing rights, consumer protection, race relations, and educational opportunities. Johnson considered the passing of this act—which prohibited discrimination in housing based on race, color, religion, and national origin by landlords, real estate agents and companies, cities, insurance companies, and banks, including lending companies—his greatest accomplishment while acting as president. The Title VII of the Civil Rights Act, as amended, states that all employees and job applicants must be protected from employment discrimination based on race, color, religion, sex, and national origin. It was the beginning of what was to come.

Then, the women got involved. In fact, nine months prior to Parks's refusal to give up her seat, Claudette Colvin, a fifteen-year-old girl riding the same Montgomery bus transport system, had refused to give up her purchased seat for a young white woman. When the bus driver ordered Colvin to stand, she replied that she could not as "history had me glued to the seat." In school, they had been learning about Harriet Tubman and Sojourner Truth and she had felt their presence in that moment. She was arrested but at age sixteen challenged the law and became part of the landmark *Browder v. Gayle* case that successfully ended bus segregation laws in Alabama. According to the civil rights activist and attorney who represented both Colvin and Parks, "The whole of history of the civil rights movement may have been different but for Claudette."[2]

When women see women in history, inspiration and courage always follow.

THE MARATHON WOMAN

In 1967, Kathrine Switzer simply decided to enter into a race. But that decision led to international news and set off massive debates about gender equity and femininity. More than fifty years later, Switzer is still mystified by it all.

It began while attending Syracuse University as a journalism student. Switzer loved to run and had been running since she was a preteen, so once she discovered there was no women's team at Syracuse she approached the men's coach, Arnie Briggs (1916–2000), who was more than happy to have a woman run (unofficially) with his team. Switzer was, in fact, the first. Briggs, a World War II veteran and reservist with the National Guard and Army Reserves, was a seasoned marathon runner who loved to tell Switzer stories as they ran. He was also the founder of the Syracuse Running Club and participated in an astounding twenty-four Boston Marathons. But when Switzer, becoming stronger and stronger with each training session, suggested she run the marathon, Briggs was aghast.

No woman, he assured her, could run a marathon. As she argued with her unofficial coach, Briggs shouted, "No dame ever ran the Boston Marathon!" Under pressure, however, he conceded that if Switzer could run 26.2 miles with Briggs, he would train with her for the marathon. Not only did Switzer complete a marathon but as they neared the end of their course, Switzer suggested adding another five miles. At mile thirty-one, Briggs was thoroughly defeated and Switzer was on course to change history.

In reality, a woman named Arlene Pieper Stine (1930–2021) ran the Pikes Peak Marathon in Colorado in 1959, becoming the first known woman to complete a marathon, from start to finish, though there was no official entry or time. Stine entered the race, famous for its 8,000 feet of vertical gain to the 14,115-feet summit, as a publicity stunt for a health club that she owned. It would be almost sixty years later that Stine would learn that her run had been historic.[3] Stine was inducted into the Colorado Springs Sports Hall of Fame in 2016.

And in 1966, Roberta Bingay Gibb (1942–) had actually run the Boston Marathon for three consecutive years but always unofficially. While there is no official statement from marathon officials regarding Gibb, it is presumed that racing officials paid her little notice as her statistics would never be documented. Such circumstances have been repeatedly told by numerous female runners who, simply wanting to run, unofficially entered races, sometimes in disguise.

On April 19, 1967, it was a brisk thirty-four degrees and Switzer, her team, and almost everyone else were in layers, hiding not only racing bibs but also Switzer's gender. While Stine's amazing run had been for publicity, Switzer had hoped to run under the radar. After filling out the application, she paid the fee, got the required physician's note that she was physically fit to enter, and received her racing bib number. In 1967, the Boston Marathon had no official record stating that women could not race; it simply wasn't considered. But as the race began and everyone stripped protective layers, the media truck quickly identified Switzer. They shouted questions to her as she ran: *why did she want to run, what was she trying to prove, did she think she could even finish the race?* Racing official Jock Semple, however, was not nearly so enthusiastic. He jumped off the press truck and charged Switzer.

Marathon woman attacked. *Courtesy of Kathrine Switzer*

A photographer with the *Boston Globe Herald* caught the act in which Switzer's then boyfriend, a former All-American linebacker, pushed Semple off balance, allowing Switzer to run on. It all happened so fast, and Switzer was scared, then embarrassed, humiliated, then angry. As she later recalled, "The distance, as it always does, gave me time to think and dissipate my anger. Jock Semple didn't take me seriously" and had assaulted her.

As she ran, she wondered why other women did not run. Was it that they lacked the support system to try, or did they believe the myths like "running ruins your reproductive organs"? As Switzer settled in, finding her own rhythm in the race, she was anything but settled. Her own parents had always encouraged her and, she knew, without Briggs, she would not be running the Boston Marathon. "I wasn't so special after all; I was just lucky."

As she ran, she realized "the reason there are no intercollegiate sports for women at big universities, no scholarships, prize money, or any races any longer than 800 meters is because women don't have the opportunities to prove they want those things. If they could just take part, they'd feel the power and accomplishment, and the situation would change."

Switzer later recalled that as she continued the race, she began to feel an overwhelming purpose to represent female athletes. She felt protective for all female athletes who had been denied the opportunity she was undertaking. "I felt responsible to create those opportunities. I felt elated, like I'd made a great discovery."

She was not alone.

THE RACE TO TITLE IX

The same year that Switzer ran the Boston Marathon, President Johnson signed an executive order forbidding discrimination in federal contracts. Under pressure from the National Organization of Women (NOW), founded in 1966, Johnson signed Executive Order 11375, which required that all organizations, institutions, corporations, federations, and companies receiving federal contracts must adhere to fair and equal hiring processes and employment for men and women.[4] While Title VII, the Civil Rights Act of 1964, prohibited discrimination based on race, color, sex, religion, or national origin in the arena of employment and public accommodations, it had not included discrimination against people in educational institutions.

Sex had not been a condition of nondiscriminatory practices among employers and coworkers. This seemingly small legal loophole allowed for discrimination, harassment, and abuse to continue not only in the workplace but within the educational system, which would, again, include yet another component—athletics. Before Title IX, too few opportunities existed for female athletes. It was why Switzer had been forced to run with the men's team and was never allowed to be officially recognized as an athlete or have her own team, and why she had been assaulted during a race.

Prior to Title IX, in addition to educational opportunities being denied to women based on gender, there were no athletic scholarships afforded to women, no championships for women's teams, and no or too few training facilities, coaches, and equipment provided despite each school or institution receiving federal financial assistance. The National Collegiate Athletic Association (NCAA) had been created to help regulate football but over time had become the ruling body of collegiate athletics. While the NCAA made adjustments to men's sporting events over time, women's sports were dismissed.

In 1973, while Congress weighed just what it meant to have equal education within the United States, the "Godmother of Title IX" was about to enter her own marathon. Bernice Sandler (1928–2019) wrote extensively about sexual and peer harassment toward women in college campuses, and coined the phrases "gang rape" and "the chilly campus climate." She earned her master's in clinical and school psychology and then her EdD from the University of Maryland in counseling and personnel services where she was denied a full-time position because, she was told, "you come on too strong for a woman."

It was the late 1960s and Dr. Sandler had not considered herself a feminist; she "halfway believed the press descriptions of its support-ers as 'abrasive,' 'man-hating,' 'radical,' and 'unfeminine.'"[5] But as she began to do more research, she found that it was not illegal at that time to discriminate based upon gender in education. In a single footnote to a scholarly article, Sandler found a reference to an executive order in Title VII that prohibited organizations with federal contracts from gender bias or discrimination. It was all she needed.

She contacted the Women's Equity Action League, formed in 1968 with the purpose of combating discrimination against women in the employment and education sector, and together they filed a class ac-tion suit in 1970 on behalf of all women in higher education. It had been their intention to file against all the college and universities, claiming an "industrywide-pattern" of discrimination against women—a bold move that rocked the education system.

At its inception, Title IX had been created to even the playing field in education, with respect to admissions, financial assistance, and opportu-nity. Title IX opened doors for women to have greater access toward a degree in law, in medicine, or even at the high school level, but Sandler began to identify more roadblocks and even criminal actions levied against women in education.

She ensured that the prohibition of sexual harassment and assault were then built into Title IX and all institutions receiving federal assistance were required to take steps to prevent misconduct and take action against it. It was then that Sandler understood that not only was discrimination prevalent within college athletics but dangerously and fraudulently so. Sexual assault and harassment against women went unchecked and unre-ported or, in the cases when a report was filed, the claim was never fully investigated. From there, Sandler and others would begin compiling just how woefully negligent institutions had been in providing adequate and safe equipment, facilities, and instruction (coaching), as well as medical treatment for female athletes.[6]

In 1970, Sandler presented her findings to Rep. Edith Green of Oregon (1910–1987), who had chaired hearings on sexual discrimination in educa-tion, and served notice to more than 250 institutions that were identified as being noncompliant with the law and violating the rights of American citizens.

From there, Rep. Patsy Matsu Takemoto Mink (1927–2002) spearheaded the 1972 Title IX Amendment of the Higher Education Act. She was the first woman of color and the first Asian American woman elected to

Congress in 1964 and was all too familiar with sexual and racial discrimination. It was she who introduced the Early Childhood Education Act, which included the first federal child care bill; worked on the Elementary and Secondary Education Act of 1965; and became the first person to oppose a Supreme Court nominee on the basis of discrimination against women. She initiated a lawsuit that challenged and changed protocol to presidential authority under the Freedom of Information Act in 1971. Her crowning achievement, however, was the 1972 Title IX Amendment of the Higher Education Act, which she coauthored but would later be renamed the Patsy T. Mink Opportunity in Education Act, in 2002.

In 1971, the women found a timely ally in Senator Birch Bayh (1928–2019) who had been working on related legal issues to women's employment and sex discrimination. Introducing the Higher Education Act of 1965 to the Senate floor coincided nicely with the revised draft of the Equal Rights Amendment (ERA) with which he had hoped to gain more support, explaining that its introduction was "an important step in the effort to provide for the women of America something that is rightfully theirs—an equal chance to attend the schools of their choice, to develop the skills they want, and to apply those skills with the knowledge that they will have a fair chance to secure the jobs of their choice with equal pay for equal work."[7]

BATTLE OF THE SEXES

On June 23, 1972, President Richard M. Nixon (1913–1994) signed the bill. Despite the fact that Title IX was and has always been an antidiscrimination, civil rights bill, it was steeped in controversy and misrepresentation much like most issues regarding women's rights had been over the centuries. It was popularly referred to as a sports-equity law, but, on this, most female athletes were happy to accept it along with the rights they were due.

Fifteen months later, more than 50 million Americans and an estimated 90 million people worldwide watched the sporting event of the century on national television with another thirty thousand fans in the Houston Astrodome. Dubbed the Battle of Sexes, it was a tennis match of the ages between self-proclaimed "male chauvinist" Bobby Riggs (1918–1995), a retired tennis champion who had once been the number one player in the world for three consecutive years, and women's professional tennis star Billie Jean King (1943–). It was an exhibition that had by far the greatest cultural impact of any known match. It was a spectacle, reported to be one of the most watched events of all time, that produced a record number of souvenirs, T-shirts, buttons, and stickers while bookies placed bets and the world picked a side.

King had initially refused the offer to play Bobby Riggs in what had been presented as simply an exhibition. Winner of thirty-nine Grand Slam titles—twelve in singles, sixteen in women's doubles, and eleven in mixed doubles—she and Karen Hantze (1942–) also became the youngest doubles team to win Wimbledon Doubles history in 1961. She was the founder of the Women's Tennis Association, one of the cofounders for the Women's Sports Foundation, and became a publisher of one of the most progressive women's sports magazines, appropriately titled *WomenSports*. In 1975, *Seventeen* magazine (the leading teen publication for girls) conducted a poll in which its readers named Billie Jean King the most admired woman in the world while *Time* magazine named her one of its "Persons of the Year." In 1972, prior to the Battle of the Sexes, King was the joint winner of *Sports Illustrated*'s coveted "Sportsman of the Year," alongside basketball great John Wooden.

It had been King who pushed for women's advancement in sport—not just tennis but all sports. By 1968, King, along with other big-name players, organized a women's tennis circuit for better treatment and pay. What became known as the Virginia Slims Circuit, named after its sponsor,[8] King continued to push the boundaries for women in a sport she loved so much.

Playing into Riggs's hype for show was not something King believed would be good for her sport. When, however, Margaret Court (1942–), one of King's greatest competitors, accepted then lost to Riggs in what the press called the "Mother's Day Massacre," King knew she had to respond. Not only had Riggs's constant remarks about women ("women belong in the bedroom and kitchen, in that order") bothered her,[9] she also worried about how Court's loss to Riggs would impact women's tennis and Title IX. She understood that with the recent passing of Title IX came great responsibility. "I thought it would set us back 50 years if I didn't win that match. It would ruin the women's [tennis] tour and affect all women's self-esteem. To beat a 55-year-old guy was no thrill for me. The thrill was exposing a lot of new people to tennis."[10]

Despite all of Riggs's outrageous stunts and statements, King beat Riggs handily in straight sets, 6–4, 6–3, 6–3, and took home the prize of $100,000. But, she maintains, that was not what it was all about. While women and many men rejoiced, many sports columnists peddled the idea that Riggs had thrown the match or that witnesses existed who could substantiate that Riggs owed money to the mob and was forced to take a dive to pay off debts.[11]

Despite unprecedented victories for women and despite a new wave of feminism and cultural/societal changes for women, Title IX was similar to the Civil Rights Act (and so many others laws) in that it was met with great opposition. Self-interest groups, bigotry, misogyny, and indifference served as a disconnect between what had become law and implementation of said law.

Title IX did not officially go into effect until mid-1975, but the social, political, and economic impact leading up to and after that historic game sent a clear signal to high school and collegiate sports that female athletes were exciting, profitable, and formidable.

TEN

Media Relations and the Second-Wave Woman

A second wave of feminism (1960–1970s) spread quickly throughout the United States and other Western countries. It focused on equality and discrimination but also representation—the treatment of females in the media.

Title IX gave women renewed strength, but, in fact, strong women have always existed. As early warriors, they were skilled combat fighters and riders, nomadic women who literally fought for survival. As competitors, they began to appear in the eighteenth and nineteenth centuries.

Catarina "Katie" Brumbach Sandwina (1884–1954) tested social norms regarding women, strength, and femininity. Born in Austria to a family of circus performers—Sandwina's father was 6'6" and her mother was six feet tall with sixteen-inch biceps—Sandwina presumably had little concept of what the ideal beauty was as a child. At age thirteen she, too, was six feet tall and two hundred pounds in a time when the average male height was approximately five feet, six inches tall.[1] She performed feats of strength and wrestled any (male) challengers. Many challenged her, but no one ever won.

In 1902, Sandwina was a star.

It was not until 1985 that her record of a three-hundred-pound lift was broken by powerlifter Karyn Marshall (1956–).

In between those years, strongwomen such as Miriam Kate Williams (1874–1946), Josephine "Minerva" Blatt (1869–1923), and Ivy Russell (1907–) broke down barriers regarding women and (muscular) power. Russell was introduced to weightlifting as a way to regain strength as she had been stricken with tuberculosis, an infectious disease that ravaged entire communities at one time.

Abbye "Pudgy" Stockton (1917–2006) became the face of women's weightlifting and bodybuilding in the United States in the 1940s. But the 1950s and '60s "kept women strength athletes hidden" until Title IX and "second-wave feminism" emboldened women to venture into previously male-dominated sports.[2]

Billie Jean King's victory in 1973 had been thrilling, but female athletes were slow to speak out about mistreatment, not yet convinced of their right to be in the sports world, particularly in academia. There was no question that women not only had the talent but incredible strength, but Title IX brought about a new kind of activism.

In 1976, Yale University had grudgingly expanded its prestigious rowing program to include women. While both Harvard and Princeton had committed funds for their women's rowing teams to include sufficient facilities, Yale had not, relegating its female athletes to sit on a bus, cold and wet, while the men's team was allowed to take hot showers and change at the boathouse.

Emboldened by their own successes and lack of any championships from the men's team in over a decade, the women repeatedly attempted to garner better equipment and accommodations. Repeatedly, they had been dismissed. On March 3, 1976, they—future Olympians, doctors, lawyers, professors, national champions, and CEOs—took a stand. To ensure their message would be heard, the team had arranged for the editor of the school paper and a photographer to be present as the women's rowing team entered the office of the director of physical education.

Team captain Chris Ernst (1953–) recalled how the secretary had reacted. "She said, 'Oh, hi, Chris,' and then she looked behind me and said, 'Uh oh.'" Behind Ernst were nineteen other women, all of whom had removed their shirts and stood naked with "TITLE IX" or just "IX" on their skin.

For Ernst and fellow teammate Anne Warner (1954–), both also training for the first-ever inclusion of women's rowing for the 1976 Montreal Games, the protest was not just about the Yale team but for all female athletes. It was what Virginia "Ginny" Gilder (1958–), Olympic silver medalist and co-owner of the Women's National Basketball Association's (WNBA) Seattle Storm, called the team's "Declaration of Accountability." The *New York Times* picked up the story and soon reporters appeared from everywhere.

Female athletes around the world celebrated the protest and, within the United States, the Yale women's rowing team had reenergized the cause of Title IX. Yale issued a public apology, and the women's program was given adequate locker rooms and training.

SECOND-WAVE LEADERS

In 1992, Nancy Woodhull (1945–1997) and Betty Friedan (1921–2006) founded Women, Men and Media, a national organization that monitors how media covers and represents women. But it was long before this time that Woodhull understood the importance of how the press depicted not only female athletes but all females as it directly impacted women and community in all facets of life—politically, economically, and socially. Within the media world, Woodhull was and is an icon. Throughout the 1960s and '70s, she worked her way up to the editor's title on numerous publications and was the first managing editor for news at *USA Today* and senior vice president at the *Freedom Forum*, which dedicated itself to protecting free press and free speech. She was the vice chair of the International Women's Media Foundation (IWMF), chair of the Peabody Radio and Television Awards, and former president of the National Women's Hall of Fame in Seneca Falls, New York.

Betty Friedan cofounded the National Organization for Women (NOW) in 1966, organized the nationwide Women's Strike for Equality, and was credited for igniting the second wave of feminism in the United States. It was Friedan's book *Feminine Mystique* that became the emblem of feminism and earned Friedan the "Mother of Modern Feminism" title. But it was Gloria Steinem (1934–) who became the *face* and *legs* of feminism.

Alongside Dorothy Pitman Hughes (1938–), Steinem cofounded *Ms.* magazine, a media outlet that went beyond recipes, housekeeping, and beauty tips for women. It introduced national and international news, politics, even articles on car maintenance and home repairs. It was one of the first magazines for women that was also owned and produced by women.

Finding advertisers, however, had been a significant challenge as most did not believe a magazine could be run by women. The "sexual revolution" headlined newspapers and magazines across the nation while educators, medical professionals, psychologists, politicians, and church officials weighed in on how the female's new sexual freedoms negatively impacted the nation. *Ms.* magazine unapologetically tackled it all.

Later, Steinem became a co-convener of the National Women's Political Caucus in 1971 and helped found the Ms. Foundation for Women, which assists underprivileged girls and women, the following year. Though the credit for the term "gonzo journalism," a style of journalism in which the reporter interjects him- or herself into the story without any claims of objectivity, is most attributed to Hunter S. Thompson when he went undercover with the Hell's Angels in 1970, it was Gloria Steinem who first pioneered this reporter's tactic in 1963 when she went undercover as a Playboy bunny to expose the hypocrisies and dangers of female exploitation. Today, Steinem is now credited in major journalism courses as an example of undercover reporting.

Although it was British fashion designer Mary Quant (1934–) who created and coined the name "miniskirt" in the early '60s, it was Steinem who became the visible activist who led the fight for equality and sexual liberation (with the emergence of the birth control pill) and against the patriarchal ideals of proper feminine behavior—all while wearing a miniskirt. For the women of the 1960s, the miniskirt was a symbol of their fight—*you can't tell me how to dress.*

SECOND-WAVE ATHLETES

As Billie Jean King once said, "visibility matters." By the 1960s, 90 percent of Americans and three-quarters of the population in the United Kingdom owned a television,[3] allowing female athletes to be seen in ways they had previously not. Roller derby—an intense, grueling sport of speed, endurance, and power—began conversations in earnest about female athletes in the 1960s and '70s. Though it had been around since the 1920s, teams of men and women skating together, "jamming" or sprinting, on tracks in full-out brawls became extremely popular once televised.

It was the successes of roller derby during the '60s and '70s that taught promoters and showed the media the economic and cultural value of female athletes in sport.[4] Roller derby worked because the female athletes played up their femininity or their characters to audiences. Yet more trailblazers of this era were triumphant as they broke into more sports, setting new records and shattering myths as to what a female athlete should look like.

With television exposure came new fans (and scrutiny) of female athletes.

Most certainly, this would include track sensation Wilma Rudolf. Perhaps even greater than her achievements on the track was the media focus she garnered following the 1956 and 1960 Olympic Games. She became a role model. Unlike any other time, this Black athlete became a role model for not only Black girls but all girls. She was stricken with polio as a child but went on to win three gold medals at the 1960 Olympic Games in Rome in the 100- and 200-meter dash, and the 400-meter relay. She was nicknamed the "Black Gazelle" for her graceful style of running; was named the Associated Press Female Athlete of the Year for 1960 and 1961; became the first Black woman to win the James E. Sullivan Award, America's highest honor in amateur sports; and has been repeatedly credited for elevating women's track and field in the United States.

Following the Games, she became one of the most recognized athletes in the world. Rudolf retired in 1962 and became a dogged activist as a civil rights and women's rights leader.[5]

Rudolf's record-setting performance was tolerable because, as the track analogy allows, she stayed in her own lane. Women's track and field was acceptable. Diane Crump (1948–), however, had gone off course. In 1969, Crump became the first female jockey to compete as a professional in a parimutuel race in the United States, also becoming the first woman to compete in the Kentucky Derby. Initially, crowds were so angry by her entry that she and her horse required a police escort to the track. "The hecklers were yelling, 'Go back to the kitchen and cook dinner.' That was the mentality at the time. They thought I was going to be the downfall of the whole sport, which is such a medieval thought."[6]

The year prior, two other female jockeys had entered a race but were forced to withdraw when all the other male jockeys boycotted the race. Later, they reported that the male jockeys even threw rocks at the women's trailers, threatening them to leave not only the race but the sport.[7]

In 1975, Margo Oberg (1953–) became the first professional female surfer in the world at the age of twenty-four. Donna de Varona (1947–) also made history as the youngest member of the 1960 U.S. Olympic swimming team at age thirteen. Four years later at the Tokyo Games, de Varona set an Olympic record in the women's 400-meter medley and won a second gold in the 100-meter freestyle relay. At just seventeen years old, she appeared on ABC's *Wide World of Sports*, becoming the youngest and one of the first women sportscasters for a national network. She cofounded the Women's Sports Foundation with Billie Jean King, served five terms on the President's Council on Physical Fitness and Sports, and remained a staunch advocate of Title IX.

Shirley "Cha Cha" Muldowney (1940–), also known as the "First Lady of Drag Racing," and Janet Guthrie (1938–), the first woman to qualify and compete in both the Indianapolis 500 and the Daytona 500 in 1977, had, along with Oberg, de Varona, and others, become the new faces of what a female athlete looked like.

But it was Joyce "Micki" King (1944–), the 1974 Olympic gold medalist diver, who caused the greatest stir. She was a phenomenal diver who, the media frequently discussed, also filled out a bathing suit very nicely. She was also an officer in the U.S. Air Force (from 1966 to 1992). Her appearance at the Munich Games was a media conundrum. Reporters routinely spoke of female athletes' bodies, but King's title of U.S. military officer caused fans—male and female—to complain when hers was mentioned, opening new discussion of why the female athlete's figure was discussed at all.

Through her own actions, King would demand respect. In 1973, she became the first woman to hold a faculty position at the U.S. Military Academy and the first coach of any sport to train a male athlete to an NCAA championship. She was named Coach of the Year for the NCAA Division II, winning four titles, and retired as a full colonel from the U.S. Air Force. However, her greatest legacy in women's sports is one of which both she and Wyomia Tyus have received little recognition. King and Tyus joined Donna de Varona and Billie Jean King in cofounding the Women's Sports Foundation. Regarding Tyus (1945–), not only did she become the first Olympian, male or female, to win back-to-back gold medals in the 100-meter (1964 and 1968), but also she is the first recorded Olympian to protest for human rights as a (Black) female athlete. History ignored her triumphs. Twenty years later, U.S. sprinter Carl Lewis (1961–) was publicly awarded the distinction of back-to-back champion.[8]

These women were no longer stories in the news but images that appeared in living rooms across the country.

While Sharon Sites Adams (1930–) became the first woman to sail solo across the Pacific in 1969, the first-ever nationally televised women's college basketball was aired in 1975 (Immaculata vs. University of Maryland) and Lucy Harris (1955–) became the first woman to be drafted by an NBA team (New Orleans Jazz) in 1977.

Althea Gibson (1927–2003) was an athlete who transcended her sport during times of racial inequity and violence. According to Billie Jean King, who knew and respected Gibson from the tennis circuit, "I never saw her back down."[9] Gibson became the first Black athlete, male or female, to win a Grand Slam title. She won both Wimbledon and the U.S. Nationals and was voted Female Athlete of the Year by the Associated Press in 1958 yet was still not allowed to play in certain tournaments because of her race. She went on to win eleven Grand Slam tournaments, five singles titles, five doubles titles, and one mixed doubles title. Then, in 1964, she became the first Black woman to earn her Ladies Professional Golf Association (LPGA) player's card.[10]

Hers was an achievement not lost on Katrina Adams (1968–), the first Black president of the United States Tennis Association (USTA), who said, "This is not just a player who won a ton of titles, this is someone who transcended our sport and opened a pathway for people of color. If there was no Althea, there'd be no me, because tennis would not have been so open to me."[11]

NOT GOOD ENOUGH

When Gibson turned to golf, she was mistaken if she believed things would be easier for a woman. In 1963, the first LPGA championship tournament was televised and won by Mary Kathryn "Mickey" Wright (1935–2020), but not everyone was impressed. Golf, a sport steeped in tradition in which working men played the fairway on weekends to be free of family, only grudgingly allowed women and minorities to enter the game. Legendary golf instructor Marshall Smith (1926–2013) unapologetically penned the article "Please, Lady, Get Off My Golf Course" in a 1966 publication of *Life* magazine, in which he described women as silly and "dawdling," in one paragraph, then vicious and vindictive in the next.

Women, he warned, threatened the integrity and traditions of the game, where "the subtleties of the game escape them."[12]

It was a popular attitude—the cover of the *Life* magazine took care to run a teaser "Advice to Lady Golfers: Get Lost!"—also shared by golfing associations and officials, and all the more notable when women achieved leadership positions in the game.

Althea Gibson. *Everett Collection Inc./Alamy Stock Photo*

It was 1977 before the PGA (Professional Golfers' Association) of America voted to allow female members and almost twenty years later before the first woman, Judy Bell (1936–), became the president of the United States Golf Association (USGA). The year prior, Marcia Chambers (1940–2018), widely credited for exposing the golf world for its continued race and gender discrimination, wrote her expose *The Unplayable Lie: The Untold Story of Women and Discrimination in Golf* and forced changes for minority groups, particularly women.

Another nineteen years later, Suzy Whaley (1966–), the first woman to qualify for both the LPGA and PGA in 2002, was elected as secretary of the PGA Board of Directors in 2014, becoming the first female officer in its history. Two years later, Diana M. Murphy (1950–) became the sixty-fourth president (only the second woman) in the USGA's 121-year history while Suzy Whaley became the first female president of the PGA of America in 2018.[13]

But, before all that, came the 1976 Montreal Olympic Games.

THE PERFECT "10"

Nadia Comaneci (1961–) of Romania was just fourteen years old when she became the first gymnast in the world, male or female, to receive a perfect 10 as a score. When the first "10" appeared on the scoreboard, however, there was brief confusion until it was understood that Comaneci had seemingly done the impossible. This would happen six more times. Overnight, Comaneci became an international sensation. But Comaneci did something far more impressive than score seven perfect 10s.

Not since Babe (Didrikson Zaharias) had reporters around the world taken to calling an Olympian by his or her first name. Reporters, broadcasters, promoters, Olympic sponsors, and advertisers all scrambled to make contact with the young star who rarely smiled and seemed elusive and mysterious.

She hadn't just earned a perfect score, she had changed the sport of gymnastics forever. She changed the judging standards and introduced new techniques and fundamental changes, showing audiences moves no one had ever seen before, much less thought possible. She also became the movement for an entire new generation of athletes—male and female. Moreover, it was not just gymnastics: As Nadia became the talking point of the Montreal Games, she symbolized what it was to be an Olympian, a "10."

Still, the patriarchal hegemonic feminine ideal was so strong that even as Comaneci rewrote Olympic standards, broke records, and changed an entire sport in mere days, the press could not refrain from discussing her small *girlish* frame, her ribboned ponytail and shy smile while Olympic standouts such as American boxer Sugar Ray Leonard (1956–) and decathlete Bruce Jenner (1949–) were noted for their aggression and power. While the champion male athlete has historically been portrayed as domineering and commanding, the female athlete was and still is measured by her appearance and emotions.

THE SPORTS BRA

Lisa Lindahl (1948–) wasn't an elite athlete; she just wanted to run: "1977 was the jogging craze," Lindahl said, but as much as she wanted to be part of it, "it was too painful." She had complained to her sister that women should have jockstraps, too, just in the way of breast cups. And so began what *Runner's World* magazine called "the greatest invention in running—ever,"[14] with the sports bra prototype (two jockstraps sewn together as a bra) in the archives of the Smithsonian's National Museum of American History.

Together, she and a childhood friend, Polly Smith (1949–), tried a variety of new designs with Lindahl running around "to see how much they [breasts] bounced." Smith, who worked as a costume designer, and later, her assistant Hinda Schreiber Miller (1950–), ultimately helped to create the final "JogBra" design, and history was made.

At the time, there were no athletic products for female athletes (the first women's athletic shoe was created in 1982), and securing a loan for a bra was, Lindahl said, "laughable. No bank was going to loan us money." After securing a patent in 1977, it did not take long before women realized theirs was a bra specifically designed for exercise, "and we couldn't keep up with the demand."

In 1990, Lindahl and her partners sold the JogBra to Playtex. Their invention created a $25 billion industry[15] on the backs of Title IX and an empowerment that came from such images as televised female athletes running, jumping, and diving.

Both Woodhull and Friedan had been right to create a national organization that monitors how media covers and represents women. Great strides had been made throughout the 1960s and into the 1980s with exciting new female athletes, but media coverage continued its relentless push for the feminine ideal and, more often than not, even worse.

THE STORY OF BEV FRANCIS AND RACHEL MCLISH:
FIRST OR LAST

And so it was for the first-ever documentary on female bodybuilders.

For the production of the 1983 bodybuilding docudrama *Pumping Iron II*, photographer George Butler chose Raquel Livia Elizondo (1955–), who would later become Rachel McLish, a Texas native who had grown up in cheerleading, and Australian powerlifter Bev Francis (1955–) as his two stars.

By 1980, still a relative newcomer to the sport, McLish won the first-ever title of Ms. Olympia and, for the next five years (of which she was only competitive for four), no other competitor was on more magazine covers or featured in more health articles. As was repeatedly noted, her "sexy" appearance made her highly promotable.

As the 1983 competition approached, Butler then found the woman he wanted to add to the cast of competitive women, an unknown to the bodybuilding world but an accomplished world powerlifting champion who had won the title of "Strongest Woman in the World" for two consecutive years.

Bev Francis was everything McLish was not. She grew up playing every sport she could, became a champion shot putter, and broke the Australian shot put record in 1977. She was accomplished in discus throw, javelin,

Pumping Iron II. Everett Collection, Inc./Alamy Stock Photo

and the 100-meter sprint. She set world records in bench press and squat, becoming the first woman to press over three hundred pounds, and when Butler saw a picture of Francis he knew she had to be in his film.

Francis, however, had to be convinced. "At that time, I had become so strong in powerlifting, I had been in a lot of magazines," Francis said. "I had no interest in bodybuilding. To me, it was pointless. You just went out to hit poses, just showing off. I was an athlete who used the body with purpose."

As an athlete, however, there were some interesting components to Butler's offer. He had told Francis that he wanted an array of female bodies and abilities for the film, "that he didn't just want a fluff movie." It would be an opportunity to show what she could really do, expose more people to the true power side of bodybuilding, but it would also be a test for Francis. Additionally, the preparation of bodybuilding for Ms. Olympia would be a kind of training and test that Francis had never experienced. She was in.

At once, Francis caused a commotion. No one had ever seen such a muscular woman before, and throughout the film and actual competition, the age-old questions of *what is femininity?* and *how muscular should a woman be?* were repeatedly asked. In one particularly unflattering review, the two women were characterized as the "Incredible Tease" and the "Incredible Hulk." In the same review, the author pens, "McLish turns out to be a clever little vixen, padding the top of her bikini and covering it with glitzy material, both contrary to contest rules. And all the while she talks about the power of religion in her life."[16]

Francis spoke often about her own concerns that, despite what the competition espoused, the championship was less about muscle development and symmetry and more about being a beauty pageant. In the end, Carla Dunlap (1954–) was chosen as the winner, becoming the first Black woman to win Ms. Olympia, while McLish came in third and Francis came in eighth.

Despite the fact that Dunlap was the new Ms. Olympia of 1983, it was McLish who graced the cover of the film's poster. It was also McLish who went on to star in movies, make the late-night television circuit, grace countless more magazine covers, model, and write two *New York Times* best sellers. McLish's success lent to a comment Francis made years after the showdown: "When I came in as the most muscular competitor at that 1983 Caesar's Palace contest . . . I should have been first or last."

The intent that Ms. Olympia was to be judged equally in the manner men were judged, based upon muscle definition and symmetry, was another female fallacy. The expectations of the female competitors were medically implausible—to be hard and lean but also curvy, busty, and soft. By the late 1980s, competitors were heavily encouraged to get breast

Bev Francis poses. *Courtesy of Bev Francis*

implants. According to sociologist/author Maria R. Lowe of *Women of Steel*, 80 percent of female fitness and bodybuilding athletes had breast augmentation. Never had any competition within the sports world shown such disparity in judging and harmful standards to the human body as women's bodybuilding and physique competitions.

In regard to the "first or last" comment in 1983, Francis was, of course, right. First or last, she would have been judged on muscular appearance or societal ideal standards of femininity.

"STRONG" WOMEN INTO THE NEXT GENERATION

The importance and contributions of the *strongwoman* in women's history cannot be overstated. One of the most common arguments about a woman and her rights throughout time has been about her physical strength or lack thereof. But as these pioneering women outlifted and outperformed men, breaking both records and societal norms, they showed just what women were capable of doing.

Janice "Jan" Todd (1952–) was one of those pioneers and a beneficiary of Title IX who changed the image of female powerlifters. As a professor in kinesiology, Todd practiced what she preached, bringing both media and academic attention to what female athletes can and have done. Throughout the 1970s and '80s, Todd set more than sixty national and world records, appeared in the *Guinness Book of Records*, and was the first woman inducted into the International Powerlifting Hall of Fame.

Todd is credited with much of the progress made for women in strength training, along with such weightlifting legends such as Karyn Marshall, Judy Glenney (1949–), and Diane Fuhrman (1962–), who made huge lifts and even bigger strides to bring women's weightlifting to the forefront.

In 1995, at just 4'11", Carrie Lynn Boudreau (1967–2020) not only made sports history but also medical history when she held the record for lifting a total of 1,154.72 pounds in three lifts: bench press, squat, and deadlift— deadlifting alone 491.72 pounds. Both the *Guinness Book of World Records* and *Medicine & Science in Sports & Exercise Journal* named Boudreau, at 123 pounds, as "pound for pound the world's strongest woman."

An athlete who said she "thrives on things stacked against" her, who suffered from asthma and scoliosis as a child, felt a new kind of empowered as she transitioned into weightlifting. Krista Ford (1966–), a twelve-time national and seven-time world powerlifting champion throughout the 1990s and early 2000s, shared this sentiment as one of the first Black women to compete in "an otherwise white sport." In their own ways, both Ford and Boudreau helped to transform both the sport and the image of females through their own lifts, and, by 2000, weightlifting was officially an Olympic sport for women at the Sydney Games.

CrossFit and strongwoman competitions around the world were held annually and, at last, not only breaking records and changing norms but providing role models.

As is the constant in women's history, however, the need for beauty and that feminine ideal to quell patriarchal worrying that sports or, in this case, lifting would harm a woman's image and health was answered by none other than six-time Ms. Olympia Corinna "Cory" Everson (1958–). During her reign as Ms. Olympia, she never lost, became the first female bodybuilder to receive the Lifetime Achievement Award in 2007, and was inducted into the National Fitness Hall of Fame the following year. Much was made of her beauty and "clean lines" during her competitive years, but it was in 1989 that Everson announced her retirement, noting that the look of competitive lifting had changed.

For her sisters of iron and women's sports, Everson acknowledged that a new kind of brawn had entered women's sports. Women were bigger and stronger than ever before. Powerhouse Robin Coleman (1973–), best known as "Helga" on the popular television series *American Gladiators*, once stunned a crowd in England during a strongwoman competition when she squatted a car fifteen times. Similarly, Becca Swanson (1973–) with her 17.5" biceps and 27" quads, officially became the strongest woman in the world when she squatted 854 pounds, bench pressed 600 pounds, and deadlifted 694 pounds.[17]

As a product of the second feminist wave, women were, at long last, choosing their own feminine ideal, the best version of themselves.

As for Francis, she continued to lift and compete following the disappointment of *Pumping Iron II*. To be clear, she was never disappointed in herself. She had done what she set out to do. As a child, she had craved more female role models, "someone who looked like me." For Francis and her fellow competitors, all the lifts and broken records are not for individual athletes but for everyone. "Women have changed politics, policies and societies every time we show what we can do," Francis said. "People have to realize women are so much more capable when given the right to be."

Eleven

The Third Wave and the Women of the 1980s and 1990s

After centuries of arguing that women could not only endure long-distance running, but also triumph at it, American Joan Benoit Samuelson (1957–) became the first female Olympic marathon champion in 1984. At the last mile, as she emerged from the tunnel into the stadium, the roar of applause from 77,000 fans reassured members of the IOC and the medical community who still believed women could not handle the grueling event.

In the 1980s and '90s, the history of women in sports and society saw great successes. By the 1950s, one of every three American women worked outside the home; by the 1990s, three out of every five worked outside the home.[1] Yet the image of women in the workplace remained highly problematic.

Women in the workplace were still assigned gender-specific tasks, expected to adhere to different dress codes, and forced to suffer sexual harassment and intimidation. Women were (and are) paid less with less opportunity for advancement. The workplace was (and is still) a male domain.

In 1975, Paulette Barnes, a federal employee demoted after refusing sexual advances from her employer, became one of the first known women to benefit from Title VII (emboldened by Title IX). At the time, discrimination and sexual harassment of a woman in the workplace was so foreign to the legal system that the courts initially denied Barnes, arguing that her refusal to have sex with an employer demonstrated "an inharmonious personal relationship" that "does not evidence an arbitrary barrier to continued employment based on appellant's sex." Sexual harassment was so common in the workplace most women did not understand they had legal protection. Sexual harassment had been considered women's "personal problems" as they certainly had to know what they were getting into by entering the male domain.[2] But a federal court found in Barnes's favor, sending the clear message that sexual harassment was a form of discrimination, negatively impacting a person's rights, and was legally prohibited.[3]

119

Ironically, the director of the Equal Employment Opportunity Commission (EEOC) and his adviser would become the center of one of the most notable cases of sexual harassment in history, bringing on the third wave of feminism in the United States.

THE THIRD WAVE

In 1991, attorney and law professor Anita Hill (1956–) stood before a Senate Judiciary Committee to testify against Clarence Thomas, who had been nominated to the U.S. Supreme Court. Hill had been called before the Senate to answer rumors that Thomas had sexually harassed women he had worked with. She had initially refused, knowing how such inquiries played out for women. But deciding it was her duty to provide factual information to the panel, she testified.

In the end, the all-male panel confirmed Thomas to the Supreme Court, outraging and dividing the American people. Hill's testimony brought about public conversations about a previously taboo topic; women suddenly understood that they were not alone in their mistreatment and harassment at work while many more were outraged by the behaviors of a member of the "'good ol' boy'" system within the U.S. Senate who had acted most inappropriately with Hill.

Phones reportedly "began ringing off the hook" at the National Women's Law Center asking for legal advice. Hill's bravery ignited sexual harassment claims with the EEOC, forcing Congress to pass the Civil Rights Act of 1991, which gave victims of sexual harassment in the workplace more legal recourse.[4]

Writer and activist Rebecca Walker (1969–) was one of the millions to witness the Senate hearing spectacle and, like so many, was outraged. Following the hearing, she wrote an article for *Ms.* magazine, "Becoming the Third Wave."

Credited for coining the phrase, Walker wrote, "So I write this as a plea to all women, especially women of my generation: Let Thomas's confirmation serve to remind you . . . the fight is far from over. Let this dismissal of a woman's experience move you to anger. Turn that outrage into political power. Do not vote for them unless they work for us. Do not have sex with them, do not break bread with them, do not nurture them if they don't prioritize our freedom to control our bodies and our lives. I am not a post-feminism feminist. I am the Third Wave."[5]

Although Hill had been a pillar of strength, her voice had been dismissed. But she had started a movement, and it extended to female athletes who, again and again, helped showcase the strength of women, the draw of female athletes, and the certain fact that they were not going away.

THE SCANDAL OF WOMEN

Seven years prior to Hill's testimony, two women engaged in a contest, steeped in political overtones, that became one of the most enduring and talked about events at the 1984 Olympic Games.

It was called the most infamous fall in Olympic history. It was the story of an eighteen-year-old runner from South Africa, Zola Budd (1966–), who ran barefoot against her idol, the seasoned world record holder in the mile, 5,000-meter, and 10,000-meter races, Mary Decker (1958–).

Decker was the first woman in history to break 4:20 for the mile, set thirty-six U.S. National records in long-distance events, and only the second woman in history to be named "Sportsman of the Year" by *Sports Illustrated* after she won the 1,500 and 3,000 meters at the 1983 World Championships in Helsinki.[6]

Heavily favored to win gold at the 1984 Olympic Games in the 3,000-meter event, Decker had a strong lead into the second half of the race. Midrace, however, the barefoot Budd attempted a pass and disaster struck.

Budd, already controversial as she circumvented politics by running for Great Britain rather than her own nation, was a sensation in her own right. At age seventeen, she broke the 5,000-meter world record with a time of 15:01.83 but, because the event took place in South Africa, the International Association of Athletics Federations (IAAF) would not ratify the time. South Africa was still under inhumane apartheid rule (racial segregation). Understanding that the track phenom, a white athlete, would never succeed in South Africa, her family moved to and obtained citizenship from Great Britain. In 1985, under Britain's flag, Budd smashed the existing record with a time of 14:48.07, but, for the 1984 Los Angeles Games, her eyes had been on Decker.

The buildup to the race between Decker and Budd had been so intense, other serious contenders such as Romania's Maricica Puică (1960–) were completely omitted from conversation. It was a race about racism. It was America vs. apartheid.

When it happened, then, cameras were already in focus.

Budd made the move to take the lead coming out of turn four. Her bare feet clipped Decker's, causing Decker to lose balance, and as she fell, she reached out to grab hold of something and tore off Budd's bib number, but it was too late. Decker went down. Budd immediately understood what happened and, on instinct, continued to run until she ultimately collapsed into tears. Few people remember who actually won the race (Puică of Romania); it is still largely remembered for the collision and iconic photographs.

As photographer David Burnett described it, "The pain in Mary Decker's face—so raw, and apparent—was something that almost should have remained the ultimate private moment. It was the anguish of a moment seen by 75,000 in the stadium, and millions around the world via television. Never have I witnessed such a raw public-private moment. . . . Yet it was played out before the world. It became Mary's worst day."[7] As it would be Budd's.

For the business of sport and the modern Olympics, however, it was pure gold. Its female athletes were the most talked about, debated, cherished, and scandalized topics of the time, proving they weren't only capable, they were exciting, they were controversial; they were moneymakers.

Exactly one decade later, another female rivalry came to light in unimaginable ways. It was called the "the scandal of Olympic proportions," and the "whack heard around the world."

It was January 1994 when Nancy Kerrigan (1969–) and then-thirteen-year-old Michelle Kwan (who would go on to become a two-time Olympic medalist, five-time world champion, and nine-time U.S. champion) came off the ice together following a practice session two days before the Olympic trials. Out of respect, the younger Kwan (1980–) let Kerrigan go first, and Kwan stopped to speak to her coach as Kerrigan disappeared behind the blue curtain leading to the locker and training rooms.

Dana Scarton, a reporter with the *Pittsburgh Post-Gazette*, had also been present and had followed Kerrigan to get a quote, becoming one of the best eyewitnesses to the assault. Scarton asked Kerrigan for an interview when a large man charged Kerrigan from behind, striking her "with something that looked like a crowbar," first on one knee, then again on both legs. As Kerrigan went down, "I heard her crying and screaming," Kwan said.[8]

What the world saw was Kerrigan, sitting on the floor of the hallway, crying in pain, "Why? Why? Why?" captured by a Chicago-based film crew on assignment to cover Kerrigan. Her final cry of "Whyyy me?" would be used again and again for years to come with still images of her on the cover of all major newspapers and magazines, many not known for sport. It was a moment in history that transcended sport.

The drama was spectacular.

Fellow figure skater Tonya Harding (1970–), always second fiddle to Kerrigan, was immediately a suspect in the attack. Later, Harding's ex-husband, Jeff Gillooly, and her "bodyguard" would be implicated, along with several other men, and arrested for the assault on Kerrigan. Gillooly pleaded guilty to planning the assault (and later implicated Harding). Harding was banned from skating only to be reinstated by the United States Olympic Committee (USOC), though it pointedly deferred any mention of her innocence involving the assault, stating: "We are appalled still by the attack on Nancy Kerrigan, which was not only an attack on the athlete, but an assault on the basic ideals of the Olympic movement and sportsmanship."[9]

Harding won the U.S. national title after Kerrigan withdrew from competition for medical reasons (i.e., severe bruises sustained due to assault by a club).[10] But in a plot perfect for a made-for-TV movie, Kerrigan arrived in Lillehammer, Norway, at the Olympic Games in time to earn a silver medal. Harding would place eighth.

For those in attendance, few remember who the other competitors were (Russian skater Oksana Baiul [1977–] won the gold), but they can still envision the media circus that surrounded the games. Suddenly, everyone wanted to watch not only the competition, but even the practice sessions, in hopes of spotting drama between Kerrigan and Harding. The practice sessions were so packed with media from around the world that added security was needed. TV ratings for the 1994 Winter Olympics skyrocketed and the skaters became worldwide celebrities.

THE STORY OF FLO-JO AND THE PED CONTROVERSY

Into the 1980s, sports fans were looking for someone beyond pixie-like gymnasts and victimized runners. That someone came in the way of controversy, grace, and muscles.

Florence "Flo-Jo" Griffith Joyner (1959–1998), known as "the fastest woman of all time," burst from the starting blocks—literally—in the 100- and 200-meter races. At the 1984 Olympic trials, she had put up the second-fastest time after Evelyn Ashford (1957–), but an injury for Ashford opened the door for Griffith Joyner to earn a silver medal in the 200-meter race at the Games.

Later that year, Flo-Jo married Al Joyner (1960–), an Olympic triple jump champion. This union brought about one of the most powerful and much talked about families in track history. Al Joyner was the brother to Jackie Joyner Kersee (1962–), considered by many to be the greatest female all-around athlete in history (gold medal–winning heptathlete and long jumper), who was married to none other than Florence Griffith Joyner's coach, Bob Kersee.

Prior to the 1988 Olympic trials, Ashford was back and still held the three best times (10.76 was the fastest recorded time) for the 100-meter with Griffith Joyner racing a 10.99 in the race. In the quarterfinals of the trials' qualifiers, however, Griffith Joyner stunned her fellow competitors when she set a new world record of 10.49, while also setting an American record in the 200-meter with a time of 21.77. Then, at the Olympic Games, Griffith Joyner stunned again, breaking two Olympic records and running a 10.54 in the 100-meter and a 21.34 in the 200-meter while also running in the 4×100 meter and 4×400 meter events.

The 1988 Olympic Games, as it turned out, was ensconced in a drug scandal that swept American sprinter Flo-Jo into the fold as both her physical metamorphosis and surprising times were subjects of speculation. Fellow competitors argued that her use of heavy makeup was done to cover acne brought about by her steroid use.[11] Despite the rumors, the press was told that Flo-Jo tested negative on every performance-enhancing drug (PED) test she was given.

When it was announced the following year that all athletes would be subjected to random drug tests, Griffith Joyner announced her retirement. Both announcements, one on the heel of the other, only heightened suspicions among those who claimed Flo-Jo had been doping. A decade later, Marion Jones (1975–), who would later be stripped of her medals for steroid use, put up the second-fastest time for a female track athlete in the 200-meter event with a time of 21.62, 0.28 seconds slower than Griffith Joyner's time of 21.34.

When Flo-Jo suddenly died in her sleep in 1998, those rumors resurfaced again with much speculation that the PEDs had been the root of her death. The coroner report, however, listed her cause of death as suffocation during a severe epileptic seizure, complicated by a cavernous hemangioma, a congenital vascular brain abnormality, and no conclusive evidence of drug use was found. Still, her name resurfaced again following a series of studies in 2015 on how long-term use of performance-enhancing drugs can cause significant brain structural and functional abnormalities, and lead to more devastating effects.[12]

That same year, in 2015, Victor Conte (1950–), founder of BALCO, Bay Area Laboratory Co-Operative, held responsible for dispensing steroids to hundreds of well-known athletes and later convicted of distributing illegal steroids for athletes, claimed that Flo-Jo and Joyner Kersee, among others, had positive drug tests covered up at the 1988 Olympics.

Year later, a whistleblower leaked data revealing that of the documented twelve thousand blood tests between 2001 and 2012, approximately five thousand track-and-field athletes showed "suspicious" blood tests, which, according to Conte, only proved that the politics and economics of sport outweigh the Olympic creed.[13] But the image of Flo-Jo had been particularly important to many.

Sports Illustrated's Frank Deford (1938–) had understood this. In a 2013 interview on NPR, he shared, "In 1988, at the Seoul Olympics, I saw a side-by-side video of Flo-Jo from 1984 and that present time. She looked and sounded like a different person. The comparison was so shocking that the producer told me he feared it would be an ugly bombshell back in the USA, if such incriminating evidence were shown about an American heroine. So, NBC shelved the tape."[14]

Many more see Flo-Jo's records as a detriment to women's track and field. No female athlete has been able to come close to Griffith Joyner's 100- and 200-meter times since 1988. For Gwen Torrence, a 200-meter Olympic champion, she refuses to acknowledge those records. "To me, they don't exist and women sprinters are suffering as a result of what [Flo-Jo] did to the times in the 100 and 200."[15]

In terms of women in sport, Flo-Jo was and is important. She was controversial and exciting. Famous for her personally designed one-legged

Florence Griffith Joyner. *PCN Photography/Alamy Stock Photo*

outfits; her long, flowing hair; and outrageously long and colorful nails (said to measure four inches), she was also muscular and sculpted.

This visibility, well after her retirement when she pursued fashion, would also forever change the sport of basketball. In 1989, an unpaid intern named Rebecca Polihronis, who had followed Flo-Jo's career, suggested that the NBA's Indiana Pacers contact the former Olympian regarding a new "look" for the team. Flo-Jo not only changed the Pacers but the entire NBA, bringing about the baggier, longer shorts and larger jerseys.[16]

HOOPS, SWOOPES, AND PRODUCT PLACEMENT

By the 1990s, a true sign that a male athlete was both successful and marketable was when he got a shoe deal. But it had always been a "he" deal. However, as more and more girls and women entered athletics, the politics and social issues and economics of the sports world began to change. This would include the world of advertisers and marketing.

In 1995, Nike teamed up with Sheryl Swoopes (1971–) prior to the 1996 Olympic Games to create the first Nike shoe to be named after a female athlete—Air Swoopes. Two years earlier, Swoopes was named Player of the Year, was an NCAA champion, and held the most points (male or female) in a national title game of forty-seven. It is a record that remains unbroken.

She caught Nike's attention when Michael Jordan (1963–) invited Swoopes to work at his summer youth camp. The two played a game of one-on-one that was caught on camera. It was later aired on NBC to the musical soundtrack of "Anything You Can Do (I Can Do Better)" but, with the formation of the WNBA in 1995, everything seemed to fall into place.

After winning Olympic gold and two championships playing with the Houston Comets, Swoopes signed contracts with Kellogg and Discover Card, she made personal paid appearances, and Air Swoopes went into a third version (by 1999, Air Swoopes had five versions of the shoe). She also had three Swoopes basketballs, a Swoopes jersey, three Swoopes children's books, a Swoopes coffee-table book, a Swoopes trading card, a Swoopes phone card, and even a Swoopes action figure, all pulling in an estimated $1.2 million—believed to be the most money a female athlete who played a team sport had ever earned in one year.[17]

Swoopes showed just how marketable female athletes were. While no women's basketball shoe has had greater success than Air Swoopes, there were others. Dawn Staley (1970–), Lisa Leslie (1972–), Rebecca Lobo (1973–), and Chamique Holdsclaw (1977–) all had their own shoes and opportunities to market directly to female athletes.

For Dawn Staley, at only 5'6", a shoe line was much more than visibility; it empowered others. Not much of a Jordan fan while growing up, Staley wore Charles Barkley's signature line as there were no such shoes for women.[18]

The three-time Olympic gold medalist and Hall of Fame player and coach understood the value of quality shoes, not only for female athletes but for everyone. A self-described "sneakerhead," Staley cofounded the nonprofit Innersoles to provide new sneakers to underprivileged children to inspire confidence and hope. By early 2020, Innersoles had given away more than twenty-five thousand shoes with the personal message from Staley to "dream big." The Nike Air Zoom S5 was an acknowledgment of Staley's place in sports history.[19]

For the shoe movement itself—including female athletes in the game of apparel and profit—however, there remained disappointment that as more women's shoe lines came out, sizes were so limited that many female basketball players had to continue to buy men's basketball shoes. Shoes designed specifically for female athletes did not always have shoes in the size that most bigger, taller, basketball-playing women wore. Even today, WNBA players routinely wear men's shoes because of the lack of larger women's shoe sizes.

ALONG CAME GABBY (AND OTHER GAME CHANGERS)

The 1990s were a critical time for not only female basketball players but all female athletes wrestling with size and femininity vs. marketability. Again and again, unlike male athletes, females had to contend with the hegemonic feminine ideals vs. their own reality. At 6'3", volleyball player Gabrielle Reece (1970–) was truly a game changer. She is credited as one of the first superathletes to change how men and women viewed female athletes. Hers was an aggressive style of play few had ever seen.

While playing volleyball for Florida State University, she broke records that still stand today, leading the program's all-time solo blocks (240) and total blocks (747), and was named to the FSU Hall of Fame. She went on to play professional beach volleyball and was named a two-time Offensive Player of the Year (1994–1995), while leading the Women's Beach Volleyball League for four consecutive years (1993–1996) with the most kills and in blocks in 1993. She went on to lead her team to victory at the Beach Volleyball World Championships and also the Olympic 4-on-4 Challenge Series.[20]

Reece became Nike's first female athlete to design a shoe, and Nike's first-ever female cross-training spokesperson in 1994. While Swoopes's distinction was to be the first female athlete to have a shoe bear her name,

Gabrielle Reece. *Zuma Press, Inc./Alamy Stock photo*

Reece's Air Trainer (1994), Air Patrol (1995), Air GR (1997), and Air GR II (1998) not only were her own designs but also became the first women's shoe line to outsell Air Jordan.

As luck and opportunity would have it, Reece was also noticed by a modeling agency in New York. Not wanting to pass up the chance to make money ("and have a little fun"), Reece signed on. While it was far more work than fun, Reece worked doggedly to improve her game, help her team, and also establish herself in the world of fashion and business.

The unthinkable began to happen: A 6'3", 175-pound woman was named by *Elle* magazine as one of the five most beautiful women in the world, one of "America's Most Beautiful People" by *People* magazine, and *Rolling Stone*'s "Wonder Woman of Sport." Reece was a cover girl for the most popular magazines of the time and was a millionaire by age twenty-five.

Her physical prowess earned her a place in sports history, but she also understood that success for a female athlete was "tricky sometimes. A male athlete can just slam-dunk above the rim and that's that—he's a hero. If you're a woman, you've got to do the sexy thing and you've got to do the nice thing. It's reality."[21]

She understood this at an early age. By the age of twelve, she was already six feet tall, was "different" from everyone, and used this to her advantage, not shying from the ideal feminine beauty but redefining it.

She penned two books, appropriately titled: *Big Girl in the Middle* (1997) and *My Foot Is Too Big for the Glass Slipper* (2013). In her first book she laments, "I don't like this 'Fear of Being Big' thing because it feeds into the general female thing of wanting to be less—less powerful, less assertive, less demanding, less opinionated, less present, less big."[22]

Before Olympic beach volleyball players Misty May-Treanor (1977–) and Kerri Walsh Jennings (1978–), Gabrielle Reece was the face of beach volleyball, bringing in big corporate sponsors and legions of fans. But May-Treanor, 5'9", and Walsh Jennings, 6'2", built upon the beach volleyball fan base, becoming a dominating team called "the greatest volleyball team of all time,"[23] bringing home three gold Olympic medals in 2004, 2008, and 2012—the first beach volleyball players to win three consecutive Olympic Games. Upon her retirement in 2012, May-Treanor was named as the most successful female beach volleyball player with 112 individual championships. Walsh Jennings played on for one more Olympic Games in 2016, earning a bronze, and amassed a total of 133 victories and over $2 million by 2016.[24]

PICABO PASSES THE BATON

Before there was Lindsey Vonn (1984–), the greatest downhill skier of all time,[25] there was Picabo Street (1971–). Known as a fearless, sometimes reckless skier whose all-out style made her a legend on slopes, she did not bother with niceties but focused only on the mountain. Growing up in the small town of Triumph, Idaho (population: fifty), there were only eight children in town; Street was the only girl. For her, there were no constraints of proper female or unladylike behaviors, and so she rode dirt bikes, boxed, played tackle football, and lost a few teeth just like everyone else. But it was skiing that she loved most and, at the age of seventeen, Street made the U.S. national ski team in 1989. She also loved to party, and soon enough, excessive drinking and lack of training got her booted from the team.

"That woke me up," Street said. Through hard training, Street earned her spot back six months later so that in 1993 she earned a silver medal at the World Championships and another silver at the 1994 Lillehammer Games.[26] It was at those 1994 Games that the world was enthralled with figure skaters Nancy Kerrigan and Tonya Harding. With such headlines as the *Baltimore Sun*'s "Dynamics Are Different When Women Clash: Catfight Fever," and the *Chicago Tribune*'s "Great Catfight on Ice," Street was the perfect reprieve for the more serious journalists and sports fans.

She was cocky, funny, and sometimes late for her own events. There was something wild and exciting about Street that defied the characteristics of the typical female athlete audiences had come to know and expect.

Over the next three years, she became the first American skier to win a World Cup, capturing six straight World Cup downhill titles (1995 and 1996) and a gold at the 1996 World Championships. Street was seemingly unstoppable until a crash that tore the anterior cruciate ligament (ACL) in her left knee in December 1996. She continued to compete, but just weeks prior to the 1998 Olympic Nagano Games, clocked at seventy-five miles per hour, she lost control and crashed, knocking herself unconscious. Miraculously, Street won gold at the Games in the giant slalom (Super G), an event she had never once won before.

After the Games, as the season was winding down, Street suffered another crash, this time breaking her femur in nine places, tearing the ACL in her other knee, and putting the question of her future in everyone's minds. Street would go on to compete in the 2002 Salt Lake Games but the results were not what she had hoped for. After the race, the thirty-year-old Street announced her retirement from competitive skiing. But, of course, she never really left the sport.

While making an appearance in Minneapolis in 1995, Street noticed a ten-year-old girl working her way through a crowd to meet the Olympian. Later, Street would say of little Lindsey Vonn, "She stayed focused on the task at hand, which was to meet me and . . . I said to myself, 'I better get ready for her because she is coming with it, and I will need to bring my A-game too.'"[27]

In 1999, Street marveled at the fifteen-year-old Vonn's performance and knew "the sky was the limit for her."[28] Together, they made history: Street became the oldest member of the 2002 U.S. Olympic team at thirty; Vonn was the youngest at seventeen.

For Street, the 2002 Games would be her last but not before she passed the proverbial baton to the youngest member of her team. Street became Vonn's mentor. Following a crash during a downhill run at the 2006 Torino Games that resulted in Vonn being airlifted off the mountain, Street brought pasta to Vonn's hospital room where they shared a meal but, mostly, cried, fearing what Vonn's long-term injuries might be. Briefly, doctors feared her back might be broken, and Street told stories of her own injuries to inspire Vonn onto recovery. Street understood the kinds of pressures Vonn was under as *Sports Illustrated*'s Olympic Preview issue predicted Vonn as "America's Best Woman Skier Ever" in 2010. Now a gold and bronze medalist from the 2008 Vancouver Games, the pressure was on from the media, fans, and sponsors while Vonn was quietly nursing yet another "excruciating" injury. Again and again, while Vonn overcame and conquered each new challenge, injury, and downhill run, Street lavished praise while, in turn, Vonn hoped to emulate Street. "I want to give the girls of the next generation someone to look up to, just like I looked up to Picabo Street."[29]

BREAKING THE ICE: MANON RHÉAUME

Manon Rhéaume (1972–), too, was a pioneer in women's sport. Rhéaume, a Canadian hockey goaltender, is the only woman to play in a National Hockey League (NHL) exhibition game. She won a silver medal in the 1998 Nagano Games (the first Olympic Games to allow women in hockey), after winning gold medals at the 1992 and 1994 International Ice Hockey Federation's (IIHF) Women's World Championships.

As a child, she had already made sports history when she became the first girl to play in the Quebec International Pee-Wee Hockey Tournament, a prestigious annual event that has hosted future NHL Hall of Famers for decades. In 1991, she again became the first female to play in the Quebec Major Hockey League for the Trois-Rivières Draveurs, but she made international news the following year when she was invited to play for the NHL's Tampa Bay Lightning in the 1992 and 1993 preseasons.

She also made sports history, signing a minor-league pro contract and playing with men for the next six years. In her debut on the ice, she played a shutout game, and yet one reporter would later ask her if she cracked a nail while another asked, "How do you feel when you have your period?"

"That's when I play my best," she said plainly, unwilling to appear bothered by the question.

Much was made of her physical appearance, and *Playboy* magazine invited her to pose. She refused, stating that this did not move women, women's sports, or her own values in a positive direction.

What Rhéaume always wanted was fair play and equal opportunities for all athletes; following the Olympic Games, she served as a marketing director to develop and promote girls' hockey equipment, including the production of women's hockey skates and, in 2008, created a scholarship program through her own foundation.[30]

Rhéaume remains the only female NHL hockey player in history.

WOMEN IN THE RING

In 1988, the Swedish Amateur Boxing Association sanctioned fights that finally opened opportunities for female boxers. In 1993, only after a series of lawsuits, USA Boxing sanctioned women's amateur boxing, with Russia, Norway, Denmark, Finland, and Hungary to follow. The United Kingdom, however, refused to issue licenses to women until 1998, citing PMS (premenstrual syndrome) would make women too unstable to fight. It was Jane Couch (1968–), five-time world champion, who fought the British Boxing Board of Control and paved the way for women.

Women such as Dutch fighter Lucia Rijker (1967–), aka "the most dangerous woman in the world," Irish fighter Deirdre Gogarty (1969–), and Sumya "the Island Girl" Anani (1972–) are just a few who fought for little or no money, too little press coverage, but for the love of the sport. Fighters such as Mexico's Laura Serrano (1967–), who challenged an ordinance from 1947 prohibiting women from boxing in Mexico, and Germany's Regina Halmich (1976–), who popularized women's boxing throughout Europe, are believed to be some of the more impactful athletes.

By the end of the 1990s, bigger, stronger women arrived. Chevelle "Fist of Steel" Hallback (1971–) and Ann Wolfe (1971–) brought in a new kind of power and intensity to women's boxing. These athletes paved the way for future fighters, but Christy Martin (1968–) is credited as the pioneer and trailblazer in women's boxing.

Martin, who made her boxing debut in 1989, fought hard both in and out of the ring for media coverage and respect. During her reign, she was the most prominent female fighter in the United States, bringing in promoters, drama, and publicity while she wore high heels and everything pink.

On March 16, 1996, a pay-per-view fight introduced millions of fans to women's fighting on the undercard of the Mike Tyson vs. Frank Bruno fight. An estimated 30 million viewers in over one hundred countries were stunned by the Christy Martin vs. Deirdre Gogarty fight—a vicious, very bloody, nonstop-action fight that made both women overnight stars. Martin retired in 2012 with a record of forty-nine wins, thirty-one of which were knockouts; only seven losses; and three draws.

WOMEN IN SKI JUMPING AND BOBSLEDDING

As in boxing, women had been ski jumping beside men for decades, although recreationally. Karla Keck (1975–) excelled in ski jumping, almost always beating the boys. When she turned eighteen, however, she saw that these same male friends were looking to the Olympics and she was just "supposed to go away." Instead, she became one of the leading pioneers for women's Nordic ski jumping and, certainly, the best known. Once ranked second in the world, she also became the first international jumper to be invited to an exclusive school in Austria for competitive jumpers. She was just one of only two women at the school, competing against men.

In ski jumping, competitors stand atop a 120-meter (394-feet) tall ramp and ski down the specially designed ramp to achieve the longest jump possible. The athletes are judged not only on the distance of their jump but also style and form, typically traveling farther than the length of a football field, up to sixty miles per hour. Although Keck excelled at this, she was repeatedly told that competitions would be unsafe for her.

"It's just like any pioneering sport," Keck said, noting that like so many others have before her, she became a "feminist." The propagandized image of a feminist, a hard woman making unreasonable demands, remains a stopping point for many females until feminism becomes about leveling the playing field and creating opportunities for everyone. When Keck saw opponents make one excuse after another to support their own discriminatory biases, she knew she had to fight. She was told the hard landings in ski jumping were dangerous to women as they would, "you know, damage their ovaries because they're hollow inside," Keck said with a laugh.[31]

In 2009, the British Columbia Supreme Court ruled that the IOC exhibited gender discrimination with the exclusion of women's ski jumping from the Vancouver Games yet did not enforce women's inclusion. Keck fought on until it was announced that women's ski jumping would be included in the 2014 Games in Sochi. By then, Keck had retired but had joined forces with ski jumpers Lindsey Van (1984–) and Jessica Jerome (1987–) to sue the Vancouver Organizing Committee (VANOC) to ensure that future female jumpers would have their opportunity.

Like boxing and ski jumping, women had been bobsledding along with men for well over a century, most often recreationally. Competitively, bobsledding was a mixed sport that required female team members. By 1924, women began to be banned from competition, but in 1940, the Amateur Athletic Union (AAU) reopened the sport to women, and Katharine Dewey won the U.S. National Four-Man Bobsled Championship.[32] In doing so, Dewey became the only woman in the history of bobsledding or any other amateur sport to win a national championship in open competition against men. Days later, the AAU reversed its decision and ruled that women could compete against other women and stripped her of her title. For the next fifty-three years, women were told that, for safety reasons, females could not slide.

By 1993, the pressure was on many national governing sports bodies to become inclusive for women. The previous year, the IOC voted to approve women's hockey as an Olympic event and determined that it would debut at the 1998 Games. Other female athletes saw an opening in otherwise male-only sports. After a series of complaints and requests, the IOC and the USOC reached out to the United States Bobsled and Skeleton Federation (USBSF). In January 1994, the USBSF held the first-ever women's bobsled camp and on September 24, 1994, history was made when the first-ever United States women's bobsled team was officially selected.

The athletes made sports history before a small crowd, including a reporter from *Sports Illustrated*, who also reported that two of the sliders had a second "sports history" to their credit: "Alexandra Allred, 29, of Westerville, Ohio, and Liz Parr-Smestad, 32, of Shoreview, Minnesota, finished first and second, respectively. . . . When each of them pushed, the sled should have had a *Baby on Board* sign: At the time both Allred and Parr-Smestad were several months pregnant."[33] Additionally, Allred and teammate Michelle Powe were sisters, the first American bobsled sisters to compete in a World Cup.

Victories were short lived, however. The women, many of whom upended personal lives and professional careers to make their bobsled dreams come true, were told the first official team had simply been show for the USOC and IOC. The assigned coach to the new women's team told them, "There will never be women in the Olympics in my lifetime."

Undeterred by the USBSF's unwillingness to comply with the USOC's ruling, the new team created their own bylaws, named their own manager, raised funding, fought for equipment and slide time, and saw one of their own make it to the 2002 Olympic Games. Sliders Christine Spiezio (1969–), Elena Primerano (1971–), Jean Racine (1978–), Krista Ford, Patty

Jill Bakken driving bobsled and brakewoman Vonetta Flowers. *Courtesy of Jill Bakken*

Driscoll, and Laurie Millet, along with Parr-Smestad, Allred, and Powe, were the first American women to compete internationally in World Cup competitions.

All the early U.S. women's bobsledders, except one, retired before they would see the Olympic Games. That one team member, Jill Bakken (1977–), the "baby of the team," not only made it to the Olympics in Salt Lake City, but she won gold—the first-ever women's bobsled gold medal. But as is so often the case in women's sport history, Bakken's tremendous achievement was all but omitted from history.

With the announcement that women would be included in the 2002 Olympic Games, the women were to be officially funded for the first time, but "from the beginning, middle, and end, there was never enough equipment."

Through it all, Bakken was one of the few athletes who avoided any media or personal conflicts. Always quiet, bobsleigh's favorite little sister flew under the radar; but, for those closely watching the women's bobsled circuit, Bakken was a threat, and eight years after attending the first-ever women's bobsled camp, Bakken became the champion no one really knew. After beating out the Germans by 0.30 second for gold, Bakken did what no other male or female driver had done in bobsled history for his or her country—she broke a fifty-year gold medal dry spell while also becoming the first-ever Olympic female champion in the sport of bobsled.

As she did as a competitor, Bakken was equally humble as an Olympian. "There were just so many people who played a part in this," she said. As so many pioneers before her noted, "it was all the people who came before the medal, who did the hard work," that the "nicest girl on the circuit" honored with her historic run.

Bakken took a year off from the sport, graduated from college, then returned to the one thing she thought she knew—competition. She met her future husband, Canadian former Olympic athlete and bobsled coach Florian Linder. For Bakken—who had once told a reporter who asked about her medal, "It's here [in the house] somewhere"—it had never been about winning gold but the pursuit of excellence. A true female pioneer, she had forever changed a sport and the Olympic Games.

TWELVE

Exploitation of the Female Image

In decades past, the few female aviators, explorers, and athletes who appeared in media inspired fellow females. When these role models appeared in print, everyday women saw women who dared to drive cars, wear pants, cut their hair short, even work. These "influencers" stood against patriarchal values and changed social norms.

In the 2000s, however, an influx of social media celebrities and influencers brought about a new wave of objectification and stereotyping of females that negatively impacted how girls and women viewed themselves. Influencers chose to glorify antiquated societal norms, while reaping financial gains—and girls were collateral damage.

In regard to women's bodies, society and the media have always focused on particular body parts of the female form, often countering medical validity and/or safety. A 2015 study found that adolescent girls who spent considerable time on social media were at great risk of developing eating disorders and negative, unhealthy body images.[1]

This made them the perfect audience for an influencer-led thigh-gap challenge that would trend less than two years later, promoting the thigh gap as a "healthy" beauty ideal that represents frailty and femininity. It is only achievable by girls or women who are underweight with "muscle waste" in their legs because of unhealthy lifestyles. Medically speaking, a "healthy" thigh gap is only attainable by someone with wider-set hips and healthy weight.

"Try telling that to an impressionable girl who has consumed unattainable images of beauty since the age of five," said psychologist and author Lucie Hemmen, who points out that the internalization of images of what society expects of women and how beauty is perceived is so strong that it overrides medical advice.

This was evident in 2020, when women who suffered from potentially dangerous eating disorders turned to an online influencer rather than licensed practitioners. Fitness and "health" influencer Brittany Dawn, with close to 1 million TikTok followers, a half-million Instagram followers,

and a successful YouTube channel, had lied about her professional certifications and scammed thousands out of money, billing herself as an expert
on eating disorders. She negligently sold "nutrition plans" to unknowing
victims. When caught, she explained to *Good Morning America* that "I
jumped into an industry that had no instruction manual." She quickly
rebranded her expertise as spiritual counseling.[2]

With the use of social media growing from just 10 percent of Americans
in 2008 to almost 80 percent in 2018, there is no escaping the images we
see. Celebrity endorsements have always played an important role in
social and consumer attitudes but, since 2013, the "microcelebrity," an
everyday person who attains celebrity-like status through huge follow-
ings, has proven to be even more economically and socially powerful.
These "celebrities" are seen as more trustworthy, more friendly than
elusive Hollywood stars while, in reality, influencers have been found to
portray luxurious lifestyles of high-end material items and travel that are
misrepresentations or obtained through advertising deals unknown to
the followers.[3] In regard to mental health, fitness, nutrition, and overall
wellness, most popular influencers are not properly certified, educated,
insured, or licensed.

Another celebrity influencer promoted diet supplements, including
an appetite suppressant in the form of a lollipop that was banned in the
United Kingdom,[4] as well as "waist trainers," a throwback to the Victorian corset. While the promotion was a big hit in the fashion and beauty
industry, it was also another hit against women and their health. Like the
Victorian corset, not only is there no health benefit to waist trainers but,
with long-term use, they cause irreversible damage to muscle, skin, the
liver, spleen, kidneys, digestive tract, even lungs.[5]

Over the past decade, a litany of scholarly works was devoted to how
damaging social media is to mental health, most particularly to girls
(including studies on the mental health of social influencers so heavily
invested in their own platforms).[6]

THE STORY OF MARY CAIN AND NIKE

For many years, the endorsement of Nike was considered a sign of success for athletes. For Mary Cain (1996–), the "fastest girl in America," it
seemed the opportunity of a lifetime. Cain set world junior indoor records
for both the 1,000-meter and 3,000-meter races and was the youngest
American athlete to represent the United States at the World Championship in 2013. She was seventeen years old and well on her way to Olympic
greatness when Nike invited her to join Nike's Oregon Project, a prestigious track program for the best and the brightest of rising track stars.

Yet, under Coach Alberto Salazar (1958–) and an all-male Nike coaching staff, Cain was body-shamed and humiliated to the point of self-harming and contemplating suicide. In 2019, Cain revealed her story through the *New York Times* and the response was immediate.[7] While Nike denied the allegations, others all too familiar with the scenario rallied with hashtags emerging: #FixGirlsSports, #WomenEmpowerment, and #Awareness.

While at Nike, other athletes knew of Cain's abuse by Salazar; they knew she was self-harming but "didn't want to get involved." Her isolation and abuse, and the thought of losing her spot in the most elite running program in the country, immobilized her.

"When I first arrived, an all-male Nike staff became convinced that in order for me to get better, I had to become thinner. And thinner. And thinner. This Nike team was the top running program in the country and yet we had no certified sports psychologist, there was no certified nutritionist. It was really just a bunch of people who were Alberto's friends."[8]

Cain said that Salazar "chose an arbitrary number of 114 pounds" as her competitive weight and began the practice of weighing her in front of her teammates, publicly shaming her if her weight was off Salazar's track. He also tried to prescribe birth control pills and diuretics for her to lose weight, a practice that was not allowed in the sport. It was then that Cain realized that there was more than her physical health and racing performance that were at risk.

"But here's a biology lesson I learned the hard way. When young women are forced to push themselves beyond what they're capable at their given age, they're at risk for developing RED-S."[9] RED-S syndrome, or relative energy deficiency in sport, occurs when an athlete suffers from insufficient energy intake. It is a condition that affects both male and female athletes, but Salazar and his team had caused it in Cain by decreasing her diet, resulting in poor racing times and, more importantly, dangerous consequences to the athlete.

In reality, female athletes perform better with a higher-fat diet. Dietary fat is 15 percent more satiating in women than men. Female athletes with more fat in their diet burn more calories during exercise, have greater strength and energy, and are more efficient.

In athletic training, not just food quality but calories are essential as the body requires energy (from calories) needed for the actual demands of the sport as well as residual energy or energy availability (EA) for recovery. For Cain, her EA fell well below what was needed for her own body composition and age, leading her to a medical condition known as low energy availability (LEA).

Although this medical condition had been identified by the International Olympic Committee in 2014, Cain's coaches missed all the signs. Cain had not had her menstrual cycle in three years. She had low bone density and suffered from five bone fractures. She was depressed and lethargic.[10] Her symptoms were what experts call the female triad: LEA, menstrual dysfunction, and low bone density.[11]

For Cain, that her body seemed to be turning against her only added to her misery. In her op-ed piece with the *New York Times*, Cain explained that she still held on to the belief that Salazar and the Nike staff knew what they were doing, yet no one ever reached out to an OB/GYN or a female coach to ask what was going on with Cain.

During a race in 2015, a thunderstorm forced athletes, coaches, and officials to huddle in a tent. There, Salazar began yelling at Cain in front of everyone, accusing her of gaining five pounds prior to the race. Witnesses turned their backs on the scene. Later, in a desperate attempt for her coach to understand how badly things were spiraling out of control, she confessed to Salazar that she had had suicidal thoughts and had been cutting herself. Salazar's response was to walk away.

"And I think for me, that was my kick in the head where I was like, 'this system is sick.'" Cain quit the team, packed her bags, and flew home.[12] In 2021, Cain became the CEO and president of Atalanta NYC, a nonprofit organization that employs and supports professional female runners: "We educate and inspire female athletes to use running and movement in a healthy and lasting way."[13]

WHAT IS THE FEMALE TRIAD?

The female triad—a combination of energy availability (eating enough), menstrual cycles, and bone strength—is directly tied to food pathologies. When female athletes do not eat properly, the entire system is disrupted. As the body tries to preserve muscle, the hormonal system is affected, energy is depleted, and, when menstruation is stopped or altered, calcium from the bones is absorbed into the body, allowing for stress fractures and increased injuries.

Existing nutrition studies for athletes are primarily focused on males, leaving coaches/trainers with the idea that females should follow the same meal plans. In fact, female athletes require *more* protein.[14] In particular to team sports such as lacrosse, soccer, and basketball, the explosive lateral (side-to-side) and stop-and-go movements place intense wear and tear on the body. The wider pelvis of the female causes a downward angle of the thigh bones and knees, which then place additional stress on the ACL, one of the key ligaments that help stabilize your knee joint. Women are two to ten times more likely to experience ACL injury than men.[15] Because biological females also have more elastic ligaments than males, who have stronger and thicker ligaments, more protein is required for the female athlete. However, female athletes tend to ingest *less* protein—the very thing that enables the body to recover more quickly following the demands of sport.

Why?

Research has found female athletes in sports requiring formfitting or revealing uniforms typically adopt "energy restriction practices," such as eating fewer calories (fewer proteins, fats, and carbohydrates), just as many female athletes are pressured to conform to a certain look and weight "that put them at a higher risk of nutritional deficiencies."[16] Female athletes in "leanness" sports are 60 percent more likely to feel pressure from coaches concerning body shape and size.[17]

All of this can contribute to eating disorders and/or nutritional deficits. Fifteen to 35 percent of female athletes are iron deficient, while an NCAA study found that over 21 percent of female athletes have abnormally lowered vitamin D measures.[18]

Simply put, the female body is most negatively impacted when denied proper nutrition and calories, even creating irreversible damage. Science, not *trends*, must be followed. As women push for greater medical care, nutrition and the female form must be part of that conversation.

GAMERS

In the world of gaming, however, conversations regarding the female athlete (or her health) was rarely considered. Until recently, the female image was highly sexualized and demoralized. In media images, advertisements geared for boys emphasize adventure and action while images for girls are passive with girls mostly posing with the goal of being *seen*.

Across the board, both boys and girls are impacted by the sexualized images of females as researchers have noted a change in sexual attitudes, beliefs, behaviors, and sexual aggression among preteens and teens.[19] This includes the gaming world, which had been predominately male and misogynistic. By 2015, more than 40 percent of gamers were female and finally using their true gender. Prior to that time, most females kept their gender a secret for safety reasons.

Within the machismo environment of video gaming world, which included overly buxom female caricatures, a culture of typically nonathletic, unmacho males were emboldened to display aggression and bully others.

Attitudes toward female gamers were so aggressive, filmmaker Shannon Sun-Higginson created the documentary *GTFO* depicting how prevalent the sexual harassment, including rape and death threats, against female gamers had become. And, like Cain, the female gamers who won most often were afraid to lodge complaints for fear of losing their positions (or rankings as gamers) within the industry.[20] While a skilled male gamer may be called harmless names, usually comical yet respectful remarks, similarly skilled female gamers were met with something far more disturbing. The following are only some of the remarks documented from just one incident in which a female gamer recorded her victory against her male peers:

> "@____, I'll rape you and put your head on a stick."
> "@____, suck' ma [expletive], u a slut."
> "Why don't you kill yourself and make a video about it?"
> "The only place for a woman is in chains in my kitchen."
> "@____. Suck my c#@# and cook me a steak."
> "Wouldn't it be funny if five guys raped her right now?"
> "Why did the feminist cross the road . . . TO SUCK MY D#%#."[21]

Even as the gaming industry touts e-sports to be the only mixed-gender professional sport, harassment and discrimination in gaming continues. At a For the Women Gaming Summit in February 2021, female e-sports athletes revealed how their relationships to teams, viewers, even sponsors changed once their gender was revealed.

Despite the fact that e-sports history is one of sexual objectification and violence against women and unregulated online communities can remain anonymous (emboldened by unchecked behavior), there have been no real policies set in place to curb dangerous, discriminatory practices. Even as e-sports executives vie for greater status as a sport, they ignore such antidiscriminatory policies set by the International Olympic Committee and other international sports agencies. The IOC's Prevention of Harassment and Abuse in Sports (PHAS) was implemented to create policies and procedures for national governing bodies of sport (NGBs) to combat harassment and safeguard participants, yet e-sports have resisted any formal policies or structure to shut down predatory behavior or ensure the safety of its competitors.[22]

Within the world of e-sports, female characters were one of the biggest problems for serious female gamers in 2015 as the higher her [gamer] level rose, the less clothing and armor her character received. "A starter female character gets one set of body-covering, generic-looking armor. But as the character ranks up, the armor available and the armor best-suited for staying alive gets smaller and 'sexier,' giving the player no choice but to don the look of a sex goddess or die in combat." According to gamer Kayleigh Connor, while the male characters were properly suited and armored and had reasonably proportioned bodies, the female was hypersexualized, only reinforcing to male gamers that she (both character and gamer) was not to be taken seriously.[23] When this gamer/

character beat out male opponents, it was doubly insulting in the male-dominated, masculine culture that was so prevalent.

The hypersexualized female character is far more dangerous than previously believed. It is not just a game. Fifty percent of college-aged female gamers experienced body dissatisfaction and reported lower self-esteem. Female gamers who used an oversexualized character felt significantly worse about themselves, while male gamers were not impacted until they also used an oversexualized (very muscular with unrealistic body proportions) male character. By 2018, more millennial and Gen Z male gamers were choosing female characters in quiet protest of the oversized armor and proportions of male characters. With the oversexualized male character, male gamers reported a decrease in their own body image.[24]

The e-sports industry reached over $1 billion in revenue by 2019 and gaming profits reach nearly $140 billion annually with very clear marketing agendas that target boys and men with sex and violence—two proven marketing gimmicks for male audiences. Despite the damaging effects of these images, which include hostility, even violence, toward female gamers online, studies have shown "that box art which contains sexualized, non-main female characters is correlated with higher sales, and box art that depicts the central female character (sexualized or not) or female characters in the absence of male characters has a negative association with sales."[25]

Central female characters (in primary roles) also present a problem in comics, particularly with superhero themes. Arguably, the two entertainment/media formats most overwhelmingly associated with a male consumer base were also most demoralizing and abusive to women in the quest to keep theirs a "no girls allowed" culture. Online threats against women, ranging from torching homes and stalking family members to rape and murder, were so persuasive that legal intervention was necessary—all to keep women from gaming and fictional female characters from becoming too "good."[26]

SEXUAL VIOLENCE AND DC COMICS

Researcher Kylie Mathis (1996–) tracked similar discriminatory practices in the comic world, noting that only recently has DC Comics released more empowered female characters with story lines independent of male superheroes such as Jessica Cruz, a Mexican American and Honduran American and member of the Green Lantern and the Justice League; BumbleBee, also known as Karen, the first Black female superhero; and Hawk Girl, Black Canary, Catwoman, and Wonder Woman, who appeared in the 1940s. Only Wonder Woman stood independently while the other women were partnered with male characters or suffered traumatic events (the hysterical woman syndrome) that forever changed them. Within the highly sexualized world of comics, characters such as Barbara Gordon, Poison Ivy, Mera, Cheetah, and Batgirl had to be demoralized and victimized (i.e., put in their place) before they could develop stronger roles. Most importantly, hers was a supporting role to larger characters.

Mathis cites the recurring trope, called "Women in Refrigerators," used to propel the male story line and character by degrading, maiming, assaulting, raping, and/or killing a female character. The refrigerator reference came from the *Green Lantern* #54 issue, published in 1994, when the hero finds his girlfriend upon returning home, strangled and stuffed in a refrigerator, thus allowing the Green Lantern to truly grow into his superpowers.

Mathis's findings, while not surprising, "only reinforced the idea that women's bodies are meant to be violated," a statement validated by the plotline's global approval with cosplays and fan art approving its message. Frustrated by the continued misogynist theme regarding female characters, comic writer Gail Simone (1974–) created a website called Women in Refrigerators in 1999 to openly discuss the treatment of female characters. While the conversation garnered national attention, no real changes were made within the comic world (or elsewhere).[27]

Mathis found it is not only heterosexual women who are victimized in media but also those within the queer and transgender communities, as well as men who do not prescribe to the male-superiority culture. But when images (comics, television, theater, music, etc.) are targeted to the mainstream, it is the women in refrigerators who best sell a male-driven plotline, leaving Mathis to ask, "What is it about women's bodies that allows creators to violate them again and again and again?" She says, "I did absolutely bawl my eyes out when Wonder Woman leapt out of the trenches and took down a bunch of Nazis with the kind of raw strength that is only reserved for male heroes. I was also thrilled to see Harley Quinn's costumes in *Suicide Squad vs. Birds of Prey*." But she worries that it is the other images—the prevalent, ever-popular, helpless female victim—that will continue to overshadow true warrior women.

Mathis concludes that writing critically about media "is crucial because it will never exist in a vacuum. It is never 'just a movie' Or 'only a comic issue.' Reality informs fiction. Our world is shaped by violent systems of oppression. We see them reflected in the media we consume. We can't afford to be complacent, even over something as trivial as comic books!" We need to showcase our living, athletic female warriors.

KILLING US SOFTLY

The average American is exposed to upwards of ten thousand advertisements and/or digital images in some varying form every day,[28] and at the center of most of these images was the ideal female—thin, tall, light skinned, with cosmetically or digitally altered measurements of unrealistic proportions and airbrushed to perfection.[29] Back in the 1960s, author and activist Jean Kilbourne (1943–) began what is considered groundbreaking work on the image of women, particularly in advertising. Kilbourne began researching (and speaking out about) the link between advertising and violence against women, eating disorders, internalization of objectification, and addiction. Truly, she was ahead of her time to assert such connections, and she was right. She created the film series *Killing Us Softly: Advertising's Image of Women*, which was released in 1979 and has been updated and rereleased four more times with newer, more startling statistics.

By the mid-1980s, more than 50 percent of girls, some younger than five years old, were conscious of their weight because of the incessant images of the ideal female form. As Kilbourne pointed out, the push by Western advertisers (in keeping with society's expectations) was so powerful that it changed other cultures as well. It was no longer just American women who felt an unexplained urgency to fit a certain mold. When television became available to the people of Fiji, a remote country in the South Pacific, women and girls soon began dieting for the first time, suddenly believing who and what they had always been was wrong. Advertisers did not just promote unhealthy appetite suppressants, relationships with food, perceived cattiness between women, and an unrelenting surplus of blond, busty women; airbrushing—the technique that allows photo edits to change body and skin tone to a desired state—became a standard in the beauty, fashion, and advertising industries, making unhealthy physical expectations even more unrealistic and unattainable.[30]

THE MIGHTY INVISIBLE BODY SHAMERS

It is not just the media and advertisers who feel the compulsion to monitor and regulate how a woman looks, but society as a whole. The first known use of the term "body-shaming," the act or practice of subjecting someone to criticism or mockery for their body or size, was in 1997.[31] The practice has been widely accepted and rarely challenged throughout history, but the internet gave it a name and greater power. Following the successes of her first movie, *Clueless*, actress Alicia Silverstone (1976–) landed the role of Batgirl for *Batman and Robin*, released in 1997, and was quickly dubbed "Fatgirl" by the media.[32] Twenty-five years later, a picture of Silverstone was posted on the internet with yet another fat-shaming caption: "Alicia Silverstone Candid Fat Photo." This time, however, Silverstone responded by posting that same image on TikTok with a smile and the middle finger.

For female athletes conscious of sponsors, such gestures are not permissible, and most simply endure the abuse. Mexico's gymnast Alexa Moreno was called "fat" at the 2016 Rio Games, with a fan posting that Moreno was "the body of two gymnasts." Moreno was ninety-nine pounds. Serena Williams (1981–), arguably one of the greatest tennis players of all time, had her weight and size critiqued on national television following the birth of her daughter.[33]

Because women's bodies have always belonged to society, advertisers, patriarchs, politicians, art, and literature, there is a sense of entitlement that comes with body-shaming, photoshopping, demeaning, and degrading. American track-and-field hammer thrower Amanda Bingson said, "Everybody wants to fit that skinny, ideal picture that we see on billboards all the time, and people would always remind me that that wasn't me." In 2013, Bingson set a new American hammer throw record with a distance of 75.73 meters, over 248 feet, in a sport that had only recently opened up to women. For Bingson, her superpower is in her size. "I never knew I was the fat kid in school until a boy told me that I was too fat. I thought, 'What does that mean?' I had always been so athletic and into sports."[34]

So it was especially empowering when Bingson posed for ESPN's "Bodies We Want" in 2015. But of course, body-shaming trolls went on the attack, unable to accept that 1) her body was named a body "we want," but also 2) that Bingson appeared to be proud of herself.

Bingson enjoys her strength more than she does external approval. "I'll be honest, I like everything about my body." This is part of Bingson's strength, and for those who would try to body-shame her, she said, "You just grow a thick skin. Like I said, I'll still whip your [expletive] if we ever get into a fight."[35] This was Bingson's proverbial finger.

ROLE MODELS WHO COUNTERED THE FEMININE IDEAL

While women such as Bingson "like everything" about their bodies, it is more *permissible* that a hammer thrower defy the hegemonic idealism of petite and slender than other athletes. With traditionally "female" sports, however, comes far more critical expectations.

When U.S. gymnast Mary Lou Retton (1968–) took the gold and astounded audiences with a kind of power the gymnastics the world had never seen, sports reporters and commentators continuously referenced Retton's "stocky," "thick," "blocky" form, noting that she had the "wrong kind of build" for a sport that expected petite and pixie-like athletes.[36] She did not look like gymnasts are *supposed* to look.

Similarly, Kim Zmeskal (1976–), who helped the United States win its first-ever world championship and was the first American female gymnast to win the all-around title at the World Championships as well as the first to win any medal in the all-around, was routinely noted to be more "square" and "compact" than the typical gymnast.

But no gymnast knows the pressures of the feminine ideal better than Katelyn Ohashi (1997–). The UCLA gymnast's floor routine video "broke the internet"[37] with nearly 240 million views after her "10" in a 2019 performance became a YouTube sensation. She was also demeaned and humiliated on multiple social media platforms. "I was told I didn't look like a gymnast. I was told I looked like I'd swallowed an elephant. Or looked like a pig."[38] At 4'10" and 105 pounds, Ohashi felt vulnerable each time she appeared before audiences and judges wearing traditional gymnast leotards. Unlike male gymnasts, female competitors have not been allowed to wear shorts and pants and are left to be objectified in a manner that their male counterparts are not.

To watch Ohashi perform her electric routine,[39] it seems impossible that she could feel insecure yet, "as gymnasts, our bodies are constantly being seen in these minimal clothing leotards. I felt so uncomfortable looking in the mirror. . . . I hated taking pictures. I hated everything about myself."[40]

In her prime, she had outscored Simone Biles (1997–). When a coach told Ohashi that she was an embarrassment to the sport, Ohashi walked away from the sport she had loved so much.

In college, she returned to compete for UCLA, but at a meeting with her new coach, Ohashi said, "I just don't want to be great again." Ohashi understood that by being the best, she would be in the spotlight of public scrutiny and vicious remarks, that striving for greatness brought on expectations (the hegemonic feminine ideal) she could not meet.[41]

WHO APPROVES CONTENT?

While the stories of Billie Jean King, the All-American Girls Professional Baseball League, and Wilma Rudolf made for positive, uplifting stories, publishers have traditionally leaned on tragic female figures in the sports world rather than empowered athletes. Stories of abuse, both mental and physical, within the sports of women's ice-skating, dance, and gymnastics, for example, are too numerous to count.

Hair pulling, of all things, reveals the stark contrast of men vs. women media coverage for acts of aggression. When NFL player Ricky Williams was dragged to the ground by his dreadlocks twice in a 2003 game, the NFL established what became the "Ricky rule," making it legal to take a player down by his hair. By 2015, 14 percent of all players had hair long enough (beyond the collar of the uniform) to be affected by the Ricky rule. When Troy Polamalu, known for his "long, wavy Samoan hair," was violently taken down by his hair in 2015, it was named as "one of the most memorable tackles in NFL history,"[42] but the act of hair pulling was and is rarely discussed among players. But on November 5, 2009, when Elizabeth Lambert (1989–), infamously known as "the hair-pulling college soccer player," of the University of New Mexico, jerked and then threw Brigham Young University's Kassidy Shumway (1989–) to the ground, it was the "ponytail tackle heard 'round the world."[43] Footage of the game has been viewed more than 6 million times, launched petitions and Facebook accounts calling for Lambert's ban from the sport. The hair pull made national news, including the morning talk shows, ESPN, and nightly news, with more articles appearing in all the major newspapers and sports magazines. Topics included aggression in women's sports, competitiveness in women's sports, the erosion of femininity in women's sports, and so forth. If the female athlete was not a victim, she was a villain.

Holly Kondras (1968–) recognized this dichotomy of coverage years earlier, and in 1999 founded Wish Publishing, the first book publishing company exclusively promoting titles for women's sports, health, and fitness. It began when Kondras, a veteran in the industry, noticed one particular letter. "In one of those piles of manuscripts was a letter from a girl who wanted to find a book about becoming a football player. . . . That got me thinking about how hard it is to be a pioneer—not everyone is brave enough to be the first person to do something, and sometimes just knowing someone else has been out there can give you the courage to try." Kondras saw that very few sports books were written for women with even fewer written by coaches of female sports.

"There was also always an undercurrent that the coaches of women's sports were second class, that even other women's sports coaches would rather get tips and techniques from the men's coaches," Kondras said, recalling a time she had attended an American Library Association (ALA) conference where a librarian had warned Kondras of the dangers of publishing and promoting female athlete books because such titles were perceived to be for the less academically inclined and, therefore, limited in marketability.

Kondras knew better. "Female collegiate athletes' GPAs elevate the entire athletic department in most cases. Many of the women who contributed to our WNBA series had finished degrees early and started graduate programs during the four years they played college ball. Many had degrees in pre-medical, pre-law, and other rigorous academic programs. I felt that the views that librarian expressed showed that even the most tuned-in professionals in the book business might not understand our audience and that, even if I explained it, their view of who would be interested would not change."

Kondras began a women's sports publishing company "for women who don't want to learn how to watch football, but how to play it," including women's sports biographies, sports skills development for girls and women, coaching texts by and about coaches of women's sports, and inspirational titles for athletes, and, in doing so, she became a pioneer herself. Through the vision of Kondras, female athletes were given a book publishing platform in which gender equity content was in the hands of female athletes, coaches, and health experts.

"MEAN GIRLS"

For the fully vested *mean girl*, however, hashtags mean nothing. While girls were three times more likely to be cyberbullied than boys in 2020, according to the National Center for Education Statistics, there remains too little data on how adult females are impacted and, more importantly, just who is doing the bullying.[44] Males most often use sex to degrade a female online (this includes all forms of violence), while female cyberbullies use physical appearance and shame as their weapon of choice.

In the case of Ohashi, the bullies were overwhelmingly female, women unhappy with their own bodies. Indeed, more than 90 percent of women are, in some measure, unhappy with their bodies. With the reality that only 5 percent of women naturally possess the current American hegemonic feminine ideal portrayed in media, the bullying of Ohashi was all the more ridiculous. And harmful.[45]

The term "mean girl" was popularized in the 2004 movie *Mean Girls*—a story of a girl who must navigate her way through the social hierarchy of a traditional American high school and its mean girls. In research, the term "mean girls" is a subgrouping of females who target another female.

Only in the early 2000s, after a number of girls hanged themselves following aggressive cyberbullying by mean girls, did experts, educators, and parents become aware of just how dangerous it could be.

Reasonably, one could ask, for all women have been through in history, why would we continue to turn on each other?

Anthropologists explain that bullying among boys/men is most frequently to establish dominance, but females most often bully to garner social status among both males and females and to "gain male attention."[46]

As dangerous as it has been to dismiss males for sexually harassing, stalking, and assaulting females with the explanation "boys will be boys," it is equally dangerous to defend female bullying with the derogatory "you know how girls are" explanation. It is not natural but taught behavior for girls to attack each other—a social construct by the patriarchal system to ensure female devotion. Each time females turn on another female for not living up to the hegemonic feminine ideal, more harm is brought to girls and women.

THIRTEEN

Modern Medicine for the Modern Woman

It was not until the 1950s that people's lifestyles were connected to heart disease and not until the 1960s and 1970s that the correlation between exercise and diet was connected to heart disease in middle-aged men. Two national clinical trials (1982 and 1995) then linked high cholesterol to heart disease and aspirin use to the reduction of heart attacks, using 34,937 men. Not one woman.

Into the twenty-first century, a study found that women were less likely to get any diagnoses for heart-related illnesses despite rising risk factors among this population. This came about because of the work of cardiologist Bernadine Healy (1944–2011), the first female director of the National Institutes of Health, who launched the NIH Women's Health Initiative to study causes, prevention, and cures of diseases that affect women.[1] It took a female physician to recognize and begin to rectify ongoing medical issues that are unnecessarily costing lives; "heart disease is also a woman's disease, not just a man's disease in disguise."[2]

Heart disease is the number one cause of death for women in the United States; yet not until 2016, when the American Heart Association released findings and proper guidelines on female cardiovascular disease, did the medical community begin to pay more attention to treatment specific to biological females.[3]

THE HISTORY OF WOMEN IN THE MEDICAL COMMUNITY

Women are affected differently by autoimmune diseases, gastrointestinal disorders, depression, even migraines. In fact, the differences between men and women are far more expansive than anyone previously understood. According to a 2017 Israeli study, researchers found sixty-five hundred genes of an approximate twenty thousand that were "biased toward one sex or the other."[4] These impact not only skin, hair, and cardiovascular diseases, but also Parkinson's disease and varying forms of dementia, underlining the differences in men's and women's patterns of behavior.

These findings support the argument for gender-specific medical treatments for disease.[5] Yet women, though scrutinized in almost every aspect of their lives, are completely neglected as patients. As Dr. Stacey Rosen, senior vice president of Katz Institute for Women's Health, explains, treating women like "little men" is not only insufficient but dangerous. "We can't blindly expect women to conform to a male model of health. We now know that male and female physiology differs well beyond the body parts covered by a bathing suit. These differences can be traced right down to our cells."[6]

BIKINI MEDICINE

The term "bikini medicine" came about as more and more female medical students and patients both saw and felt the disparity in treatment in the medical community. The body parts covered by a bikini were believed to be strictly female, but all other aspects of the female form were equal—medically speaking—to the male anatomy. Modern medicine traditionally used a 154-pound male as the typical human measurements by which medication and anesthesia were dispensed and treatments were offered.

This is dangerous. Even something so seemingly inconsequential as sleeping aids make a difference between the sexes. Women metabolize Ambien more slowly than men, leading to a higher risk of "next-morning impairment" for females. Conversely, women who are sedated with propofol for medical procedures are known to wake up sooner than men and therefore require more dosing. With many if not most physicians still unaware and uneducated about females metabolizing medications differently, female patients are vulnerable to potentially dangerous mishaps due to misdiagnosis.

The problem is females have been actively omitted from medical clinical trials. In 1993, at the urging of the National Institutes of Health, Congress enacted a federal law that biological sex had to be considered as a biological variable in studies (both in human and animal subjects). Still, by 2016, almost 70 percent of biomedical research papers published did not report on the sex of subjects. Some of the least sex-related documentation was in medical areas where there are greater disparities between males and females such as hematology, the study of disorders of the blood and bone marrow; immunology; and pharmaceutical medications.[7] This is significant because physicians cannot safely suggest medications to their female patients, not knowing the outcomes of clinical trials for female subjects.

In 2015, a national survey of U.S. medical students revealed two important indicators regarding the past and future when it comes to women's health: an overwhelming 96 percent of respondents were concerned about the lack of information in treatment of female patients and hoped to have sex and gender medicine curriculum as part of their training. Yet, by 2018, the differences between genders were still not being addressed in most medical schools. One of the first notable schools to do so was the Laura W. Bush Institute for Women's Health of the Texas Tech University Health Sciences Center in 2007, recognizing that "research proves that some diseases react different[ly] in men and women, which challenges health care professionals to design special approaches that provide women's health information, disease diagnosis and treatment."[8]

However, in 2018, both the Association of American Medical Colleges and the American Medical Association refused to recognize the value in requiring continued education and research on sex and gender differences and, instead, put the onus on medical students to "learn to recognize and appropriately address gender and cultural biases in themselves, in others, and in the health care delivery process."[9] What this did, then, was allow all students to continue to diagnose and treat women according to the 154-pound-male model, leaving women to fight for women.

One such woman is Dr. Jan Werbinski, 2020 president-elect of the American Medical Women's Association (AMWA) and national spokesperson for greater education and training and research for sex- and gender-based medicine, who is calling for a "revolution in the delivery of healthcare to women."[10]

Werbinski, whose career has spanned over forty years in women's health, along with her colleagues at AMWA's Sex and Gender Health Collaborative, has worked diligently to raise awareness with medical institutions and leaders in the medical field regarding women's health. "It really boils down to how physiology, evaluation, and treatment of disease is different in women than it is in men. . . . We know now that there are differences in the sexes in every disease and every cell and every organ system," Werbinski said. "What I urge the students to do is ask one question in every medical venue they attend—how would a particular condition or disease look in the opposite sex?"[11]

As long as the medical community continues its practice of what has been called one-sex medicine or gender-blind medicine, female patients will continue to be harmed by this negligence. According to Dr. Marjorie Jenkins, a cofounder of the Laura W. Bush Institute for Women's Health, "We need to stop ignoring the mountain of evidence that we have that men and women are different."

In emergency rooms across the world, women who suffer with acute abdominal pain in the emergency room wait longer, on average, than men as the pain of men continues to be seen as more serious.[12] Men also receive more proactive and faster care during heart attacks.[13] To Jenkins's point, science has shown that women's immune systems are more robust and complicated than men's, explaining why women are more likely to suffer from autoimmune conditions yet are often dismissed by doctors, labeled hypochondriacs.

During the 1990s, studies in the United States revealed that as many as 30 to 50 percent of female patients were misdiagnosed with their depression, an issue compounded by the fact that many times the depression and anxiety were symptoms of other medical issues.[14] By 2010, female patients were reportedly taking multiple medications, one often counteracting another, without accurate diagnoses. A 2013 study in the United Kingdom noted that more than twice as many women as men had to make more than three visits before their primary physician would refer them to a specialist, that is, take their concerns seriously.[15]

In the case of two of the most elite female soccer players in the world, they had to find their own treatments as their symptoms did not present as the typical 154-pound male.

THE CONCUSSED MICHELLE AKERS AND BRIANA SCURRY

In the 1990s, Olympic gold medalist, FIFA world champion, and U.S. Soccer Hall of Famer Michelle Akers (1966–) began to suffer migraines and feel exhausted and disoriented. She suffered a concussion in the 1999 World Cup final that essentially ended her soccer career. In April 2010, fellow Olympic gold medalist, FIFA world champion, and U.S. Soccer Hall of Famer Briana Scurry (1971–) received a brutal concussion that sent her down a medical rabbit hole. Both athletes were misdiagnosed for years. No one considered that either athlete had chronic traumatic encephalopathy (CTE), a progressive, degenerative brain disease believed to be caused by repeated blows to the head and repeated concussions (most commonly associated with NFL players), based simply on gender.

Akers was the first female soccer star in the United States. Her reputation for nonstop aggression on the field was unmatched. She was the first female soccer player in the United States to earn a shoe endorsement and was named FIFA Female Player of the Century. She has been called "the best woman that has ever played the game."[16] A publication by the International Federation of Association Football (FIFA), the highest governing body of the sport, said of Akers, "No one, before or since, man or woman, was more competitive or committed."[17]

She led the United States to victory in 1991 for its first appearance in a World Cup, scoring ten goals. In fact, Akers scored the first-ever goal for the U.S. women's national team in 1985. Of her own legendary performances, Akers once said, "I took risks on the field. I was competitive with myself and I'd go into tackles hard when we were up 7–0. It drove my coaches crazy."[18]

Her competitive risks made her an international star but also brought about significant damage. In her playing days, Akers had a dozen knee surgeries, numerous head injuries, and knocked-out teeth.

When asked to identify just how many concussions she suffered in sport, Akers is uncertain. Her best guess was "into the double digits." In a PBS film titled *Bell Ringer: Michelle Akers on Concussions*, the athlete recalls feeling foggy, experiencing headaches and migraines following games, "and I always felt like my head was kind of swollen."

What made national headlines regarding Akers's health was not her multiple concussions but the plethora of varying diagnoses. Dating back to 1991, she began to feel exhausted and disoriented following the World Cup. Doctors told her she was simply fatigued and needed rest. When things worsened, she again sought medical advice but it was not until 1993 when one of the world's strongest and reputable female athletes collapsed on the field that red flags were raised. With her national team and international reputation to back her up, no one was going to call Akers "hysterical." Even then, after a year of echocardiograms, heart stress tests, and blood tests, she was first diagnosed with infectious mononucleosis, also known as mono, then with the Epstein-Barr virus, and, finally, with chronic fatigue and immune dysfunction syndrome (CFIDS).[19]

It took one of the biggest stars in the sports world to normalize CFIDS, a disorder that is two to four times more prevalent among women but was dismissed even into the early 2000s. That wasn't the only thing wrong with Akers; yet, despite her migraines and memory loss, she had never thought about CTE until she was watching a 2017 documentary about former English soccer star Alan Shearer and his research into CTE and his own symptoms. She started doing research on her own to see what studies were being done for female athletes in the United States. There were none.

She got in touch with Boston University professor of neurology Dr. Robert Stern, clinical research director for BU's CTE center, and initiated a first-of-its-kind study on the long-term effects of head trauma on female soccer players.[20]

Briana Scurry's career-ending injury would not occur until her professional career with the now-defunct Women's Professional Soccer League's Washington Freedom in 2010. As goalkeeper, Scurry came out of box to scoop up a "low ball" as she had done thousands of times. "I never saw the forward coming," she said. The opposing player attempted to beat Scurry to the ball; instead "her knee smashed into the side of my head."

It was just one too many concussions for the legendary goalie unafraid to challenge offensive players. But that knee to the head in 2010 was—in every sense—a game changer.

"I couldn't focus on anything in my own living room!" What began as a headache and clouded judgment worsened into extreme sensitivity to light, sounds, and movements. She had insomnia, her balance was off, and she began to have anxiety attacks. She had difficulty finding words, expressing her feelings, and performing the most basic day-to-day activities. She did not tell anyone how bad it had become. That is, until thoughts of suicide began to overtake her.

"My brain chemistry had changed," she explained. "It was like my mind was broken." Finally, "I gave myself the greenlight to talk about it." She began seeing doctors—many doctors. Again and again, she was told "this is how it is" and that she needed "to learn to live with it." Instead, Scurry acted as her own champion, eventually finding doctors familiar with traumatic brain injuries (TBIs) (and how symptoms present in females) who were able to help her.

She learned that 50 percent of girls who play soccer will suffer at least one concussion during their athletic careers and that female athletes are more susceptible to concussions. While men and women have always been treated the same when it comes to concussions, new evidence shows that women take longer to recovery from TBIs and may have more symptoms. Because women more frequently have weaker neck muscles, they may experience a ricochet effect during impact. Changes in estrogen and progesterone levels during menstrual cycles can also affect how severe concussions (and symptoms) may be for females. Most recently, the NIH and funding agencies in Canada and Europe have acknowledged that there is insufficient data regarding concussed female patients and clinical treatment.

While males most typically experience short-term amnesia and disorientation, females more frequently experience prolonged headaches, dizziness, vomiting and/or nausea, and difficulty concentrating. Additionally, females are more likely to die from a head injury than men in head injuries by vehicle collisions, assault, and sport-related injuries.[21] It is not just NFL players who suffer concussions but also female athletes in soccer, cheerleading, basketball, and football, to name a few.

With this knowledge, Scurry began speaking publicly to better educate the public and medical community about concussions. Like Akers, Scurry remains an iconic role model in women's soccer, and she used that platform to go beyond sport and to begin speaking to the medical community, to trainers, coaches, and, in 2014, Congress. "Today, I stand here before you to share my new mission with you. My new mission is to provide a new face and voice to those who have and may suffer the long and difficult recovery of a devastating concussion."[22]

As seen again and again, women have had to speak out for other women to the medical community.

THE PILL

Within the sports world, the oral contraceptive (the pill) has been invaluable for athletic performance. For female athletes who menstruate, "the pill" has helped them to track and better control their own physical performance. No one knows this better than professional long-distance runner Sarah Crouch (1989–). Logging as many as 140 miles per week, the thirteen-time NCAA Division II All-American dutifully tracks her diet, nutrition, water intake, sleep patterns, routes she runs, even the weather. But one of the most frustrating things for a female athlete to contend with is her menstrual cycle. While more than 60 percent of female athletes confirm that their performance can be impacted by their menstrual cycle,[23] too few feel comfortable speaking about it with coaches, trainers, and even teammates.

Through research, Crouch hoped to learn the effects of various types of birth control on runners. Instead, "I pulled up absolutely nothing. I was shocked. It was like nobody had ever studied it."[24] When she posted her frustrations on a group site that included sixty other elite female distance runners, the response was immediate and overwhelming. All of the women shared how they were forced to experiment on themselves to see how their bodies (and performances) would react to different forms of birth control.

"It made me a little angry," Crouch said. "To know that women would reach 25, 30 years old as professional athletes, with every aspect of their lives controlled and tweaked down to an inch but in this one area, there was no research and no answers. It's a difficult and lonely landscape."[25]

Because coaches and athletes have been left to perform their own research in women's biology, inconsistencies remain. Canadian Olympic running coach Wynn Gmitroski insisted that his female athletes not take the pill as it can lower levels of testosterone and thereby slow his runners. In one study of 123 elite female skiers and biathletes, 72 percent reported weight gain, loss of muscle strength and endurance, and mood instability, also reporting a loss of their competitive edge while on the pill.[26] None had been warned of these possible side effects by their attending doctors.

Other elite athletes, however, feel they had more control over their bodies and, therefore, their performances, as the pill helps the fluctuation of hormones and controls cramping, headaches, and heavy bleeding.

The reality is, there is insufficient research and evidence regarding birth control and performance for women. Remarkably, it has been found that the female subjects used in previous studies of hormonal impact on athletic performance were not athletes. This is essential, as researchers from Penn Medicine and Northwestern University warn that "manipulating the menstrual cycle to avoid performance changes may have dangerous consequences," which include the female triad, levels of testosterone, and the long-term impact on the female musculoskeletal system. "The bottom line," says Dr. Ellen Casey, codirector of the Penn Center for the Female Athlete, "is that hormonal shifts that drive the menstrual cycle can affect multiple parts of the body, including muscle, bone, endurance, energy level and attention." Women's hormones and the hormones in birth control pills, she says, needs to be better explored in regard to injury prevention and performance enhancement.[27]

A 2020 review of forty-two separate studies on the effects of oral contraceptives on exercise performance in menstruating athletes remains largely inconclusive as the effects were too "trivial and variable."[28]

Despite unanswered questions about those "trivial and variable" issues of the female body, consumers were assured that the pill was safe. Certainly, it did give women new independence—but it also came with costs. Throughout a woman's lifetime, she is faced with numerous decisions unique to women, including the medical/pharmaceutical intervention of and for birth control, pregnancy, childbirth, and later, menopause.

In the United States alone, nine hundred thousand people are affected by blot clots each year with as many as one hundred thousand dying. More people die from blood clots than breast cancer, HIV/AIDS, and car accidents combined. Women are more susceptible to blood clots during childbearing years, with birth control pills containing estrogen and progesterone or progestin increasing the levels of clotting proteins in a woman's body. Despite these facts, pharmaceutical companies are now manufacturing birth control pills that pose a risk two times greater than the older pills.[29]

In addition to blood clots, studies in the 1970s revealed increased risk of ischemic strokes linked to oral contraceptives containing high-dose estrogens. Sixteen studies from 1960 to 1999 found increased risk of stroke (with those risks rising in consideration to age, smoking, and high blood pressure), with a more recent study from 1995 to 2009 citing lower risks of stroke with low-dose ethinyl estradiol formulations of oral contraceptives.[30] Studies have found women with epilepsy have increased instances of seizures while taking oral contraceptives. For women using the hormonal patch, instances of seizures increased greater than 68 percent; 62 percent higher with progestin-only oral contraceptives.[31] Yet another study has found that birth control pills may alter women's brains by leading to less brain cell growth, with women taking the pill having a smaller hypothalamus than women not taking the pill. The researchers found that a smaller hypothalamus is associated with increased anger and symptoms of depression.[32]

At least 150 million women and girls worldwide use oral contraception, for reasons ranging from birth control to controlling acne and/or post-menstrual symptoms. Yet the American College of Obstetrics and Gynecology claims the pill is safe while also acknowledging it is associated with increased risks for blood clots, breast cancer, and, after prolonged usage, possible difficulty conceiving. The World Health Organization (WHO) called the pill a "carcinogenic."[33]

In 2013, twenty-three Canadian women, all under the age of twenty-six with two just fourteen years old, died from the use of the oral contraceptives Yaz and Yasmin, highlighting what was happening around the world, including an astonishing number of young women surviving but living with long-term health issues associated with the pill. That same year, American Alexandra Rowan, twenty-four, collapsed, then "crashed three times on the operating table" before dying from "massive pulmonary embolisms" as a result of birth control.[34]

For perspective, when six women (out of 6.8 million) collapsed and one died because of blood clots after receiving the Johnson & Johnson vaccine for coronavirus disease 2019 (COVID-19), the federal government intervened to stop further administration of the vaccine until more research could be done—because the vaccines were for both men and women. Yet one in one thousand females experiencing dangerous (even fatal) reactions to the birth control pill is medically satisfactory.

For award-winning research psychologist and professor (with expertise in women's health) Sarah Hill, this is not satisfactory. "We're not calculating risk the same way with the vaccine as we are with birth control. In some ways, I think that this is evidence of how cavalier we are about birth control and its impact on women's health."[35]

One more example of putting profits over women's health is the push by hospitals and insurance companies to convince women that the baby they carried was too large for their birth canal, that a day over their due date could cause problems in the labor and delivery room, and that they would recover more quickly from a C-section. In reality, hospitals working in conjunction with insurance companies find C-sections to be more lucrative and time efficient than natural or vaginal births. The National Bureau of Economic Research found that obstetricians are paid more when they perform a C-section, which may be an incentive to push the faster procedure that also allows for more bed space in hospitals.[36]

Worse, the numbers of deaths (for mothers and babies) related to C-sections are on the rise, more than the number for natural births. And

women who undergo C-sections are less likely to understand that recovery following the procedure is more difficult than vaginal birth, that
bleeding and infection rates are higher with more scar tissue that can be
problematic years after giving birth.

WOMEN HAVE ABORTIONS . . .

"Every female athlete I know has had an abortion." It was a bold statement made by U.S. sprinter and five-time Olympic gold medalist Sanya
Richards-Ross (1985–) following the release of her 2017 book *Chasing
Grace*. In it, she writes, "Everything I ever wanted seemed to be within
reach." She had learned just weeks prior to the 2008 Olympic Games that
she was pregnant. "The culmination of a lifetime of work was right before
me. In that moment, it seemed like no choice at all."[37] It is called "abortion doping," an inconceivable practice in which athletes purposefully
become pregnant prior to an athletic event, and time it so that they are approximately eight to twelve weeks pregnant for performance-enhancing
benefits. Following the event, the athlete then has an abortion. By the
mid-twentieth century, there were rumors of Soviet, East German, and
Chinese athletes engaging in this practice for the almighty gold medal.

Certainly, there are benefits that come from pregnancy. In the first
trimester, there is a natural surplus of red blood cells, known as the "steroidal effect" that supports the growing fetus but also supplies the mother
with an extra boost of hormones, including testosterone. However, morality aside, the "morning sickness," exhaustion, interrupted sleep patterns,
and more fluctuating hormones make it unlikely that any elite athlete
would be willing to endure these negative side effects for such a gamble.[38]

Stories of abortion doping officially took hold in 1988 when a Finnish
physician wrote about athletes using and then terminating pregnancy for
performance benefits in sport. No evidence was offered, merely speculation, yet it was widely believed that abortion doping was a regularly practiced technique with communist countries. In 1994, Russian gymnast Olga
Karasyova, a 1968 USSR gold medalist, reportedly gave an interview in
which she revealed she was forced to get pregnant and was at ten weeks
during the 1968 Games. The caller, however, was later found to be an
imposter.[39] Instead, by 2021, a new study came to the same conclusion as
no new evidence has been revealed.[40]

With one in every four women having an abortion before the age of
forty-five in the United States,[41] and six out of every ten unwanted pregnancies being terminated worldwide, abortion is a deeply personal and
hotly debated subject, shrouded in secrecy, shame, judgment, and patriarchal laws. But it was not always that way.

Dating back to writings of Aristotle and Plato, the conventional thought was, until the birth of a child, it was not yet a member of society. This, historians believe, may be due in part to the high mortality rate among the unborn, newborns, and mothers in labor. It may also be an attitudinal reflection of the unspoken—how often women and female children were raped and, left pregnant, took measures to terminate pregnancies.

The state of a woman's pregnancy was far less important in English law as seen in 1557: "The thing killed must be in part of the world of physical beings"; therefore, "if one kills an infant in its mother's womb, this is not a felony."[42] While shocking, it demonstrates what was more important to the state. Literature, from Aristotle to William Shakespeare, has told of midwives using herbs and plants to help with morning sickness and labor pain, but also offering forms of birth control, spontaneous miscarriage, and abortions. These were known practices as were the realities of rape and incest.

The Roman Senate of Caesar Augustus's era was not concerned about population growth but, rather, the economic consequences of declining birth rates. Abortions and all forms of birth control were outlawed based not on religion, morality, or any concerns about females, but on economics.

During the Middle Ages, it was economics again that drove the Church to punish any who engaged in any form of abortion or birth control. Yet with the never-ending search for food and survival, most historians agree that the most reasonable explanations for the many dramatic declines in population were contraceptives and "morning after" treatments of herbs to eliminate risks of pregnancy[43] as well as infanticide, a practice more commonly held in societies that valued male babies over females. This theory has been supported by the high percentages of male to female births.

In a piece about historical attitudes regarding abortion and religion, historians have found that abortion was accepted in ancient Greece and Rome, and that the Old Testament has several legal passages that refer to abortion, but they deal with it in terms of loss of property and not sanctity of life.[44]

Despite common myths that abortion is a relatively new form of birth control, abortion has been a last-recourse option for many women throughout time. From ancient texts to current research, it is clear that reasons for abortion have ranged from fear, anxiety, medical, religious, and political to private or group decisions. The first known evidence of induced (nonsurgical) abortion comes from the Egyptian medical text Ebers Papyrus (1550 BC).

Ancient civilizations around the world all used methods that would eventually evolve into more expansive medical practices in colonial America and beyond. In 1650, in New England, abortion was not only legal but so prevalent that both legal and medical documentation of this era has provided historians with much information about political, social, and religious attitudes. When the U.S. Constitution was written, abortion was a legal medical practice.

At that time, an abortion could be obtained legally until the "quickening," the first time a mother feels the baby kick, typically between fourteen and twenty-six weeks in pregnancy. Because laws against any premarital sex were so rigid, victims of rape and incest carried out abortions in secrecy to escape judgment, punishment, and shame.

It is not just rape but the societal shame and ostracization of women that have led and continue to lead women to discreetly "end a pregnancy." According to a 2015 study among Christian congregations in the United States, more than four in ten women who had an abortion were regular churchgoers. Only 7 percent discussed their decision to have an abortion with church officials. Sixty-five percent said church members judged single pregnant women; 54 percent believe the church "oversimplifies" fair and/or realistic options for pregnant women, with fewer than 41 percent having confidence they would receive proper help for unwanted pregnancies.[45]

In 2021, Texas governor Greg Abbott signed into law a measure that bans abortion after six weeks (before most women even know they are pregnant), even in the cases of rape and incest, despite 56 percent of Texans (including pro-life and pro-choice voters) supporting a woman's choice in the event of rape or incest or if the life of the mother is threatened. By early 2022, neighboring state Oklahoma reported a "massive influx of women from Texas" seeking abortions[46] then, just weeks later, also banned abortion after six weeks.[47]

For the 3 million girls and women who become pregnant as a result of rape,[48] being forced to carry a pregnancy to term can be harmful beyond the financial and physical aspect. Already without their sense of safety and control, these victims are further violated by a law that does not consider them or their worth, making recovery even harder.

After 50 years, however, the U.S. Supreme Court shocked the world with its decision to overturn *Roe v. Wade*, the court's own landmark decision in 1973, putting abortion rights in the hands of state legislators. Less than a month later, controversy began as a 10-year-old rape victim was transported across state lines so that she might have an abortion and begin the slow process of healing (both emotionally and physically).

True to women's history, the news spread quickly throughout the world with many celebrating their cause but far more protesting that once again, women had no say regarding their own bodies, even if their lives were threatened, even in the event of a crime. Always political, often extremely difficult, the history of women in sports and society is as complicated as it is interesting and will never *not* be talked about. The issue of women and their bodies remains, historically, a favorite topic.

WOMEN HAVE PERIODS . . . .

However, few wanted to talk about her menstrual cycle.

Roman author and philosopher Pliny (AD 23/24–79) wrote that "on the approach of a woman in this [menstrual] state, meat will become sour, seeds which are touched by her become sterile, grafts wither away, garden-plants are withered up, and the fruit will fall from the tree beneath which she sits."[49]

In reality, because early male doctors and religious leaders did not understand the importance and value of the menstrual cycle, they decided it must be a punishment. The Church frequently shamed women for their cycles and disallowed any pain relief remedies to women during menstruation and childbirth to remind them of Eve's original sin.[50]

Before there were sanitary pads or tampons, women balled up clothing and bled into rags (thus the expression "on the rag") and wore herbs around their necks and waists in the attempt to neutralize the odor of blood. The first disposable pads were invented in 1888, yet today women and girls in rural Nepal are banished from their homes during their periods and forced to sleep in windowless, poorly insulated "menstruation huts." Every year, girls and women die of exposure, animal bites, or smoke inhalation after lighting small fires to keep warm. This *chhaupadi* ("impurity") is imposed on women to prevent them from spreading disease, disaster, or bad luck among their neighbors. It is also strictly forbidden for a menstruating woman to handle any food.[51]

Women around the world remain uneducated about their own bodies because the topic is so taboo. In 2016, China manufactured eighty-five billion sanitary pads but not one single tampon. All feminine hygiene products are banned on television during lunchtime and prime-time viewing as such things are considered "disgusting" by China's media regulator. In addition, lack of sex education for females regarding their bodies and fears of tampons breaking their hymen and "robbing" their virginity are prevalent.[52] Throughout India, Russia, and the United States, to name a few, even elite female athletes do not always fully understand how they are impacted both psychologically and physically during menstruation . . .

. . . AND CYCLES

The menstrual cycle begins when the lining of the uterus (endometrium) is shed, a natural occurrence for the nonpregnant female with each monthly cycle. The endometrium is designed to nourish a fetus, with increased levels of estrogen and progesterone thickening its walls. When fertilization (from the male sperm) does not occur, the endometrium along with blood and mucus from the vagina and cervix are shed from the body through the menstrual flow.

At the beginning of the follicular phase (or "low hormone" phase), estrogen levels slowly increase. The first spike of estrogen, the "middle" of the cycle, is then followed by the release of the egg (oocyte), as well as the highest level of estrogen and progesterone.

These biological changes can produce cramping, back aches, headaches, and bloating, as well as fluctuations in metabolism, inflammation, body temperature, fluid balance, mood, and memory. This can impact strength, increase injury risk, and lower energy.[53] In other words, a period is not a curse or punishment but a medical event that happens once a month to females and can create real physiologic changes and disturbances that should be understood (and fully appreciated).[54] For this reason, Dr. Stacy Sims (1979–), an exercise physiologist and nutrition scientist, lectures extensively on the menstrual cycle.

As a former elite athlete, Sims understands that for too long females have been told that when they have their period they should expect to feel poorly and, as athletes, underperform and, so, they should sit out. Sims argues that the menstrual cycle is actually an opportunity to increase the intensity of training sessions. In her lectures, she often tells the audience, "As we have this conversation, we kind of giggle and laugh. I want everyone in this room to turn and say, 'Women have periods.'" Each time, the audience members burst into laughter. To Sims's point, why, in the twenty-first century, does this make men and women so uncomfortable?

Through lore and history, women's menstrual cycles have been treated as a punishment when, medically speaking, menstruation offers tremendous benefits to women. A woman's cycle (heavy or light) is an indicator of well-being. Lack of menstrual cycle can flag issues of heart disease, diabetes, reproductive issues, and even cancer. A regular, healthy cycle is a strong indicator of good health.

During a woman's cycle, her estrogen levels will rise, also releasing endorphins for mood elevation and increased alertness,[55] but menstruation also helps cleanse and flush toxins from the body naturally, which also helps reduce risks of cardiovascular disease and excess iron.[56] And beyond identifying possible medical issues, a regular menstrual cycle slows the process of aging.

Two studies in 2013 and 2017 on Muslim women before, during, and after Ramadan, with its strict fasting rules, concluded that cycles were affected by fasting.[57] These studies are not only valuable regarding nutrition and energy stores but, on the whole, are valuable as too little medical attention has been given to women and their cycles—especially for female athletes who have been left to figure it out on their own, including how to deal with social stigmas about menstruation.

During the 1996 Atlanta Games, U.S. sprinter Gwen Torrence (1965–) turned to see Pauline Davis (1966–) of the Bahamas pointing down to Torrence's shorts. Her tampon string was showing. Mortified, Torrence attempted to tuck it back inside the seam of her shorts. The baton was passed off to the second leg while Davis shook her head at Torrence. It was still showing.

Davis then actually crossed over her line into Torrence's lane. In one of the biggest races in Olympic sports with the race well underway, two women of opposing nations, both favored for the gold and silver, huddled together in Torrence's lane, trying to hide a tampon string. Finally, a frustrated Torrence said, "Oh, forget it!"

Once the baton was in hand, Torrence won gold for the United States while Davis ensured a silver, making it the first time in Bahamas history that women medaled in any sport. Reporters later asked Torrence what she and Davis had been doing during the race. "I told them, 'It was a female thing,' and that was that."

In the case of record-setting race car driver Lyn St. James (1947–), the first female to win the Indianapolis 500 Rookie of the Year and former president of the Women's Sports Foundation, things did not go so smoothly.

She had won the Kelly Services Races, which meant she would receive an award before a large audience. But when she refused to climb out of the car, her pit crew believed she was simply being modest—again. Sitting in the winner's circle, people began to swarm her car, and her pit crew yelled for her to get out. "Nope," she said, shaking her head. "I'm not getting out." The crew chief stuck his head into the car, ready to pull her out, when she grabbed his head and turned it so that he could see that her once all-white racing suit was soaked in menstrual blood. "He said only three words," St. James recalled. "Oh, my God!'"

Immediately, he rallied the crew and they pushed St. James's car out of the pit area and smuggled her into the locker room. Not another word was said about that incident, but the crew did pitch in to buy her a gift—an all-black racing suit.

In 2016 at the Rio Olympic Games when Chinese swimmer Fu Yuanhui (1996–) took on the taboo subject, she became an internet sensation, winning legions of fans despite her own loss in the 4×100 medley relay. When her team came in fourth place, a reporter asked the disappointed Yuanhui about the loss. She responded, "Actually, my period started last night so I'm feeling pretty weak and really tired," adding, "but this isn't an excuse."[58] It was what it was.

For more than a century of documented sports articles, athletes from every known discipline have easily explained away poorer performances due to illness, injury, or distraction, but a woman's menstrual cycle has always been too biologically gender specific and personal to discuss. That is, until Yuanhui simply allowed both biology and frustration to be heard. By the closing of those Olympic Games, #MenstruationMatters was trending.

Yuanhui had opened the door for female athletes, and six years later, New Zealand's professional golfer Lydia Ko (1997–), ranked third in the world, did not flinch when a reporter noted that she sought treatment from her physical therapist during competition and asked if she had any long-term concerns.

"I hope not," Ko said. "It's that time of the month. I know the ladies watching are probably like: 'Yeah, I got you.' So, when that happens my back gets really tight, and I'm all twisted." While the reporter was at a loss for words, social media was filled with them, praising Ko for her honesty about women's cycles and women in sport.[59]

While one Twitter user wrote, "'It's that time of the month. My back hurts.' Male reporter: '. . .' Imagine being a sports reporter and never discussing a major aspect of female players' performance," forensic pathologist and Twitter user Dr. Judy Melinek added, "Love this! Let's normalize talking about our periods."

SCIENCE MEETS PREGNANCY AND SPORT

Prior to 1985, sixty years after women got the vote, eighty years after the first women competitors were allowed in the Olympic Games, and thirty-seven years after Fanny Blankers-Koen showed what could be done while pregnant, women had no clear guide on what was safe and how much was too much in terms of activity while pregnant. The American College of Obstetricians and Gynecologists (ACOG) advised against high-impact activities, recommended a heart rate no greater than 140 beats per minute, and a core body temperature no greater than 100.4°F/38°C. As it turns out, this would be both a blessing and curse for elite female athletes.[60]

By the late 1980s, a significant number of studies were conducted on pregnant women and the correlation between exercise/activity to the birth weight and development, long-term health of the baby, and benefits to the mother during labor and postpartum.

Dr. James Clapp III, a leader in research and studies in women's athletics and pregnancy, studied 250 pregnant women, one of the largest studies at the time, and found that 80 percent of the exercising women gave birth on or before their due dates, compared with 50 percent of the control group of nonexercising women, which is significant as gestation that continues past the due date increases the chances of inducement of labor. Additionally, Clapp learned that 70 percent of the exercising women who delivered vaginally completed their labors in less than four hours while only 30 percent of the control group took so little time.

In short, women who exercised were far more likely to have happier, healthier pregnancies with faster recoveries while their children had higher marks for verbal communication and coordination four years after birth.[61]

THE HEART RATE AND INNER CORE TEMPERATURE DURING PREGNANCY

Following ACOG's 1985 guide for female athletes, however, professionals within the medical fields—both male and female—paid little attention to the entirety of ACOG's recommendations. By and large, the medical community focused simply on a heart rate no greater than 140 beats per minute.

For the recreational athlete or a pregnant woman who simply wanted to walk, this was a solid recommendation that she could easily follow. For the Olympic, professional, or otherwise competitive athlete, this half information was harmful. In the 1990s, elite athletes such as two-time Olympian swimmer Angel Martino Sims (1967–); Evelyn Ashford, a three-time track and field Olympian with four gold medals and one silver and the first female to run under eleven seconds in the 100-meter dash (at the 1984 Los Angeles Games); fellow track athlete Sandra Farmer Patrick (1962–), a three-time Olympian in hurdles and silver medalist, were deflated by the prospect of training at 140 bpm.[62] They knew they could do more, but their doctors were telling them differently. With the 1985 exercise recommendations of a restrictive heart rate zone of 140 for a duration no longer than fifteen to twenty minutes, many athletes became so frustrated they simply stopped.

In 1994, ACOG revised its recommendations again based on prenatal studies in which it placed almost no restrictions on maternal physical activity and eliminated parameters for heart rate and the duration of exercise for elite athletes, stressing that they (elite athletes) should be analyzed individually.

Clapp's revolutionary studies that included nonactive women, recreational exercisers, and elite athletes provided the much-needed, full scope of women in sport. Most elite athletes studied were long-distance runners, but no one had studied pregnant women performing plyometrics or heavy weight lifting until this time. It was then that Dr. Clapp took on a United States bobsled athlete training for a sport in which athletes were tested on the 40-meter and 100-meter sprint, shot put, vertical leap, and a timed 425-pound sled push. The mother-athlete was connected to a fetal monitor, EKG (electrocardiogram) leads attached to the chest to measure heart rate and analyze PVCs, and an EKG exchange while the fetal monitor watched for any change or distress in the baby. An oxygen mask was also required to measure the mother's oxygen intake and returns as well as a rectal thermometer to register her inner core temperature.

Clapp's research was presented to the International Olympic Committee as new safety guidelines and recommendations for pregnant athletes in training, as it impressed the importance of monitoring the inner core temperature and allowing the athlete's heart rate to go beyond 140 bpm in intervals. For the elite athlete, this is a safe measure. Additionally, Clapp found that for those athletes who still engaged in challenging workouts, their labor and delivery were faster and easier with greater recovery after birth and fewer incidents of postpartum depression.[63]

WHEN WOMEN PRACTICE MEDICINE

The history of medicine regarding women has always been based more in assumption than science—its roots in marginalizing women's health, the knowledge of the female anatomy and her psyche pitted against political and social norms. Medicine of antiquity held that women who remained celibate for an extended period of time would become victims of a wandering womb as her uterus was believed to be a "living animal," eager to produce children. While Aristotle taught that woman's sole contribution to childbirth was serving as host to the male's seed, medieval physicians believed the uterus caused female diseases, calling it a "sewer," a site of noxious poisons that caused disease. By the fifteenth century, the greatest amount of interest, discussion, and debate centered around the male genitals and sperm. It was the beginning of physicians treating the female anatomy as male. For centuries prior, physicians believed that women had internal penises and testes. By the mid-1600s, William Harvey (1578–1657), a well-respected English surgeon, anatomist, and physiologist, noted that women and eunuchs were essentially the same and could, therefore, be treated as men.[64]

Dr. Elizabeth Blackwell (1821–1910) is best known as America's first female doctor. She was inspired to study medicine when a dying friend told her she might have been saved had she had a female doctor. Indeed, Blackwell called out the grievously negligent practices of the treatment of females. She was one of the first to practice preventive care and personal hygiene (noting that male doctors often spread infection and disease by neglecting to wash their own hands between patients) and also saw medicine as an opportunity to bring about social and political change through and for women.

Her thesis, which was on typhoid fever, was the first medical article published by a woman and was both praised as empathetic toward human suffering while also calling for economic change and social justice, and criticized by the medical community for being "feminine" in its opinion.[65]

Blackwell established the New York Infirmary for Women and Children with her sister, Dr. Emily Blackwell (1826–1910) in 1857 and the following year opened a medical college in New York City, which Emily ran while Elizabeth permanently moved to London, becoming a professor of gynecology at the London School of Medicine for Women.[66]

The Blackwell sisters believed it would be women who would best help women and change the world. Other female doctors persisted in the need for gender-specific research, also calling for medical journals to reject studies that excluded women. It is a fight that continues today as an astounding 70 percent of medical faculty stated they did not have a formal sex- and gender-specific integrated medical curriculum. Even upon a directive by the U.S. Congress that sex and gender medical differences be included, women were ignored by our most prestigious institutions of higher education and medical training.[67]

While great strides have been made, the disturbing trend of willful medical negligence continues regarding women's hormones, the training of elite pregnant athletes, how to medicate female patients, and the need for proper sport and exercise science research, including the highly debated conversation about the fairness of allowing transgender female athletes in sport.

FOURTEEN

The (Recognized) Entry of Lesbians in Sport

Historically, male and female athletes have always hidden their sexuality when it did not align with mainstream America. For that matter, athletes around the world did the same, fearful of losing their standing on or with a team, or incurring backlash from media, religious, and political leaders, as well as possible sponsorship. Interestingly, well-known female athletes such as Billie Jean King and Christy Martin initially denied their homosexuality from the public and press, believing the only way they could safely navigate their sport was to conform to the ideal feminine image—a protection that did not and does not exist.

THE HISTORY OF LESBIANS AND SPORT IN THE MODERN WORLD

For centuries, patriarchal societies had warned that participation in athletics would alter femininity and, if left unchecked, ruin women. But as more and more benefits were derived from women participating in athletics, figureheads had to decide *which* athletics were acceptable. Even then, it appeared that women could (and did) participate in all sports without any life-altering consequences.

With the passage of Title IX in 1972, however, came rumors that the new law would allow "homosexuals" to gain greater entry into mainstream sports, and three years later, the *Washington Post* ran a four-part series on "homosexual" men and women in sport. Despite Title IX, Rene Portland (1952–2018), head coach of the women's basketball program at Penn State University, openly practiced homophobic sentiments against her lesbian and bisexual athletes. In 1985, during an interview with the *Chicago Sun Times* about lesbians in athletics, Portland was quoted to say, "I will not have it [lesbianism] on my teams."[1]

While male and female athletes had always hidden their sexual identities in the past, tennis sensation Martina Navratilova (1956–) came out in a *New York Daily News* interview in 1981, identifying herself as bisexual—

both a brave and risky career move for any athlete.[2] She had asked the reporter, Steve Goldstein, not to reveal this information as news broke that Billie Jean King had been slapped with a lawsuit from her former hairdresser and lover. Navratilova had feared that the two news headlines about gay tennis players would hurt women's tennis and "Avon might pull out" as a sponsor. Goldstein and the *Daily News* ran the story anyway and Avon dropped its sponsorship.[3]

The Czechoslovakian-born American (retired) Navratilova was selected by *Tennis* magazine as the greatest female tennis player from 1975 to 2005, and is widely considered to be one of the best players of all time. At a time when more than eighty countries around the world criminalized homosexuality, Navratilova had to consider her own legal standing (and safety) when she competed overseas. Most other players were not willing to take such risks. By 1992, she had become a pioneer, speaking openly at the National March on Washington for Lesbian, Gay and Bisexual Rights.

The year following her public "coming out," the Federation of Gay Games was established with the first Gay Games in San Francisco in 1982, with the sole purpose of bringing people together from all over the world "with diversity, respect, equality, solidarity, and sharing"; the fundamental principle of the Games was (and is) inclusion.[4]

While the 1982 Gay Games began (to be repeated every four years, following the tradition of the Olympic Games), the NCAA's Women in Sports Conference actively refused to use the word "lesbian" in organizing agendas, also the same year that Betty Baxter (1952–), a Canadian athlete and coach, was fired when local media reported that Baxter was gay. She later served as a board member of the 1990 Gay Games in Vancouver and cofounded the Canadian Association for the Advancement of Women in Sport and the National Coaching School for Women.[5] Later in her career, Baxter became an antibully and antiharassment activist in the public schools.

While Baxter entered into the political arena to create change, Navratilova stayed the course in the world of tennis—but not without problems.

WOMAN VS. LESBIAN

Much like ancient Amazons, evidence of lesbians was rarely shared by Greek (male) scholars in ancient Greece;[6] but throughout history, art, most often, depicted female relationships. The lesbian figure became more evident into the sixteenth and seventeenth centuries in Europe. By the eighteenth century, English law actively ignored female homosexual activity "out of male fears about acknowledging and reifying lesbianism."[7]

By the nineteenth and early twentieth centuries, what came to be known as "Boston marriages," involving two women living together, independent of men, was actually practiced around the world. Most women remained closeted, but those who were in the public eye, particularly athletes, drew public scrutiny.

During the years 1981 to 1989, despite the fact that Navratilova was one of the best, most aggressive players in the world and a big draw at tournaments, she could not get corporate endorsements. At the same time, Anna Kournikova (1981–), a successful tennis player in doubles, was once said to be "the best and worst thing to ever happen to women's tennis." Without ever winning any significant titles, Kournikova, who was known on the circuit as "Pornikova" for her sexy pictorials and image, made far more money off the court than on. In 2002, she made $10 million a year in just endorsements.[8]

Her beauty notwithstanding, Kournikova's blatant sexuality made corporate America and patriarchal societies feel just a little better about women in sport. And when tennis star Hana Mandlíková (1962–) told reporters following her 1985 upset over Navratilova, "It was difficult playing against a man," it endeared Mandlíková to male viewers. Worse than throwing her own opponent under the proverbial bus, worse than using language meant to degrade Navratilova not only as an athlete but as a woman, was the fact that Mandlíková herself would come out in 2001.[9]

So rampant was the fear of being ostracized from sport, Mandlíková's behavior was more normal than not, for the media was a constant watchdog of behavior, appearance, and all things female. Early on, female athletes—gay or straight—have understood that media portrayals of female athletes shaped public and corporate opinions of what and who they were.[10]

For the female athlete who did not fit the hegemonic feminine ideal or, more importantly, did not care to play to the prescribed feminine ideal, marketability was far more difficult. This would, of course, include the female fans.

It was why the WNBA actively chose to ignore who many of its fans and its own players were. The decision, the WNBA wagered, was one based on economics. On April 24, 1996, the "We Got Next" announcement was made when the NBA Board of Governors gave the green light to a women's league—the Women's National Basketball Association (WNBA). Owned by the NBA, the WNBA was launched the following year. Its then-NBA owners focused on the economic, social, and cultural aspects of creating a successful brand in which they could draw in male viewers, with the assumption that a strong female fan base already existed. Already an economic powerhouse, the NBA drew upon its own marketing and advertising successes, which included General Motors,

Sears, Nike, and Mattel as examples, and played upon the feminist rhetoric—girl power—to excite both investors and fans.

Early warnings from the "front office" had been to stay clear of the "gay issue," even as Sue Wicks (1966–) of the New York Liberty came out as the first publicly open gay player in the WNBA. It was news but not overwhelming, and the focus remained on making the WNBA a family affair. The 2005 announcement by Nike darling Sheryl Swoopes, however, bought more press than the most seasoned NBA marketing agent could ever dream of when she came out.

The pressure had been building before Swoopes's announcement. According to former coach and author Pat Griffin, whose first published work "How to Identify Homophobia in Women's Athletic Programs" (1988) long argued that lesbians had been a huge economic fan base of women's sports, including professional golf, tennis, soccer, and basketball, "Everybody knows that they are a good portion of the folks putting their fannies in the seats, but the league has been ashamed of them and scared of them. They've been two-faced about the issue."[11]

It was at a New York Liberty game in Madison Square Garden in August 2002 when the self-described "Lesbians for Liberty" fans staged a "kiss-in" in which for every time-out on the nationally televised game, fans would kiss each other for the kiss cam. The kiss-in had been orchestrated to publicly address the "homophobic denial" represented by upper management of the Liberty team and the WNBA and NBA offices. Despite the fact that this particular fan base had exhibited a powerful economic boon for the Liberty in both tickets and merchandise, the NBA/WNBA remained convinced that recognizing lesbians could be too costly. For far too long, lesbians and bisexual women have felt invisible within their own community but also women's sports.

To their advertisers, the NBA/WNBA could claim ignorance by stating, "I am not aware of that. . . . We don't take attendance that way. The league does not discriminate," as the chief marketing officer for both the NBA and WNBA once did in 1997.[12] It was not until 2014 that the WNBA, becoming the first American pro sports league to openly recruit gay athletes, finally recognized its faithful lesbian fan base. In the year prior, Brittney Griner (1990–), celebrated as one of the most heralded collegiate players in women's history, had come out in a press conference before she ever set foot on the professional court (for the Phoenix Mercury), arguably a tipping point for the front office of the WNBA. Until then, "the marketing was all about urging families to go to games: Dads, bring your daughters!"[13]

By 2018, "the out and proud WNBA players send invaluable messages to young women that achieving your dream is possible regardless of who you are and who you love," said GLAAD president and chief executive

Sarah Kate Ellis. "I love attending WNBA games with my wife and our children because the WNBA and its teams have created an accepting environment for all families to cheer for the talented athletes."[14]

THE ECONOMICS OF LESBIANISM

Rather than shrink away from the jabs made by her fellow competitors, French tennis star Amélie Mauresmo (1979–) came out, saying she did not want or plan to run from who she was or be in fear of how it might impact her career.[15]

The concern that religious, political, and community leaders espoused for lesbian women had, in reality, nothing to do with the welfare of individual women as much as it was about society preserving its own ideologies of femininity and masculinity. What made Mauresmo worrisome to so many was not so much that she was a lesbian (as this had been suspected), but how unafraid she had been to "come out."

Further, Mauresmo had no interest in the traditional tennis dress and made no apologies. That she came out in the height of her career—an unprecedented move in an athlete's career—was all the more stunning.

There were no repercussions, in the eyes of the old guard, as Mauresmo did not lose any sponsors. In fact, she became more popular on and off court. Mauresmo revealed a new marketing trend of sports consumers who supported lesbians. What had always been the white, male, heterosexual market was no longer. Before Mauresmo's coming out, even the WNBA had actively ignored the lesbian market, hoping to attract more white, heterosexual male and female fans but by 2001, saw the value in courting lesbian supporters as well.[16]

However unintentionally, Mauresmo showed that an athlete could, at the top of her game, come out and still keep her fan base and endorsements. Moreover, she did not have to put on lipstick and a dress.

FEMINISM VS. LESBIANISM

When women began to organize for the right to vote, fought against law citing husbands as owning their wives, and demanded equal treatment in the legal and medical communities (this would include receiving assistance when beaten/raped by a husband), this first-wave feminism essentially ended with the passage of the Nineteenth Amendment in 1919 when women were given the legal right to vote.

Second-wave feminism focused on equity and discrimination issues, and as more and more women entered the workforce, it sought higher education and better opportunities, adopting the slogan "The Personal Is Political," meaning the social/cultural, economic, and political inequities were directly related to their personal lives.[17]

But it was the third wave of feminism that recognized how the second wave mostly benefited upper-middle-class white women, while females of color and/or lower socioeconomic status were left behind. This also included those in the LGBTQ+ communities. (In recent years, the "+" was added to also encompass everyone within the sexual identifying spectrum.)

During the first- and second-wave feminist movements, however, lesbians remained in the closet as coming out could mean violence upon their person; ostracism from family, friends, and neighbors; the loss of employment; and harassment. Even into the 1980s, homosexuality was viewed as deviant behavior.

Yet such pioneers as Del Martin (1921–2008) and Phyllis Lyon (1924–2020) founded the first advocacy group for lesbians, called the Daughters of Bilitis (DOB), as early as 1955 to serve as an organization that offered lesbians a sense of community but also took on social and political issues. Martin and Lyon lived what they preached, becoming the first same-sex couple to legally marry in 2008, after fifty-five years together.[18]

Historically, lesbians have been both active and instrumental in the suffragist and feminist movements while downplaying their own struggles for equality. During the second wave, greater emphasis was placed on civil and gay rights with changing attitudes about sexuality. Among their gay (male) peers, lesbians were subject to overt sexism, and within the women's movement, there was resistance. Betty Friedan, founder of the National Organization for Women, once called lesbians within the movement the "lavender menace," asserting that lesbians would distract from the message and sully the work heterosexual women had put in for respect and equality.[19]

Lesbians found themselves marginalized and disconnected from the two movements they were most invested in. Within the field of women's studies, for example, when lesbian history was provided, it was a history in the context of the broader women's history. Even then, most lesbian studies were folded into gay studies that had been traditionally written and taught by gay men who, while they did fight for gay rights, always had the right to vote and had access to educational and employment opportunities. Throughout time, gay men could simply choose to live their life as a bachelor, without scrutiny, owning property, even entering into politics, religion, higher education, and business. With more money and power, they also had a stronger voice within the gay community.[20] The only true recourse for lesbian feminists was to create their own organizations for outreach and education programs, and pursuit of inclusion and equality.[21]

For the women of the WNBA, the silence was deafening. Once again, female athletes were forced to wait for time to catch up to who and what they had always been.

WHY SOCIETY CARES

Historically, of course, lesbians (including Amazon and Scythian women of antiquity) were held responsible for the erosion of social structures. Lesbians, then, had to be further degraded to justify their dissatisfaction with males.

In 2009, the book *Sexual Fluidity: Understanding Women's Love and Desire* made waves, from the pulpit and political arenas to pop culture and sport, as author/psychologist Lisa Diamond (1971–) analyzed how and why women love in gender research. Diamond followed one hundred women over the course of a decade, who at one time or another experienced same-sex attractions. As Diamond called for "expanded understanding of same-sex sexuality" she also called into question those "LGBT activists who hold that sexual identity is fixed and antigay groups who believe sexuality is chosen."[22] Just as women were historically diagnosed and treated by the medical community based on what male doctors knew of the male anatomy, the female's sexual desires, attractions, and habits were also so prescribed.

A gender-fluid female or a person who may identify as cisgender, bigender, or another nonbinary identity can be threatening to those who hold conservative, conventional ideals regarding sex and gender, but in a postmodern era when women's sexuality has been relegated to "how to please your man," Diamond revealed that women's sexual desires are not strictly geared for males but are far more complex, proving that more expansive studies need to be done on female subjects. In fact, Diamond's theories, while valuable, are not new.

In the 1949 book *The Second Sex*, French author/philosopher Simone de Beauvoir (1908–1986) wrote that "one is not born, but becomes a woman," lamenting that society, not biology, creates female behavior.[23] The classic feminine characteristics of conformity, passivity, and grace are not necessarily innate but taught. It was a patriarchal society that determined the scale of femininity and then, by all means, held them to it. And it is for this reason that lesbianism, in the eyes of men, is both fascinating and worrisome. When lesbian activity is sexually arousing for males, with a promise that they might be included in sexual acts, it is acceptable. If, however, the lesbian is unattractive, she carries less value from a marketing and/or sexual standpoint. But when women love women, what are men to do?

Whether hetero- or homosexual, the reality is, dating back to the early Amazons, women have a strong bond with one another. A 2020 study found that women in heterosexual marriages reported the highest levels of "psychological distress,"[24] while female couples are mostly likely to evenly share housework, child care, and financial duties. Because same-sex partners are raised in mostly heterosexual households and have been exposed to the gender roles played in normative homes, females are more apt to share evenly with their partner.[25] In a survey administered in Austria, Belgium, France, the Netherlands, Norway, Sweden, and Australia, same-sex participants displayed higher levels of equality compared to different-sex couples.[26]

To the lesbian point, conformity has been the common theme within the patriarchal structure, which is reliant upon compliant females. To the patriarchal society, lesbians, in particular, are problematic in that they not only defy the gendered role of childbearing and continuing the male's legacy but are viewed as anti-male. Amazon or Scythian women of antiquity were nomad warriors who dwelled in hunter-gatherer communities that shared roles; however, over time, the legacy of the Amazon became one in which man-hating women lived on a remote island. It was, in the realm of patriarchs, the only reasonable way to explain strong independent women caring for one another.

FIFTEEN

The Closing of the Twentieth Century

From beginning to end of the twentieth century, the demand for femininity of women in sport was incessant. In the early 1900s, with the threat of
women receiving the right to vote, their foray into athletics was doubly
troublesome to the patriarchal system. Sports equated to strength, endurance, independence—all qualities unwelcome in women.

When the flapper girl arrived in the 1920s, such fears were confirmed.
However, the style, while considered *too* liberating, flaunted makeup and
sexual appeal, which helped to ease patriarchal fears as dressing to be attractive *for* men has always been essential criteria for females.

By midcentury, an AAU poll was produced to show sports fans and
sponsors alike that indeed female athletes were heterosexual, publicizing
that 91 percent of former female athletes had married. Not only was the
female athlete's appearance important but so, too, was the idea that she
was wholly heterosexual and attracted to men. It was not just the wartime
All-American Girls Professional Baseball League but also professional
and semipro basketball and softball teams that held beauty contests and
other promotional stunts to display how attractive and feminine players
were.

Again, this persistent show of sexual "allure" was and is completely
unique to women's sports as male athletes have never been asked to do
anything but play their sport. Still, sexual allure was heavily promoted,
as the "most acceptable athletes were the women whose beauty and sex
appeal 'compensated' for their athletic ability."[1]

Leading into and even after the passing of Title IX, worries resumed
as female athletes expanded their interests and talents into long-distance
running, extreme sports, race car driving, and other previous male-only
sports. At the same time, the sexual revolution, which included mini-
skirts and pants, was a social movement that challenged the treatment of
women, sexuality, and interpersonal relationships. For those who deeply
clung to the patriarchal system as a guide for behavior and appearance,
these were tumultuous times. And yet, how a woman dressed, how the

female athlete looked in her uniform tied heavily to her femininity, her sexuality, and her successes.

By the end of the century, incredible progress had been made in women's sports. By the 1990s, it was female athletes who dominated the Olympic Games. The media focused on individual athletes such as soccer players Mia Hamm (1972–) and Julie Foudy (1971–), volleyball sensation Gabrielle Reece, basketball star Sheryl Swoopes, track athlete Florence Griffith Joyner, ice-skaters Nancy Kerrigan and Michelle Kwan, and golfer Annika Sorenstam (1970–). The twentieth century had been one of achievements of and for women in sport and society, but there were always stars who shone for upholding the feminine ideal.

THE TROUBLE WITH BEING SEEN

The coverage of the *ideal* female athletes was a continued practice of cherry-picking female athletes who men enjoyed watching. It was also a time period in which the death of Hollywood actress Rebecca Schaeffer (1967–1989) shocked a nation and brought the term "stalking" into focus. In 1989, a stalker who had become obsessed with the actress acquired her home address through a detective agency and eventually killed her. Schaeffer's murder led to the first antistalking law in the United States when the state of California passed it in 1990. By 1996, then-president Bill Clinton signed the Interstate Stalking Act, making it a crime for any person to cross a state line with intent to injure, harass, or threaten another person. In that same year, stalking and sexual harassment were so prevalent on college campuses across the nation that the U.S. Department of Justice, the Bureau of Justice Statistics, and the National Institute of Justice created the National College Women Sexual Victimization study.[2]

In the early 1980s, Olympic swimmer Nancy Hogshead-Makar (1962–) was abducted while running and raped for two and half hours by a stranger she would later say "clearly hated women." She believes that she was picked because she was a well-known and respected world-class athlete and was being punished. Other well-known athletes such as tennis star Anna Kournikova, golfers Michelle McGann (1969–) and Laura Davis (1963–), gymnast Shannon Miller (1977–), swimmer Summer Sanders (1972–), ice-skater Katarina Witt (1965–), and U.S. track athlete Sheila Taormina (1969–) all had aggressive stalkers during their careers, some more violent than others, including that of Taormina (the first-ever female athlete to qualify for the three different sports of swimming, triathlon, and modern pentathlon), whose stalker eventually mailed her a letter promising how he would assault her. He was later arrested, but it was the 1993 stabbing of tennis sensation Monica Seles on live TV that stunned the world.

Monica Seles (1973–), at nineteen years old, had dominated the women's tennis world and was, according to most sports analysts, on track to become tennis's greatest champion ever, but on April 30, 1993, while taking a water break at the Citizen Cup in Hamburg, Germany, a warm-up to the French Open, she was stabbed in the back by a fan upset that Seles had taken the championship from tennis star Steffi Graf (1969–).

She had been ranked number one in the world for 178 weeks, a nine-time Grand Slam champion; she is said to be first of "big hitters" in women's tennis and was on a historic run, repeatedly beating Graf. No one, it seemed, could beat her, until she was attacked. In her book *Getting a Grip*, Seles writes:

> It's strange how the tiniest thing can have the most impact on your life. Doctors later told me that if I hadn't bent forward at that precise second, there was a good change I would have been paralyzed. The cup had barely touched my lips when I felt a horrible pain in my back. Reflexively, my head whipped around towards where it hurt and I saw a man wearing a baseball cap, a sneer across his face. His arms were raised above his head and his hands were clutching a long knife. He started to lunge at me again. I didn't understand what was happening: for a few seconds I sat frozen in my chair as two people tackled him to the ground. He had plunged the knife one and a half inches into my upper left back, millimeters away from my spine. I stumbled out of my chair and staggered a few steps forward before collapsing into the arms of a stranger who had run onto the court to help. . . . I heard someone yelling for help, calling for paramedics. It was chaos. I was in shock but I remember one thought clearly racing around in my head: Why?[3]

Seles would not return to the game, thus giving Steffi Graf a comeback that would allow her to dominate once again. Sadly, through no fault of Graf, her fan got his wish. It is important to note that Graf played no part in the assault. Graf and Seles remain friends, but according to tennis historian Richard Evans and fellow tennis stars, sports history would look very different today had Seles not been attacked.

Assault on women is not new. Throughout history, women have been used as political tools and emotional warfare, or simply assaulted for being female. But as recent as 2020, while much has changed for women in politics and society, females of all ages are still attacked, and those living within the sports world are not exempt. In fact, 84 percent of female runners report that they have experienced some kind of harassment or threat against their safety while running. This would include being followed (on foot or by car), flashed, verbally threatened, and/or touched. More disturbing, according to the nonprofit Stop Street Harassment, and in conjunction with the University of California, San Diego, Center on Gender Equality and Health, and the Bureau of Justice Statistics regarding rape and sexual assault, 68 percent reported being harassed on public streets, trails, and parks. While most are equivalent to lewd comments, the number of women sexually assaulted or murdered is rising. Another 16 percent reported "constantly" thinking about being assaulted while exercising.[4]

Though these cases are the most horrific and extreme, they become a part of the female athlete's psyche. *Could this happen to me? I should have a running partner but I like to run alone. Am I safe? When should I run? Where should I run?*

"People minimize street harassment because they don't see it as sexual harassment [since] it's not rape or battery," says Joan Cook, PhD, associate professor of psychiatry at Yale School of Medicine in New Haven, Connecticut. But the seemingly innocent catcalls, she says, are toxic fumes that seep into the psyche.

There remains yet another component that, again, is unique to the female athlete. Not only is the female athlete expected to be attractive, but her beauty then also "explains" why she might be stalked, assaulted, even killed. In an article by the Sportster staff titled "15 Female Athletes You Didn't Know Were Stalked by Creeps," it is explained "that it only makes sense" the women were stalked by the level of their "hotness." In describing the stalking incidents of Summer Sanders, the author(s) included, "Add to the fact that Sanders was one of the most beautiful women in the world at that time, and she was bound to have an obsessed fan." Of Katarina Witt, it was explained that "Witt is also one of the hottest women back in her time," and that Maria Sharapova (1987–) was "also one of the prettiest and hottest women in the world today. So it makes sense that she has a stalker."[5]

As female athletes bought into fan-based, sponsor, and media acceptance (an economic reality), they also paid the price of the "she was asking for it" rationale.

THE COST OF BREAST IMPLANTS

While launching *Ms.*, Gloria Steinem recalled a time a male executive spat on an issue of the magazine in defiance of the idea of a women's publication discussing equality. It was a concept so inconceivable, even offensive, that *Ms.* used "The Beauty of Health" on its cover "hoping that our readers would see the 'health' and the advertisers would see the 'beauty.'"[6]

Media—the very thing that women and girls relied upon to learn about all things female, from femininity to empowerment, from education to medical treatment—has also been damaging, if not dangerous.

Enter the importance of plastic surgery.

In 1895, Austrian German surgeon Vincenz Czerny (1842–1916), known as the "Father of Plastic Surgery," performed the first breast implant surgery at the University of Heidelberg, but it had been done for reconstructive purposes following the removal of a tumor. It was 1945, following World War II when prostitutes in Japan began injecting silicone directly into their breasts to appeal to U.S. military men serving overseas. But it was Timmie Jean Lindsey (1932–) who became the first woman to undergo the first silicone-based implant.

The procedure was marked as a success, and fourteen years later, the U.S. Food and Drug Administration (FDA) began regulating the production and standards of silicone breast implants. Surgeons and manufacturers saw the instant value in such cosmetic surgeries and began marketing the desirable female form in women's magazines. By 1982, the FDA, noting "reports of adverse events in the medical literature,"[7] tightened regulations on silicone-based implants.

Throughout the 1980s and '90s, thousands of lawsuits against manufacturers for body deformations, failing health, and rising medical costs were won. By the mid-1990s, despite claims that the procedures were safe, over 440,000 women who became sick after getting silicone implants registered in a global settlement.

Meanwhile, advertisements for plastic surgery promising safe and immediate results became the most lucrative advertisers for women's health, fashion, and home magazines. Because most cosmetic surgeries were and are not covered by medical insurance and often occur outside a hospital setting, hard statistics are historically difficult to obtain. The only information available is provided by physicians' professional associations. From this information, we learn that from 1970 to 1996, the number of medical doctors who turned to plastic surgery quadrupled. Of these, only 62 percent were board certified in plastic surgery with too little information provided outside hospitals. According to the American Board of Medical Specialists (ABMS), there was a 700 percent increase in the number of cosmetic surgery procedures from 1992 to 2004.[8]

By 1998, the most popular women's magazines refused to run articles that would provide accurate research to warn consumers against silicone implants. That same year, a surgical nurse at Mount Sinai Hospital who assisted physicians in the removal of implants revealed just what they saw when removing the implants. Described as "black gunk" that leaked from the implants and attached itself to "everything inside the body," it was shocking to see how much damage was caused to the human body by the small implants.

Still, despite the fact that Germany, France, the United Kingdom, and United States had periodically pulled silicone implants from the market, pending further research in lieu of growing lawsuits and medical scares, the breast implant industry was far too lucrative to stop.

By 2012, the United Kingdom banned France's Poly Implant Prothese (PIP) hydrogel implants when it was discovered that the implants were not filled with medical-grade silicone but industrial-grade silicone (used for mattresses), linked to cancer.[9]

By 2022, thousands of women around the country were having implants removed each month in the United States, citing medical and emotional reasons, including such celebrities as Chrissy Teigen (1985–), Ashley Tisdale (1985–), and Rachael Finch (1988–).

At long last, the largest study of long-term health conditions for patients with breast implants was conducted at the University of Texas MD Anderson Cancer Center without interference from the private sector in 2018. It found that silicone implants are associated with rare diseases, autoimmune disorders, and cancers, including scleroderma and melanoma. For clarity, the researchers stipulated that an exact causative relationship has yet to be established, but senior investigator Mark W. Clemens noted, "This is important safety information for women to consider when thinking about cosmetic or reconstructive surgery with breast implants. It also underscores the need for more research in this area."[10]

Better still, a 2020 study not only substantiated what thousands of victims have felt but added more findings or "devastating effects" of breast implant illness (BII), also naming the condition. New studies have affirmed the link to higher instances of rare cancer of the immune system and inflammatory reactions but have also added breast pain, hair loss, skin irritation, memory loss, and breathing issues, as well as varying aches and pains on a day-to-day basis, including internal inflammation.

What is most startling about this new study is that it includes the investigation and reporting of saline implants, of which many of the shells contain silicone. Researchers found that with these revolutionary (safe) new implants, patients still experience capsular contraction, or the tightening of the chest, long associated with breast pain, difficulty in breathing, and muscle aches and stiffness. Moreover, the authors of the study suggest that restorative health was possible with the removal of the implants and also recommend that manufacturers of breast implants be required to use box warnings to inform patients that breast implants are not "lifetime devices, and that complications can increase over time."[11] However, given the history of both women and American businesses, as long as a product is lucrative, too little attention is given to the health and welfare of women.

BUYING INTO THE HEGEMONIC FEMININE IDEAL

It wasn't just the cosmetic and fashion industry that pushed the feminine ideal for profit but also sports and sports magazines. The promise for female consumers was beauty; the reward for industries promoting beauty was monetarily astronomical. While the eyelash, makeup, cosmetic surgery, and diet industries were worth billions (each), the *Sports Illustrated* swimsuit issue became the single best-selling issue for Time Inc., the parent company of *Sports Illustrated*, and its entire magazine franchise. The 2005 issue generated an estimated $325 million in advertisement sales whereas the regular *Sports Illustrated* sales is estimated at roughly $3 million for subscribers and is read by 23 million each week, while the swimsuit issue sells ten to fifteen times more copies on newsstands.[12]

Through heavy promotion, women were sold the idea that appearing in the magazine was empowering, and female athletes, hopeful of creating a large fan base, bought in. Into the new century, however, there was a shift in what is feminine beauty among female athletes. Female athletes who still participated in the celebrated swimsuit edition wanted to showcase more muscular bodies, including the appearance of Megan Rapinoe, the first openly gay woman, but also larger-framed women, and the first openly transgender woman, Valentina Sampaio (1996–). Letters to the editor make it clear that the leaner, more muscular, more athletic, including gay and/or transgender females, however, did not live up to the hegemonic ideal. By 2018, sales were down among male readers and *SI*'s owner, Meredith Corporation, put *Sports Illustrated* up for sale in 2018, dropping its original asking price of $150 million to $100 million in 2019–2020.

BODY-SHAMING AND BOOTYLICIOUS BECOMES OFFICIAL

Body-shaming has never been new for women, but the official name "body-shaming" appeared in 1994. By 2004, the same year "bootylicious" was formally recognized as an official word of the English language, researchers found that the message of thinness and beauty in children's media was so prevalent that children, especially girls, were compelled to emulate what they saw.

The twentieth century had been one of mixed messages in regard to equal rights, the value of women, and the female image. This would hold true of female athletes as well.

The images of players such as Mia Hamm, Kristine Lilly (1971–), Julie Foudy, Joy Fawcett (1968–), Brandi Chastain, and Abby Wambach (1980–) of the U.S. women's soccer team—all lean, tanned, and pony-tailed, had been very popular.

Specific to Hamm, she was America's golden girl, holding records in career assists, twice named FIFA World Player of the Year in 2001 and 2002, and U.S. Soccer Female Athlete of the Year five consecutive years. She appeared on the Wheaties box in 1999 and was dubbed "the Reluctant Superstar" on the cover of *Sports Illustrated* in September 2003.

Hamm not only changed women's sports, she was the face of U.S. women's soccer and, some have argued, the face of soccer everywhere. Her #9 jersey was a top seller and her popularity soared, beyond her retirement, to a level that rivaled some of the best-known male athletes.[13] During the 1990s, otherwise known as "Mia Mania," she unwittingly fed the patriarchal ideal; her "good-natured way, clean looks and undeniable passion made young girls throughout the United States take notice of a sport that was a blip on the radar screen."[14]

Hamm, for her part, never wanted the role of star; but for sports marketing and advertising agents, Hamm was perfect, and yet another reminder to all other female athletes who did not fit the mold of the early 2000s that they would never garner that same kind of attention.

Decades later, WNBA star Sue Bird (1980–) said, "Women's soccer players, generally, are cute little white girls while WNBA players, we're all shapes and sizes." Although the topic of the interview had been about players in the WNBA speaking out about social activism, Bird also discussed how the WNBA and its players had felt more scrutiny, noting that female athletes are all too used to "being judged on virtually everything": "When you're a male athlete, you're allowed to just play your sport," while women, she said, were judged on everything else.[15]

In fact, it's been that way throughout time. Unique to women's sports, women have never been allowed to *just* play.

It was by design that "bootylicious" was born.

It was validation that a new hegemonic ideal had arrived. And it was far more inclusive.

Beyoncé Knowles-Carter (1981–) never fit the hegemonic feminine image, but when weight gain earned her harsh criticism, "I wrote the song [Bootylicious] because I was getting bigger and bigger and I just wanted to talk about it. I like to eat and that's a problem in this industry."[16]

With the lyrics, "I don't think they can handle this," and "I don't think you're ready for this jelly . . . cuz my body's too Bootylicious," the song became the anthem of body positivity before there was ever a hashtag, rising to No. 9 on the Billboard Hot 100 in the United States and No. 2 on the UK Singles Chart.[17]

It was not just a popular song but the beginning of a movement. By 2010, the average pant size for American women was a 12–14 while standard fashion models were a size 0. Plus-sized models were a size 8.[18] While the average size for women in the United States has gone up to a 16–18 in 2020, the fashion standard has not moved for fashion models who fit what is perceived to be the norm. Plus-sized models broadened to sizes 12 and up, depending upon the advertiser, but the overall message remains in place: thinness equates to beauty. Bootylicious, however, opened new dialogue to how industry and media standards impacted public health, including that of female athletes.

Bootylicious, however, remains mere lyrical fantasy as sponsors, advertisers, and public opinion are so invested in the female form that even coaches, race and event officials, trainers, and agents, not to mention sports journalists, feel compelled to pressure athletes to fit into that hegemonic female form. Mary Cain's experience at Nike became a very public example of that issue, but it happens around the world at all levels for female athletes.

In September 2019, a seventeen-year-old American high school student from Anchorage, Alaska, was disqualified from her race after a racing official ruled that her swimsuit did not fit her properly. Breckynn Willis (2001–) had not just participated in the 100-meter freestyle event but had won. Her disqualification sent shock waves among racers and coaches, including Lauren Langford, a swim coach from a different school district whose own team competed against Willis's. Langford protested the ruling, calling Willis's disqualification an act of body-shaming and racial profiling. Langford argued that simply because Willis's body was curvier, fuller figured, and "look[s] different than [her] willowy, thin, and mostly pallid teammates," she was punished. But, in fact, Langford argued, then all the competitors were punished. "What's clear is that these girls' bodies are being policed—not their uniforms."[19]

For Willis, the ruling was ultimately reversed and she was properly awarded her victory, but the damage was done. Even one of the most powerful athletes in the world, Serena Williams, has revealed that she often feels insecure when stepping onto the court before a large audience, sure that people are scrutinizing her appearance far more than her performance.[20]

THE NUMBERS GAME

Because it is women's bodies that are discussed, measured, and analyzed, it tracks that numbers mean so much more. While women's larger frames are referred to as "plus sized," men's inferences are more appealing to the male ego—big and tall. But the emphasis on size has also allowed for the entire fashion industry to reassign sizes interchangeably to fit the female ego. It is called "vanity sizing," a practice that began during the depression when the U.S. government tasked statisticians to measure and calculate the average size of the American woman by measuring fifteen thousand women.

In a surprise only to the men who ran the National Bureau of Standards (later becoming National Institute of Standards and Technology [NIST]), which helped manufacturers size clothing, women had very diverse body types. The project was abandoned until the 1950s when, in addition to the fifteen thousand women previously measured, they also included information on females who served in the military during World War II.

In 1958, the "Body Measurements for the Sizing of Women's Patterns and Apparel" was published. Sizes ranged from 8 to 42, with a size 8 measuring as a thirty-one-inch bust, twenty-four-inch waist, and a weight of ninety-eight pounds. Hips were not a measurement requirement, following the male model, and the problem was immediate. Varying breast and hip measurements invalidated the current sizing system, and, by 1983, the government abandoned its effort. Today, the American Society of Testing and Materials (ASTM), which took over the responsibilities from the NIST, has left it to the private sector to size clothing as it sees fit.[21]

Although the mission statement of the ASTM is to "positively impact public health,"[22] today's vanity sizing is harmful. By 1995, what had been a size 8 in 1958 became a size 2; by 2011, those same measurements were a size 00.[23] Women were already bombarded with confusing, often unhealthy messages about their bodies; clothing manufacturers played to their need to feel smaller than what they actually are. In reality, different manufacturers can vary as greatly as five inches on material in size yet be labeled the same size.

While initial attempts to "size" women by using male measurements were abandoned, far too many things, from medical research to cell phones, continue to be sized for the male consumer.

In March 2019, NASA's first all-female spacewalk was canceled because two medium-sized spacesuits fitted for a female were needed in the International Space Station but NASA—with a budget of $22.6 billion—only had one female spacesuit for its sixty-five current female astronauts in that same year. Just as smartphones, backpacks, and the size of tools are fitted to the average male hand, even fitness equipment is calculated to the male frame, leaving females subjected to injury. More concerning is how armor protection, radiation vests, and bulletproof vests are manufactured to fit the male form but when marketed for female consumers, the only alterations made are shades of pink and more "soft, sensitive, and beautiful" descriptive words while males consumers are targeted with words like "ultimate, classic, and professional," while also enjoying a lifesaving fit.[24]

ARE WE STILL TALKING ABOUT PANTS?

Not even the color pink, however, could change patriarchal attitudes about pants. An informal dress code had been enacted in 1916 when the first woman of the House of Representatives, Jeannette Rankin (1880–1973), was elected. During the 1940s, when more women were elected to the House of Representatives, self-imposed monitors made sure the women were dressed appropriately.

One such bureaucrat was J. Edgar Hoover (1895–1972), a frequent visitor in the halls of the U.S. Senate and first director of the Federal Bureau of Investigations (FBI), who "manifested a 'visceral, public hatred' for notable women."[25] It was only after Hoover died in 1972 that women at the FBI were allowed to wear pants, as he allegedly hated seeing women in pants.[26] Hoover held particular disdain for Eleanor Roosevelt for her liberal views and, no doubt, penchant for wearing pants. In fact, Hoover doggedly investigated the First Lady to undermine her, and to this day his file on Eleanor Roosevelt is considered to be one of the largest files in FBI history on a single person.[27]

No one crossed the line within the House or Senate until 1969 when Republican Rep. Charlotte T. Reid (1913–2007) appeared wearing a bell-bottomed pantsuit. It was a mistake she would not make again.[28]

Even in the 1980s when female senators could and did wear slacks into their private offices, if there was an urgent call to the U.S. Senate floor, they would have to quickly change into a dress and, if they did not have one, borrow one from someone else.

Senate doorkeepers, a position held by men who enforced dress codes, determined who could or could not enter the Senate floor, but even that had become so discretionary between different doorkeepers that a group of female Senate aides wrote a letter of protest in 1972, simply asking for a written dress code that all doorkeepers would adhere to.

It was not just female politicians but also the wives of politicians who adhered to unwritten rules of feminine etiquette without question—mostly. Technically, it was First Lady Lucy Hayes (1831–1889) who was the first to wear pants in 1880 though the evidence was never made public until the early 2000s. First Lady Florence Harding (1860–1924) wore pants in December 1920 when she was invited to fly in a seaplane. Wearing a helmet, goggles, and a protective duster with pants that went over her dress so that she could climb into the plane, this photograph was a private, not public affair. It was Eleanor Roosevelt (1884–1962) who was frequently seen in her riding pants; one of the most famous examples occurred during the Easter Egg Roll at the White House in 1933. Roosevelt had been riding earlier, lost track of time, and arrived to the White House event with no time to change.

By the 1960s, Jackie Kennedy (1929–1994) wore slacks regularly. However, she was not only considered a fashion icon but was of the younger generation that wore slacks, and she was generally forgiven for wearing pants. Although it was Hillary Clinton who made the pantsuit-wearing politician image most famous, First Ladies Pat Nixon (1912–1993), Betty Ford (1918–2011), Rosalynn Carter (1927–), Nancy Reagan (1921–2016), and Barbara Bush (1925–2018) would wear pants in private or very informal affairs. Only Clinton regularly wore pants as casual, dress, and business attire.[29]

No one, however, made as big an impact than incoming senator Carol Moseley-Braun (1947–). Newly elected in 1993, her entrance was historic. Not only was she the first Black woman elected to the U.S. Senate, but she came in wearing pants. "I had no idea there was a stricture or an unwritten rule in the Senate about women not wearing pants. I thought I was all decked out in this nice pantsuit, you know? I thought I looked good. And everyone started whispering and whispering," Moseley-Braun said.[30]

As it happened, there were four female senators by 1992 and, like Moseley-Braun, they did not understand the pants rule. Senator Barbara Mikulski (1936–) soon joined Moseley-Braun, as did Senate staffers, but when the doorkeepers took issue with the pantsuits, complaints were brought to the Senate sergeant at arms, who happened to be the first-ever woman to hold the position. Martha Pope made a slight adjustment to the dress code: To "Women are required to wear business attire, i.e., dress, skirt and blouse or business suit," Pope added, "coordinated pantsuit (slacks and matching blazer; no stirrup pants)."[31]

At that time, it had been well over a hundred years since Dr. Mary Walker (1832–1919), the first female U.S. Army surgeon of the Civil War, a prisoner of war, and the first woman to receive the Presidential Medal of Honor, was also arrested for wearing pants in public. It was in New Orleans in 1870 when she famously responded, "I don't wear men's clothes, I wear my own clothes."[32]

That women wore pants could be so problematic for men carried far more troubling issues than simply discriminatory restrictions against women. It told of senior male politicians who had been empowered and entrusted to serve all people yet were only vested in upholding archaic ideals that discriminated against women. The transparency of the pants issue is directly related to how women are viewed.

Within the sports world, women's lacrosse and field hockey players were required to wear skirts during games without any reasonable explanation other than it was "tradition." When the British athlete Constance M. K. Applebee (1873–1981) introduced field hockey to a class at Harvard University in 1901, all the participants were dressed in the traditional floor-length dresses. Applebee established the United States Field Hockey Association in 1922, as well as the U.S. Women's Lacrosse Association in 1931, but no formal dress code demanded the players perform in skirts. It is hard to imagine that Applebee, who remained in athletics and education, retiring at the age of 94 (and lived to be 107 years old),[33] would have required skirts in modern times.

Constance Applebee. *Bryn Mawr College Special Collections, Ida W. Pritchett photograph album*

In fact, the only true tradition to the lacrosse and field hockey skirts comes from the age-old patriarchal push for what was "sex-appropriate" sports for women, that is, individual sports that required grace and beauty over brawn. Given the aggressive play that does exist in these sports, the skirt serves to soften what spectators may perceive as too masculine. Female athletes who engage in female-appropriate sports are photographed far more than often those who participate in contact sports, with their images presented in a more suggestive and provocative form for audiences.[34]

"YOU CAN'T TELL ME HOW TO DRESS!"

By the end of the century, the hegemonic feminine ideal continued to thrive despite the 1960s rally *"You can't tell me how to dress!"* Cosmetic procedures alone made clear how important the feminine ideal was socially and economically. Many well-known female athletes continued to pose for men's publications to subsidize the unequal pay scale they found among male and female athletes.

Case in point is American basketball player Lisa Leslie. She became the first woman to dunk in the Women's National Basketball Association (WNBA), was a three-time WNBA MVP, played for eleven seasons before retiring, and is a four-time Olympic gold medalist. Inducted into the Women's Basketball Hall of Fame, Leslie also had a successful career as a model; yet when her agent worked on a shoe endorsement deal, the company did not believe in her star power as a female athlete. Instead, sports companies like Under Armour and Puma have signed celebrities such as Rihanna and Gisele Bundchen over female athletes.

The message is loud and clear when sports companies actively choose singers and models for women's sports apparel over actual female athletes.[35] It is precisely why so many female athletes, if given the opportunity, willingly pose for male viewers, feeding into the very institution that diminishes their achievements as athletes (and that of their sister athletes).

Even in the twenty-first century, female athletes are offered endorsements based on "marketability" that is directly correlated to their appearance while male athletes' value is based upon batting averages and touchdowns, and the media reinforces these gender roles based on beauty as the former, power and strength as the latter.[36]

During the 2018 season, skier Lindsey Vonn earned just over $128,000 for her performances with the International Ski Federation (her best season was 2012 when she earned more than $592,947), while her net worth was approximately $12 million.[37] Because print media, for both men's and women's magazines and online sites, portray female athletes as sex symbols, opportunity for greater exposure and advertising is too enticing for many female athletes to turn down.

Following the 1999 World Cup championship game in which Brandi Chastain famously ripped off her jersey, the image appeared in newspapers and magazines across the world. Following that victory, she then posed nude for *Gear* magazine, saying that she had chosen to do so not to "objectify her body," but that she had earned the right to show it off following all her hard work.[38] It must be asked, however, when has any male athlete, upon achieving his greatest athletic feat, then rewarded himself by posing nude for the world?

In closing of this era, women were still told what to wear and how to look, but a change was coming. A new athlete, a fourth-wave woman having lived through #TimesUp and a renewed effort to strip women of their rights, understood that until the *controllers of women* were stopped, women and girls would never fully enjoy equal status in society.

After centuries of fighting for equality and the right to play, the history of sexual abuse persisted. The shame and stigma of sexual abuse kept women silent, further empowering their abusers and keeping the patriarchal system intact. Even today, the majority of underage victims do not report the crime. A 2018 study in Germany found that of 165 child sex abuse victims, it took an average of 24 years from the time of assault(s) to speak up. A 2014 study found that the average age for reporting a crime was age 52.[39]

Sixteen

Sports and Abuse

By 2015, four U.S. female gymnasts slated to be the "brightest stars" of a generation in their sport were also identified as "Athlete B," "Gymnast 1," "Athlete A," and "Gymnast 3" during the investigation of a doctor with the U.S. national women's gymnastics team. Larry Nassar (1963–) was found guilty of child pornography and tampering with evidence for which he was sentenced to 60 years in prison while given another 40 to 175 years to be served in Michigan State prison for seven counts of sexual assault of minors and an additional 40 to 125 years in Michigan State prison after pleading guilty to an additional three counts of sexual assault. Six years after the investigation and one year after the guilty verdict of Nassar, those once anonymous athletes stepped forward. Gymnasts Simone Biles (1997–), McKayla Maroney (1995–), Maggie Nichols (1997–), and Aly Raisman (1994–) appeared before the U.S. Senate Judiciary Committee to share how not only USA Gymnastics and the U.S. Olympic and Paralympic Committee failed to protect female athletes but so, too, had the Federal Bureau of Investigation.

The gymnasts revealed that beyond the reprehensible inactions of USA Gymnastics and the USOC, the intentional neglect of the FBI had felt most damaging. As Raisman explained, "The FBI made me feel like my abuse didn't count. I'm still navigating how I feel from this. I don't think people realize how much this affects us. . . . I'm often wondering, am I ever going to feel better? . . . I'm sick from the trauma."[1]

WHEN WOMEN SPEAK

Larry Nassar is believed to have sexually assaulted, groomed, and abused as many as 500 or more girls, some as young as six years of age, and women over two decades, with 332 of those victims being named in a $500 million lawsuit to be paid by Michigan State University, as it was found complicit in Nassar's crimes.[2] On January 24, 2018, Nassar was

Biles, Maroney, Raisman, and Nichols at U.S. Senate hearings. *Reuters/Alamy Stock Photo*

sentenced to 175 years in prison after pleading guilty to seven counts of sexual assault of minors. Six months earlier, he was also sentenced to an additional 60 years for child pornography, and on February 5, 2018, he also pleaded guilty to sexually assaulting three more victims, adding another 125 years to his sentence.

There had been complaints about Nassar's behavior dating back to the early 1990s at Michigan State University where Nassar worked as the sports doctor, specifically with the gymnastics program. Although Nassar pleaded guilty specific to those cases brought before the courts, more than 250 women and girls testified in court how Nassar assaulted them in his campus office, at his home, at tournaments and competitions, in locker rooms, even in hallways. Nassar was emboldened by his position of power, reputation, and the continued protection of officials, muting his victims until Rachael Denhollander (1984–) and Jamie Dantzscher (1982–) found the courage to stand.

Denhollander was first assaulted in 1999 when she was just fifteen years old. It would not be until 2015–2016 that she reported Nassar's crimes to the Michigan State University Police Department and filed a Title IX complaint with the university. It was then that the world began to learn of Larry Nassar and just how corroded the USA Gymnastics system was.

Beyond being the worst sexual abuse scandal in sports history, it is not just about gymnastics. Like any predator, Nassar was an opportunist and victimized women and girls from other sports, including figure skating, soccer, softball, cheerleading, rowing, diving, dance, track and field, and wrestling, though well-known Olympic gymnast gold medalists Jordyn Wieber (1995–), Aly Raisman, Gabby Douglas, McKayla Maroney, and Simone Biles are the most recognizable.[3]

Jamie Dantzscher, a bronze medalist from the 2000 Sydney Olympic Games, became the very first to publicly detail what Nassar had done to her and is credited for opening the proverbial floodgates that encouraged other victims to speak out. But so vested was USA Gymnastics, as well as other coaches and institutions connected to Nassar, that Dantzscher became the target as USA Gymnastics turned on its athletes, working to discredit their names and reputations rather than address the issue of abuse within its own system.

In regard to Dantzscher, USA Gymnastics reached out to all of her ex-boyfriends and associates for information they could use against the gymnast[4] while they forced other athletes like McKayla Maroney to sign nondisclosure agreements (NDAs) and threatened to sue her if she were to speak out against USA Gymnastics or its coaches. While NDAs are not all that unusual in business, what makes the transaction between Maroney and USA Gymnastics, as well as many more athletes and coaches, questionable is why the NDAs were even put in place. USA Gymnastics knew years prior to 2018 that there was a problem.

THE INVESTIGATION

Bela and Martha Karolyi created a world-famous training facility in Houston, Texas, that generations of parents had come to trust to make their sons and daughters world champions. It was also a place where Larry Nassar preyed on victims and was never questioned about his methods.

Following an examination in which Nassar shut the door and closed the blinds to his training room to treat a fifteen-year-old Maggie Nichols, she immediately knew that how he touched her was very wrong, but more disturbingly, he never put on gloves. This would be a detail repeated by hundreds of victims. It was 2015 and Nichols was a top contender for the 2016 Olympic team when she sustained an injury. It was then that gymnastics coach Sarah Jantzi overheard Nichols asking a fellow gymnast, "Does he do this kind of stuff to you as well? Is it normal? Like, does he do it to everyone?" But unlike all the other adults, Jantzi wanted to hear more. When she had heard enough, she called Nichols's mother.

Jantzi also contacted USA Gymnastics on June 17, 2015, to report Nassar's "sexual abuse/sexually inappropriate treatment" of Nichols, but when the information was given to Steve Penny, USA Gymnastics CEO, it was dismissed.[5] This would mark the first official complaint that was ignored, even rebuked, while hundreds and hundreds of more victims fell to Nassar's perversion. When Rachael Denhollander bravely spoke up that same year, Nichols knew two things: if she spoke up publicly, her Olympic dreams would be over, and those who had spoken out were terribly mistreated. After keeping her true identity sealed for three years, Nichols finally found the courage to speak out following the testimony of so many others, but it was Nichols along with McKayla Maroney and Aly Raisman who helped lend credibility to Rachael Denhollander's initial report that would launch the July 2015 FBI investigation of Larry Nassar.[6]

However, two years passed while Nassar remained free and continued to molest and rape female athletes. In an interview with NBC News, Raisman says when the FBI called her more than a year later after the reports of sexual assault, she asked what had taken them so long and the response was, "Oh, we wanted to wait until the Olympics were over." When Simone Biles was asked how she felt about the FBI's delay in investigating a serial rapist, she tearfully added, "You literally had one job and you couldn't protect us."[7]

Sara Teristi (1974–) was first abused by Nassar in 1988. She had already been victimized by her gymnastics coach, John Geddert (1957–2021), so her sense of self-worth and confidence was gone. By the time Nassar began volunteering to help with Geddert's girls, Geddert had created a culture in his gym in which parents and athletes did not question what they saw and little girls were routinely body-shamed. Worse, according to Teristi, Geddert watched as Nassar assaulted her.[8] Teristi, who was fourteen years old at the time of the sexual assault, was regularly verbally abused by Geddert who made sexually charged jokes like "the boys would love me because I couldn't keep my legs together."[9]

By the early 2000s, male gymnastics had been phased out of Geddert's gym so that it was only girls, which, according to his gymnasts, left the empty boys' locker room as the place where Geddert would pull girls in to abuse them, verbally and otherwise. Amanda Smith, a gymnast who had trained with Geddert since she was nine years old, said in her victim impact statement, "That was a daily thing," Smith said. "It was like Dr. Nassar had the back room, and [Geddert] had the locker room. We were terrified to go in there. Even if you didn't know what happened in there, it was very clear when girls came out and were hyperventilating because they were so scared."[10]

Not only was he aware of Nassar's abuse, victims claim, but Geddert had been investigated by police in 2011 and 2012 for intimidation and assault charges. It was in 2013 that he was investigated again for physically assaulting a gymnast. When, in 2018, USA Gymnastics suspended

Geddert, fifty-three other coaches had multiple complaints from athletes, parents, even other coaches on charges that ranged from dangerous and negligent behaviors in training to body-shaming, intimidation, and/or inappropriate physical contact, yet no investigations were ever conducted. Three years later as prosecutors filed twenty-four different charges against Geddert, he committed suicide.

Within the culture of athlete-coach relationships in the sport of gymnastics, brainwashing and punishment were far more prevalent than anyone wanted to admit—including the same governing bodies set in place to protect the athletes. Coaches would often "ignore" an athlete, which had devastating effects on training. No training meant no competing and no competing meant no career. This included dieting, medical treatment, even activities outside the gym, including school. By normalizing this behavior, the girls (and their families) learned to internalize what was happening, creating a culture so toxic that victims did not believe they could speak out and, more often than not, did not even understand that they had been victimized.

THE KAROLYI RANCH

During the congressional investigation of how such abuses could have gone on for so long, despite complaints, law enforcement investigators of the Texas Rangers were called to investigate allegations of abuse and assault at the Karolyi Ranch. Both the FBI and the House Committee on Oversight and Government Reform were looking at USA Gymnastics, the United States Olympic Committee, and Michigan State University.

It was bittersweet for Dominique Moceanu (1981–), who had sounded the alarm of abuse in 1998 against both the Karolyis and the culture within gymnastics. "I remember as a 10-year-old being terrified of those people. I wasn't even allowed to ask to go to the bathroom. That's how afraid we were."[11]

For Moceanu, who had come from a family of domestic abuse, the Karolyis, she alleges, used that against her to keep her frightened and compliant. For gymnast Mattie Larson (1992–), it was a "win-at-all-cost" philosophy that allowed Nassar to come in and prey on the girls.[12] Even in 1999, when more athletes and families spoke openly about the treatment of the Karolyis, including stories of malnutrition (the female triad), training while injured, and emotional abuse, USA Gymnastics named Bela Karolyi as national team coordinator, which meant the only way to make the Olympic team was to go through the Karolyi Ranch. After the Karolyis defected from Romania to the United States, they helped USA Gymnastics win forty-one Olympic medals, thirteen of which were gold, over a span of three decades and earned millions of dollars for and from USA Gymnastics.[13]

It was why the abuse was ignored and when any one girl or woman had the nerve to speak out, her reputation and name was attacked. Moceanu's character and career were destroyed the moment she began speaking out. It was, she said, a culture in which an abuser was able to thrive in the normalization of abuse and the internalization that victims learned to endure to survive.[14]

THE NORMALIZING OF HOLLYWOOD, POLITICS, AND SPORTS

In 2006, Tarana Burke (1973–) created the #MeToo movement when she was working with many young women of color who, she found, had no voice. With no resources, little support, and no confidence in the judicial system, Burke wanted to create something that would allow survivors of sexual assault and abuse to tell their stories. As a lifelong activist and community organizer, Burke understood the value in the #MeToo movement.[15] The movement did not reach the global stage until actress Alyssa Milano (1972–) used it in a tweet during the sexual assault investigations of Hollywood director Harvey Weinstein (1952–). Even as Weinstein was found guilty of rape in the third degree and a criminal sexual act in February 2020, following a two-year investigation, more women came forward.[16] Over one hundred women have reported they, too, were victims of Weinstein. Much like the story in gymnastics, dozens and dozens of people in Hollywood, from film crew members to famous producers and actors, knew of Weinstein's behaviors and did nothing.

But when Milano tweeted the #MeToo hashtag, the movement Burke had always dreamed of went international. While *Time* magazine named Burke its "Person of the Year" in 2017, Harvey Weinstein, alongside comedian and serial-rapist Bill Cosby, went to trial, and USA Gymnastics, the USOC, Michigan State University, the Karolyi Ranch, and other organizations continued to fight against the victims as too much money and reputation was on the line.

By 2016 and 2017, more than two dozen women had stepped forward and named Donald Trump as their attacker in sexual assault and/or harassment. Well before Trump famously bragged about sexually assaulting women in a tape recorded in 2005 with *Access Hollywood* (in which he laughed about grabbing women by their genitals, doing so quickly before they could react),[17] his alleged victims included models, Miss Universe and Miss Teen USA contestants, businesswomen and associates, actresses, even a photographer from *People* magazine. Trump denied knowing his accusers, despite more than half offering witnesses and/or photographic evidence to prove otherwise.

Such powerful men have always seemed untouchable, including former presidents Bill Clinton and John F. Kennedy. Clinton's gross abuse of his office and extramarital affair with twenty-two-year-old Monica Lewinsky and Kennedy's affair with nineteen-year-old intern Marion "Mimi" Beardsley (1943–) occurred while in office.[18] In both cases, not only did partisan parties conceal or deny abuse of power, but in the case of Kennedy, the press corps turned a blind eye. Women were simply collateral damage.

Given the extent of Trump's alleged victims, not to mention his own admission to assault on the *Access Hollywood* audio, the Women's March and pink hats of 2017 became a safe way of speaking out in a culture that did not want to hear about women's rights. It became a worldwide day of demonstrations to support gender equity, civil rights, and other issues that demonstrators feared would be challenged under newly inaugurated Donald Trump.

When U.S. Supreme Court nominee Brett Kavanaugh (1965–) met with accusations of sexual assault stemming from the 1980s, the culture of "reputation, money, and politics" over all else became the issue once more. Despite the fact that the American Bar Association and three Republican governors called for the delay in Kavanaugh's nomination until a more thorough investigation could be made, despite the fact that the Catholic magazine *America* withdrew its nomination for Kavanaugh and more conservative groups such as Mormon Women for Ethical Government noted that Kavanaugh's behavior "raises a red flag," despite the fact that numerous Republican senators privately conceded that Christine Blasey Ford had testified honestly, calling her a more "credible witness," it was *his* word over *hers*.[19]

Critics saw accuser Christine Blasey Ford (1963–), a professor of psychology, as a political weapon. Not only did Ford answer questions openly and pass her polygraph that was administered by the FBI, but her placement of people and time were verified, while Kavanaugh refused to answer many questions, pleaded ignorance, and became defiant. Yet it was Ford who was repeatedly attacked by political figures, including the sitting president who mocked her character, personal life, and testimony.[20]

Ultimately, Kavanaugh was confirmed, inspiring more women to speak up and tell their own stories. The hashtag #WhyIDidntReport trended, along with #MeToo, #YesAllWomen, #NotOkay, and #BelieveWomen.

As for Nassar, he decided that he was actually a victim after all and, before a stunned, packed courtroom in 2018, admonished his victims, the judicial system, and presiding judge Rosemarie Aquilina (1958–) for his treatment. The girls and women, he argued, had misunderstood his treatment.

For the girls and women who told stories of endless nightmares, thoughts of suicides, ruined relationships, mistrust of all medical professionals, and fears of human contact, Nassar adopted the word "treatment" in replace of rape and sexual assault.

Each time the reasons for rape are justified or explained, not only is violence against women condoned but the value of females is further diminished.

Such euphemisms as "warrior" and "hero" are used in men's sports when a linebacker charges successfully down the field or a basketball player leads his team to victory, but it is the women who took down Nassar, who testified in court, who petitioned for change at the risk of losing everything just to make something better for the next person, who are the real warriors, our heroes.

Such a warrior is Nancy Hogshead-Makar (1962–). At age fourteen, she was the number one swimmer in the world. Hogshead-Makar became the first recipient of a swimming scholarship from Duke University and later won three gold medals and a silver at the 1984 Olympic Games. She was inducted into six Halls of Fame, including the International Swimming Hall of Fame and the International Scholar-Athlete Hall of Fame. She served as president of the Women's Sports Foundation, graduated from Georgetown Law, and specialized in Title IX cases with a private practice.

But before all her successes, Hogshead-Makar had been brutally kidnapped and sexually assaulted. She suffered from posttraumatic stress disorder (PTSD) and was redshirted by Duke, allowing her time for recovery. Hogshead-Makar had not yet won any Olympic medals, as the United States had boycotted the 1980 Games, but she had garnered significant national and local attention, having set her first American record at age fourteen and having been predicted to win multiple medals at the Games. But by 1982, she wasn't sure she was ready to go back or, if she even wanted to go back. It was then that her coach offered her something too good to pass up—Duke's first scholarship in swimming.

Hogshead-Makar returned to swimming, and Olympic history was made. But it gave her something else. "Of course, sports are so important to us all. It teaches how to win, learn to be part of a team, how to postpone short-term gratification and to achieve longer-term goals but, for me personally, it was a wonderful way to recover from being raped. It helped me reclaim my body.

"It [swimming] allowed me to become the author of my body again. I could set sports goals and meet them. This is a very common feeling among rape victims, women feel very out of control of their own bodies. I was taking it back. Every day I was trained, every day I swam I got a little back. And, it gave me a socially acceptable way to vent anger. I could scream under water. I could channel anger. I could be very mad at the East Germans for using steroids," she said with a laugh.

She devoted herself to fighting against sexual abuse. Tragically, the Nassar/gymnastics scandal was not the only story of abuse in sports. In 2020, six women from USA Swimming filed lawsuits against the program. Debra Grodensky (1969–), Suzette Moran (1966–), and Tracy Palmero (1974–), as well as three other swimmers who remained anonymous, identified in court how they were groomed and/or stalked, and sexually and psychologically assaulted as minors, ranging in ages from twelve to sixteen. Like the Nassar case, the former U.S. Olympic and national team coach Mitch Ivey (1949–), former U.S. national team director Everett Uchiyama, and former coach Andrew King had been known within the swimming community but also by USA Swimming for sexual misconduct with children yet ignored it, allowing a "culture of abuse."[21]

These are the women, among countless others, the army of survivors, the athletes turned activists who stand on the front lines to make change in women's sports and society to ensure that we continue to move forward. However unwittingly, these were the women who emboldened the fourth wave.

SEVENTEEN

The Fourth Wave in
Sports and Society

A fake fourth wave of feminism was launched in 2014 by antifeminist internet trolls plotting to create a "pro-sexualization, pro-skinny, anti-fat" movement that would cause discourse between the third and fourth wavers and ultimately bring down the feminism movement. But, as author Fernando Alfonso writes, "feminism is too complicated for a site full of historically ignorant dudes,"[1] and the plan did not work.

The website 4chan, an anonymous imageboard created back in 2003, began spamming social media on January 6, 2014, with images of thin women in bikinis achieving the "bikini bridge" (a term for the space between the bikini bottom fabric to the hip bone when lying down). It was pitched as "the next big thing," replacing the thigh gap. Despite it being a hoax, it caught on. #Bikinibridge was suddenly trending and mentioned on news programs around the world, and so 4chan took it to the next level, proclaiming #bikinibridge a catalyst for Operation Fourth Wave Feminism, a movement for attractive and sexualized skinny and fit female bodies. The idea was to pit the fourth wave against the (heavily implied) unattractive third wave to demoralize the feminist movement. But as writer Alfonso explains, 4chan was too historically ignorant to understand that third-wave feminists fought to empower all women to be proud of their sexuality. There was also another problem that 4chan didn't recognize: the real fourth wave of feminism was already underway.

Most historians date the beginning of the fourth wave of feminism between 2010 and 2012, which focused on reproductive rights, equal pay, body-shaming, and sexual assault (similar to the third wave), but it is best recognized for its focus on empowerment of women, sexual minorities, and other oppressed groups as well as the use of the internet and technology to educate and uplift women and girls around the world.

WOMEN CONNECTING

Also in 2010 came the development of Orreco, a bio-analytics program located in the National University of Ireland that developed a female-focused performance platform for athletes with the ability to track menstrual cycles, its symptoms, and specific guidance for training and nutritional needs based around the cycle. With early investors such as Fitbit and Peloton, elite athletes such as U.S. swimmer and four-time Olympian Allison Schmitt (1990–) began to have "unthinkable" results. Through technology, Schmitt said, "we realise just how important it is to focus on women separately. Honestly, until I was introduced to the work that Orreco are doing, I had no idea just how impactful hormones are."[2]

There remains a certain irony that science and technology have ignored women when female entrepreneurs were historically infused in its successes.

It was codebreaker Elizebeth Smith Friedman (1892–1980) who was single-handedly responsible for intercepting Hitler's plans on destroying an Allied supply ship, saving over eight thousand soldiers' lives (J. Edgar Hoover took credit for this, and only after her death was the truth revealed by historians). It was actress Hedy Lamarr (1914–2000) who created and patented the Secret Communication System, otherwise known as frequency hopping, a design meant to prevent the enemy (the Nazis) from detecting messages sent through radio. It is today the basis for Wi-Fi, GPS, and Bluetooth. And it was female "human computers" who made it possible for NASA to put American astronaut John Glenn into orbit in 1962—women such as Mary Jackson (1921–2005), Katherine Johnson (1918–2020), and Dorothy Vaughan (1910–2008), Black mathematicians working under strict segregation.[3]

Most impressively, it was Ada Lovelace (1815–1852) of the Victorian "hysterical woman" era who wrote the world's first computer program that is now used by the U.S. Department of Defense. In her honor, the program is called "Ada," the most commonly used language for mission-critical defense software today.[4]

These pioneers of programs and digital progress helped to facilitate the giving and receiving of information and connectivity that quite literally changed the lives of girls and women hidden from the world. Through the new age of technology, there came greater insight and the need to act. By the fourth wave, it was clear that social media platforms presented greater misogynistic threats than previously realized, but the internet also revealed just how oppressive and dangerous laws and societal ideas were for many non-Western women. As fourth-wave responders sounded the alarm, women's sports provided a solution.

ESPNW AND THE U.S. STATE DEPARTMENT

On the fortieth anniversary of the passage of Title IX, then–secretary of state Hillary Rodham Clinton (1947–) not only celebrated but emboldened the landmark federal civil rights legislation prohibiting sex discrimination in education—she went global. Clinton understood the importance of sports and politics. She understood how politics and equality fuel economic gains for everyone. Using both sport and education, she teamed up with ESPN to launch Empower Women and Girls Through Sports.

According to the United Nations, when girls participate in sport, they are also more likely to stay in school and engage in their community. For girls and women in culturally conservative and misogynistic countries such as Bangladesh, Afghanistan, and other Middle Eastern nations that carry restrictive laws against basic freedoms, suicide rates, human trafficking, and abuse remain very high.[5] Clinton was certain that the outreach and inclusion of sport not only creates societal, political, and economic change but can save lives.

While this is certainly not new information in Western cultures, it is for some of the more remote regions of the world. In societies and cultures in which females have been restricted from the most civil rights and freedoms, the image of girls engaged in sport is empowering. Each ball that is hit or kicked, every race that is run, every rope climbed leads to greater things. Girls who play sports are more likely to excel in school, in business, and in leadership.

Laura Gentile (1972–) knew this firsthand. The founder and senior vice president of espnW and Women's Initiatives, a council member on the U.S. State Department's Council to Empower Women and Girls Through Sports, Gentile is credited for building the world's biggest sports brand for women.

As a former athlete herself—a successful field hockey player for Duke University in which she led Duke to its first-ever appearance in the NCAA Tournament, was named All-American and All-ACC honors, and was a two-time team captain—Gentile explained, "I innately knew how female athletes felt."

Many years prior to Clinton's Empower Women and Girls Through Sport initiative, Gentile noted that women and girls were much more than just sports fans. Women were athletes, women were pioneers in sport, and, as ESPN's fan base revealed, women were a powerful economic demographic.

Gentile saw and felt that female athletes had been overlooked in the sports media industry and knew it was time for change. By 2011, research showed that females comprised nearly 50 percent of the fan base; and with 70 percent of all financial and/or consumer decisions made by

Laura Gentile, All-American turned founder of espnW. *Courtesy of Laura Gentile*

females, sports marketers were paying attention. The NFL was the first league to offer an exclusive female clothing line and quickly earned financial reward.[6]

Gentile saw more. With more than 80 million sports fans (at that time), Gentile worked to create the first espnW Summit in 2010 with the idea of inviting the most influential women in sport to discuss the sports industry. It became so much more with business and sports industry leaders, athletes, coaches, and journalists creating a network of women "which really never existed before." Gentile's goal was not only about "getting women a seat at the table," to make decisions within the sports industry, but mentoring girls, educating athletic directors and student athletes about campus sexual assault, and using sport for greater "athlete activism" for social change.[7]

Clinton's invitation arrived in 2012 with the proposal of a global mentoring program in which women from around the world would be brought to the United States "to be mentored by incredible women in sport." In partnership with espnW and the University of Tennessee Center for Sport, Peace, and Society, the U.S. State Department selected international delegates for a five-week training program. Each delegate was paired with female (senior) executives within the sport industry and "given a seat at the table," Gentile said.

As delegates arrived from such nations as Uganda, Egypt, and India, Gentile, under direction of the U.S. State Department, employed cultural sensitivity programs as "many of these women were coming from a place where women did not contradict men, where they did not have an equal seat at the table." Gentile was humbled when many of the delegates expressed dismay when female executives countered male voices during meetings, "and I remember one time, I was talking to a woman named Fatima from Pakistan." Gentile asked the woman how she would describe her experience while in the United States and Fatima replied, "I just feel safe. Just walking around, I feel safe."

It was a stark reminder for Gentile of the power of the initiative. Through sport and education, women can and should expect gender equality; through sport and education, equal treatment then empower women to stand up, speak out, lead others, dispel "feminine" stereotypes and claim their right to opportunity.

#REPEALTHENINETEENTH

In 2016, the antifeminist/antifemale #RepealTheNineteenth began trending, an online movement that referenced the U.S. Constitution's amendment granting women the right to vote. While #RepealTheNineteenth gained moderate popularity in the United States, a global gender solidarity countermovement had already taken shape in the form of #HeforShe, created by UN Women, including actress and activist Emma Watson (1990–), which garnered more than 1.3 billion commitments by 2018.[8]

The bigger issue was the sentiment that, in empowering the other half of a population, those "in power" were threatened. By 2020, four out of every ten American men believed empowerment to women came at the expense of men and that it was the workplace that gave females this advantage of equality. Speculation as to how women fare in the media, politics, fashion, and sport are not considered.[9]

Unsurprisingly, as a new assault on women began in 2016, the majority of the world's media outlets slowly disabled their reader comment sections due to dangerous and hateful rhetoric, most of which was directed at women. In particular, if the article centered on a woman, on female issues, or was authored by a woman, misogynistic language and threats of physical violence dominated conversation.

As just one example, when British fashion vlogger and activist Victoria Magrath (1989–) decided to post "Happy International Women's Day" in celebration of empowering women to cheer her global sisters, she was forced to disable the comment capability from her site as she and other women were repeatedly threatened with rape.[10] Similarly, when a sports fan used the day to commemorate the WNBA on Twitter, there came a barrage of hateful messages regarding the WNBA players, leaving other sports fans to wonder why there remains such a visceral reaction to the celebration of women.

Just as it is important to celebrate International Women's Day as a way to acknowledge and honor women around the world, it is also important to understand that the men's rights movement (MRM), among other such movements, has legitimate social and legal issues that are not antifeminist in nature but focused on the issues of men, such as suicides, domestic abuse against men, circumcision, and certain health policies. Additionally, the rights of men are important in child custody, alimony, and distribution of property in divorce cases—all legal issues that men's rights groups contend have been unfairly stacked against them in the court system.

However, whatever progress was made regarding men's legal rights, the MRM was soundly shut down with the rise of male supremacy groups whose single goals were (and are) to restrict women's civil rights. The International Centre for Counterterrorism (ICCT) began tracking male supremacism as a right-wing extremist ideology as their misogynistic views and terrorism began to morph together. The ICCT has determined that male supremacy holds two core misogynistic views: Men are entitled to sexual access to women but have become victims of "involuntary celibacy" as women withhold sex which then justifies (mass) violence as retribution, and the "belief that feminists are a malevolent force controlling society at the expense of men."[11]

Historically, 1989 is considered by scholars and law enforcement to be the beginning of the Incel Movement, an antifemale online subculture that blames women for denying them sex and/or romantic relationships. That same year, a male student at a Montreal engineering school murdered 14 female students, then blamed feminism for ruining his life in a suicide note. Nine years later, a dozen women were shot and three of them killed in an aerobics class by a man who claimed "involuntary celibacy" for his actions. When, in 2014, almost two dozen people were shot, six of them killed, the killer had previously written, "One day incels will realize their true strength and numbers, and overthrow this oppressive feminist system. Start envisioning a world where women fear you." But of his murderous spree, he explained, "loneliness, rejection, and unfulfilled desires all because girls have never been attracted to me."[12]

The takeaway here is, despite fewer chances for promotions in the workplace and the continuing wage gap (in 2022, women are still only making 83 cents to every dollar men earn[13]), the inattention of females toward males in a patriarchal society remains intolerable for a small but dangerous group.

While some of the previously listed grievances of unfair treatment must be evaluated in earnest, there remains the mindset that in sharing privilege, those who already have it will lose their own. Economically, the poorest, most poverty-stricken, uneducated countries in the world have the most restrictive rules placed upon women. Empowering all members of society, however, brings greater economic power to a nation.

When a society holds its citizens to gender-based roles, it is difficult to see them as champions or warriors or even politicians.

(MOST) NATIONS MOVE FORWARD

From countries that have been the most restrictive regarding women in sport, the Olympics offer a glimpse in how opportunity creates change. At the 2012 London Games, Saudi Arabia, Qatar, and Brunei, the last three countries in the world to have banned female athletes, sent female representatives, making a total of 158 women from the Middle East. Tunisia's Habiba Ghribi (1984–) became her nation's first female athlete to medal when she won a silver in the 3,000-meter steeplechase.

At the Rio Games in 2016, several Middle Eastern nations sent female athletes. Egypt made its debut with its first female beach volleyball team and player Doaa Elghobashy (1996–) became a media sensation with her head-to-ankle-covered body. For Elghobashy, it was not about clothing but opportunity, saying, "It doesn't keep me away from the things I love to do."

Ines Boubakri (1988–) of Tunisia won Africa's first women's Olympic medal in individual foil (fencing) and dedicated her bronze medal to "the Tunisian woman, the Arab woman . . . who has her place in society," while fencer Ibtihaj Muhammad (1985) of the United States won the bronze in sabre, making history as the first American to compete in a hijab.

Sprinter Kariman Abuljadayel (1994–) became the first female athlete from Saudi Arabia to compete in the Olympic 100-meter dash.

Mary Al-Atrash (1994–) of Palestine, who had never had full access to an Olympic-sized pool, competed in the 50-meter freestyle event.

Kimia Alizadeh Zonouzi (1998–) won the bronze in tae kwon do, becoming the first Iranian female athlete to win an Olympic medal. For

Egyptian Doaa Elghobashy. *dpa picture alliance/Alamy Stock Photo*

Zonouzi it was opportunity that went beyond sport. "I thank God that I made history with my bronze to pave the way for other Iranian women."[14]

Beyond individual experiences for these female athletes, their nations were rewarded for their participation as the International Olympic Committee, individual governing bodies (for individual sports programs), and the United Nations work toward inclusion that, beyond sport, promises economic reward.

When Tahmina Kohistani (1989–) became Afghanistan's first female Olympic athlete, competing in the 100-meter in track at the 2012 London Games, her race was far braver than most people could understand. What the world saw was a 5'3" woman wearing a traditional headscarf, covered head to toe, hoping only to finish with a respectable time. Before the cheering crowd of sixty thousand with so many more congratulating Kohistani for being there, she was also receiving threats on social media and faced backlash at home. During her training, she was threatened, heckled, even kicked out of a taxi (she was not allowed to drive) when the driver discovered she was training for the Olympic Games.

On the day she learned she had made the Olympics, she said she cried for every girl who was told she could not run; she cried because those girls would never "know the joy of moving with the wind." And she cried again after losing in the first heat as one of the slowest runners in the game—not because of her time but because "I achieve my dream and my dream come true." Then, despite all the abuse, threats, fear tactics she had endured, Kohistani did something spectacular. Using the Olympic platform, she spoke to her countrymen and women:

> There are a lot of bad comments about me in my country and there's lots of people not ready to support me. But I think I will make the nation of Afghanistan proud of me and they are going to never forget me. I just opened a new window, a new door, for the next generation of my country. . . . There are lots of girls in Afghanistan. Because of some social problems, because of family problems, they cannot do sport. But I'm going to say for them: Come and join me, Tahmina, and we can make a very big and strong sport network in our country.[15]

Sisters Shabnam (1992–) and Sadaf Rahimi (1993–) trained at the Ghazi Stadium, once used by the Taliban as a place of public punishment where women were routinely stoned to death, along with a growing number of other girls hoping to learn to box.[16] But before they could ever gain traction, not to mention acceptance, the sisters fled to live and train in Spain.

"In Afghanistan, women have no rights, no life," Shabnam Rahimi said. "We went out to box in the mornings and we didn't know if we would get back alive at night."[17] When a member of Afghanistan's boxing federation warned Sadaf, "If I find you alone in the street, I am going to throw acid on you," she knew they had to leave. In 2012, Sadaf became the first female boxer from her country to be invited to complete in the 2012 Olympic Games.

In February 2020, when the United States and the Taliban struck the "U.S.–Taliban Peace Deal," it was not just their Olympic dreams that faded but all the rights and freedoms women had gained in the past two decades. Many had feared that the withdrawal of Western troops could signal a revival for the Taliban, an ultraconservative political and religious organization that uses extreme military tactics to impose its laws, which is a threat to all women. In August 2021, the Taliban gained control and women went back into hiding, making the visibility of the empowered female athlete around the world all the more important.

THE "SEXY" IN SLAM DUNKS

When, in 2006, ESPN commentator Bill Simmons (1969–) wrote, "The vast majority of WNBA players lack crossover sex appeal," what he meant was, the skill of female players did not matter. He wanted and needed to feel attraction to the women he watched. Otherwise, what was the point? "That's just the way it is," he wrote. "Some are uncomfortably tall and gawky. . . . The baggy uniforms don't help. Neither does the fact that it's tough for anyone to look attractive at the end of a two-hour basketball game."[18]

In other words, male viewers are willing to watch strong females (in entertainment or sport) so long as they are attractive and offer some kind of gratification to the viewer and do not encroach on male domain. What is known in the media world as "the male gaze" is really a description of how female portrayals uphold the hegemonic masculine and feminine ideals. In respect to sports, the "male gaze" is important to both the media and sponsors who promote specific athletes (or sports) for greater viewership. Women's soccer, volleyball, and gymnastics, for example, have much higher male viewership than traditionally more masculine sports, which includes basketball, boxing, or race car driving. A quick Google search of the words "female athlete" brings about countless lists of "50 hottest females ever" (which will include gymnasts under the ages of eighteen), "most beautiful," and "greatest bodies." It is a fact the sporting industry and media are well aware of.[19]

In a 2021 study, Nike was used as the model in how gender stereotypes are used to portray and sell the "male gaze." Although Nike's mission statement is "to do everything possible to expand human potential," it also relies heavily on the "male gaze" for sales.[20] It is important to note that while Nike was used in this particular study, this promotional tool is extremely popular across the sport industry and media. However subtle, by reinforcing masculine and feminine traits within the sports world, not only does the overlap into everyday society exist and persist, but so too does the unconscious (or conscious) belief that women should only engage in certain sports and, therefore, hold more feminine characteristics.[21]

Studies show that when the female athlete or sport does not support the male viewers' perception of gender roles, there is less interest in watching that sport or athlete. Interestingly, female viewers, however, want to see more barrier-breaking endeavors by female athletes, no matter their appearance.[22]

There is no threat in traditional female sports that show more skin, but a tall, strong female basketball player does not attract the male gaze. The WNBA, in fact, actually considered an overhaul of its "unflattering" uniform. But with the fourth wave came a newer, more brash kind of athlete—one less interested in the antiquated ideal and more interested in power and performance.

"I hate how they try to use sexy on us," said Brittany Griner (1990–), the only NCAA basketball player, male or female, to score two thousand points and block five hundred shots, a three-time All-American, named the Player of the Year by the Associated Press and Most Outstanding Player of the Final Four, who went on to turn pro and make the U.S. Olympic women's team. At 6'8" and wearing a men's U.S. shoe size 17, Griner was just one of the WNBA players asked to consider a more feminine look for her game. "Like that's the only way women can get people to watch our sport or see anything we're doing. You'll never hear a guy say, 'I gotta be sexy.' You'll hear a guy say, 'I gotta go hard, be raw, be fierce.'"[23]

While it's unlikely that the male gaze will ever go away, in the fight for greater respect and understanding of the female athlete there remains an undeniable need for greater female leadership in women's sports.

WOMEN WHO COACH

Around the world, females were stepping into positions of coaches, referees, and athletes in male sports. With such coaches as Notre Dame's women's basketball head coach Muffet McGraw (1955–) who racked up 936 wins, nine Final Fours, seven championships, and two national championships during her thirty-three-year career and coach Kim Mulkey (1962–), also an Olympic gold medalist and first player in NCAA women's basketball history to win a national championship as a player, an assistant coach, and a head coach, female athletes had real mentors to look to. C. Vivian Stringer (1948–); volleyball legend Mary Wise (1959–); and softball coach Carol Hutchins (1957–), the youngest Division I coach in the NCAA's history[24] and, winningest head coach—male or female—as head coach in NCAA Division I softball with more than fifteen hundred wins, empowered today's athletes and coaches.

As for Pat Summit (1952–2016), everyone knew who she was. Whether they were a fan of basketball, women's sports or not, the name was as big as sports itself. The third-winningest coach in women's college basketball (Tara VanDerveer is the most), Summit won eight national titles and was the first college basketball coach—male or female—to reach one thousand wins, and never had a losing season in thirty-eight years.

Hers was incredible run, that included first a career as an athlete at both the collegiate and Olympic level, then as a national, Olympic, and collegiate coach, becoming the first U.S. Olympian to win a medal as an athlete and a coach.

She won seven NCAA Coach of the Year Awards, was inducted into six different Halls of Fame. She was the only female coach to make the 50 Greatest Coaches of All Time in all sports, coming in eleventh place in 2009.[25] But perhaps one of the most notable things about Summit was her "100 percent graduation rate among her players who completed their athletic eligibility," an honor President Obama attributed to her when he awarded her the Presidential Medal of Freedom in 2012.[26]

As for McGraw, she also created the first all-female coaching staff at Notre Dame and made no apologies, saying simply, "People are hiring too many men." When asked if she planned on ever hiring a male coach again, she said, "No." From her vantage, there are no better coaches and no better role models for female athletes than other female athletes.[27]

As has been the mission of the U.S. State Department's Council to Empower Women and Girls Through Sport, the Global Sports Mentoring Program, and such associations as the NCAA's Women Coaches Academy, Australia's Change Our Game, or the Female Coaching Network, all have embraced "you cannot be what you cannot see" to elicit real change in women's sports.

HASHTAGS: AN AWAKENING BUT NOT CHANGE

Within the sports world, women and girls have broken ground in new ways—not because they have only discovered new talents and passions; rather, this is what happens when opportunities are earned—opportunities are taken. As both Hillary Clinton and Laura Gentile had imagined with a global mentoring program, when girls and women believe, anything is possible.

One such and most exciting believer appeared in 2014 when, at the age of thirteen, American Mo'ne Davis (2001–) captured the attention of the world in her Little League World Series appearance. In fact, she dominated. She became the first girl to pitch a shutout in the celebrated tournament and the first Black girl to play in the Little League World Series.

It was not because of her gender but raw talent and intimidating presence on the mound that commanded attention. She threw a seventy-mile-per-hour fastball, combined with numerous off-speed pitches that left opponents swinging blindly or too stunned to move at all that made Davis a superstar, which landed her on the cover of *Sports Illustrated* and an invite to the White House.[28] Best of all, her "That's throwing like a girl" national commercial reinspired the hashtag #ThrowLikeAGirl.

Davis both became a part of and renewed a movement. In the summer of 2014, while Davis shut down batter after batter, Procter & Gamble, the manufacturer of Always, a feminine hygiene product, began its #LikeAGirl campaign, which culminated into an Emmy Award–winning commercial that debuted during the 2015 Super Bowl.

It was historic.

It was the first time a feminine hygiene product ran in the Super Bowl. In a sixty-second advertisement, sponsored by Always, the message was really about what #LikeAGirl means. Before an audience of 115 million viewers, documentary filmmaker Lauren Greenfield (1966–) asked a variety of people to run, throw, and fight like a girl. The responses were demeaning. When a male adolescent was then asked, "So, do you think you just insulted your sister?" the boy responds, "No, I mean, yeah . . . insulted girls, but not my sister."

That defining moment highlighted how not only the boys but young women and men had also acted out unflattering directives "as a girl," while the girls—each one—tried their very hardest to show strong throws, kicks, hits, and sprints.

We do not mean to insult girls but, socially, we have been trained that it is acceptable to demean those who are not taken seriously. The commercial became an overnight sensation with more than 85 million views, was ranked #1 Super Bowl Spot by Adweek,[29] #1 Super Bowl Spot by Advertising Age,[30] and in the year to come, would receive over three dozen different awards, including Outstanding Directorial Achievement in Commercials by the Directors Guild of America.[31] The message from the advertising and marketing world was clear but, aside from physical awards, what changed?

After the sixty-second film, 76 percent of viewers said they would no longer view the "like a girl" phrase as a negative, and two out of three men said they would refrain (or try to) from using "like a girl" in the form of an insult. In February 2014, #LikeAGirl was trending.[32]

Others, however, asked if it was appropriate to have an Always-sponsored commercial about girl empowerment during the Super Bowl, the implication being that this was a topic just for girls. But as women drive upwards of 80 percent of all consumer purchasing and are 46 percent of the Super Bowl–watching population, why not?

Chief creative officer Judy John, the visionary behind the Always #LikeAGirl global sensation, was compelled to use the brand as a "confidence" platform because when girls hit puberty, their confidence drops significantly and rarely regains what they once felt as a child, unlike their male counterparts. "As a brand that champions girls' and women's confidence, we knew we had to do something about this,"[33] but no sooner did the ad run when self-proclaimed "meninists," men who believe their own rights are being taken from them as women vie for equal treatment, complained about the treatment of boys. Almost immediately, a new hashtag #LikeABoy was trending with comments such as:

"Hopefully one day men can have equality and treated the same. #LikeABoy."
"Can we get a #LikeABoy commercial too please?"

"Seriously #LikeAGirl is the most insulting commercial ever and there better be a #LikeABoy commercial."
"#LikeABoy because I can actually run and throw."[34]

Despite the long and undeniable history of discrimination and degradation of women, despite the fact even as the commercial aired women were not given equal status to men in the U.S. Constitution or in the form of earned wages, there came the knee-jerk reaction of anger when girls were given a moment to shine. Still, many, many more truly listened and took note:

"Seconds after #LikeAGirl started trending, someone created #LikeABoy bc masculinity needs constant reassurance & attention."
"The difference between like a boy and like a girl is that #LikeABoy has never been used as a generalized insult against men."
"If you seriously are trying to make #LikeABoy happen, you need to grow up. Don't be threatened by strong women, be inspired."
"When women get a commercial dedicated to feminism and empowerment, get annoyed and start making fun of it #LikeABoy."
"Throw a tantrum that there's ONE commercial about girls in 4-hour event centered around masculinity #LikeABoy."
"To boys making fun of the #LikeAGirl commercial: I hope God blesses you with a baby girl and I wanna see you tell her what shes incapable of."[35]

What had merely begun as a message from a feminine hygiene company to embolden young girls to keep and nurture their self-esteem and confidence by phrasing "like a girl" as a positive description rather than an insult became a male issue in just sixty seconds. As one person questioned, "People up in arms over #LikeAGirl commercial. What's so wrong with telling little girls they can do anything regardless of what society says?"

In an answer, "#LikeAGirl is the best thing to happen. Ever," was posted. It was only the beginning of the hashtag movement.

EIGHTEEN

Transgender Female Athletes in Sport

Before discussing the issue of transgender female athletes in women's sport, it is essential to briefly discuss the history of the transgender community. Never have transgender people been more visible than in the twenty-first century, but their history is not new. The history of the LG-BTQ+ community is one of societal- and religious-imposed shame, self-shame, confusion, hate, and violence. Theirs is not a history of life gone awry but one of self-discovery. Despite prevalent myths, one does not become transgendered for attention or on a whim.

THE NONBINARY THIRD GENDER

Evidence of transgender or third genders (a term used to categorize people who do not identify as male or female, identify as both, or as the opposite of their assigned or biological gender) dates back forty-five hundred years ago throughout Europe and Africa. Grave markers, art, and texts have revealed goddess-centered priesthoods who self-identified as "neither man nor woman" or eunuchs imitating traditional female behaviors. Throughout the Greco-Roman, Akkadian, and Sumerian (ancient Middle East) Empires, into contemporary India and Pakistan, self-castration was not unusual for "spiritual men" and/or devotees of the Mother Goddess cults. The galli (ancient Roman priests) and hijra (most directly identified with Shiva, a sexually ambivalent figure in Hinduism as Ardhanarish-vara, or half-man/half-woman) are well established.[1] In April 2019, the Bangladeshi government legally recognized the hijra (a growing population of more than a half-million in 2019) as a third gender, allowing them to legally vote as such.[2] Such depictions of half-man/half-woman or third genders, as well as literary references, have been discovered throughout Southeast Asia and the Americas.

The first successful sex reassignment surgery was conducted in 1952, thanks largely to groundbreaking research in human gender and sexuality and surgical procedures made decades earlier by Dr. Magnus Hirschfeld (1868–1935). The first successful surgical transgender was Christine Jorgensen (1926–1989), who also underwent hormone therapy. Upon her return to the United States (the surgeries took place in Copenhagen, Denmark), both the media and public treated her well while Hollywood welcomed her, offering film and advertising contracts to which she once said, "I guess they all want to take a peek."[3]

Renee Richards (1934–), a professional tennis player, however, did not receive such a welcome following her surgery. While hers was not the first sex reassignment surgery, she is believed to be the first transgender woman to play a professional sport. While playing a match in 1976, a local television reporter outed her "as a man," and Richards was banned from the tournament. Following that outing, multiple female players refused to play in any tournaments Richards was in, citing her muscular frame as unfair.

Richards petitioned for her right as a woman to play while the United States Tennis Association began requiring genetic testing of its female athletes. Richards refused the test and sued. In a landmark case for transgender rights, the New York Supreme Court ruled in her favor. She played professionally for four years and quietly retired, also refusing to act as a spokesperson for transgender rights. What makes Richards interesting is that she believes that gender is binary (male or female), rather than fluid (how a person identifies).

"I like the difference between men and women. I live the concept of male and female. There is no such thing [as gender fluidity]. The population doesn't repopulate itself from fluidity. It's what the world is all about, right?"[4]

Richards also argues against third genders, saying no such genders exist, but science disagrees.

THE REASSIGNED DNA

Gone are the once simple XX and XY chromosome explanations of girl and boy. New research shows that biological sex is far more complicated. It is and has been scientifically possible for XX individuals (female) to have male gonads, and for an XY individual to have ovaries through a group of cells known as bipotential primordium and a gene labeled SRY or Sex region Y, a region on the Y chromosome that is the testis-determining factor.

As an embryo develops, a group of cells form the bipotential primordium. Not yet identified as male or female, the formation of the SRY, as well as genes DMRT1 (also important for the development of testes)[5] and

FOXL2 (important in ovarian development and determination of the female sex),[6] determine the development of an individual's biological sex. It is only later, as the individual develops, that secondary sex characteristics (penis, vagina, even appearance and behavior) arise, all influenced by hormones, genetics, environment, and so forth.

Just as no one person is the same, science has discovered that same reality holds to genetic makeup and biological sex of individuals. Nearly one hundred years after Dr. Hirschfeld found that trans- and homosexuality were natural, science is finding that even the brain structure affects how sex and gender interact. For example, one study found that transgender individuals are similar to cisgender individuals with the same gender identity in certain brain regions.[7] Still more studies have found that hormones, the introduction of hormones, and the natural occurrences of puberty have far more profound effects on individuals than previously believed. During prepubescence and puberty, certain sex hormones like estrogen (even in males), progesterone, and testosterone do not just impact the person but the individual's genetic makeup. The sex hormone levels in one individual may vary greatly from another, which may then be further impacted depending upon environmental, social, and behavioral factors. Interestingly, current ongoing studies are linking chemicals found in manufactured foods and drink to "a variety of abnormalities in human sexuality, gender development and behaviors, reproductive capabilities, and sex ratios."[8]

In short, biological sex and societal gender norms on females, males, cisgender, bisexual, and transgender people are as varied as they are complex. Transgender people must be afforded civil rights, health care, and service in the military, like anyone else. They must be provided their own space in sports, as well.

But is that space in women's sports?

THE CONVERSATION ABOUT WOMEN'S SPORT

In keeping with the history of women, the topic of women's sports has become a political, religious, and legal cultural war where conversation leans away from science and the need for more studies and toward the economic value for the Olympics (and other lucrative sport agencies), all of which makes great fodder for media opinion pieces. Along the way, however, cisgender female athletes were excluded from conversation about their own history and space in the world of sports.

The world of women's sport historically has been inclusive (since the world outside of sports has not been so welcoming for women), but the issue of the forced inclusion of transgender female athletes in women's sports threatens to negatively change women's sports forever.

The conversation has not been about her ovaries but of testosterone levels. Such is the history of women. When cisgender females have spoken out in protection of women's sports, which includes the need for coaches and trainers to learn about the female triad or scientists to include biological females in medical trials that will ultimately be prescribing medication to women, supporters of transgender females have called this phobic and hateful. Yet, the reality is scholarships, state titles, Olympic dreams, high-dollar endorsements, equal playing field, the historically negligent medical care of cisgender women, and so much more are all on the line.

TRANSGENDER IMPACT ON WOMEN'S SPORT

Individuals designated as males at birth competing in women's sports has become a hot topic in the new century. Donna Lopiano (1946–), former president of the Women's Sports Foundation, explained, "I don't know of a woman athlete who doesn't want trans girls to be treated fairly. But the cost of treating her fairly should not come at the cost of discrimination against a biologically-female-at-birth woman."[9] Caitlyn Jenner who, as Bruce Jenner, had been a former football player, then two-time Olympian who won gold in the 1976 Montreal Games in decathlon, agrees. The press named Jenner an "all-American hero" and "world's greatest athlete," yet forty years later, after transitioning into a female, Jenner believes allowing transgender females in sport "just isn't fair."[10] She would know about biological differences.

With politicians, religious leaders, celebrities, and athletes all weighing in, the lack of guidelines has only complicated an already complex issue. Rules vary from state to state with each sport governing body leaving the participation or expulsion of transgender athletes to individual interpretation. For example, in Texas, Louisiana, Idaho, Nebraska, Indiana, Alabama, and North Carolina, athletes can only participate in a gendered sport that matches their birth certificate, whereas the NCAA and Olympic Committee require the completion of one year of testosterone suppression treatment and testing for testosterone levels.[11] In Connecticut, however, athletes are allowed to compete according to their own gender identity without any restrictions. The Connecticut High School Association's legal position stated that as long as federal courts and government agencies refer to "sex" as "ambiguous," theirs is not the position to deny a transgender athlete from competing.

In reality, transgender females moving into and impacting women's long history of sport had gone unnoticed until it became a talking point in politics. In 2004, with almost no credible research, the IOC officially gave approval to allow transgender females into sport without ever looking at hard science. It only stipulated athletes who transitioned were required to have reassignment surgery followed by two years of hormone therapy. By 2015, the IOC ruled that transgender athletes could complete in the Olympics and other international events without undergoing sex reassignment surgery even as more research was coming in. By 2020, the ramifications of their negligence was an embarrassment they were not willing to face, announcing all responsibilities and/or recourse belong to individual sporting agencies.

The problem with this (as mentioned in chapter 13) is that, although women and men have different medical needs and react differently to medicines and treatments, by 2016 over 70 percent of medical clinical trials still did not differentiate by gender; and by 2018, both the Association of American Medical Colleges and the American Medical Association refused to do continued education and research on sex and gender differences. So, where exactly were these individual sporting agencies supposed to get scientific data when so little data exists for women?

THE DIFFERENCES OF BIOLOGIES

As the subject of female transgender athletes participating at competitive levels against cisgender females is debated, so, too, is the scientific research. The American Civil Liberties Union (ACLU) has stated that not only is the language within Title IX ambiguous but that science supports the idea that athletes who were assigned male at birth can fairly compete as females. However, by 2020, more data began to show that even after years of testosterone repression therapy, transgender female athletes hold significant physical advantage.

Higher muscle mass and residual strength in biologically recognized males continued to be detected after two years of testosterone suppression therapy. A study at the Boston University School of Medicine found that "medicine alone" does not completely suppress testosterone levels,[12] as 75 percent of transgender women failed to suppress appropriate levels of testosterone,[13] leaving more research to be done on female athletes, in particular.

As male athletes go through puberty, the physiological playing field does change. Males have greater muscle mass, higher ratio of muscle to body weight and strength, and greater bone density. Not only is the biological male skeletal system larger, but transgender females/cisgender males also have thicker and stronger ligaments, larger organs, less body fat (without the fluctuating hormones that biological females have or widening of hips, which can change gait and performance), as well as larger hearts allowing for greater oxygen-carrying capacity. No medicine can or will ever change these biological facts.

After doing its own research, World Rugby banned transgender women from competing in global competitions, becoming the first international sports governing body to do so. As Ross Tucker, a South African exercise physiologist, stated, the guidelines regarding transgender athletes competing in women's athletics was "sport's unsolvable problem."[14] As head scientist for World Rugby, however, the decision for safety and player welfare had to come first.

World Rugby reportedly reviewed and analyzed data for nine months and determined that transgender women could cause serious harm to cisgender athletes. The decision was made following the release of the Swedish study that revealed only a 5 percent loss of muscle mass among transgender athletes after one year of testosterone repression therapy, also supporting other studies that muscle strength and mass gives female transgender athletes a significant advantage over cisgender athletes. The decision, according to Tucker, was made not only for the safety of athletes but for the sports itself. "If sports don't take care of the safety issues, sports will die."[15]

However, despite the growing number of international studies dispelling the hormone repression therapy argument, despite the fact of the larger size of the male-born heart, skull, and bone structure, as well as bone density, ability for greater oxygen intake, along with muscle and cartilage design, the IOC continued to rely on hormone repression therapy in 2020, stating that transgender female athletes can participate in the Games if their serum testosterone levels are reduced below 10 nanomoles per liter for a year and continue to stay low during their athletic careers. The average male has 300 to 1,000 nanograms per deciliter (ng/dL) while the average female has 15 to 70 ng/dL (which can change during menstrual cycles), and in sport, this still allows much higher levels than elite cisgender female athletes. As a means of comparison, according to the international World Athletics and its track and field governing body, the average testosterone range for cisgender women is 0.12 to 1.79 nanomoles per liter whereas the average for men (after puberty) is 7.7 to 29.4.

This means a transgender female athlete can compete with testosterone levels of 9 nanomoles—more than five times the level of even those female athletes who presented with the highest levels of testosterone.

The disparity is evident as science repeatedly explains why female athletes must retain their own space within the world of sports.

TRANSGENDER FEMALE PIONEERS IN SPORT

CeCe Telfer (1995–), a Jamaican-born U.S. citizen, moved to New Hampshire at age twelve and was later recruited to run for Pierce Franklin University's Division II men's 400-meter hurdles. While competing on the men's track and field team, Telfer put in a time of 57.34 and was ranked 200th and 390th in the 2016 and 2017 Division II seasons, respectively. Telfer competed again in 2019 as a transgender female and became a national champion with a time of 57.53. The second-place finisher came in at a very distant 59.21, and Telfer became the first transgender female to win an NCAA title. An aspiring model, activist, and Olympian, however, Telford was ruled ineligible in 2020 and disqualified from the United States in 2021 from competition for failure to meet testosterone level requirements to compete in women's sport. Telfer, feeling the effects of muscle deterioration, maintains that she is at the disadvantage in running while undergoing testosterone repression.

Despite the disqualification, Telfer hopes to serve as a role model to other transgender females to "live an authentic life," and strive for happiness.[16]

Lia Thomas is a transgender female swimmer at Penn State University. As a male swimmer, Thomas was ranked 554th in the 200-meter. As a transgender female, she is the first known transgender athlete to take an NCAA swimming championship after breaking record after record and by April 2022, was on par to break the long-standing records of Katie Ledecky (1997–) and Missy Franklin (1995–), two beloved U.S. Olympians.

Thomas had only gotten into the sport of swimming following her older brother; but while swimming, she realized she was a transgender female in 2018 and began hormone replacement therapy in 2019. She came out as a trans woman her junior year in college to friends, family, coaches, and both the men and women's swim team at Penn. "I was struggling, my mental health was not very good. It was a lot of unease, basically just feeling trapped in my own body. It didn't align," Thomas said. It was then that she decided to come out.[17]

After two years of hormone therapy, Thomas, who transitioned well after puberty and still has male genitalia, noticed that her strength was not the same and fat had also redistributed within her body. And yet no cisgender female came close to Thomas's times.

During an interview with *Sports Illustrated*, Thomas hit upon an important point when asked about her dominating women's swim, saying, "The very simple answer is that I am not a man. I'm a woman so I belong on the women's team. Trans people deserve the same respect every other athlete gets."

She is not alone in this feeling. While Thomas's cisgender female team-mates were told they would face disciplinary measures if they spoke to the media, several parents have been vocal. "We support Lia as a trans woman and hope she leads a happy and productive life, because that's what she deserves," one parent of a Penn swimmer says. "What we can't do is stand by while she rewrites records and eliminates biological women from this sport. If we don't speak up here, it's going to happen in college after college. And then women's sports, as we know it, will no longer exist in this country."[18]

THE (DIS)ADVANCES OF WOMEN IN SPORT

According to the World Health Organization, transgender people and other gender minorities comprise approximately 0.5 percent of the world's population, and experience disproportionately levels of anxiety, depression, and other mental health issues. They endure discrimination, violence, bullying, ostracization, and barriers to health care with nearly 40 percent of respondents in a 2019 survey reporting that they had attempted suicide at least once in their lifetime.[19]

A 2021 study from Australia found two in every three transgender and nonbinary youth reporting symptoms of major depressive disorder,[20] while a rise of anti-transgender sentiment has risen around the world over the fight of transgender women in women's sports. While many have focused on simply the science behind biology in regard to sports, many more have used this debate to launch an all-out assault on the trans community and their rights to better health, more studies, greater understanding, and inclusion.

Without proper support or any positive outlet, the risk factor of transgender men and women succumbing to substance abuse, sex work, gender dysmorphia, unemployment, and violence remains significantly high.[21] But in particular to youth, a critical period when all individuals must negotiate puberty, changing hormones, and identity, social networking and/or finding a community is invaluable. Beyond the physical benefits of sports (weight control, bone health, increased cardiorespiratory and muscular fitness, reduced risk of diabetes, etc.), children and teenagers experience lower rates of anxiety and depression. Youth athletes in sport have increased self-esteem and confidence, and they are less likely to engage in substance abuse or other risky behaviors while establishing more healthy relationship with their peers and/or teammates. Youth athletes report feeling improved psychological and emotional well-being, particularly those with disabilities or within the LGBTQ communities.[22]

For example, there remains a high percentage of body dysmorphia among transgender males and females, but studies continue to show a consistently high pattern of transgender females engaging in disordered eating for gender-affirming purposes.[23] However, transgender and nonbinary high school youth athletes in school districts that have policies supporting their identity had higher grades than those who did not participate in sport, are associated with lower suicide risk, and reported feeling safe or safer at school.[24] Something as innocuous as using the restroom in the middle of the day has become a significant stressor for transgender people.

While the debate rages on, members of the LGBTQ+ community, particularly trans youth, remain incredibly vulnerable and at risk. As the debates continue, transgender and nonbinary youth feel the brunt of a growing global anti-trans sentiment. Even transgender former athlete Caitlyn Jenner, born Bruce Jenner, who won Olympic gold in decathlon at the 1976 Montreal Games, called Lia Thomas "one of the worst things to happen to" and "bad publicity for" the trans community.[25]

Though hard words, perhaps Jenner has a point. For those who argue against transgender female athletes in women's sports, Thomas's biological advantages were and are evident. For transgender athletes and those who support their entry into women's sports, Jenner was right again in that without clear guidelines from the IOC, the NCAA, and all NGBs, attacks on the transgender community will never stop. Still again, Jenner's comments ring true for the undecided in this global debate as Thomas, who transitioned well after puberty and still has her male genitalia intact, provided more questions and scrutiny. *If an athlete transitions after puberty, should they be allowed to participate in women's sports? Is it a full transition with male genitalia intact? What is the science on testosterone levels for fully and nonmedically transitioned transgender females?* and *Is she really a trans female without full transition?*

The argument is not going to go away until clear guidelines are given. By 2020–2021, twenty states had introduced bans on high school transgender athletes participating in sports.[26] By 2022, fifteen states and Washington, D.C., adopted policies allowing transgender students to participate in high school sports without requirements of medical or legal transition.[27] Other states have offered no guidance either way, allowing for different school administrations to determine rules regarding transgender athletes not only about participating in sports but even which bathroom they can use and how they are to be addressed by faculty and staff. The uncertainties only add to the anxiety of the adolescent.

To repeat, the IOC only exacerbated the issues when it initially allowed transgender females to participate in the Olympic in accordance to their identity, then decreed that transgender athletes must transition before puberty and be fully (medically) transitioned or going through the process before competition. Then, just a few short years later, the IOC disregarded studies and declared that no medical transition was necessary.[28]

For proponents and opponents of transgender female entry into women's sports, there remains no clear answers. Historically, "sex" and "gender" have been used interchangeably, which has only added to the confusion and, it has been argued, either watered down science or has finally empowered the trans and nonbinary communities.

As transgender female athletes fight for a place in women's sports, many feel that cisgender female girls and women are being forced out of sports.

"This is the problem," said Fiona McAnena, marketing consultant, former rower, and volunteer with Fair Play for Women. "The transgender community is demanding that we make space for them. Why won't they make space for us?"

In a 2020 poll in which more than one hundred elite cisgender female athletes were asked if the inclusion of transgender female athletes is "good for their sport," the response was overwhelming. When the athletes were allowed to remain anonymous, 100 percent reported concerns of long-term negative impact and fairness of women's sports and individual female athletes. They feared retribution from sponsors, sporting agencies, and the public, if they were to speak publicly. More than 60 percent of those athletes added that they did not want to prevent transgender female athletes from "experiencing the joys of team sports or competing," but the fairness of biology was both a fact and factor.[29]

Professional and Olympic female athletes from across the globe also took issue with the "women don't need to be saved" argument. Ronda Rousey, arguably one of the most feared and respected athletes in MMA, refused to fight transgender fighter Fallon Fox (1975–), the first openly transgender athlete in the MMA, in 2014 (at the height of her domination), expressing concern over the fact that Fox had already gone through puberty, thus benefiting from the testosterone boost, not to mention her greater lung and heart capacity, denser bones, and thicker/larger skull. A well-aimed punch would not impact Rousey and Fox equally.

Former cycling champion Victoria Hood concurred after Veronica Ivey, aka Rachel McKinnon (1982–), a transgender cyclist, demolished track records. "It is not complicated," Hood said. "The science is there and it says that it is unfair. The male body, which has been through male puberty, still retains its advantage; that doesn't go away. I have sympathy with [transgender female athletes]. They have the right to do sport but not a right to go into any category they want." Orthopedic surgeon and competitive cyclist Jennifer Wagner-Assali, award-winning track athlete and coach Cynthia Monteleone, and International Swimming Hall of

Famer and lawyer Sandra Bucha-Kerscher (1954–) also spoke out about transgender females competing in female sport with the shared sentiment of Monteleone that the performance of transgender females who went through puberty "is greatly enhanced compared to females, due to basic physiological differences."[30] But as many female athletes have discovered, speaking out earns them physical threats, including death threats for Wagner-Assali, as well as threats of loss of team membership and sponsorship.

"No one needs saving but integrity needs preserving," said a former U.S. national athlete who only spoke on the condition of anonymity. "Everyone is angry right now. I get it. But it has gotten so that cisgender females are not even allowed to express their views in their own sport."

Only now are female athletes beginning to openly discuss their menstrual cycle and its impact on athletic performance. It is implausible that transgender female athletes can be fairly entered into women's sport when we do not fully understand cisgender female athletes. In 2022, British sprinter Dina Asher-Smith called for more research on how periods affect athletic performance when she finished last in a race she typically dominated. "More people need to actually research from a sports science perspective because it is absolutely huge," she said. In fact, only 6 percent of sport and exercise studies specifically focus on female athletes.[31]

"I actually support all LGBTQ+ and trans rights," the athlete said. "I'm proud that trans are now being recognized as lawful partners and parents but in terms of athletic rights for women, we need to take a step back. Women have been fighting for decades—well, honestly, centuries but, in modern times, for decades—to have the right to play in sport, to be represented fairly in the media. To have these rights trampled on by a small group of athletes who are shattering records and times is not right."

Katrina Karkazis, an anthropologist at Amherst College and coauthor of *Testosterone: An Unauthorized Biography*, explained that history "has for a very long period not been at the forefront of gender equality, inclusion so it's no wonder that we're having this kind of debate."[32]

INTERSEX ATHLETES FACTOR IN

If things were not complicated enough, the story of Mokgadi Caster Semenya (1991–), a South African middle-distance runner who reached international stardom, is a particularly difficult one. Semenya became famous not for her gold medal at the 2009 World Championships in the 800-meter event or for her gold medal in the 2016 Olympic Games but for her sex. Or, the question of her sex.

As an intersex cisgender, Caster (her preferred name) Semenya was assigned "female" at birth. Born with XY chromosomes and naturally elevated testosterone from a condition known as hyperandrogenism, characterized by high levels of androgens in females, which include elevated testosterone levels, increased body or facial hair, and infrequent or absent menstruation, Semenya came under increased scrutiny as she dominated the track world.

The International Association of Athletics Federations (IAAF), now formally known as World Athletics, withdrew Semenya after an imposed sex testing in 2009, but she was cleared the following year to compete.

In 2019, when the then IAAF ruled that intersex and transgender athletes could not compete in the 400-, 800-, and 1500-meter events unless they underwent testosterone suppression therapy to lower testosterone levels, Semenya was also diagnosed with 5-alpha-reductase deficiency, which equates her testosterone levels to the equivalence of a male athlete. According to the IAAF, "46 XY 5-ARD (5-alpha-reductase deficiency) athletes"—such as Semenya—have "circulating testosterone at the level of the male 46 XY population and not at the level of the female 46 XX population. This gives 46 XY 5-ARD athletes a significant sporting advantage over 46 XX female athletes."[33]

Intersex athletes, male and female, born with biological factors that cannot be controlled, have also pushed sports agencies to qualify guidelines. Following the IAAF's 2015 ruling that intersex athletes must undergo testosterone therapy, the Court of Arbitration for Sport (CAS) called for more research to be done on the matter.

More scientific evidence revealed that, in fact, hypoandrogenism, which is also known as a difference of sex development, does increase muscle mass, strength, and hemoglobin, which affects endurance for athletic performance, further dividing the sports world regarding intersex and transgender athletes.

For these athletes, the IAAF has argued they should be required to reduce their testosterone levels even lower than the mandated 10 nanomoles per liter to levels lower than 5 nanomoles per liter for middle-distance runners, something that IOC may also be requiring in the future. In the meantime, transgender female athletes with biological advantages continue to be allowed to dominate women's sports.

As one elite athlete noted, "This is a difficult subject because so many within the transgender community are looking for some footing, a place to call their own but in their quest to be equal (as women), they are literally taking us back 100 years.

"What other group besides white men in our society has not had to fight for everything they have in society? Women, all non-whites, those with disability, every group has had to fight. Female athletes are ready to stand with the transgender community. We'll help you fight for what you need but not at the expense of our own progress; not at the expense of seeing the brilliance of female athletes competing against one another. There must be a solution for everyone. But not at the expense of taking from us, our blood, sweat and tears, our records and titles."

WHAT'S THE ANSWER?

Dr. Nicola Williams, a research scientist specializing in human biology, proposed that there remain just two sporting entities: open sport and women's sport. For all biologically nonfemale athletes, open sport is available without question of (natural) testosterone. In elite sport, if the athletes are successful, they will make the team. It is a theory that goes well with what transgender female athletes such as Valentina Petrillo (1974–), Rachel McKinnon (aka Veronica Ivey), and Terry Miller (2002–) have said about simply "being good enough."

Miller, one of two transgender female athletes who claimed fifteen state records in girls' track, responded to complaints of unfairly dominating girls' high school sport by saying that cisgender athletes just needed to try harder.[34] In many respects, when transgender female athletes have made such remarks, it is not done so with disrespect to their fellow sister athletes but truly not understanding the biological differences between male and female muscular, skeletal, integumentary, and nervous systems.

For open sports, the argument would allow all athletes with biologically male consistent levels of testosterone and other physiologies without then unfairly changing women's sport. As Williams points out, "Being a transgender female athlete means they will get medical drugs for hormone repression that are banned for women." More complicated, "the monitoring of these drugs and testosterone levels is not routine. It would take years for a robust system to be put in place" in which governing bodies could test and ensure testosterone levels were regulated and legally accurate. "The reality is, most sports at high school level will never have such testing."

Even then, this does not change the advantages of larger organs, including the heart, allowing for greater oxygen capacity to a more substantial muscle mass, says sports physicist Joanna Harper, a female transgender and former competitive runner. Harper, a Loughborough University PhD researcher in England and the author of the 2019 publication of *Sporting Gender: The History, Science, and Stories of Transgender and Intersex Athletes*, served as an adviser to the IOC and other governing sports bodies and warned of such advantages in sport. During an interview with WebMD, Harper stated that after reviewing research, there was "absolutely no question in my mind that trans women will maintain strength advantages over cis women, even after hormone therapy."[35] She concedes, "What needs to happen over the next 10 to 12 years is we need to get some transgender athletes into exercise labs." More research is needed.[36]

In November 2018, transgender female powerlifter JayCee Cooper (1988–) signed up for two powerlifting meets in Minnesota, including a Therapeutic Use Exemption form that, if approved, allows for the athlete to compete despite taking medication (not allowed for cisgender female athletes). In the case of Cooper, the medication was spironolactone, a testosterone-suppressing medication. When her participation form was denied "because," Cooper said, "'transgenders' have a supposed advantage," there was no recourse but to complete "untested" in another event.[37]

Cooper won state but, four days later, United States Powerlifting (USPL) banned transgender women from competing against cisgender female lifters. As a possible solution, the USPL offered an MX category in which anyone could compete but Cooper declined, stating this "othering" category was unfair and discriminatory. In January 2021, Cooper filed a lawsuit against the USPL for violating the Minnesota Human Rights Act. As Cooper describes it, "I was gutted. I had been training for months and up until that point had experienced so much love and community around the sport."[38]

While Cooper had felt "gutted," so, too, did Beth Stelzer (1985–), who had also used sports (training for years, not months) as a platform to overcome PTSD from a dangerous and abusive relationship that also left her emotionally battered. When she discovered powerlifting, she flourished. When she finally competed, she had the bad luck to do so against Cooper.

When Stelzer spoke up against transgender female athletes competing in the sport, she was harassed both in competition and online, which "really put me down this rabbit hole." Transgender female athletes had been nowhere on her radar. She had only been focused on empowerment through sport when the venue of sport itself became threatening.

"All I had wanted was an event that was a celebration of strong women," she said. "I was a victim . . . a victim of stalking. I needed that space, that safe space to be comfortable around other women, not look over my shoulder, and I'm being screamed at" by transgender athletes' advocates.

Meanwhile, the parents of Penn State swimmers have been speaking anonymously on behalf of their daughters who are too afraid to speak out against their transgender teammate; and national and Olympic athletes from around the world will only speak on the record anonymously out of fear of aggressive transgender advocates and of losing sponsorships—all because they want to have a fair shot in their own sport.

Because Dr. Nicola Williams is also gay, she initially struggled with this issue, asking, "'Why can't people live and let live?' I fully support the right of trans people to live free of fear and discrimination just the same as everyone else, but this isn't the same as the fight for gay rights. When I looked at the facts more closely, I could see this was very different. There was a fundamental conflict between the demands some trans lobby groups were making and the rights of another vulnerable group—women and girls.

"If someone wants to live as though they are the opposite sex, that's their choice and I fully support their right to do so. But . . . to compete against women and girls in sports, and women have no choice about that, that takes away women's most fundamental right; the right to say no to male-bodied people entering our spaces."

Throughout the United Kingdom and United States, what women's rights advocates were hearing (and saying) is, in the continued conversation about testosterone, women had no voice. In willfully omitting hard evidence and medical research, women had no voice. In ignoring the biological differences between male and female bodies, women had no voice.

The conundrum is historic. For centuries women have been told to simply "be sweet" and endure. But as more cisgender females have begun to speak up to preserve female sports on the basis of science, anatomy, and the history of women, if not for a safe space for themselves, they are reminded that women's sports do not belong to them but to sponsors, political platforms, and an extremely small but effective minority group.

When New Zealand powerlifter Laurel Hubbard (1978–), a transgender female, began outlifting all other female competitors at the age of forty-three (an age in which cisgender females become perimenopausal, biologically impacting muscle development and retention, strength, cycles, metabolism, and even memory), easily taking a spot on the women's Olympic team, former lifter Tracey Lambrechs (1985–) spoke up and was quickly told to "be quiet."[39] Among the cycling community, the story is the same. With a rising number of transgender females in a sport in which they excel, cisgender female athletes have been directly ordered to remain quiet at the risk of losing sponsors and/or a place on their own team.

"Women have fought for decades to have access to similar resources as male sports, similar media coverage, pay parity in professional sports—and now that we are actually starting to gain some ground, that's all being put at risk," said Katherine Deves, spokesperson for Save Women's Sport in Australia. Australian track and field Olympian Tamsyn Lewis (1978–) has used her platform to encourage transgender people "to play sport and stay healthy while protecting female sport as a category for girls and women." Until more conclusive research is done, Lewis worries that the rush for inclusion could do more harm than good.[40]

Deves added, "At no time has anyone said people who are transgender or gender diverse can't play sport, but there needed to be a conversation about this and we needed to look at the research, and we needed to hear opinions from everybody." For Deves and so many others, greater frustration comes from the fact that "this has been done without any (mainstream) community consultation or knowledge, no parliamentary or ministerial oversight, no media scrutiny whatsoever."[41] There has been no attention to science.

It was why Stelzer created Save Women's Sports in 2019. "We're back in this toxic environment where women are being told to be quiet about their own bodies and their own rights. We're the silent majority," Stelzer said. This issue, she says, "is the most important thing to happen to women's sports since women's sports began. This is the true beginning of the end of our rights."

THE TRANSGENDER SKEW IN SPORT

Certainly, the rights of women have always been challenged and their voice always silenced for the "good" of others, but in the case of transgender females in sport, what of trans youth whose own health and a place in society remains in jeopardy? Caitlyn Jenner had not been wrong in her assessment of Lia Thomas in terms of negative publicity and blowback upon the trans community, just as Dr. Nicola Williams's "open sport" proposal offers sound solutions. And yet, it does still discriminate against transgender female youth so vulnerable and in need of a support system.

As previously stated, a real solution can only come about when all sporting entities gather for an international summit to establish solid rules, hearing both sides of the debate. In a recent national poll, 38 percent of U.S. adults said that greater acceptance of people who are transgender is generally good for our society, while 32 percent believe it is "bad" and another 29 percent were undecided.[42] In yet another national poll, more Americans supported the idea of allowing transgender men and women in the military, at 66 percent (notably down from 71 percent in 2019), but when asked about transgender females in sport, the vast majority of Americans believe that athletes must play on teams that match biological gender.[43] Even with more Americans identifying as LGBT,[44] the confusion over science, self-identifying, and discriminatory practices throughout educational and sporting agencies regarding transgender females in women's sports is creating negative feelings with long-term impacts on society. Sports, the gateway to acceptance and achievement in society, should be open to everyone.

Creating a "transgender skew" or "TS" that allows transgender athletes, both male and female, to engage in sport where they are most comfortable then recognizes fair play and inclusion. It is the Women's Sports Policy Group, whose mission statement rejects "both the effort to exclude" transgender female athletes from sports as well as the effort to have cisgender female athletes compete against them, that has suggested an asterisk for the sports record books. Says member and tennis legend Martina Navratilova, "It's not about excluding transgender women from winning ever. But it is about not allowing them to win when they were not anywhere near winning as men."[45] At minimum, it is the beginning of a conversation for the inclusion of all athletes with respect to both sport and individuals.

NINETEEN

Title IX in the New Millennium

Prior to Title IX, men's and women's athletic programs operated as two different entities, but when all sports then legally fell into one department, male directors took control. In 1972, 90 percent of the coaches for women's collegiate sports were women. By 2016, just over 40 percent of coaches were women.[1] It is an interesting and repetitive history in women's sports that women have never had full control of their own space. Such is the story of Joanne Washburn.

A "GIANT" IN COLLEGE ATHLETICS HISTORY

For thirty-nine years, Joanne "Jo" Washburn (1937–2020) served as athletic director for women's sports at Washington State University (WSU). In 1979, she joined in a landmark lawsuit against the university that she loved so much when she, along with twenty-one other coaches and thirty-nine athletes, saw how the university responded to the passage of Title IX. There were no full-time female coaches, no full-time (female) assistant coaches, not even separate locker rooms for the individual female athletes. While male athletes took chartered buses to away games, female athletes carpooled in their own cars, paying for gas and food and sleeping as many to a hotel room as possible to save expenses. That was when track athlete Karen Blair Troianello (1958–) became the lead student plaintiff in *Blair vs. Washington State University*—a case that would set a precedent for all public four-year colleges and universities in the state.

After years of litigation, the university settled with three female complainants—Jo Washburn, Sue Durrant (1937–), and Marilyn Mowatt, who had been denied equal pay based on gender. Washburn, however, would pay a penalty of her own. In 1982, when the two athletic departments merged, Washburn was (temporarily) terminated, in spite of the fact that during her time as women's athletic director, she did the seemingly impossible: she "presided over unparalleled growth in the program that supported eight varsity program sports—volleyball, basketball, field hockey, skiing, tennis, track and field, gymnastics and swimming—and saw its budget grow from $2,000 to eclipsing $1 million."[2]

Only through more legal action were Durrant and Washburn reinstated to teaching positions, but neither would hold positions of head coach or director again. Instead, they established women's athletic scholarships at WSU and brought on full-time coaches for women's athletics teams; and women's locker room and training facilities were added, including buses. For Washburn, she was able to see the Sport Management Program that she developed grow from six to more than two hundred majors when she retired in 2004.

In 2012, Washburn was inducted into the WSU Athletic Hall of Fame, also noted for the Washington State University's Sport Management Program that Washburn founded in the early 1980s and still continues today. Washburn is credited for establishing WSU's strong women's athletic program, called "a giant in college athletics history," where Washburn "fought tirelessly for gender equity and ultimately impacted change that continues to benefit generations of student-athletes."[3]

As we celebrate the victories of women, there have been so many more who, as victims of discrimination, simply walked away or, as in the case of Washburn, were forced onto a new path. For all that it felt like Washburn lost in her battle against gender inequity, she created much change. The fight that Washburn, Durrant, and Mowatt, in particular, brought to WSU was not about themselves or the school but for all women.

"We wrote reports, reports, reports, trying to get the University to see that we could be the leader here. Well, we ended up being the leader, but not how we thought we were going to be," Washburn said.[4]

MYTHS ABOUT TITLE IX THAT PERSIST TODAY

When intercollegiate sports opened to women, the number of participants multiplied by five, validating that if given the opportunity, more females become engaged in sport.

Still, the myth that, by enforcing Title IX, schools must cut men's sports programs continues to exist. What has happened, however, is that schools *elect* to drop programs like men's gymnastics, soccer, or wrestling rather than take money from basketball and football program budgets that already consume 75 percent of the average men's athletic expenses.

In 2001, a study supported this with several findings:[5]

- San Diego University decided to "address its $2 million budget deficit" by cutting into its men's volleyball program rather than "cutting slightly" into the $5 million football budget. Just four months later, the football team was outfitted with new uniforms, including brand new titanium facemasks.

- Rutgers University spent $175,000 on hotel rooms for just six football games, totaling more than the entire budget of the men's tennis team, which had previously been eliminated (for the sake of the men's football program).
- Brown University spent $2.5 million to buy out the contract of the football program's head coach, cutting two women's tennis teams to save $64,000.

These universities are only a few examples of dozens of such practices among state universities when it comes to preserving men's basketball and football programs above all else, which leads to yet another myth: men's basketball and football programs finance other sports in colleges. In fact, the costs of these teams do not generate enough revenue to pay for themselves. Certainly, men's basketball and football do not and cannot then afford to cover the costs of other programs. In particular to football teams, rosters boast upwards of 70 (traveling) players with an average of 120 players on the roster. Airline tickets, hotel accommodations, food and ground transportation, not including stadium and bowl fees, are astronomical.

Additionally, it is the culture of the machismo sports that allows for special demands that universities are all too happy to accommodate. When the University of Texas spent $120,000 to repanel the football coach's office in mahogany, no one questioned the Athletic Department's response that there was no money in school coffers to add any programs for women. Nor was it questioned when the University of Oregon spent $3.2 million on a two-story locker room, complete with three sixty-inch plasma televisions, Xboxes, and specialized lighting throughout to allow players to better adjust to sunlight outside.[6] Schools like Oregon State and the University of Oregon, for example, benefit exponentially from outside agreements with private companies. By 2020, Nike was still in an eleven-year, $88 million contract with the University of Oregon that entitles Nike to free "broad and prominent" brand exposure, including three full days of access to the football and basketball head coaches for publicity events while student-athletes must wear the Nike logo and apparel in practices, games, photoshoots, interviews, and press conferences. In 2013 when economist Tim Duy analyzed college athletics, focusing on both football and the University of Oregon, his findings exposed massive debt driven by the football program.

While some of the money from NCAA's Division I sponsorship deals are put back toward scholarship programs promised by the universities, the reality is the majority of the money from the corporate sponsorship deals is funneled into luxury items, such as games and plasma televisions, but also, for the University of Oregon, a $68 million football performance center that boasts handwoven Nepalese rugs and stone imported from China while coaching contracts are into the millions.

In return for lavish stadiums and centers, schools go into debt. The University of Oregon's Athletic Department, for example, spends 17 percent of its budget on interest, which, according to payments scheduled for the next twenty-four years, exceeds $144 million for just three projects. Those numbers "not only worry lenders and hurt the university's credit" but create a relationship in which the university is indebted to private companies more than its mission statement to serve its students and make identifying "quantifiable outcomes of college athletics . . . elusive."[7]

By 2020, the average salary for a NCAA I football coach was $4.3 million in the SEC Division, $3.4 million in the Big 12, $3.1 million in the Big Ten, and $2.7 million in both the ACC and Pac-12.[8] In comparison, the average annual salary for NCAA women's basketball coaches was $41,667.[9] The total cost to universities (and all other sport programs) are further damaged with such contracts as Auburn University's $43 million buyout of its head football coach.

Title IX is not meant to eradicate football. One should not affect the other. This is an important distinction. The practices and expenditures of the University of Oregon described here are done so only to illuminate how the moneymaking machine of its football program is profitable only to the business of football, not students or the institution of higher education. Worse, blatant disregard of federal law has been a persistent problem regarding football and Title IX.

However, football is not the only offender. The NCAA continues inequity with its treatment of other sports, such as baseball and softball. While Baseball's College World Series is one of the NCAA's marquee championships, drawing an average of twenty-two thousand fans per game to Omaha every spring to watch future pros play baseball, the Women's College World Series draws nearly as many television viewers as baseball. In 2019, the softball tournament drew an average of 1 million viewers.

Yet women do not get rest days or weather delays and must play multiple doubleheaders. Until 2011, there were no locker rooms at the tournament; players changed into their uniforms at their hotels or on the bus. There were no bathrooms in the stadium dugout, forcing players to run along the baseline or into the stands to share bathrooms with fans.

Carol Hutchins (1957–), the head softball coach at Michigan, described a longtime sentiment among women's college coaches: "The NCAA never asks, 'What's the least we can do for the men?' With the women, that is always the question. We have to fight to get things. We are fighting with the NCAA, and it all comes down to they do not want to spend the same on the women."[10]

THE MISEDUCATION MISREPRESENTATION

Upon its fortieth anniversary, Title IX had still not lived up to its intended beneficiaries. Schools, on all levels, had and have not properly complied with the laws mostly by fault of miseducation. As long as educators, administrators, coaches, parents, students, and even federal government employees do not understand the scope and range of Title IX, it cannot be as effective. Before Title IX, one in twenty-seven girls participated in sports; by 2015, two in every five girls were playing sports. When funding was granted equally to female athletes, there was a 545 percent increase in the percentage of women in collegiate sports and a 990 percent increase in the percentage of girls playing high school sport.[11] Still, Title IX complaints have risen in the past fifteen years. Athletic complaints were among the fewest while allegations of schools mishandling sexual harassment and/or sexual assaults began to rise in 2006, then rose significantly in 2009.[12]

In 2014, Senator Claire McCaskill (1953–) released findings that suggest more than 20 percent of educational institutions allow the athletic department to investigate sexual assault cases involving their athletes[13] with 40 percent of colleges responding that they "had not conducted a single investigation of sexual assault case in the past five years"—an assertion that the senator, rape crisis centers, and statisticians find "unbelievable."[14]

In 2016, Baylor University's president, Kenneth Starr (1946–), was demoted while its head football coach, Art Briles (1953–), was fired when an independent law firm hired to investigate sexual assault allegations found more than fifty examples of alleged assault in which Starr and Briles were complicit in burying the information, sacrificing the welfare of the victims over keeping a full roster for the Baylor Bears football team. Starr, who became a household name in the United States during the 1990s in his dogged pursuit for "morality" issues of the "Monica Lewinsky Affair," did knowingly "discourage complainants from reporting," engaged in "retaliation against a complainant," and ignored predatory behaviors on campus as president.[15]

In 2017, one lawsuit named over thirty members of the football team as responsible for having committed up to fifty-two rapes, but this was not the first time such incidences or these names came up. In 2013, a Baylor female volleyball player told her coach that she had been gang-raped by five members of the football team. The coach, armed with all five names, reported the incident to Coach Briles who reportedly said, "Those are some bad dudes. Why was she around those guys?"

The rape had happened the prior year and the victim was only beginning to talk about what had happened. Baylor had not yet established a Title IX coordinator, and so the victim's mother approached the university's athletic director who told her that, because her daughter had not reported the crime at the time, there was nothing he could do. This is incorrect. In yet another example, Briles, the athletic director, and police conspired to keep an incident of assault and subsequent death threat "quiet."[16]

At the conclusion of the investigation, there were multiple convictions of players, terminations, and resignations among the Athletic Department and Board of Regents, and a national scandal.

HOW PERVASIVE IS SEXUAL ASSAULT ON CAMPUS?

By 2016, the scandal at Baylor University appeared to have blown over. Two years later, however, more allegations of assault were made, more victims stepped forward, while on-campus results from a national survey showed that Baylor reported just four rapes on campus in the year 2014.[17]

In 2018, Title IX filed a lawsuit against the university on behalf of the victims, both named and unnamed, also revealing just how deep the problem was. According to an affidavit filed in a federal district court in Texas, the Board of Regents former chair Richard Willis (1960–) made a statement that the reason Baylor had "such good [expletive] football players" was because "we have the best blonde-haired, blue-eyed p***y in the State of Texas."[18]

The affidavit also identified ten women who alleged the university mishandled their sexual-assault complaints, as well as evidence of how long the university resisted a Title IX coordinator to be staffed on campus— three years. Patty Crawford, a Title IX coordinator, testified that during the years 2014–2016, she personally witnessed how sexual-misconduct matters were handled and attested that numerous board members, administrators, and "powerful" faculty members "didn't see Title IX compliance as a priority; some were opposed to the federal gender-equity law on religious grounds." Crawford was routinely discouraged from tracking or maintaining any "formal records of Title IX-related things." She said, "It was a pattern of things—we don't want things documented."[19]

Yet, when the independent investigation released its findings, Willis officially responded, saying, "We were horrified by the extent of these acts of sexual violence on our campus. This investigation revealed the University's mishandling of reports in what should have been a supportive, responsive and caring environment for students."[20] This was the same Willis, who stood on a religious, moral high ground opposing gender equity, displaying surprise at the misogynistic culture on campus yet was all too pleased to serve up "blonde-haired, blue-eyed p***y" for his football team. Unfortunately, the problem is far greater than Willis, Starr, Briles, and/or Baylor; this culture thrives on campuses across the nation. Had these universities and faculty understood the benefits of Title IX, gender equity, proper training, and education, and implemented and followed its policies, many such stories would have very different endings.

CHANGING (TITLE IX) HISTORY

Title IX was introduced to end discrimination on the basis of sex. The focus was education because education offers more opportunity. By 1975, however, its interpretation on athletics stirred far more controversy than allowing women on campus. The language itself was clear. For example, if 50 percent of the students are female, those students should then receive 50 percent of athletic scholarships. Instead, institutions claimed that females were not that interested in sports and, therefore, the majority of the money should be allocated to the male sports.

Legally, not only colleges but elementary, secondary, and high school programs, from physical education classes to club and varsity athletic programs, including equipment, coaching, and facilities must be equal. For decades, the unspoken practice was simply to not offer those opportunities to females. Citing a *Harvard Law Review* article with the subtitle "Using Title IX to Fight Gender Role Oppression," Ninth Circuit judge Cynthia Holcomb Hall (1929–2011) stated that Title IX "recognizes that, where society has conditioned women to expect less than their fair share of the athletic opportunities, women's interest in participating in sports will not rise to a par with men's overnight."

In fact, this is what happened. But when more opportunities became available, the number of female athletes—of all ages—rose dramatically. As Judge Hall explained it, women's attitudes toward sports were socially constructed and historically limited through practices of discrimination, peer pressure, gender stereotyping, even guilt. "Congress passed Title IX to combat such discrimination and stereotypes, thereby changing the social environment in which girls and women develop, or do not develop, interests in sport."

One of the biggest problems, however, is "fewer than 50 percent of educators understand what Title IX covers and . . . only a miniscule percent of students and parents are aware of their rights under Title IX." A 2007 study conducted by the Mellman Group revealed that 80 percent of those surveyed strongly supported Title IX but 60 percent did not know what steps to take to enforce compliance.[21]

Ironically, within the sport world, certifications and continued education are part of the job. As part of professional development, coaches at NCAA institutions are required to learn the rules governing recruiting and pass an exam before they are permitted to recruit athletes. Yet 60 percent were uninformed as to how Title IX compliance works. Arguably, however, it should not take a certification to understand what equal treatment looks like.

In a presentation by civil rights attorney Nancy Hogshead-Makar (1962–), the founder of Champion Women and named as one of the most influential people in the history of Title IX by *Sports Illustrated*, equal treatment of athletes means simply that men's and women's sports would be equally featured, with equal prominence, on school and athletic department websites and social media with equal support, marketing, and promotional dollars.

Schools would invest equally in cameras and production equipment for women's and men's sports, also to include sports jerseys, apparel, and memorabilia. They should have equal medical care, athletic training access, including nutritional guidance and access to dining halls.

Though seemingly obvious, the continued references to women's appearance over performance among commentators should stop, including prioritizing sports by gender. To this, the practice of displaying "basketball" (to mean "men's") and women's basketball should be equally presented as "men's basketball" and "women's basketball."

Coaches, trainers, and competition officials should be given equal compensation with the school's band and cheerleaders also supporting women's athletics.

WOMEN WHO STAND

Soccer legend Kristine Lilly (1971–), who made the U.S. Women's National Team (USWNT) at age sixteen, had no real female role models to look to in her own sport growing up. When she made the 1987 U.S. team, she suddenly found herself surrounded by role models. "It was pretty amazing to see women like me who loved the game, who wanted to compete, wanted to be the best."

For Lilly, who retired in 2011, it is the *image*—not the athlete—that needs to change in women's sports.

Women and female athletes, in particular, have long been aware of the long-term damage of sexualized female images, yet very little research has been done on how males respond to nonobjectified female images.

In 2011, Dr. Heidi Wartena and Dr. Elizabeth Daniels of the Center for Critical Sports Studies examined the responses of U.S. boys between the ages of twelve and seventeen to images of performance [female] athletes, sexualized athletes, and sexualized models.

When subjects were shown a picture of Brandi Chastain, for example, she was described as "sporty," "powerful," and "talented," illustrating how "youth make instrumental evaluations of female athletes when they are portrayed playing a sport" while sexualized images were objectified, scrutinized, and minimalized.[22] When shown sexualized female athletes who posed for *SI*'s swimsuit issue and covers for men's magazines, their athletic abilities and accomplishments in sport were diminished. This is significant as many female athletes today view sexualized media opportunities as a positive marketing tool, not understanding that their objectified boost in visibility carries negative consequences. The greater a female athlete's sexual image, the lessening of her perceived ability in sport occurs.

Brandi Chastain. *Reuters/Alamy Stock Photo*

Each time an athlete buys into the idea that she must pose to please, the wedge of equality between men and women is widened. Female athletes who accept objectification as empowerment do so at a social cost. Their own self-objectification reinforces the male/media focus on appearance over ability, increasing self-esteem and worth issues among females while also alienating female viewership and athletes from the sport conversation. Females are expected to accept provocative female role models in sport as ideal.[23]

As a strong female role model, Lilly sees the need to empower both boys and girls through leadership. "We need to show boys and girls that women can stand before you and coach the game. Girls see this and say, 'I can do that,' but boys will also say, 'Oh, they can do that, too.' It is so important for kids to see women before them."

The women of the U.S. soccer team did just that when they took yet another stand for equal pay. The U.S. women's soccer team long dominated the international women's World Cup, medaling in every World Cup and Olympic tournament from 1991 to 2015. However, one of their greatest achievements as a team came in 2017 when U.S. Women's Soccer and U.S. Soccer ratified a collective bargaining agreement (a written agreement regarding rights and conditions of employees, i.e., female soccer players, through negotiations with management) to include the fight for equal pay. Ironically, while the USWNT were outselling and outperforming the men's team (including merchandise, ticket sales, fan base, and medals), they would not yet see equal pay. By 2018, the U.S. women's soccer team had won four Olympic gold medals and three World Cups; the U.S. men had not won any. Yet the men, despite the fact that the U.S. women's soccer team also played more games and brought in more revenue in 2017, were paid significantly more than female players.[24]

The image of the female athlete is not just one of ability but one who can and does stand up for her rights, elicits positive change, and fights for others.

WHEN WOMEN TAKE A KNEE

On August 14, 2016, during a preseason NFL game, San Francisco 49ers quarterback Colin Kaepernick (1987–) took a knee as the national anthem played. It was his silent protest in response to increased violence he perceived against Black people on the part of police in the United States. It was not his first time to take a knee, but it was the first time it garnered national attention.

#TakeAKnee4Me and #TakeTheKnee hashtags designed to bring attention to social injustices became a gesture that was both instantly controversial and deeply misunderstood. Suddenly, there were #Stand-ForTheFlag and #BoycottNFL hashtags as counterprotests that claimed greater patriotism. In fact, Kaepernick's decision to take a knee came from the advice of former NFL player and former active-duty U.S. Army Green Beret Nate Boyer. Kaepernick had been looking for a way to protest the situation, not his nation, so "we sat in the lobby of the team hotel, discussed our situation, our different opinions," Boyer said. "And that's where the kneeling began."[25]

Mere days after Kaepernick took a knee, the entire team of WNBA's Indiana Fever took a knee. They would be the first team in any professional, collegiate, or high school sport to take the knee in complete solidarity, after which their coach, Stephanie White (1977–), told them, "I'm proud of y'all for doing that together. That's big. It's bigger than basketball."[26]

What made the gesture all the more heroic was, unlike Kaepernick who was earning almost $12 million a year when he kneeled (and would later earn a deal with Nike, netting him a reported $39.4 million),[27] the women had much more to lose. Kaepernick was earning more than 150 times the WNBA women who took a knee. In fact, female athletes, particularly WNBA players, have taken up social causes for years, risking their careers as the league struggled because they were the mothers of "believe in something, even if it meant sacrificing everything." Minnesota Lynx and New York Liberty team members wore #BlackLivesMatter shirts at a press conference, for which they were all cited for uniform violation and initially fined.

When the Los Angeles Sparks, again as a team, elected to stay in their locker room during the national anthem for "unity and solidarity,"[28] they did so with the understanding of just what they were sacrificing. They did not have megamillion-dollar sponsors, corporations, high-profile politicians backing them. Earning salaries less than what most computer programmers make, theirs was a stand (or kneel) for social justice, willing to risk it all. Yet their voices, their actions, even their names were invisible in the media while far bigger male names were highlighted as they began to kneel a year later.[29]

By the sheer fact that these athletes had fought so hard for their right to play ball, they were already seasoned activists.

In 1968, the historic raised-fisted protest by Tommie Smith and John Carlos at the Olympic Games was not the only protest; two Black cheerleaders also raised their fists during the national anthem in protest of racial discrimination. Just as women have fought to ride a bicycle, wear pants in public, compete in the Olympic Games, go to college, join the military, and earn equal pay, Black cheerleaders simply wanted to cheer.

During the 1950s and '60s, Black girls, already limited in athletics, began to fight for their right to join cheerleading squads. Using local

NAACP chapters, students and parents threatened legal action and reminded schools of constitutional laws that prohibited discrimination. By the 1960s, in a quest to have fair representation among cheerleading and majorette squads, Black Americans picketed, staged walkouts and sit-ins, and wrote to their state representatives and school superintendents for something that was already legally theirs—the right to cheer in their own schools. Yet the fight for inclusion persisted well into the 1970s. As one student noted during a walkout in Gastonia, North Carolina, "They want our boys to play on their teams and win the games but they don't want our girls to cheer for them."[30]

Black girls and women persisted in their rights to cheer and it came (slowly) to fruition not on moral or legal grounds—for across the country, particularly in the southern states, schools actively ignored law—but to combat interracial dating. As more colleges and universities filled its rosters with Black male athletes, and later added Black studies courses and (minimally) Black faculty, the Black cheerleader was added.

It was two Black Yale cheerleaders who stood before the teams and fans at a 1968 Yale vs. Dartmouth football game and raised their fists and still more Black cheerleaders from Northern Illinois University who protested the treatment of Black students by walking off the basketball court during the national anthem, as well as Black cheerleaders from Brown University who refused to stand during the national anthem in 1973.[31]

But the first known athlete to protest was track and field athlete Eroseanna "Rose" Robinson (1925–1976) during the Pan American Games in 1959. Robinson was "consumed" by the injustices she saw around her and decided to use her athletic platform to cast an unflattering light on segregation, inequality, and war, all of which she vehemently opposed.

These were not her first acts of protests, however. In the early 1950s, Robinson led protests at a segregated skating rink, zigging in and out of the white-only crowd, using her athletic prowess to forcibly integrate the rink.[32] When angry white skaters broke Robinson's arm, it only steeled her resolve. Yet, despite such contributions to sport and activism, Robinson has been forgotten.

According to Harry Edwards, founder of the Olympic Project for Human Rights and professor of sports sociology at University of California at Berkeley, this loss is not a surprise as female activist athletes are "often not mentioned . . . They and their activist contributions typically have been diminished if not completely dismissed, ignored, and forgotten by the sports media and even many sports historians."

The visibility of women, or lack thereof, would be challenged still by the new female athlete less interested in traditional sports. She is the game changer, the Wonder Woman, the Amazon, the Rose Robinson of modern times.

TWENTY

Game Changers

Introduced as a "Real-Life Lara Croft,"[1] American Lauren McGough (1987–) is one of the original game changers in women's modern history. A pilot, skydiver, anthropologist, and falconer who travels the world, McGough defies the hegemonic feminine ideal.

Awarded a Fulbright Scholarship in 2009 to live and train with the Kazakh Berkutchi, a nomadic people of Mongolia, McGough began to perfect the craft of falconry with eagles and embodied the history of ancient female hunters.

As McGough's reputation grew, she became one of the most widely respected Western falconers—male or female. Media images of falconers are usually male royalty, military figures, or tribal leaders, not women and certainly not a ponytailed American woman who began her craft as a child in Oklahoma.

Lauren McGough taps into ancestral roots. *Photo by Robert M Palmer*

"For a lot of falconers, we were born falconers; we just didn't know it," McGough said. That is, until that sprit was awakened. "At 14, I didn't know [falconry] was a thing," but once she did, she was singularly focused. She devoured books, studied, became a licensed falconer, built an aviary, found a mentor, traveled, and trained. She earned her PhD in anthropology, and she learned to hunt.

The practice of working with birds of prey originated between 4000 and 6000 BC but has only recently been acknowledged as a likely form of hunting for females. While Greek mythology depicted Amazon warriors working with birds of prey, archaeological discoveries across ancient Scythia (today's Ukraine and southern Russia into China) revealed that the nomadic women of the steppe also hunted on horseback with dogs and raptors.

An ancient gold ring (ca. 425 BC) displayed at the Boston Museum of Fine Arts in 2014 depicted an image labeled as "Amazon," with a nomadic horsewoman, a dog in the image of a sight hound known to hunt with eagle hunters in Central Asia, and a large bird flying overhead. Until this time, the bird was thought merely decorative. Then photographs were published of Makpal Abdrazakova (ca. 1997–), the only known female golden eagle hunter in Kazakhstan,[2] and historian Adrienne Mayor (1946–) linked the images.[3]

During McGough's falconry career, there has been a significant growth among female handlers, but when she began in 2000, "there were no real female mentors," although she did follow the career of Frances Hamerstrom. "She died in 1998 so I never got to meet her [Hamerstrom] but just knowing about her, [that] she flew eagles, was inspiring."

Frances "Fran" Hamerstrom (1907–1998) was an author, naturalist, and ornithologist, and known for her "unladylike" behavior. Rather than adhere to the conventional feminine pursuits of interest, Hamerstrom liked to hunt, keep wild animals, and wear pants. She often hid her outdoor attire in poison ivy, something she was immune to, to keep her family from taking her "gear."[4]

Like Hamerstrom's, McGough's and Abdrazakova's commitment to birds of prey transcends societal norms. It's a beautiful image—the image of a lone female falconer, tracking and hunting with just her bird, both contented and confident to strike out on their own, honing ancestral skills of a centuries-old sport. It is an image we cannot afford to lose.

THE GIRLS OF WRESTLING

Perhaps equally important is the image of the Spartan woman engaged in the early sport of wrestling. Khutulun (1260–1306), great-great-granddaughter of Genghis Khan, was not only a fierce warrior, but also a champion wrestler. When she was instructed to marry, she agreed to do so only if a man could best her in a wrestling match. Her conditions: Win and she would marry; lose and you owe 100 horses. According to historians who witnessed the matches, including Marco Polo (1254–1324), Khutulun quickly amassed 10,000 horses—and no husband.

Following the passage of Title IX in 1972, a few brave girls entered wrestling contests, but it was the 1990s that saw the greatest rise in high school female wrestlers. By the new millennium, they had found a home. Yet, as female wrestlers entered into the sport, coaches noted boys were leaving wrestling. Wrestling advocates blamed Title IX and female participants for declining numbers, but the reality is, across the nation, there had been a 70 percent drop among both boys and girls in organized youth sports by adolescence.[5] According to *Open Access Journal of Sports Medicine*, by the age of fifteen, as many as 80 percent of teenagers leave sports.[6]

Girls had not strangled the sport of wrestling but saved it. As the number of male wrestlers left, girls—who have historically looked for athletic opportunities beyond the socially acceptable formats—took to the wrestling mats. From 1994, the number of female high school wrestlers grew from 804 to 16,562 in 2019, with numbers still rising. In 2020, twenty-eight states had official girls' wrestling programs with sanctioned state championships, with forty-six colleges and universities sponsoring women's wrestling at the varsity level, according to the National Wrestling Coaches Association.[7]

Michaela Hutchison (1989–) made history in 2006 by becoming the nation's first girl to win a state high school championship against boys, and her victory opened doors for other girls in wrestling. She went on to wrestle in college (as a four-time All-American and three-time Women's Collegiate Wrestling Association National Champion for the Oklahoma City University) and now coaches wrestling at McKendree University Stars.[8]

Mildred Bliss, also known as Mildred Burke (1915–1989), was one of the true pioneers of women's professional wrestling. Her career began in 1934 as she and her husband/manager traveled on the carnival circuit, offering $25 (more than $300 today) to anyone who could pin Burke in under ten minutes. No one ever could or did.

From 1935 to 1954, Burke took on over 150 men and five thousand women, becoming so well known that she graced the cover of *Life* magazine, appeared in *Ripley's Believe It or Not*, became a regular on radio talk and sports channels, and single-handedly brought credibility to women's wrestling. She was a three-time women's world champion, she won the first-ever National Wrestling Alliance (NWA) Women's Championship, and she is in the Professional Wrestling Hall of Fame. Her record was

5,149 wins and one loss that remains contested as, following a bitter divorce, her husband used wrestling connections to guarantee the loss as a punishment to his former wife.[9]

Sixty-five years after Burke's last fight, Cassy Jakoubek (1996–) introduced herself to a Denver high school girl's wrestling team for the first time. For the girls, however, the name meant nothing until the coach offered her wrestling name—Cassy Herkelman, the first girl in her state's history to win a contested match when her opponent refused to fight a female. Almost instantly, Herkelman-Jakoubek said, the phones came out and she watched as her new student-athletes googled her name. "You could see the lights go on. They were like, 'Oh, OK,' as they read 'first girl to win a match at the Iowa state tournament,' 'Cadet national champ and two-time Junior national finalist,' and 'two-time All-American.'"[10] Like Hutchison, Jakoubek is helping other girls to succeed in wrestling.

The impact of female athletes in wrestling is another example of the symbiotic relationship between women and sport. Not only have they helped save one of the oldest known sports in history but, in return, they now had new educational, social, and economic opportunities through collegiate scholarships, competitive opportunities, coaching careers, and, with the inception of women's wrestling in the Olympic Games (2004), potential sponsorship and marketing deals.

THE WOMEN OF THE WPFL

In 1926, NFL teams had female football players take the field at halftime to entertain the fans.[11] Female athletes also participated in exhibition games in 1930 and 1931. Despite evidence of "financial success," the idea of women playing a full-contact sport was denounced as "exploiting womanhood," when the truth was there were more volunteers than the female rosters could hold. Women always wanted in, it was just a matter of organization and *permission*.

Just as women's basketball went through a number of professional formats—such as the American Basketball League (ABL), the Women's Basketball Development Association (WBDA), the Women's American Basketball Association (WABA), and finally, the Women's National Basketball Association (WNBA)—so too has women's football. The Women's Professional Football League (WPFL), created in 1965, was resurrected in the '70s, and once more in 1999. There were also the National Women's Football League (NWFL) in 1974, the American Football Verband Deutschland (American Football Association of Germany; AFVD) in 1986, the National Women's Football Association (NWFA) in 2000, and the Independent Women's Football League (IWFL) in 2002.

Women's professional football found its footing by 2002. While the WPFL struggled to reestablish itself, the NWFA grew to twenty-one teams in five divisions. Originally called the NWFL, its owner, Catherine Masters, who was inducted into the American Football Association's Semi Pro Football Hall of Fame in 2006, was forced to change the name in 2002 to the NWFA. By 2009, however, the NWFA was dissolved,[12] allowing the more profitable Women's Football Alliance (WFA) to step in.

A hiccup for serious footballers was the establishment of the Legends Football League (LFL) in 2003—a new league in which players wore lingerie. Its participants argued that they were every bit as strong and athletic as their full-gear/full-tackle, fully clothed female counterparts while *McCall's* magazine wrote, "It's offensively exploitive and sexist. Women who want to play full-contact, tackle football and be taken seriously should wear what men wear. It's that simple. So many people have worked hard to put women's sports on the map and create opportunities for female athletes. This league is a step backward."[13]

Coach Dee Kennamer (1957–) was a serious pioneer determined to showcase female athletes as legitimate football players. Hers is a story that is both legendary and commonplace within the world of women's football. Approached about the WPFL Texas team Austin Rage, Kennamer and partner Donna Roebuck believed the timing was right and bought in. Fully. They bought the equipment and jerseys needed, they leased a stadium, paid for the electricity, paid for staff, tickets, and so forth. "We knew we would never see that money again," Kennamer said, but they hoped that investing in the future would pay off. The following year, however, the WPFL front office had no explanation for lack of funds, unpaid bills, and zero marketing plans. Money that had been pooled by individual franchise owners for marketing and advertising had disappeared. Without sponsors, marketing or any media awareness, the dream was over.

PLAYING WITH RAGE

On paper, Kim Mott (1964–) should not have been a football player. Historically, there were many things the 5'2" female should not have been. She should not have been in the U.S. Army or served as a heavy wheel mechanic or done construction in the late 1980s. Yet, when she stepped onto the field after she and a group of friends answered a flyer for "try-outs" for the WPFL, her life changed.

Mott, like her Austin Rage teammates, never earned a paycheck. "But that's not why I played. It was for the opportunity, to do something I loved." Twenty years later, Mott is the quintessential female athlete who made lifelong friends and continues to support all female sports and athletes because "when you allow one female into anything, to whatever, there has always been progress. Always." Opportunity, though the women of the WPFL were given so little, changed everything.

It is not just the female athlete but those female leaders—coaches, politicians, pioneers—who took up the game or race so that others could simply experience opportunity. Mott says that bodybuilder and pioneering powerlifter Bev Francis helped her, Mott, first realize her own power. She also credits Kennamer and Roebuck for giving her the opportunity to play professional ball. "They gave us a voice." Although Kennamer and Roebuck never personally saw their investment "pay off," their planting the seed of professional female football players did take root.

It was from the shoulders of the women of the WPFL, the NWFA, and all the other prior leagues that the Women's Football Alliance, the largest and longest-running women's tackle football league in the world, prevailed. With forty-seven teams, however, the league is still "all passion, no pay," with players practicing nights and weekends after working full-time jobs. Yet, visibility and progress are slowly being made. In fact, the quarterback for six-time league champions Boston Renegades, Allison Cahill (1981–), is the first female QB to have her jersey enshrined in the Pro Football Hall of Fame in Canton, Ohio.[14]

THE CONCEPT OF CULTURE AND
WOMEN'S RIGHT TO PLAY AND COACH

When Kennamer's dream with the WPFL ended, she could not have imagined that, because of her, another dream would be realized. But for American football Hall of Famer and coach Chenell "SoHo" Tillman-Brooks (1966–), this is precisely what happened when she was named the first female full-time defensive coordinator for a men's semipro football league with the Virginia Crusaders in 2020.

Before joining the Crusaders, Tillman-Brooks rose through the ranks (as coach) within the WPFL and IWFL leagues, was selected as the head coach for the IWFL All-Star games, coached at the prestigious Manning Passing Academy, and was just one of two female coaches to participate in the Football Coaching Internship at Dartmouth College.

"Coming into this gig," Tillman-Brooks said of moving to Virginia to coach the Crusaders, she was certain she would have to prove herself to the male players. "But, evidently, the coaching staff in place had already placed my resume in front of the guys." The once hard-hitting player with a league-wide reputation had an equally impressive coaching reputation that transcended gender lines.

In 2021, Tillman-Brooks's team played an intense rivalry that included insults from the other team. "They were yelling, 'You guys ain't gonna stop us. You're coached by a woman! Women shouldn't coach football! Women don't know football.' Needless to say, that fired up my defense. We had their QB running for his life the whole game! Their only score came off of a breakdown in discipline. My defense had three interceptions and a fumble recovery to seal the game."

For Tillman-Brooks, greater validation for her time on the gridiron has come not only from her female athletes but the male players who fully embraced her as coach, telling her "that I can't leave and I can't go to another team . . . I'm where I'm meant to be."

Tillman-Brooks was by no means the first to break into men's sports as a coach. Lanny Moss is believed to be the first full-time female general manager in the minor leagues back in 1974.[15] In 1989, Julie Croteau became the first female to play on an NCAA men's baseball team and, though she would later quit due to persistent sexual harassment and sexism on the team, she returned for another "first," as the first female assistant coach in NCAA baseball at New England University in 1993. In 2001, Lisa Boyer (1967–) became the first female assistant coach in the NBA when she was hired by the Cleveland Cavaliers.

Chenell Tillman-Brooks. *Courtesy of Chenell Tillman-Brooks*

For decades, sports historians and women's sports advocates have called for female coaches and referees to represent all sporting venues, noting both their expertise and the need for visibility. According to sports economist Andrew Zimbalist of Smith College, women in sports have always been in an *out-of-sight, out-of-mind* predicament; "because they have been neglected as professional athletes, and their leagues have been under-advertised and under-promoted," the idea that women could lead or referee men's sports had then never been seriously entertained.[16] That is, until Donnie Nelson.

Donnie Nelson (1962–) followed in the footsteps of his father, Don Nelson (1940–), a Hall of Fame coach distinguished with the most wins of any coach in NBA history. Both Nelsons became NBA executives with an eye for talent. Donnie Nelson, in particular, was named the third-best general manager of the decade in 2009, and was credited for assembling the Dallas Mavericks 2011 NBA Championship team but also for hiring a woman to coach.

Nancy Lieberman (1958–), aka Lady Magic, had made a name for herself long before, becoming a member of the USA National team at age seventeen as well as a member of the first-ever women's Olympic basketball team. Winning a silver at the Montreal 1976 Games, having just turned eighteen, Lieberman also became the youngest basketball player in Olympic history to win a medal.

After the United States boycotted the 1980 Olympics, Lieberman turned pro in 1981; was inducted into both the Basketball Hall of Fame and the Women's Basketball Hall of Fame; and also had the distinction of being a player, general manager, and head coach within the WNBA. Lieberman's resume was outstanding. She was the first two-time winner of the Wade Trophy, awarded as women's basketball's best player, the first woman to play in a men's pro league, and when the WNBA was finally formed in 1997, then-thirty-nine-year-old Lieberman played for a season, becoming the oldest player in league history. She would return in 2008, at age fifty, to play a game just to beat her own record

Lieberman (and Nelson) would make sports history when Nelson hired Lieberman to be head coach of the NBA Development League team Nelson put together in November 2009. For Nelson, choosing the right coach had never been about male or female; he needed to choose someone well known in the basketball world, who had strong coaching experience and credibility among the players. The idea of a female had not even entered his mind. By chance, he bumped into Lieberman at a local Starbucks and wondered to himself, *Why not her?*

Lieberman would go on to become just the second woman to act as an assistant coach in the NBA in 2015 with the Sacramento Kings before she left in 2017 to become a broadcaster and also serve as a head coach for Power in the BIG3 league, leading the team to the 2018 Championship.

Until August 2014, no female had acted as a full-time head or assistant coach in the NBA, NFL, NHL, or MLB. Becky Hammon made news when the San Antonio Spurs brought her in as the first full-time assistant coach with full benefits in the NBA. But Hammon made *international* news in 2019 when the Spurs head coach, Gregg Popovich, was ejected from a game and Hammon stepped in, acting as the first-ever female head coach in the NBA. In 2021, Hammon accepted a full-time coaching position in the WNBA, returning to the very place "I come from."[17]

Chan Yuen-ting of Hong Kong became the first woman to coach a men's professional football (soccer) team in 2016, while Alhambra Nievas of Spain and Joy Neville of Ireland became the first two women referees to take charge of the men's rugby union internationals in the Rugby Europe Conference that same year.

Jen Welter (1977–) became the first female running back in a men's professional league in February 2014, when she played for the Texas Revolution of the Champions Indoor Football League. At just 5'2" and 130 pounds, she was also became the first woman to coach (part-time) in the NFL in 2015 when she interned as a defensive coach for the Arizona Cardinals during training camp. That same year the NFL also hired Sarah Thomas (1973–), the first female on-field official. (In 2012, Shannon Eastin from the Mid-Eastern Athletic Conference served as a line judge during the lockout of game officials at the start of the seasons, but Thomas would become the first full-time on-field official.)

Thomas had not started out with the hopes of officiating at the NFL level. In fact, the former collegiate basketball player had, like most NFL officials, gotten into officiating only when she realized how much she missed sports. By 1996, she became the first female referee in a Division I-A high school football game in Mississippi. By 2007, she began officiating college games, then championship games in 2010 and 2014.[18]

On February 7, 2021, Thomas became the first woman to ever officiate the Super Bowl, arguably one of the largest and most recognized sporting events in the world. For Thomas, who had been advised not to allow her blond ponytail to attract attention when she first began officiating, Super Bowl LV was no longer "about my hair anymore." For Thomas to recognize and be recognized as just another official is what progress is all about.[19]

In baseball, Alyssa Nakken (1990–) became the first woman to coach in the MLB in 2020, also becoming the first on-field female coach when she acted as first base coach during exhibition games for the San Francisco Giants against the Oakland A's. In that same year, Kim Ng (1968–) was named general manager of the Miami Marlins, becoming the first woman to serve as GM of one of the "big four" in professional sports in the United States and the first person of East Asian descent.[20]

Women have begun to break into the men's game in the front office, as well. In 2017, Kim Davis (est. 1957–) broke real barriers when she joined the NHL as the highest-ranking Black executive, male or female, as senior executive vice president, whereas Blake Bolden (1991–) became not only the first Black woman to play professional hockey in the NWHL but also the first Black woman to act as a professional scout for the NHL's L.A. Kings.

Jessica Berman (est. 1978–) left the NHL to become the highest-ranking women in men's professional sports when she became deputy commissioner and executive vice president of the National Lacrosse League (NLL) in 2019.

In 2018, Stephanie Sharpe (1980–) coached in the NFL, selected by the Atlanta Falcons before turning her attention to NCAA, where she works with Division I athletes. Deeply respected by all her athletes, like Kristine Lily, Sharpe believes standing (and coaching) before elite male and female athletes is when and where change begins.

THE WONDER WOMAN EFFECT

In 2009, a television show called *American Ninja Warrior* (*ANW*) showcased elite male and female athletes overcoming extremely challenging obstacles as a timed event. Unlike the Japanese version (which inspired *ANW*), the *ANW* competition is one of the very few in the world in which male and female athletes compete against one another, on the same obstacles with the same expectations for performance. No modifications.

Ninjas such as Meagan Martin (1989–), a former gymnast, pole vaulter, and competitive rock climber; Jesse "Flex" Labreck (1990–), a former hurdler and heptathlete; and Jessie Graff (1984–), stuntwoman, martial artist, and former pole vaulter, became some of the most popular ninjas on the circuit—male or female.

In 2017, former gymnast Barclay Stockett (1994–), at just 5'0", "may be the strongest athlete out here, male or female, pound for pound," according to commentator Matt Iseman. Stockett became the shortest competitor in *ANW* history to make it up the finish wall, make it through the spider jump, and was the shortest to conquer the warp wall in the Vegas competition. Yet Stockett was once embarrassed by her muscular arms, just as Jessie Graff tried to hide her muscularity in stunt work.

Graff had taken to wearing different "super" costumes while she attacked the ninja courses and had earned a huge fan base. Also trained in seven different styles of martial arts, including a black belt in tae kwon do and a black sash in kung fu, as well as pole vaulting, Graff mesmerized audiences, including film producer Patty Jenkins who had noticed Graff, who had been wearing a Wonder Woman costume for *ANW*, and brought Graff onto the *Wonder Woman* set to stunt.

With the 2017 release of *Wonder Woman*, which made more than $820 million worldwide, came a shift for female producers and stuntwomen dubbed "the Wonder Woman effect." Suddenly, they were more marketable. The visual of the all-female cast of Amazons, including Graff, who stunted as Wonder Woman, then brought on a new kind of #GirlPower.

What all the ninjas have found is it is not only girls and women they have impacted but boys and men as well. For Martin, the competition showcases how female athletes and ninjas come "in all shapes and sizes" and demonstrates what women can really do. "We give girls something other than looks to strive for," Martin said. "We show them that strength and agility [are] beautiful, that being confident and capable is better."

SUPER MOMS

In 2019, world and Olympic champions Alysia Montaño (1986–), Kara Goucher (1978–), and Allyson Felix (1985–) broke nondisclosure agreements to reveal "stories we athletes know are true but have been too scared to tell publicly: If we have children, we risk pay cuts from our sponsors during pregnancy and afterward," Felix shared. "It's one example of a sports industry where the rules are still mostly made for and by men."[21]

In particular to Felix, a nine-time Olympic medalist, the pay cut was 70 percent of her salary because of her pregnancy. She says she was told by Nike to "know her place" when she pushed back against the discriminatory policy. Nike later changed its contract reductions for pregnant athletes, but Felix wondered why public shaming was required for change to happen.[22]

A 2018 study revealed that nearly a quarter of women in the U.S. workforce fear telling an employer about a pregnancy, indicating maternity rights have not improved. While 78 percent of working mothers feel they must work much harder than coworkers to "get ahead," nearly half of the coworkers studied believe working mothers are 41 percent less dedicated to their jobs while believing a new father is 75 percent *more* dedicated to his job.

However, corporate leaders disagreed, stating that working mothers were harder working, better prepared, better listeners, and more willing to be team players while also handling emergency situations better than working fathers. Yet, within these same interviews, negative stereotypes about working mothers persisted.[23]

More than two dozen Olympic and professional mother-athletes interviewed each indicated that she was a better athlete *because* she was a mother. But Felix was the one to openly challenge the system. Felix left Nike and went on, ten months after her C-section, to win her twelfth gold medal at the World Championships, breaking Usain Bolt's record. At the 2021 Tokyo Olympic Games, she won bronze in the 400-meter dash, making her the most decorated female Olympian in track-and-field history, and only the second U.S. track athlete (with Carl Lewis) to win ten Olympic medals.

It took the most decorated woman in Olympic track-and-field history to showcase the strength of all mothers and fight back against sexism and discrimination.

TRAIL SISTERS

Outside Hollywood and the Olympic Games, away from media attention, Gina Lucrezi (1983–) quietly started a revolution of her own for inclusion and empowerment, tucked away on hidden trails and rocky terrain. It began not from desire but necessity.

Lucrezi had always been a runner, saying, "I hated it but was good at it." So good that she became a ten-time collegiate All-American and national champion (in the 1,500-meter) before turning professional. After earning her master's degree in sports management, Lucrezi interned at the United States Olympic Committee in Colorado Springs. That was where she discovered trail running, earned a position with *Trail Runner* magazine, and fell in love with the grueling aspect of trail running. She also began to note the disparities between how men and women runners were treated.

"I started to see how representation and opportunities for women in this sport was. Why was a guy doing the same [competition] as me, getting paid more than I was? Why do men have eight different versions of a team t-shirt while women got three? Why are men always featured first? Why are the results always starting with the men's and then trickle down to the women? Why? Why? Why? I almost couldn't stop seeing all the differences and, at times, I wished I could because it drove me nuts." But the more she saw, it became impossible to ignore.

So Lucrezi created Trail Sisters in 2016, an online site for the purpose of sharing inspirational articles. The site quickly became a platform for equity. Lucrezi's mission was simple: "Female voice and representation are essential in the future of our outdoors, impacting the role we play both on and off the trails. . . . To break through long-standing barriers, Trail Sisters generates educational content and resources, while fostering an inspirational community that encourages self-advocacy and life-long friendships."[24]

Along with seven friends, Lucrezi grew Trail Sisters to more than 130 running groups throughout the United States, Canada, and Europe, inviting all women, from novice walkers to elite professional runners who wanted a sense of community.

Since 2016, Lucrezi has been approached by some of the largest corporations in the fitness and sports world, hoping to tap into Trail Sisters' popularity, but Lucrezi returned the rewards right back into her community rather than selling her "brand."

"We're not a brand, not media; we're a community. We're the new thing." For Lucrezi, the win became about creating more opportunities for trail running and hiking "through education, inspiration and empowerment," but also changing the way the sports community sees its female competitors.

"We want to see race officials be more welcoming for all racers with equal prize money, equal podium spots, equal swag," noting that would also include no more unisex shirts but sizes and styles specifically designed for the female body.

"There should also be menstrual products on tables," Lucrezi said, pointing out that medical kits are already present at races. "Why not just add a few tampons and pads?"

There also needs to be visibility with the media for female athletes.

"When there is a picture in the paper the next day of a race, what is it? A wall of men!" As she describes it, in every big race it is the men who stand at the starting line. "There needs to be a larger push for diversity. Split the lines and encourage more women to stand at the starting line. Allow photographers to find different images."

As Lucrezi sees it, running is the most primitive sport in existence, and yet for centuries women were discouraged from this exercise "because someone decided they weren't supposed to do it." For Lucrezi and the millions of women like her, such ideals are no longer tolerable. Women have been excluded from science because of fluctuating hormones and treated by physicians who knew too little about the female anatomy. Even in 2022, women's hormones, anatomy, skeletal frame, and organ size are not discussed in the hotly debated issue of transgender athletes in women's sports; it is male testosterone.

Women have been neglected and deleted from history, excluded from sport and equal pay, while the media sexualizes their image for both fantasy and approval. In the realm of sport, continued research, studies, and

Extreme runner Gina Lucrezi. *Courtesy of Gina Lucrezi*

discussion are needed so that women can realize their full potential and dreams, something Lucrezi is helping to accomplish.

SHE RUNS FOR HER PEOPLE

While sports bring many athletes a great sense of pride, this is not so for Rosalie Fish (2003–), a member of the Cowlitz Tribe in Washington State. When she joined the Muckleshoot Tribal School's track team, she had the desire to run but had not yet found her passion.

She knew the harrowing statistics about girls and women disappearing from her region. As a toddler, her aunt Alice Looney (1966–2004) disappeared, like so many other women. Looney's skeletal remains were found fifteen months later, but her suspected murderer was never found. Looney is in the horrific company of countless other American Indian (AI) and Alaskan Native (AN) women who have simply become statistics—underreported, neglected statistics.

Around the nation, women of Indigenous communities are under assault. In 2020, the U.S. Department of Justice found that the murder rate of AI/AN women was more than ten times the national average and four out of every five AI/AN women will experience some sort of violence in their lifetimes.[25]

These staggering statistics, emboldened by the lack of police and legal intervention, only solidified Fish's worries that nothing was going to change. "Nobody is going to listen to me. As a teenage girl, nobody has to care what I say. But when I run about it, people will notice."[26]

So, she ran.

But when she saw Jordan Marie Brings Three White Horses Daniel (1988–), a former NCAA Division I runner and member of the Kul Wicasa Lakota in South Dakota, everything changed. Daniel ran the Boston Marathon in 2019, dressed in the traditional runner's attire and with a painted symbol of a red hand across her face.

The red hand face-painting was more than a symbol for Daniel who wanted to help "break into a new public consciousness."[27] As the founder of Rising Hearts coalition, an organization dedicated to defending Indigenous rights and bringing attention to the crisis that AI/AN women face, Daniel encouraged Fish, who had asked permission to also display the red hand face-painting during competition.

Seeing Daniel, who had the letters *MMIW* (Missing and Murdered Indigenous Women) on her right leg in addition to the face paint, only cemented the feelings Fish already had. In her senior year of high school, Fish unintentionally became a social media star. Making the decision to emulate Daniel, she competed at a track meet with the MMIW on her leg and the red-hand face paint across her mouth. Her courage to do so came from the lost and missing who could not speak. It was her final race in high school and she won three gold medals, a silver medal, and a Sportsmanship Award, but she did not run for any medals or awards. In her heart, each race was run for those who could no longer.

"Growing up, I knew I was a target," Fish said. Fish acknowledged that the reality and fear of being a target (four of every five women in her community would experience violence in her lifetime) "really takes away that childhood aspect; it becomes about survival . . . I didn't realize it was a nationwide or global issue until high school when I had access to social media."

When Daniel finished the Boston Marathon, she shared with Fish that the weight of "running and praying for our sisters" was a responsibility she carried with her for the entire marathon, so that they were not forgotten.

"That was my ah-ha moment," Fish said. Running was not just running. "It had given me a platform to share and amplify my voice; it became the catalyst for Indigenous representation. Running is the very minimum I can do," she said, but also noted that it is sports that has allowed her such a platform.

She still remembers what her coach Mike Williams said to her the day of her final races in high school. She had already run the 800-meter and the two-mile race, winning gold in both, and was prepping for the 400-meter. "I know your legs are tired," he said. "But you don't care. You don't care that your legs are tired . . . because you're running for more than this medal.

"You're running for Misty and Jackie and Renee and Alice. But you're also running for your little sister Solstice and your older sister Cedar and you're running for my daughters Nyala and Khalil. And you're running for all of the little girls at tribal school, and you're running for Indigenous women everywhere. . . . That matters most to you, not how tired you are."[28]

Fish runs for University of Washington and hopes to graduate with a degree in social services, dedicating her life to helping those who have been exposed to violence, to lend a greater voice to all Indigenous people, to put a spotlight on the crisis her people face, and to empower girls and women to reclaim their rights in society. "I will not stop."

WHEN WOMEN RISE

There remains a gender bias so deeply rooted in society that researchers have found when subjects are asked about prejudice toward women, survey responders denied any bias. However, when the same responders believed their answers to be anonymous, they revealed biased, even resentful or hateful attitudes toward women.[29] When they believed their attitudes could be linked to their name, they offered different responses. In the wake of being "woke," many responders understand it is socially unacceptable to hold gender bias but still hold those beliefs.

Even more prevalent is unconscious gender bias/belief that women are not able to hold positions of leadership, considered a masculine skill set.[30] The Reykjavik Index for Leadership study found that society's perceptions of male and female leaders—from twenty-three sectors in ten countries, including Canada, France, Germany, India, Italy, Japan, Kenya, Nigeria, the United Kingdom, and the United States—continues to distrust women's ability to lead.

What political and social scientists have found is the standard upon which female politicians are expected to undertake or overachieve is to both deviate from gender stereotypes while also working against their gendered norm.[31] When women were equally assertive in speech as their male counterparts, the female politician was described as "aggressive," "demanding," even "hysterical," while males were "commanding" with "strong" convictions. In particular to minority women, Black females were too abrasive while Asian women were not believed to be strong or assertive enough.[32]

Unique to female politicians and athletes, before they can prove they are qualified and competitive, they must first fight for the right to even be present. Perceptions continue to manifest in numerous and deepening inequalities across every aspect of society, government, and business,[33] including sport.

This why media images are so important for females and why strong leaders, through sport, are so important to society and future generations. The game changers can only continue to rise, women will continue to rise, when society (including medicine and science and sport and politics) changes and rises as well.

TWENTY-ONE

Where to Go from Here?

It was called *Sleevegate, Up in Arms, The Right to Bare Arms*, and *Arm-a-Gottum*. It consumed national headlines in 2009, drawing very strong opinions from political foes and allies in Washington, D.C. It was widely discussed around the world. It was, of course, the topic of then–First Lady Michelle Obama (1964–) showing toned arms.

First Lady Michelle Obama. *World History Archive/ Alamy Stock Photo*

The history of the First Lady had always been a staple in American politics and the media image. The First Lady had almost always been white, delicate, and well suited for the domestic roles of White House wife. Obama, however, was quite different. Black, tall, athletic, and a Princeton- and Harvard-educated lawyer, she was attacked in the media in unprecedented fashion.

While conservative (male) talking heads called her attire "disrespectful," American women reacted differently. Michelle Obama remains one of the most beloved First Ladies of all time. According to a 2010 Pew Research Center poll, Obama was not only more popular than her husband, President Obama, and such popular First Ladies as Laura Bush and Hillary Clinton,[1] but she appeared on the cover of twelve magazines during her time in the White House (including *Vogue* [three covers], *Glamour*, *Time*, *InStyle*, *Essence*, *Elle*, *Ladies Home Journal*, *Redbook*, and *Harper's Bazaar*) and more than one hundred since retiring to the private sector. Among the numerous "Best Dressed" awards, Obama was also the first First Lady to present at the Academy Awards (2013) while making *Forbes'* World's Most Powerful Women list. In 2020, she was named America's Most Admirable Woman for the third year in a row, while both she and Barack Obama were voted to be the most admirable man and woman in forty-two countries and territories.[2] In 2018, she penned the book *Becoming*, which quickly sold more than 14 million copies. She also was the inspiration behind numerous children's books, including the best seller *Parker Looks Up*.

Obama brought real political power to the position of First Lady. "Michelle Obama was an important symbol in American politics and that beyond any of her activities as first lady, her presence provided meaning to particular groups of Americans." First Ladies of the past partook in "noncontroversial" partisan politics while Obama initiated the "Let's Move" campaign with the uncompromising goal of eradicating childhood obesity.

Support within the medical and health industries was almost immediate, as was the endorsement of the U.S. Department of Defense and the branches of the armed forces, as obesity among recruits had increasingly become a problem.[3]

She turned to media while the fast-food industry turned to politicians to elicit support to dismantle "Let's Move!" She garnered celebrity and athlete endorsements and then turned to her intended audience—children. She appeared on the popular Nickelodeon TV show *iCarly* and the Kids' Choice Awards. She beat TV talk show host Ellen DeGeneres (1958–) in a push-up contest while also appearing on other talk shows to promote better health. Most notably, the First Lady crossed into the private sector, convincing major retailers such as Walgreens and Walmart to sell more fresh fruits and vegetables in communities that typically had fewer healthy options.[4]

Beyond healthy eating, Obama pushed hard to get children and teenagers outside, away from video games, and engaged in sport. She reached out to the NFL to pair "Let's Move!" and the NFL's PLAY 60 to fight childhood obesity.

Unlike traditional First Ladies, Obama was not an extension of her husband (and his ideologies) but an independent, successful, competitive woman in her own right who pushed (and continues to push) education for girls, equality, and healthy lifestyles. Moreover, Obama was never a showpiece but an active woman who lived up to her own "Let's Move!" platform. She worked out every morning at 5:30 a.m. and was known for her "gladiator" style routines. She ran, played tennis, jumped rope, and raced with children. She danced, bared her arms, exhibited tremendous grace when attacked, and did not back down from her own convictions.

Notably, there had been one other First Lady who stood at 5'11": notoriously independent, she wore pants and was far more interested in civil rights than the latest fashions. Eleanor Roosevelt (1884–1962), the longest-serving and one of the most impactful First Ladies in history (1933–1945), was anything but the definition of hegemonic femininity.

Much of her activities were distasteful to Americans at the time as she lobbied for civil rights, women's rights, children's causes, and women's health and wrote about such things in her daily syndicated news column, My Day. Called "the most liberated woman of the century," Roosevelt spoke for those who could not always be heard.[5]

As First Lady, she only allowed female reporters to attend her press conferences, of which there was 348 during her tenure, to ensure job security and more access to news for women journalists but, in doing so, Roosevelt also helped mold a different kind of image of women—all women—in the media.

Sixty-four years later, Michelle Obama's experience would be much different than that of Roosevelt, to which she famously said, "When they go low, we go high," a sentiment she wholly adopted.

She recognized the need for girls and women to see a strong woman in a position of power play to her strengths, not traditional behavior, and so, in 2018 when she spoke on International Day of the Girl, she reaffirmed this platform. "That's what happens with change. Change is not a direct, smooth path. There's going to be bumps and resistance. There's been a status quo in terms of the way women have been treated, what their expectations have been in this society, and that is changing."

THE STATUS QUO OF WOMEN

The assault on Obama's character was never about her sleeveless wardrobe. It was something else—something much bigger. It was her skin, her height, her boundless energy, her education, and her muscular, toned arms. First Ladies were expected to be more Athenian in nature while Obama was a Spartan.

For women of color in predominately *white* sports, Obama's reception had not been a surprise. The entry of the Williams sisters, Serena and Venus (1980–), into tennis was less about ability than simple acceptance. The same was true for swimmer Simone Manuel (1996–). "I was a tall Black girl with muscles, an athletic build. 'You must play basketball,' people would say," said Manuel. "Or, 'I bet you run track, right?'" Though she was only twelve when she became serious about swimming, she already understood the stereotype that chased her.[6] Instead, she removed those barriers, becoming an NCAA champion swimmer at Stanford and becoming the first Black swimmer to win Olympic gold at the 2016 Rio Games.

Just as prima ballerina Misty Copeland (1982–) was repeatedly told she did not have the "right" body type for ballet, French figure skater Surya Bonaly (1973–) did not fit the perceived mold for figure skating. She was a muscular, dark-skinned Black athlete who posed as a real challenge for officials who struggled with scoring. They could not accept her muscular

Williams sisters. *AF archives/Alamy Stock Photo*

legs. They interpreted (willfully) her power as unfeminine. They disapproved of her braids. But the three-time World Championship silver medalist, five-time European, and nine-time French National champion would not be ignored. To date, she remains the only Olympic figure skater—male or female—to land a backflip on just one skate and was an undisputable fan favorite.

Being seen is as important as the competition itself, if not more. Briana Scurry specifically wanted to let girls "who looked like me *see* me." When inducted into the National Soccer Hall of Fame, she was not only the first goalie to earn such a distinction but was also the first Black female athlete. "I had some girls tell me, 'I didn't even know Black girls play soccer.'"

For women of color, being *seen* has special importance while the issue of being heard is an issue for all women.

THE STATUS QUO OF EXPECTATIONS

For over two thousand years, women have endured implicit and explicit bias in the way of laws, medical treatment, and social values. It was *implicit bias*—an unconscious socially driven attitude of preexisting beliefs about women (and their abilities and purpose)—that made women complicit in their own treatment. So ingrained was the idea that keeping the home and rearing children was strictly woman's work that antisuffragists/antifeminists were able to convince women that equality meant abandoning their children, even womanhood. Women endured great physical pain from Victorian-era corsets, drowned in suffocating clothing, and remained silent after assault. They knew their sufferings were wrong, but this was how things were. Implicit bias allowed for men to believe that working mothers were not as driven. Implicit bias allowed medical science to use only males in medicine to cure everyone.

Explicit bias is *conscious* socially driven attitudes. Society recognizes its preexisting beliefs, it recognizes its prejudices, yet continues to push a misogynistic agenda for personal gain or a political/social/religious leverage. As an example, USA Gymnastics officials ("protectors") knew their female athletes were being assaulted by an employee but chose economics over human rights. Meanwhile, the IOC had heard complaints for decades regarding uniforms and the (overt sexualization) treatment from the media, but when female athletes rebelled against dress codes imposed only on female athletes, it was the women who were punished.

In the first modern Olympic games in 1900, it did not matter that the female athlete's floor-length (and heavy) dress could cause her injury. Patriarchal dress codes decreed that for "the safety of women," including that of her reputation, she must dress modestly and appropriately. By

2020, however, the new hegemonic feminine ideal called for more skin and so the appropriate dress was anything but modest. It did not matter that bikini-clad female volleyball players were on sand that reached temperatures of 120 degrees Fahrenheit. Male volleyball players were offered more protection with oversized shirts and long shorts, but economics (not safety) drove the insistence on women appearing in bikinis.

When Norway's women's beach handball team revealed its new uniform, a wider and more supportive sports bra/tank and thigh-length athletic shorts at the EURO 2021 competition, there were immediate protests. The European Handball Association's Disciplinary Commission fined the team for "improper clothing," while the IOC threatened sanctions.

It was an irony not lost on anyone. More clothing was "inappropriate" for women.

Norway, however, was not alone. Germany's women's gymnastics team debuted its unitard as a stand against the "sexualization of gymnastics." German artistic gymnast Sarah Voss (1999–) noted that as she got older, particularly after starting her menstrual cycle, she "began feeling increasingly uncomfortable." The double standard that female gymnasts face includes not only their smaller uniforms but how they are judged. An unsightly "wedgie," view of a bra strap, or underwear might also cause the deduction of score. In fact, the simple act of adjusting a uniform for greater comfort can earn a demerit of points.[7] Meanwhile, the men compete in shorts and shirts and have no point deductions for wedgies and adjustments.

The bias does not end there. "With female athletes, you would see just overt zooming in on body parts," in the same sports in which no such camerawork occurs with the male athletes, observed Professor Kim Bissell of the College of Communication and Information Sciences at the University of Alabama.

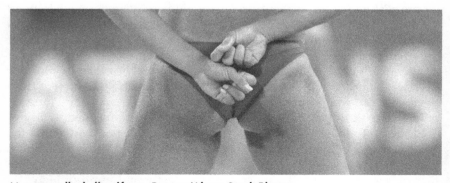

Norway volleyball uniform. *Reuters/Alamy Stock Photo*

During the International Federation of Sport Climbing (IFSC) World Championships in Moscow 2021, competitors and spectators were shocked by overt sexualized camerawork of female climbers, while male athletes were presented from a distance. The slow-motion and compromising positions were so graphic the live broadcast feed was temporarily removed from the federation's channel.[8]

These intentional acts, explicit bias against women, are so ingrained that the *offenders* do not even understand or care about repercussions. When females are more inanimate object than human, such behaviors persist. For example, in 2020, U.S. representative Robert "RJ" Regan, while discussing how to accept defeat, said, "I tell my daughters, 'Well, if rape is inevitable, you should lie back and enjoy it,'" sharing his view of women, violence against women, and even his own daughters.[9]

In 2013, during a campaign to launch Ford's new Figo car model overseas, JWT India, an advertising agency hired by Ford, created a poster with the tagline "Leave your worries behind with Figo's extra-large boot," referring to the vehicle's trunk space. The image was of former Italian prime minister Silvio Berlusconi (1936–) shown with three women in the trunk, bound and gagged and crying. The ad appeared in Italy just as several high-profile cases of gang rape shocked the nation. While WPP Group, the marketing firm that holds JWT, released a statement apologizing for the "distasteful" posters,[10] mass production and distribution was never questioned until women protested.

The image of Prime Minister Berlusconi was no mistake as he was known for restrictive and extremely misogynistic views on women.[11] Ford, too, apologized that WPP's phrasing was "never intended" for publication—a sentiment all too familiar for many civil rights activists. *Why was it ever conceptualized, much less produced?*

How women are portrayed has a direct impact on how females are valued in society. So pervasive was Italy's ideal hegemonic female image, for example, that in 2019, Italy's Justice Ministry overturned a rape conviction, citing that the female was "too ugly to be a credible rape victim."[12]

Even as FIFA announced to female football fans attending the 2022 FIFA World Cup that they might likely be raped and then face further persecution from police for attending the sporting event, the Morality Police (the modern-day version of Controllers of Women) in Iran apprehended, beat, and ultimately killed Mahsa Amini (2000–2022), citing that she did not wear her hijab properly. Women stood, igniting protests, and the first recorded female athlete, Elnaz Rekabi (1989–), disobeyed Iran's strict dress code to compete in an international rock climbing contest without a hijab.[13]

These explicit (and implicit) biases are not just wrong but dangerous as they feed into other ideas such as—if they hold so little value—why do women need specialized medical research and care?

THE STATUS QUO OF CHANGE

In 1919, the U.S. Senate approved the Nineteenth Amendment and it was ratified the following year, promising political and social equality for women. That did not come to pass, nor has it yet. To amend the problem, the Equal Rights Amendment was drafted in 1923 but was not passed until 1972. In 2019, forty years after the passage of the Nineteenth Amendment, Virginia became the thirty-eighth and final state required to ratify the amendment, but the Trump administration refused to accept its legitimacy, asserting that an earlier deadline for ratification had passed, and equal rights were stalled once again.

Of the 195 countries around the world, over 160 offer constitutional provisions that prohibit discrimination on the basis of sex and/or gender. The United States is not one of them. Of the newer countries, no constitution created since 2000 omits protections against sex-based discrimination while the nations of France, Germany, and Luxembourg amended their own to include sex equality.

This matters for females as, for example, in Nepal, a woman's rape by a husband was no longer considered his marital right but a violation of *her* rights; in Germany these constitutional rights ensured that a pregnant woman could not be fired; in Tanzania, girls could no longer be married off at a younger age than boys (who must be at least eighteen years of age). But for American women, there is no absolute guarantee for equal pay or against discriminatory practices or policies regarding health care and coverage, or absolute legal rights for victims of violence, including domestic violence.[14]

It is another example of how damaging implicit and explicit biases toward women can be as the United States lags behind the majority of the world in supporting its female citizens. On January 27, 2022, incoming president Joe Biden (1942–) stated:

> We must recognize the clear will of the American people and definitively enshrine the principle of gender equality in the Constitution. It is long past time that we put all doubt to rest. I am calling on Congress to act immediately to pass a resolution recognizing ratification of the ERA. As the recently published Office of Legal Counsel memorandum makes clear, there is nothing standing in Congress's way from doing so. No one should be discriminated against based on their sex—and we, as a nation, must stand up for full women's equality.[15]

It is a change long overdue from a society that "has conditioned women to expect less than their fair share," according to Judge Cynthia Holcomb Hall. This would include "their fair share of athletic opportunities."

It took a woman to wonder, an athlete, a fan of Wonder Woman her-self to bring about her own answers and change. Ironwoman Stacy Sims was competing at the 2002 Ironman World Championships in Kona, Hawaii—a combined 2.4-mile swim, 112-mile bicycle race, and 26.2-mile run widely considered to be one of the most difficult events in the world. Sims was fully prepared to perform well when things began to fall apart. She developed a headache and her body began to swell, so she took a couple of glucose and electrolyte tablets, but this only ignited an immedi-ate need to urinate. Only later did she learn that the sodium levels in her blood were so low she neared a hyponatremic state (a serious condition that causes the body to hold on to too much water and can be life threat-ening if not properly treated).

Already working toward her PhD in environmental exercise physiol-ogy and nutrition science, Sims had more questions than answers regard-ing her condition. It was only when she turned to fellow female athletes that she learned when females near a menstrual cycle, the female body enters near or borderline hyponatremic condition.

As an undergraduate kinesiology major at Purdue University, Sims took a break from her cross-country training and joined its rowing team. There, she said, the women's team had the "same training and race sched-ule as the men but there would be times when we were flat in the boat, even though we had the same recovery and same training schedule as the men," and she wondered, "Why?"[16]

Dr. Stacy Sims. *Courtesy of Stacy Sims*

A partial answer came during a required lab in which she, along with two other male students, had to run on the treadmill for two hours, then repeat the performance the following week. As she explained, "The first week, no problem," but the following week, Sims was in distress after thirty minutes while the two male athletes showed no difference in performances. What the tests revealed was during Sims's first run, "I was using a lot of fat as fuel, which is great because you have an opportunity to go for a really long time but in the second trial, I burned through carbohydrates,"[17] which made it difficult for her to refuel, activate, and recover.

Again, Sims asked why, "and they said women are an anomaly so we don't necessarily study women in sports nutrition or science." It was a stunning admission from researchers at one of the top universities in the nation yet not surprising given the history of women in sport and medicine.[18] It was female athletes who reaffirmed how the menstrual cycle affects an athlete's performance, not science.

The reality is because women show greater physiological variability *because* of their fluctuating hormones, more detailed, time-intensive research is required, thereby making it more expensive to study female athletes and thus providing another excuse for the exclusion of females from studies. But there is also the long history of male-only, male-dominated research studies, clinical trials, and medical practices that simply did not consider the female as she was *a part of* man. This would include only male-biology factors of transgender female athletes in women's sports.

Historically, medical professionals have missed early signs or detection of a medical event or completely (and negligently) misdiagnosed a female patient as her symptoms did not align with male symptoms. In the case of female anatomy, however, there can be no comparison between male and female menstrual cycles or the hormonal spikes of estrogen, yet there still remains too little data for female athletes.

Following the Ironman race in 2002, Sims devoted her research to understanding how hormones, from puberty and menstrual cycles to pregnancy and menopause, affect the way women metabolize nutrition and maintain hydration, regulate body temperature, train, compete, and recover. "As an academic and an athlete," she said, "it is essential to understand that there are sex differences," and how puberty, hormones, menstrual cycles, pregnancy, and menopause all relate to the female athlete's entire life cycle.[19]

Throughout her career, Sims was continuously asked why she wanted to study women. She was once asked, "Why do you want to study women when we don't know enough about men?" As Sims explains, from onset puberty, boys become bigger, stronger, more aggressive—all positive attribute by societal standards—while females' hips widen, they put on fat, their gait changes—of all which impacts her as an athlete but also disrupts confidence and self-esteem as well as athletic ability because "no one talks about it"; no one tells the pubescent child "this is just a temporary change," that she can work through it to become a successful athlete.[20]

The case of abuse of Mary Cain, "the fastest girl in the world," should never have happened, but because of negligence and long overdue research she gave a face and name to the countless female athletes before her who were subjected to the same treatment. By 2010, academic journals and data-based studies began to require gender-friendly research while new programs were founded, such as the Female Athlete Program at Boston Children's Hospital.[21] It was founded in 2012 by Kathryn Ackerman, a former national athlete turned physician for the U.S. women's rowing program and associate professor of medicine at Harvard University.

Like Sims, when Ackerman saw how many female athletes were being negligently coached, trained, and treated, she knew she had to find the solution. Called "bossy," "aggressive," even "difficult," Ackerman dug in. "I've been told that women don't contribute as much to the revenue of sports organizations or media outlets, so they don't deserve as much funding or coverage. Most female sports advocates have heard the same things."

With half the world's population, relatively speaking, deserving of gender-based research, it is the nonsensical resistance that forces such women as Sims and Ackerman to demand "their fair allocation of resources and attention." Unquestionably, female athletes compete with fluctuating hormones and cycles that biological male athletes have never had to contend with; males have never dropped out of sport or missed competition because of the natural function of their own bodies, all of which lends to the argument that it should be female athletes who deserve priority in the field of research and science. That would benefit not only the physical but psychological aspect of sport performance.

Ackerman said, "When I stopped focusing on what I hadn't accomplished, but what I *could* accomplish and spread that message to others, I was dumbfounded at how that resonated with women. One thing that surprised me most about this area of sports research is that it's created an amazing international sisterhood. The limited resources currently dedicated to women's sports science [have] caused many of us around the globe to lean in and collaborate and promote one another. It's been so fun to learn from each other, understand each other's experiences, and try to build something as a supportive network."[22]

This would include such revolutionary products as FitrWoman, an app specifically created to allow athletes to track their menstrual cycles and obtain customized training and nutritional guides tailored to the changing hormone levels throughout each cycle.[23]

This should be the direction of medical science, of medical institutions committed to caring for *all* bodies, for equality, and for better/greater representation in the media. Our laws and our Constitution should guarantee equal status just as women's sport should mandate a level playing field for female athletes. Instead, laws, wages, imposed feminine ideals, media images, even sport has often worked against us.

Former Texas governor Ann Richards (1933–2006), then the treasurer of Texas, said it best: "But if you give us a chance, we can perform." Only the second woman in 160 years to deliver a keynote address at her party's convention in 1988, Richards added, "After all, Ginger Rogers did everything Fred Astaire did, she just did it backwards and in high heels!"[24]

Met with thunderous applause, women intuitively understood this was the station of all women everywhere; there were always extra burdens. Actress/dancer Ginger Rogers (1911–1995) shared in her autobiography, *My Story*, that while choreographing dances, Astaire often forgot she was wearing high heels while creating a "backwards three-step turn-jump up the stairs."[25] That Rogers seamlessly matched Astaire's own talent yet did so in heels was not lost on artist Bob Thaves who popularized, perhaps even originated the "in heels" homage. In his comic strip series *Frank and Ernest*, the cartoon characters are seen looking at an announcement of a Fred Astaire film festival with the caption: "Sure he was great, but don't forget that Ginger Rogers did everything he did . . . backwards and in high heels."[26]

It is a certain fact that stuntwomen have always known.

While stuntmen have enjoyed padded costumes to emulate the traditionally muscular physique of the male actor or hero, stuntwomen had the opposite. Performing the same stunts, stuntwomen were (and are) more frequently in sheer clothing with short sleeves and even shorter hemlines and, of course, in heels.

It was not until the 1970s that women were brought on full-time for such shows as *Police Woman* and *Charlie's Angels*. Previously, there was little call for a female actress to have an action role, or stuntmen simply wore wigs. Pioneers Julie Ann Johnson (1939–) and Jeannie Coulter (1944–) fought for women's rights in the stunt world and were ceremoniously blacklisted, ridiculed, even harassed, but it was they who opened the doors for others, allowing for audiences to see women in action hero movies, such as *Xena: Warrior Princess* (1997–2003) and, later, *Wonder Woman*.

But the hegemonic ideal remains strong.

Without realizing it, Jessie Graff had traded out her own personal safety, athleticism, and strength for that hegemonic femininity ideal. As a stuntwoman, beyond performing extremely challenging and sometimes life-threatening stunts, she also worked hard to keep her 5'8" lean but muscular frame similar to those often too-thin, 5'5" actresses. "I didn't even really think about it at first," Graff said, "but I was suffering from body image issues."

Graff had become too focused on "bulking up, not being bigger than the actress but jumping off of and out of buildings was tearing me up. I needed to weight train. I needed to be smarter about what I was doing."

Before, Graff had focused on what the director, stunt coordinator, even actors wanted, asking, "How do you want me to be? What do you want me to look like?" It is something, Graff points out, that women and girls feel each time they stop to study the cover model of a magazine.

At last, Graff realized she needed to take care of herself. When she did, not only was she stronger than ever, breaking more records as a ninja and a female pioneer in the growing sport, but she began to get more work as a stuntwoman. "I had the confidence to say, 'You know, if I'm too big for your actress, that's okay,'" she said.

This is the story of women in sport and society.

Jessie Graff celebrates. *Photo by Mick Kelly*

Postscript

A note from the author regarding the women who participated in this book:

Some of the biggest names in women's athletics made themselves available to this work not for self-promotion but for the important subject of women in sport and society. Sports pioneers, Olympic and professional athletes, X-treme competitors, stuntwomen, ninja warriors, accredited scholars, and anthropologists all contributed to these pages for future generations and the up-and-coming athletes, determined to propel women forward.

In keeping with the unconventional, daring women who appeared in history, many of the interviews conducted for this work were done in nontraditional manners. The interviews span over nearly two decades— an interview with Sheryl Swoopes in a car, with Jackie Joyner Kersee in a dressing room, at an ESPN Fight Night with Sumya Anani (1972–), on the field with women professional football players (in full gear), and on the playground with Peggy Fleming (1948–).

ABA and WNBA player Sonja Tate (1971–) held my child during an interview; in another interview with soccer players, it was my turn to hold athletes' children so that we could talk. When the pioneer marathoner Kathrine Switzer hopped on a Zoom call during the pandemic, she spoke for nearly thirty minutes before asking, "Where are you?" I had borrowed a laptop and had been so thrilled to speak to Switzer I had not noticed the backdrop of the laptop had me speaking to the legend from what appeared to be a pork slaughterhouse. It had been a joke the laptop's owner had had with coworkers that would set the interview apart from all others when Switzer laughed and said, "Well, I've never been in a slaughterhouse before!"

Interviews were conducted on the slopes, during World Cup bobsled competitions, and at the beach. But one of the most interesting was with Gina Lucrezi, ten-time collegiate All-American, national, and professional trail runner. I first saw her outside the remote mining town of Pitkin,

Colorado. In what she described as having an "off day," she had run a strong pace at twelve thousand feet above elevation until she became too fatigued to continue. I had not yet known what a phenomenal athlete or figure in women's sports history she was; I had only noted that the same person who raced by me thirty minutes earlier had then adopted a defeated walk as she headed back toward the mountains for what I knew was more than a twenty-mile trek over rocky terrain and sheer drop-offs. It was nearing dusk, so she would also have had to risk bears and mountain lions. I offered her a ride on my all-terrain vehicle and, for over an hour, I learned about the history of women who run, the discriminatory practices of running sponsors, and her incredible fight to level the rocky paths of trail running. She remains a reminder that amazing female athletes are everywhere.

Another such athlete and figure in women's sport history is Amanda Kammes, the perfect role model to wrap up women's history in sports and society. As a graduate of private school Benet Academy outside Chicago, Illinois, Kammes went on to play for the University of Pennsylvania's (UPenn) women's basketball team as a starting point guard and team captain. After graduation, Kammes coached at American University until she decided to return to school for a nursing degree. It was then, while working as a neuro-ICU nurse, that she discovered and fell in love with the sport of lacrosse.

She started off as an assistant coach at a local high school with the single goal of mentoring other young female athletes. It was not a salaried position, but Kammes felt immensely rewarded by the job. This would continue when the high school's head coach, Kate Henwood, became just the third head coach at the University of California, Davis's women's lacrosse program and brought Kammes with her. In just their first year, the UC Davis Aggies' defense was ranked fifth in the nation. Together, they created a girls' lacrosse program with NXT Sports in Pennsylvania (where Henwood remains executive VP of girls' lacrosse), which had previously only held programs for boys. After a few years, Kammes made the move back to her home state to be closer to family. It did not take long before local sporting organizations and schools began to pursue Kammes. In short time, she accepted a position with Lakeshore Lacrosse and now serves as its chief executive officer (CEO). Not long after came the call from her alma mater, Benet Academy.

Kammes was actively recruited by Benet Academy in Lisle, Illinois, to become the girls' lacrosse new head coach. She was an athlete, a winning coach and CEO of a girls' lacrosse organization, and, of course, a graduate of Benet Academy. She was the perfect fit for Benet Academy, the perfect coach for Benet Academy's girls' lacrosse program. That is, until Kammes wrote down the name of her wife as an emergency contact on the formal paperwork after she was hired, having been overwhelmingly approved by Benet Academy staff and board members.

She was told there was a problem. "I asked if I was fired," Kammes recalled. It would take another week before she would get any definitive answers. Although the email response had been vague, Kammes had a feeling she knew the reason. "I was the most experienced candidate in the area. I was on the top of the chain," she said, adding, "[Benet Academy] recruited *me*."

When Benet Academy, a private Catholic school, released a public statement that it "respects the dignity of all human beings to follow their conscience and live lives of their choosing," the backlash was immediate for, clearly, it did not. Parents were incensed, particularly those who had specifically enrolled their daughters into the academy so that Kammes could be their coach. For Kammes, however, it was baffling.

"I mean it's 2021. C'mon." Kammes led her personal life much as she did her professional and athletic careers—openly, honestly, unapologetically. Not knowing what else to do, Kammes called the parents who had followed her to let them know she would not be their coach after all and, when asked why, she was honest.

"Even though my heart didn't want to believe it. I never thought it would be an issue until it became one."

Kammes was willing to let it go. Given her reputation, finding another job would be easy enough. The parents, students, alumni, and community, however, were another matter. They petitioned, gathering more than four thousand signatures in just a few short days. Girls from the lacrosse team took to social media, staged a protest outside the school, wore rainbow masks and T-shirts, rallied more supporters, and stepped into the centuries-old tradition of female warriors and athletes fighting for their fellow sister in the name of social justice.

As news crews lined up outside the school, the administration of Benet Academy understood the gravity of their own choices. Kammes remained silent but deeply affected by what was happening. She had become a symbol.

"It was an amazing show of support and solidarity of all walks of life. It was no longer about my job. So many people reached out to me about their own experiences. I began hearing from kids from other Catholic institutions." Ironically, Kammes was back to where she started as a lacrosse coach. It was not about monetary gains but serving as a mentor and role model to others.

Historically speaking, none of this was new. The lives of women, their bodies, rights, and activities have always been seen in the public forums of politics, sports, religion, and society. What was new was that Benet Academy reversed its decision, stating, "The Board has heard from

Amanda Kammes. *Courtesy of Amanda Kammes*

members of the Benet community on all sides of this issue over the past several days. We had an honest and heartfelt discussion on this very complex issue at our meeting. Going forward we will look for opportunities for dialogue in our community about how we remain true to our Catholic mission while meeting people where they are in their personal journey through life. For now, we hope that this is the first step in healing the Benet community."[1]

"That might be," Kammes said, "the first Catholic institution in the country to reverse its decision to hire an openly gay, married woman. Not just that, but they openly admitted they stopped the hiring process with me because of my 'life choices.' By doing that, they acknowledged my kids, the protests. They said to the kids, 'You know what? We made a mistake but we love and accept you and want to work harder to include everyone.'"

At that point, Kammes knew what she had to do. No matter how she felt about previous treatment, "I could not let down those kids. By the mere act of me accepting the job, I acknowledged that a group of people at a Catholic institution came to a solution that was right. They made a wrong right." As a coach at Benet Academy, Kammes said, she is also an ally. "There will be kids who may never talk to me, but they know I am there. I'm there."

The very day that Kammes agreed to an interview for this book, she had declined all television interviews, including the *Today Show*. She had been concerned that the "story" had become about her when, in reality, she said, this had been about her students, about social justice, about women in sport, about righting the wrongs of centuries past.

This is, at its finest, the long-embattled, frustrating, glorious, complicated history of women in sport where champions, standing upon the shoulders of other strong women, shine.

As the story of Amanda Kammes hit the news, many former student-athletes reached out to their beloved coach. "While all this was going on, one of my former students texted me." Emboldened by what her former coach was going through so publicly, "she came out to me and told me that there was one story that always resonated with her. She said, 'You told that story of when you were a kid at Benet and you hated the fact that you had to wear a skirt and you said that the day you were allowed to wear pants, it was the best day of your life,' and I said, '*That* is what resonated with you?'"

Kammes laughed that for all her speeches about rising up, being true to oneself, about work ethic and teamwork, a story about being forced to wear a skirt had been the standout for this former student. But it lends to how impactful it is for girls when societal, political, and religious values override the personal rights and choices of half the world's population. And, so, I took that moment to share a conversation I had had with biblical scholar and archeologist Carol Meyers, who wondered why girls still had to wear skirts in lacrosse. Specifically, she wanted to know why she was forced to wear a skirt to play field hockey in the late 1950s and early '60s.

Kammes's answer came quickly: "Tradition," adding, "but none of my athletes wear skirts. They wear shorts." In fact, one of her first acts as assistant coach at UC Davis had been to order new uniforms, telling the Athletic Department, "Our girls are not wearing skirts."

Kammes would have us believe that this was not a story about her. In truth, the history of women in sport and how she dressed, behaved, and upheld societal norms that were assigned to her is the story of every woman: women such as Kammes and her activist students, female falconers and American ninjas, the first to bobsled or fly solo, those who refused sexualized uniforms, those who fought for the vote and the right to wear pants, those who disrupted the hegemonic feminine ideal (which was never set by real women). These are the women whose own stories created the best history that is so rarely told.

Notes

INTRODUCTION

1. Shaiann Frazier, "North Carolina Charter School Rule That Girls Wear Skirts Struck Down as Unconstitutional," NBC News, March 29, 2019, https://www.nbcnews.com/news/us-news/north-carolina-charter-school-rule-girls-wear-skirts-struck-down-n988901.

2. Julie Brucculieri, "Women and Pants: A Timeline of Fashion Liberation," *HuffPost*, March 8, 2019, https://www.huffpost.com/entry/women-and-pants-fashion-liberation_l_5c7ec7f7e4b0e62f69e729ec.

3. Bradley Geiser, "Removing Softball from the Olympics Hurt the Sport for Years to Come," SportsCasting, January 23, 2020, https://www.sportscasting.com/removing-softball-from-the-olympics-hurt-the-sport-for-years-to-come/.

4. Courtney Withrow, "The International Appeal of Softball," Athletes Unlimited, July 13, 2020, https://auprosports.com/read/the-international-appeal-of-softball/.

5. Sean Wagner-McGough, "Ronda Rousey vs. Holly Holm Surpass 1 Million PPV Purchases," CBS Sports, December 30, 2015, https://www.cbssports.com/boxing/news/report-ronda-rousey-vs-holly-holm-surpassed-1-million-ppv-purchases/.

6. Linda Grant De Pauw, *Battle Cries and Lullabies: Women in War from Prehistory to the Present* (Norman: University of Oklahoma Press, 1998).

CHAPTER ONE

1. Giovanni Destro-Bisol, Francesco Donati, Valentina Coia, Ilaria Boschi, Fabio Verginelli, Alessandra Caglià, Sergio Tofanelli, Gabriella Spedini, and Cristian Capelli, "Variation of Female and Male Lineages in Sub-Saharan Populations: The Importance of Sociocultural Factors," *Molecular Biology and Evolution* 21, no. 9 (September 2004): 1673–682.

2. Anil Ananthaswamy and Kate Douglas, "The Origins of Sexism: How Men Came to Rule 12,000 Years Ago," *New Scientist*, April 18, 2018, https://www.newscientist.com/article/mg23831740-400-the-origins-of-sexism-how-men-came-to-rule-12000-years-ago/.

3. Patricia Nell Warren, "History: A Female Athletic Champion in Ancient Olympics," SB Nation, April 13, 2009, http://www.outsports.com/os/index.php/component/content/.

4. Edith Hall, "Citizens but Second Class: Women in Aristotle's Politics (384–322 B.C.E.)," in *Patriarchal Moments: Reading Patriarchal Texts*, ed. Cesare Cuttica and Gaby Mahlberg (New York: Bloomsbury Academic, 2016), 35–42.

5. Amanda Foreman, "The Amazon Women: Is There Any Truth behind the Myth?" *Smithsonian Magazine*, April 2014, https://www.smithsonianmag.com/history/amazon-women-there-any-truth-behind-myth-180950188/.

6. Lulu Garcia-Navarro, "Remains of Ancient Female Fighters Discovered," NPR, January 12, 2020, https://www.npr.org/2020/01/12/795661047/remains-of-ancient-female-fighters-discovered.

7. Adrienne Mayor, "Who Invented Trousers?" *Natural History* 122, no. 8 (October 2014): 28–33.

8. "Amazon Warrior Women: Interview with Dr. Jeannine Davis-Kimball," PBS, May 29, 2014.

9. Hall, "Citizens but Second Class."

10. Boniface Obichere, "Women and Slavery in the Kingdom of Dahomey," *Outre-Mers. Revue d'histoire* 238 (1978): 16–17.

11. Stanley Alpern, *Amazons of Black Sparta: The Women Warriors of Dahomey* (New York: New York University Press, 1998).

CHAPTER TWO

1. Marlene LeGates, "The Cult of Womanhood in Eighteenth-Century Thought," *Eighteenth-Century Studies* 10, no. 1 (1976): 21–39.

2. Mona Dobre-Laza, "Sport and Gender," a reproduction with permission from *The British at Play—A Social History of British Sport from 1600 to the Present* by Nigel Townson (Bucharest: Cavallioti, 1997).

3. Sundari Anitha and Ruth Pearson, "Striking Women Striking Out," *Feminist Review* 108 (2014): 61–70.

4. *Gazetteer and New Daily Advertiser*, May 21, 1767; *Ipswich Journal*, May 23, 1767; *Derby Mercury*, May 29, 1767.

5. Louis-Claude Bruyset de Manevieux, *Treatise on the Royal Game of Tennis* (1783), trans. Richard Travers (Romsey, Victoria, Australia: Historical Publications, 2004).

6. Peter Radford, "Was the Long Eighteenth Century a Golden Age for Women in Sport? The Cases of Mme Bunel and Alicia Thornton," *Early Modern Women* 12, no. 1 (2017): 183–94, Project MUSE.

7. Arthur Hayward, *Who Have Been Condemned and Executed for Murder, the Highway, Housebreaking, Street Robberies, Coining or Other Offenses: Collected from Original Papers and Authentic Memoirs* (New York: Library of Alexandria, 1735).

8. James Peller Malcolm, *Anecdotes of the Manners and Customs of London, during the Eighteenth Century* (London: Longman, Hurst, Rees, and Orme, Paternoster Row, 1810).

9. L. A. Jennings, "Elizabeth Wilkinson Stokes: Championess of American and of Europe," Vice, *Fightland Blog*, June 28, 2016, https://www.vice.com/en/article/53xgwz/elizabeth-wilkinson-stokes-championess-of-american-and-of-europe.

10. "Ann Glanville," Saltash History and Heritage, https://saltash.org/saltash-people/ann-glanville.html.

11. Leslie Heaphy, "Black Women in Baseball," Sport in American History, March 21, 2016, https://ussporthistory.com/2016/03/21/black-women-in-baseball/.

12. Susan Isaac, "The Dangers of Tight Lacing: The Effects of the Corset," Royal College of Surgeons of England, February 17, 2017, https://www.rcseng.ac.uk/library-and-publications/library/blog/effects-of-the-corset/.

13. Kristina Killgrove, "Here's How Corsets Deformed the Skeletons of Victorian Women," *Forbes*, November 16, 2015, https://www.forbes.com/sites/kristinakillgrove/2015/11/16/how-corsets-deformed-the-skeletons-of-victorian-women/?sh=1ca4db26799c.

14. Fercility Jiang, "Chinese Foot Binding," China Highlights, March 18, 2021.

15. Louisa Lim, "Painful Memories for China's Foot Binding Survivors," NPR, March 19, 2007, https://www.npr.org/2007/03/19/8966942/painful-memories-for-chinas-footbinding-survivors.

16. Ada McVean, "The History of Hysteria," Office for Science and Society, McGill University, Montreal, Quebec, July 31, 2017, https://www.mcgill.ca/oss/article/history-quackery/history-hysteria.

17. Hanna Ross, *Revolutions: How Women Changed the World on Two Wheels* (New York: Plume, 2020).

18. *The Literary Digest: A Repository of Contemporaneous Thought and Research. Periodical Literature of the World*, vol. 11, May 1895–November 1895 (New York: Funk & Wagnalls, 1895).

19. Sue Macy, *Wheels of Change: How Women Rode the Bicycle to Freedom (with a Few Flat Tires along the Way)* (Washington, DC: National Geographic, 2011).

20. Adrienne LaFrance, "How the Bicycle Paved the Way for Women's Rights," *Atlantic*, June 26, 2014, https://www.theatlantic.com/technology/archive/2014/06/the-technology-craze-of-the-1890s-that-forever-changed-womens-rights/373535/.

21. "Pedaling the Path to Freedom: American Women on Bicycles," Natural History Women's Museum, June 27, 2017, https://www.womenshistory.org/articles/pedaling-path-freedom.

22. *Encyclopedia Britannica*, "Ulrich Salchow: Swedish Athlete," April 15, 2021, https://www.britannica.com/biography/Ulrich-Salchow.

23. Beverley Smith, *Figure Skating: A Celebration* (New York: McClelland & Stewart, 1999).

24. Sarah Bond, "What Not to Wear: The Short History of Regulating Female Dress from Ancient Sparta to the Burkini," *Forbes*, August 31, 2016, https://www.forbes.com/sites/drsarahbond/2016/08/31/a-short-history-of-regulating-female-dress/?sh=58882ec958f1.

CHAPTER THREE

1. "Golf in Scotland: A Swing Through Time 1457–1744," National Library of Scotland, 2010.

2. Bonnie Morris, "Women's Sports History: A Heritage of Mixed Messages," National Women's History Museum, August 4, 2016, https://www.womens history.org/articles/womens-sports-history.

3. kwatkins9, "Significant Events for Women in Sports," Timetoast.com, https://www.timetoast.com/timelines/significant-events-for-women-in-sports.

4. Karl Lennartz, "Two Women Ran the Marathon in 1896," ISOH, 2016, http://isoh.org/wp-content/uploads/2015/04/102.pdf.

5. Tarasouleas Athanasios, "Stamata Revithi, 'Alias Melpomeni,'" *Olympic Review* 26, no. 17 (1997), Olympic World Library, https://library.olympics.com /Default/doc/SYRACUSE/353009/stamata-revithi-alias-melpomeni-by-athana sios-tarasouleas?_lg=en-GB.

6. Else Trangbaek, "Danish Women Gymnasts: An Olympic Success Story," Centre for Olympic Studies, Denmark, https://kipdf.com/danish-women-gym nasts-an-olympic-success-story_5ab82bdb1723dd329c648c6a.html.

7. Trangbaek, "Danish Women Gymnasts."

8. Sheila Mitchell, "Women's Participation in the Olympic Games 1900–1926," *Journal of Sport History* 4, no. 2 (July 1977): 208–28.

9. Marilyn Morgan, "When Culture Kills: A History of Drowning in America," Consuming Cultures, August 24, 2012, https://www.consumingcultures.net /2012/08/24/when-culture-kills-a-history-of-drowning-in-america/.

10. "History of Bathing Suits," *Victoriana* magazine, http://www.victoriana.com /library/Beach/FashionableBathingSuits.htm.

11. Catriona M. Parratt, "Athletic 'Womanhood': Exploring Sources for Female Sport in Victorian and Edwardian England," *Journal of Sport History* 16, no. 2 (1989): 153.

12. *Report on the Inter-departmental Committee on Physical Deterioration*, vol. 1: *Report and Appendix* (London: Darling & Son, 1904).

13. Hilde Lindemann, *An Invitation to Feminist Ethics* (New York: Oxford University Press, 2019).

14. Richard C. Bell, "A History of Women in Sport prior to Title IX," *Sport Journal* 21 (March 14, 2008).

CHAPTER FOUR

1. Aileen S. Kraditor, *The Ideas of the Woman Suffrage Movement, 1890–1920* (New York: Norton, 1981).

2. Jane Donawerth, ed., "Frances E. Willard," in *Rhetorical Theory by Women before 1900: An Anthology* (Lanham, MD: Rowman & Littlefield, 2002), 241–54.

3. Linda O. McMurry, *To Keep the Waters Troubled: The Life of Ida B. Wells* (New York: Oxford University Press, 1998).

4. "Viola Belle Squire," FindAGrave.com, https://www.findagrave.com/memorial/76333118/viola-belle-squire.

5. "Prefixes 'Mrs.' Without a Husband: Belle Squire Says Every Woman Has a Right to It—Explains It to the World," *Columbus Republican*, February 26, 1913.

6. "Suffrage in 60 Seconds: Ida B. Wells," National Park Service, last updated September 1, 2020, https://www.nps.gov/articles/000/suffrage60seconds_ida_b_wells.htm.

7. Morgan Greene, "Ida B. Wells Receives Pulitzer Prize Citation: 'The Only Thing She Really Had Was the Truth,'" *Chicago Tribune*, May 4, 2020, https://www.chicagotribune.com/news/breaking/ct-ida-wells-pulitzer-citation-20200505-rlt4ujeeenf7vi5z6qt7e4pmha-story.html.

8. Peggy Miller Franck, *Prides Crossing: The Unbridled Life and Impatient Times of Eleonora Sears* (Beverly, MA: Commonwealth Editions, 2009).

9. Peggy Miller Franck, "The Mother Title IX: Trailblazing Athlete Eleonora Sears," *Daily Beast*, July 13, 2017, https://www.thedailybeast.com/the-mother-of-title-ix-trailblazing-athlete-eleonora-sears.

10. "The Infamous New York Female Giants Baseball Team at the Lenox Oval in Harlem, 1913," *Harlem World* magazine, July 12, 2020, https://www.harlemworldmagazine.com/in-1913-a-new-york-female-giants-baseball/.

11. Lily Rothman and Liz Ronk, "See How the New York Female Giants Made History," *Time*, October 25, 2016, https://time.com/4539351/new-york-female-giants-baseball/.

12. Colette Dowling, *The Frailty Myth: Women Approaching Physical Equality* (New York: Random House, 2000).

13. Marty Klinkenberg, "The Edmonton Grads Were Champions Long before the Toronto Raptors," *Globe and Mail*, June 21, 2019, https://www.theglobeandmail.com/sports/article-the-edmonton-grads-were-champions-long-before-the-toronto-raptors/.

14. Elizabeth Fitzgerald, "Women and the Olympic Games: 'Uninteresting, Unaesthetic, Incorrect,'" SBS.com, May 3, 2016, https://www.sbs.com.au/topics/zela/article/2016/05/03/women-olympic-games-uninteresting-unaesthetic-incorrect.

15. "Alice Milliat Foundation," https://fondationalicemilliat.com/.

16. Fitzgerald, "Women and the Olympic Games."

17. *Nobody Loves Me—Guess I'll Be a Suffragette*, John Hopkins Library, https://exhibits.library.jhu.edu/omeka-s/s/VotesAndPetticoats/item/2375.

18. Kat Eschner, "The Surprising Origins of Kotex Pads," *Smithsonian Magazine*, August 11, 2017, https://www.smithsonianmag.com/innovation/surprising-origins-kotex-pads-180964466/.

19. Purdue Women's Athletic Association Constitution, 1926, Box 22, Folder 2, Purdue University Athletics collection, MSP 160, Series 5, Sub-series 1, Purdue University Archives and Special Collections, Purdue University Libraries, p. 14.

20. "Swimming Goggles Used by Gertrude Ederle," National Museum of American History, https://americanhistory.si.edu/collections/search/object/nmah_748874.

21. T. R. Ybarra, "Gertrude Ederle Swims the Channel," *New York Times*, August 6, 1926, http://archive.nytimes.com/www.nytimes.com/packages/html/sports/year_in_sports/08.

CHAPTER FIVE

1. "Seneca Falls Convention Begins," History.com, September 15, 2020, https://www.history.com/this-day-in-history/seneca-falls-convention-begins.
2. Sojourner Truth and Olive Gilbert, *The Narrative of Sojourner Truth* (New Haven, CT: Lillian Goldman Ban Law Library, Yale Law Firm, 1850).
3. Rosalyn Terborg-Penn, *African American Women in the Struggle for the Vote, 1850–1920* (Bloomington: Indiana University Press, 1998).
4. "Mary Ann Shadd Cary," National Women's Hall of Fame, https://www.womenofthehall.org/inductee/mary-ann-shadd-cary/.
5. "Fugitive Slave Acts," History.com, February 12, 2020, https://www.history.com/topics/black-history/fugitive-slave-acts.
6. Catherine Clinton, "General Tubman: Female Abolitionist Was Also a Secret Military Weapon," *Military Times*, February 7, 2018, https://www.militarytimes.com/military-honor/black-military-history/2018/02/07/general-tubman-female-abolitionist-was-also-a-secret-military-weapon/.
7. Blake Stilwell, "8 Amazing Facts about Harriet Tubman," *Business Insider*, April 21, 2016, https://www.businessinsider.com/8-amazing-facts-about-harriet-tubman-2016-4.
8. Alan Singer, "We May Never Know the Real Harriet Tubman," *Afro-Americans in New York Life and History* 36, no. 1 (January 2012): 64–85, Gale Academic OneFile.
9. Singer, "We May Never Know the Real Harriet Tubman," 64–85.
10. Kevin Lilley, "How Harriet Tubman's Military Service Added Up to $20—a Month," *Military Times*, April 20, 2016, https://www.militarytimes.com/news/your-military/2016/04/20/how-harriet-tubman-s-military-service-added-up-to-20-a-month/.
11. Kate Clarke Lemay, *Votes for Women: A Portrait of Persistence* (Washington, DC: National Portrait Gallery, Smithsonian Institution, 2019).
12. Patricia G. Holland, "George Francis Train and the Woman Suffrage Movement, 1867–70," *Books at Iowa* 46, no. 1 (1987): 11.
13. Martha S. Jones, "How Black Suffragists Fought for the Right to Vote and a Modicum of Respect," *HUMANITIES* 40, no. 3 (Summer 2019).
14. "About NAACP," NAACP.org, https://www.naacp.org/about-us/.
15. Patricia A. Broussard, "Black Women's Post-slavery Silence Syndrome: A Twenty-First Century Remnant of Slavery, Jim Crow, and Systemic Racism—Who Will Tell Her Stories?" *Journal of Gender, Race, and Justice* 16 (Spring 2013): 378–80.
16. Kyle Deckelbaum, "Woman Recalls Menifee's 1939 State Title," ABC 7 News, July 2, 2016, https://www.thenation.com/article/society/black-women-athletes-under-jim-crow/.

17. Dave Zirin, "Black Women Athletes under Jim Crow," *Edge of Sports* (podcast), The Nation, May 16, 2018, https://www.thenation.com/article/society/black-women-athletes-under-jim-crow/.

18. Zirin, "Black Women Athletes under Jim Crow."

19. Zirin, "Black Women Athletes under Jim Crow."

20. Tim Fitzsimons, "Rick Santorum Says 'There Isn't Much Native American Culture in American Culture,'" NBC News, April 26, 2021, https://www.nbcnews.com/news/us-news/rick-santorum-says-there-isn-t-much-native-american-culture-n1265407.

21. Patrick Kiger, "10 Native American Inventions Commonly Used Today," History.com, November 18, 2019, https://www.history.com/news/native-american-inventions.

22. Stewart Culin, *Games of the North American Indians*, volume 2, *Games of Skill*. Twenty-Fourth Annual Report of the Bureau of American Ethnology (Lincoln: University of Nebraska Press, 1992).

23. "Voting Rights for Native Americans," Library of Congress, https://www.loc.gov/classroom-materials/elections/right-to-vote/voting-rights-for-native-americans/.

24. "Voting Timeline," Aljazeera.com, https://interactive.aljazeera.com/aje/2016/us-elections-2016-who-can-vote/index.html.

25. Sally Roesch Wagner, "How Native American Women Inspired the Women's Rights Movement," National Park Service, 2020, https://www.nps.gov/articles/000/how-native-american-women-inspired-the-women-s-rights-movement.htm.

26. National Woman Suffrage Association, *Report of the International Council of Women*, Washington, DC, March 25–April 1, 1888; Section 237–40.

27. National Woman Suffrage Association, *Report of the International Council of Women*.

28. National Woman Suffrage Association, *Report of the International Council of Women*.

29. Terri Hansen, "How the Iroquois Great Law of Peace Shaped U.S. Democracy," *Native Voices* (blog), PBS, December 17, 2018, https://www.pbs.org/native-america/blogs/native-voices/how-the-iroquois-great-law-of-peace-shaped-us-democracy/.

30. "Brokers of the Frontier: Indigenous Women and the Fur Trade," Women's History Matters, December 2, 2014, https://montanawomenshistory.org/brokers-of-the-frontier-indigenous-women-and-the-fur-trade/.

31. "Sacagawea," History.com, April 5, 2010, https://www.history.com/topics/native-american-history/sacagawea.

32. Kathy Weiser, "Toussaint Charbonneau: A Dislike Trapper and Trader." Legends of America, February 2020, https://www.legendsofamerica.com/we-toussaintcharbonneau/.

33. Hansen, "Iroquois Great Law of Peace Shaped U.S. Democracy."

34. Tim Stelloh, Molly Roecker, Chiara A. Sottile, and Daniel A. Medina, "Freezing Protesters Soaked with Water in Pipeline Protest," NBC News, November 10, 2016, https://www.nbcnews.com/storyline/dakota-pipeline-protests/dakota-pipeline-protesters-authorities-clash-temperatures-drop-n686581.

CHAPTER SIX

1. Dave Skretta, "St. Louis Olympics Was Really World's Fair with Some Sports," *Washington Post*, July 24, 2020, https://www.washingtonpost.com /sports/olympics/st-louis-olympics-was-really-worlds-fair-with-some-sports /2020/07/24/0664ea78-cdc3-11ea-99b0-8426e26d203b_story.html.

2. Mark Dyreson, "American Ideas about Race and Olympic Races from the 1890s to the 1950s: Shattering Myths or Reinforcing Scientific Racism?" *Journal of Sport History* 28, no. 2 (2001): 179.

3. Teryn Bouche and Laura Rivard, "America's Hidden History: The Eugenics Movement," *Nature Education*, September 18, 2014, https://www.nature.com /scitable/forums/genetics-generation/america-s-hidden-history-the-eugenics -movement-123919444/.

4. Bill Rhoden, "Women in Sports: A Fruitful Past but a Shaky Future," *Ebony*, August 1977, 62.

5. Susan K Cahn, *Coming On Strong: Gender and Sexuality in Women's Sport*, 2nd ed. (Urbana: University of Illinois Press, 2015).

6. "Izzy Channels' Basket in Closing Seconds of Play Beats Olivet Church Five," *Chicago Defender*, April 17, 1926.

7. "Basketball," *Chicago Defender*, December 1, 1934, national edition; "Girls Colored Team Plays Northern at Rapid Tuesday; Merchants Meet Rock," *Escanaba Daily Press*, December 31, 1939.

8. Claire Brewster and Keith Brewster, "Women, Sport, and the Press in Twentieth-Century Mexico," *International Journal of the History of Sport* 35, no. 10 (2018): 967.

9. Brewster and Brewster, "Women, Sport, and the Press in Twentieth-Century Mexico," 967.

10. R. M. Gil and C. I. Vasquez, *The Maria Paradox: How Latinas Can Merge Old World Traditions with New World Self-Esteem* (New York: G. P. Putnam's Sons, 1996).

11. "Life Story: Jovita Idar Juarez," Women and the American Story, New York Historical Society, https://wams.nyhistory.org/modernizing-america/xeno phobia-and-racism/jovita-idar-juarez/.

12. "Unladylike2020: Unsung Women Who Changed America," PBS, American Masters, August 5, 2020.

13. Raquel Reichard, "Remembering Carmelita Torres, the Teenage Mexicana Who Started a Riot at the Mexican Border," *Mitú*, August 7, 2019, https://weare mitu.com/things-that-matter/remembering-carmelita-torres-the-teenage-mexi cana-who-started-a-riot-at-the-texas-border/.

14. John Burnett, "The Bath Riots: Indignity Along the Mexican Border," NPR, January 28, 2006, https://www.npr.org/2006/01/28/5176177/the-bath-riots -indignity-along-the-mexican-border.

15. Anju Reejhsinghani, "Women's Boxing in Mexico and the Caribbean," Fighting Women: A Symposium on Women's Boxing, Toronto, Canada, June 2013.

16. Jose M. Alamillo, "Beyond the Latino Sports Hero: The Role of Sports in Creating Communities, Networks, and Identities," in *American Latinos and the*

Making of the United States: A Theme Study (Washington, DC: National Park Service Advisory Board, 2013), 161–83.

17. Ryan Wallerson, "Why Women's Soccer Was Banned in Brazil until 1979," OZY.com, October 24, 2016, https://www.ozy.com/the-new-and-the-next/why-womens-soccer-was-banned-in-brazil-until-1979/72241/.

18. Wallerson, "Why Women's Soccer Was Banned in Brazil until 1979."

19. Anne-Marie O'Connor, "A Cultural Snub for Women's World Cup," *Los Angeles Times*, July 16, 1999, https://www.latimes.com/archives/la-xpm-1999-jul-16-mn-56675-story.html.

20. O'Connor, "A Cultural Snub for Women's World Cup."

21. Jorge D. Knijnik and Juliana S. Soares Souza, "Brazilian Women in the Sports Press: A Case Study," *Journal of Human Sport and Exercise* 6, no. 1 (2011): 12–26.

22. "Women's World Cup: Marta Has Record to Rival Brazil Legends Ronaldo and Pele," BBC, June 13, 2019, https://www.bbc.com/sport/football/48629040.

23. Marta Vieira da Silva, "Women and Girls in Sports Can Change the Global Game," UN.org, April 5, 2020, https://www.un.org/pt/node/65411.

24. da Silva, "Women and Girls in Sports Can Change the Global Game."

CHAPTER SEVEN

1. "Ruth Law Lands Here from Chicago in Record Flight," *New York Times*, November 21, 1916, 3.

2. "Ruth Law's World War I Liberty Bonds Leaflet," Smithsonian National Air and Space Museum, March 2, 2016, https://airandspace.si.edu/stories/editorial/ruth-laws-world-war-i-liberty-bonds-leaflet.

3. Keith O'Brien, *Fly Girls: How Five Daring Women Defied All Odds and Made Aviation History* (New York: Houghton Mifflin Harcourt, 2018).

4. Steve Sheinkin, *Born to Fly: The First Women's Race across America* (New York: Roaring Book, 2019).

5. Edward White, "The Short, Daring Life of Lylya Litvyak," *Paris Review*, October 6, 2017, https://www.theparisreview.org/blog/2017/10/06/short-daring-life-lilya-litvyak-white-rose-stalingrad/.

6. Brynn Holland, "Meet the Night Witches, the Daring Female Pilots Who Bombed Nazis by Night," History.com, June 7, 2019, https://www.history.com/news/meet-the-night-witches-the-daring-female-pilots-who-bombed-nazis-by-night.

7. Holland, "Meet the Night Witches."

8. Reina Pennington, "More Than Just Night Witches," *Air Force Magazine*, October 2014.

9. Leverett G. Richards, "Birdwoman Finally Comes Down to Earth," *Oregonian*, April 28, 1946.

10. "Claire Mae Fahy," Davis-Monthan Aviation Field Register, last revised January 30, 2014, https://dmairfield.org/people/fahy_cl/index.html.

11. Nina Anderson, *Flying above the Glass Ceiling: Inspirational Stories of Success from the First Women Pilots* (Sheffield, MA: Safe Goods, 2009).

12. Fred Erisman, *In Their Own Words: Forgotten Women Pilots of Early Aviation*, (West Lafayette, IN: Purdue University, 2021).

13. Kali Martin, "It's Your War, Too: Women in World War II," National WWII Museum, New Orleans, March 13, 2020, https://www.nationalww2museum.org/war/articles/its-your-war-too-women-world-war-ii.

14. Adam Bisno, "The Integration of the WAVES and the Navy's First Female African American Officers," Naval History and Heritage Command, December 18, 2019.

15. Susan Stamberg, "Female WWII Pilots: The Original Fly Girls," NPR, March 9, 2010, https://www.npr.org/2010/03/09/123773525/female-wwii-pilots-the-original-fly-girls.

16. Stamberg, "Female WWII Pilots."

17. Melissa Ziobro, "'Skirted Soldiers': The Women's Army Corps and Gender Integration of the U.S. Army during World War II," Army Historical Foundation, https://armyhistory.org/skirted-soldiers-the-womens-army-corps-and-gender-integration-of-the-u-s-army-during-world-war.

18. "12 Things You Didn't Know about Women in the First World War," Imperial War Museums, https://www.iwm.org.uk/history/12-things-you-didnt-know-about-women-in-the-first-world-war.

19. Ziobro, "'Skirted Soldiers.'"

20. Megan Garber, "The Many Faces of Rosie the Riveter," *Atlantic*, April 24, 2015, https://www.theatlantic.com/entertainment/archive/2015/04/the-many-faces-of-rosie-the-riveter/391364/.

CHAPTER EIGHT

1. Brendan Higgins, "A League of Their Own: The True Story behind the Classic Film," Collider, July 20, 2020, https://collider.com/galleries/a-league-of-their-own-behind-the-scenes/.

2. Kara Kovalchik, "Six Women Who Beat the Boys," CNN.com, May 27, 2009, http://edition.cnn.com/2009/LIVING/worklife/05/27/mf.women.who.beat.guys/index.html.

3. Warren Corbett, "Joe Engel," Society for American Baseball Research, July 2017, https://sabr.org/bioproj/person/joe-engel/.

4. Janna Jahn, "Mitchell Dazzled on the Mounds Decades Before Mo'ne," *Chattanooga Time Free Press*, September 21, 2014.

5. Tony Horwitz, "The Woman Who (Maybe) Struck out Babe Ruth and Lou Gehrig," *Smithsonian Magazine*, July 2013, https://www.smithsonianmag.com/history/the-woman-who-maybe-struck-out-babe-ruth-and-lou-gehrig-4759182/.

6. "Elizabeth 'Lizzie' Murphy," Rhode Island Heritage Hall of Fame, https://web.archive.org/web/20151228054153/http:/www.riheritagehalloffame.org/inductees_detail.cfm?crit=det&iid=56.

7. Joanna Rachel Turner, "Diamonds Are a Girl's Best Friend: How P.K. Wrigley Started the All-American Girls Professional Baseball League," AAGPBL.org, February 12, 1993, https://www.aagpbl.org/articles/show/36.

8. Martha Ackman, *Curveball: The Remarkable Story of Toni Stone* (Chicago: Lawrence Hill Books, 2010).

9. Ashawnta Jackson, "This Woman Shattered the Gender Barrier in Pro Baseball," Timeline.com (Medium), June 7, 2018, https://timeline.com/toni-stone -first-woman-pro-baseball-206e26cb27ae.

10. Natalie Weiner, "How 'A League of Their Own' Impacted the Way People See Women in Sports," SB Nation, December 18, 2018, https://www.sbnation .com/2018/12/18/18147135/penny-marshall-a-league-of-their-own-impacted -women-in-sports.

11. "50 Facts You Never Knew You Wanted to Know about Sports Movies," *Sports Illustrated*, February 20, 2013, https://www.si.com/extra-mustard/2013 /02/20/50-mind-blowing-sports-movie-factoids.

12. Nicole Haase, "Women's Baseball Trailblazers Reflect on the League, 75 Years after Its Founding," SB Nation, May 30, 2018, https://www.sbnation .com/2018/5/30/17407798/women-baseball-trailblazers-reflect-aagpbl-75th -anniversary.

13. Jack Doyle, "'1930s Super Girl' Babe Didrikson," PopHistoryDig.com, April 17, 2013, https://pophistorydig.com/topics/babe-didrikson/.

14. Larry Schwartz, "Didrikson Was a Woman Ahead of Her Time," Sports Century, ESPN.com, http://www.espn.com/sportscentury/features/00014147.

15. Susan E. Cayleff, "The 'Texas Tomboy': The Life and Legend of Babe Didrikson Zaharias," *OAH Magazine of History* 7, no. 1 (Summer 1992): 29.

16. Vin Burke, "Former Enterprise Sports Editor Tells Story of Babe Didrikson," *Beaumont Sunday Enterprise*, May 3, 1970, the Babe Didrikson Zaharias Papers at the John Gray Library Special Collections, Lamar University, Beaumont, Texas.

17. Pete Martin, "Babe Didrikson Takes Off Her Mask," *Saturday Evening Post*, September 20, 1947, 137.

18. Cayleff, "The 'Texas Tomboy,'" 28–33.

19. Brent Kelly, "Biography of Babe Didrikson Zaharias, Golf and Athletics Legend," LiveAbout.com, May 15, 2019, https://www.liveabout.com/babe -didrikson-zaharias-1563841.

20. Bill Lubinger, "Babe Didrikson Zaharias, 'Wonder Girl' of the Sports World Was Controversial and Decades ahead of Her Time," *Cleveland Plain Dealer*, June 1, 2011, https://www.cleveland.com/books/2011/06/babe_didrikson_zaharias _wonder.html.

21. William Oscar Johnson and Nancy P. Williamson, *"Whatta Gal": The Babe Didrikson Story* (New York, Little, Brown, 1977).

22. Cayleff, "The 'Texas Tomboy,'" 30.

23. Cindy Himes Gissendanner, "African American Women Olympians: The Impact of Race, Gender, and Class Ideologies, 1932–1968," *Research Quarterly for Exercise and Sport* 67, no. 2 (June 1996): 172–82.

24. "Berlin Olympics, 1936: Golden Memories," *Northern Illinois Alumni News* (DeKalb, IL), 1984, 1.

25. Matt Osgood, "Sports History Forgot about Tidye Pickett and Louise Stokes, Two Black Olympians Who Never Got Their Shot," *Smithsonian Magazine*, August 15, 2016, https://www.smithsonianmag.com/history/sports-history

-forgot-about-tidye-pickett-and-louise-stokes-two-black-olympians-who-never
-got-their-shot-glory-180960138/.

26. Emily Bonzagni, "Politics of Exclusion: An Analysis of the Intersections of Marginalized Identities and the Olympic Industry," Syracuse University Honors Program Capstone Projects, August 9, 2017.

27. Larry Elliott, "London's 1948 Olympics: The Real Austerity Games," *Guardian*, March 30, 2012, https://www.theguardian.com/sport/2012/mar/30/london-1948-olympics-austerity-games.

28. Jere Longman, "At the Olympics in Bombed-Out London She Forever Changed Women's Sports," *New York Times*, July 24, 2020, https://www.nytimes.com/2020/07/24/magazine/1948-olympics-fanny-blankers-koen.html.

29. "Alice Coachman," Hall of Fame, United States Olympic and Paralympic Museum, https://usopm.org/alice-coachman/.

30. "Alice Coachman, the First Woman of Colour to Win Athletics Gold," Olympics.com, last updated March 30, 2021, https://www.olympic.org/news/alice-coachman-athletics.

31. David Dunlap, "Alice Coachman, Who Won a Medal but Came Home to Segregation," *New York Times*, August 19, 2016, https://www.nytimes.com/interactive/projects/cp/obituaries/archives/alice-coachman.

32. "Dominique Dawes Biography," Biography.com, August 7, 2020, https://www.biography.com/athlete/dominique-dawes.

33. Sheng Peng, "7 Asian American Sports Trailblazers Who Changed Sports," NBC News, May 23, 2019, https://www.nbcnews.com/news/asian-america/7-asian-american-sports-trailblazers-who-changed-games-n1006201.

34. Gilbert King, "How Fanny Blankers-Koen Became the 'Flying Housewife' of the 1948 London Games," *Smithsonian Magazine*, July 31, 2012, https://www.smithsonianmag.com/history/the-flying-housewife-of-the-1948-london-games-10049278/.

35. King, "How Fanny Blankers-Koen Became the 'Flying Housewife' of the 1948 London Games."

36. "Fanny Blankers-Koen Honoured at the Meeting and Stadium Which Bear Her Name," WorldAthletics.org, May 31, 2004, https://www.worldathletics.org/news/news/fanny-blankers-koen-honoured-at-the-meeting-a.

37. Susan K. Cahn, *Coming on Strong: Gender and Sexuality in Women's Sports* (Chicago: University of Illinois Chicago, 2015).

38. Gareth Edwards, "Sport and the Russian Revolution," Culture Matters, October 31, 2017, https://culturematters.org.uk/index.php/culture/science/item/2650-sport-and-the-russian-revolution.

39. Arthur Daley, "With a Bow to Women's Liberation," *New York Times*, February 15, 1972.

40. John F. Kennedy, "The Soft American: Sport on the New Frontier," *Sports Illustrated*, December 26, 1960, 16–17.

41. OlympicTalk, "Nina Bocharova, First Olympic Balance Beam Champion, Dies at 95," NBC Sports, September 3, 2020, https://olympics.nbcsports.com/2020/09/03/nina-bocharova-gymnast-dies/.

42. Jim Riordan, "The Rise, Fall and Rebirth of Sporting Women in Russia and the USSR," *Journal of Sport History* 18, no. 1 (1991): 194.

43. Robert H. Boyle, "The Report That Shocked the President," *Sports Illustrated*, August 15, 1955.

44. "President's Council on Sports, Fitness and Nutrition," U.S. Department of Health and Human Services, https://www.hhs.gov/fitness/about-pcsfn/our-history/index.html.

45. "1959 Dallas Children's Boxing League Newsreel Archival Footage," Public DomainFootage, YouTube video, 1:23, posted October 6, 2013, https://www.youtube.com/watch?v=ni3KQYIbzqw.

46. Women in American History, "Mrs. America: Women's Roles in the 1950s," PBS, https://www.pbs.org/wgbh/americanexperience/features/pill-mrs-america-womens-roles-1950s/.

47. "1959 Dallas Children's Boxing League Newsreel Archival Footage."

48. Riordan, "The Rise, Fall and Rebirth of Sporting Women in Russia and the USSR," 195.

CHAPTER NINE

1. DeNeen L. Brown, "The Fair Housing Act Was Languishing in Congress. Then Martin Luther King Jr. Was Killed," *Washington Post*, April 11, 2018, https://www.washingtonpost.com/news/retropolis/wp/2018/04/11/the-fair-housing-act-was-languishing-in-congress-then-martin-luther-king-jr-was-killed/.

2. David Begnaud and Sophie Reardon, "Claudette Colvin, Arrested for Not Giving Up Her Seat to a White Woman in 1955," CBS News, December 16, 2021, https://www.cbsnews.com/news/claudette-colvin-record-expunged/.

3. Jill Rothenberg, "60 Years Ago, the First Woman to Complete a U.S. Marathon Ran to the Top of Pikes Peak and Back Down Again," *Colorado Sun*, August 23, 2019, https://coloradosun.com/2019/08/23/first-female-marathoner-arlene-pieper-stine-pikes-peak/.

4. "Lyndon B. Johnson: Executive Order 11375—Amending Executive Order No. 11246, Relating to Equal Employment Opportunity," American Presidency Project, UC Santa Barbara, https://www.presidency.ucsb.edu/node/239383.

5. Elizabeth Kaufer Busch and William E. Thro, *Title IX: The Transformation of Sex Discrimination in Education* (New York: Routledge, 2018).

6. Katharine Q. Seelye, "Bernice Sandler, 'Godmother of Title IX,' Dies at 90," *New York Times*, January 8, 2019, https://www.nytimes.com/2019/01/08/obituaries/bernice-sandler-dead.html.

7. Courtney Emerson, *After You Vote: A Woman's Guide to Making an Impact; From Town Hall to Capitol Hill* (Dallas, TX: BenBella, 2021).

8. Susan Ware, *Game, Set, Match: Billie Jean King and the Revolution of Women's Sports* (Chapel Hill: University of North Carolina Press, 2011).

9. Adam Augustyn, "Battle of the Sexes: Tennis Event 1973," *Encyclopedia Britannica*, September 13, 2020, https://www.britannica.com/topic/Battle-of-the-Sexes-tennis.

10. Anna Diamond, "The True Story behind Billie Jean King's Victorious 'Battle of the Sexes,'" *Smithsonian Magazine*, September 22, 2017, https://www.smith

sonianmag.com/smithsonian-institution/true-story-behind-billie-jean-king-bat
tle-sexes-180964985/.

11. "Was the 1973 'Battle of the Sexes' Tennis Match Thrown?" NPR, *All
Things Considered,* August 26, 2013, https://www.npr.org/templates/story/story
.php?storyId=215838779.

CHAPTER TEN

1. Max Roser, Cameron Appel, and Hannah Ritchie, "Human Height," Our
World in Data, 2013, updated May 2019, https://ourworldindata.org/human
-height.

2. Paulina Rodriguez, "Lifting the Bar: A History of Exclusion, Empowerment
and the Rise of Women's Olympic Weightlifting," master's thesis, California State
University, Fullerton, Summer 2016.

3. Winthrop Jordan, *The Americans* (Boston: McDougal Littell, 1968).

4. "Feminism on the Flat Track," National Women's History Museum, June
22, 2018, https://www.womenshistory.org/articles/feminism-flat-track.

5. "Trailblazing Black Women in Sports," History.com, February 4, 2010,
https://www.history.com/topics/black-history/black-women-in-sports.

6. Sheena McKenzie, "Jockey Who Refused to Stay in the Kitchen," CNN,
October 2, 2012, https://www.cnn.com/2012/09/26/sport/diane-crump-first
-female-jockey/index.html.

7. McKenzie, "Jockey Who Refused to Stay in the Kitchen."

8. Richard Retyi, "One Armed Diver Who Struck Gold: The Story of Maxine
'Micki' King," University of Michigan Sports, June 17, 2016.

9. Robert Mcg. Thomas Jr., "An Unlikely Champion," *New York Times,* September 29, 2003, https://www.nytimes.com/2003/09/29/sports/an-unlikely
-champion.html.

10. Michael Dickens, "Althea Gibson: Let Me Be One of You," Tennis TourTalk,
February 20, 2019, https://www.tennis-tourtalk.com/40502/althea-gibson-let
-me-be-one-of-you.

11. Francesca Gariano, "Althea Gibson: The Trailblazer for Modern Tennis,"
Nécessité, February 25, 2020, https://necessite.co/2020/02/25/althea-gibson-the
-trailblazer-for-modern-tennis/.

12. Marshall Smith, "Please, Lady, Get Off My Golf Course," *Life,* June 17, 1966,
105.

13. Nancy Berkley, "Learn the History of Women's Golf," Nancyberkley.com
http://nancyberkley.com/timeline.

14. Erin Ryan, "The Greatest Invention in Running—EVER—Is the Jog
Bra," *Runner's World,* August 30, 2018, https://www.runnersworld.com/women
/a22824620/the-greatest-invention-in-running-is-the-sports-bra/.

15. Maggie McGrath, "Women Supporting Women," *Forbes,* March 6, 2020,
https://www.forbes.com/sites/maggiemcgrath/2020/03/06/women-support
ing-women-the-inspiring-story-behind-one-of-the-20th-centurys-least-appreci
ated-innovations-the-sports-bra/?sh=55df40e43174.

16. Gene Siskel, "'Pumping Iron II' Develops Human Side of Bodybuilding," *Chicago Tribune*, May 31, 1985, https://www.chicagotribune.com/news/ct-xpm-1985-05-31-8502030911-story.html.

17. "All-Time Historical Women's Powerlifting World Records in Pounds/Kilograms," PowerliftingWatch.com, https://www.powerliftingwatch.com/files/PLWR-W-01-03-18.pdf.

CHAPTER ELEVEN

1. "Changes in Women's Labor Force," U.S. Bureau of Labor Statistics, February 16, 2000, https://www.bls.gov/opub/ted/2000/feb/wk3/art03.htm.

2. Anna-Maria Marshall, "Closing the Gaps: Plaintiffs in Pivotal Sexual Harassment Cases," *Law and Social Inquiry* 23, no. 4 (1998): 761–93.

3. Michael D. Vhay, "The Harms of Asking: Towards a Comprehensive Treatment of Sexual Harassment," *University of Chicago Law Review* 55, no. 1 (1988): 328–62.

4. Sarah Pruitt, "How Anita Hill's Testimony Made America Cringe—And Change," History.com, September 26, 2018, https://www.history.com/news/anita-hill-confirmation-hearings-impact.

5. Rebecca Walker, "Becoming the Third Wave," *Ms.*, no. 11 (1992): 39–41.

6. Jenna West, "Megan Rapinoe Becomes Fourth Woman to Win Sportsperson of the Year Unaccompanied," *Sports Illustrated*, December 9, 2019, https://www.si.com/sportsperson/2019/12/09/megan-rapinoe-sportsperson-of-the-year-fourth-woman-unaccompanied.

7. David Burnett, "The Real Story behind This Iconic Olympics Photo," *Runner's World*, July 24, 2020, https://www.runnersworld.com/runners-stories/a33367218/mary-decker-zola-budd-1984-olympics/.

8. Philip Hersh, "Remembering the Attack on Nancy Kerrigan at the Figure Skating Nationals Championship 25 Years Ago," NBC Sports, January 4, 2019, https://olympics.nbcsports.com/2019/01/04/nancy-kerrigan-tonya-harding-attack-25th-anniversary/.

9. Phil Hersh, "Settlement Means Harding Will Skate," *Chicago Tribune*, February 13, 1994.

10. Hersh, "Settlement Means Harding Will Skate."

11. Legacy Staff, "Florence Griffith Joyner: The Fastest Woman on Earth," Legacy.com, December 21, 2010, https://www.legacy.com/news/celebrity-deaths/florence-griffith-joyner-fastest-woman-on-earth/.

12. Mark J. Kaufman, Amy C. Janes, James I. Hudson, Brian P. Brennan, Gen Kanayama, Andrew R. Kerrigan, J. Eric Jensen, and Harrison G. Pope Jr., "Brain and Cognition Abnormalities in Long-Term Anabolic-Androgenic Steroid Users," *Drug and Alcohol Dependence* 152 (2015): 47–56; "Brain Imaging Study Suggests Long-Term Study Use Can Lead to Significant Brain Structural and Functional Abnormalities," McLean Hospital, June 15, 2015.

13. Ed Odeven, "Conte Says Coverup Protected Big Stars at Seoul Games," *Japan Times*, August 11, 2015, https://www.japantimes.co.jp/sports/2015/08/11/more-sports/conte-says-coverup-protected-big-stars-seoul-games/.

14. Steve Inskeep, "Love of Victory in the Time of Steroids," NPR, October 2, 2013, https://www.npr.org/transcripts/228194177.

15. James Montague, "Saving Flo Jo: Taking Back a Legacy," CNN, August 10, 2012, https://www.cnn.com/2012/08/10/sport/olympics-flo-jo-seoul/index .html.

16. "The Story Behind the Flo-Jo's," NBA.com, January 30, 2015, https://www .nba.com/pacers/news/story-behind-flo-jos.

17. Erin Davies, "Heir Jordan," *Texas Monthly*, June 1999, https://www.texas monthly.com/articles/heir-jordan/.

18. Erica Ayala, "The Legend of Air Swoopes and the Quest for a New Women's Signature Shoe," *Sports Illustrated*, August 19, 2020, https://www.si.com /wnba/2020/08/19/air-swoopes-sheryl-signature-shoe-nike-daily-cover.

19. Kiki Wooley, "Dawn Staley," *Columbia Business Monthly*, March 9, 2020, https://www.columbiabusinessmonthly.com/2020/03/09/300052/dawn-staley.

20. Kelsey Bibik, "Seminole Legend: Gabrielle Reece Returns to Tallahassee," Florida State University, October 2, 2018, https://seminoles.com/seminole -legend-gabrielle-reece-returns-to-tallahassee/.

21. Karen Karbo, "The Ubergirl Cometh," *Outside* magazine, October 1995, https://www.outsideonline.com/health/training-performance/ubergirl -cometh/.

22. Gabrielle Reece and Karen Karbo, *Big Girl in the Middle* (New York: Crown, 1997).

23. Blake Dorfman, "Misty May-Treanor and Kerri Walsh: Their Amazing Beach Volleyball Careers," *Bleacher Report*, August 8, 2012, https://bleacherreport .com/articles/1290605-how-misty-may-treanor-kerri-walsh-became-greatest-in -womens-beach-volleyball.

24. "Overall Career Individual Leaders," Beach Volleyball Database, http:// bvbinfo.com/leader.asp.

25. "The Best Female Skiers of All Time," Alltracks Academy, https://www .alltracksacademy.com/blog/best-female-skiers-of-all-time/.

26. Bob Phillips, "Injuries Haven't Stopped Greatest U.S. Skier," ESPN Classic, http://www.espn.com/classic/biography/s/Street_Picabo.html.

27. Seth Rubinroit, "The Bond between Lindsey Vonn and Picabo Street," NBC, February 16, 2018, https://www.ktvb.com/article/sports/olympics/the-bond -between-lindsey-vonn-and-picabo-street/277-513643703.

28. Rubinroit, "Bond between Lindsey Vonn and Picabo Street."

29. Rubinroit, "Bond between Lindsey Vonn and Picabo Street."

30. Jamie Edmonds, "Manon Rhéaume's Story: Hear from the First Female NHL Player," WDIV4, January 7, 2020, https://www.clickondetroit.com /sports/2020/01/07/manon-rheaumes-story-hear-from-the-first-female-nhl -player/.

31. Laura Yuen, "Girls Just Want to Jump," NPR, *Fresh Air*, March 18, 2008.

32. "Sports: Bobbers," *Time*, February 26, 1940, http://content.time.com/time /magazine/article/0,9171,763250,00.html.

33. Candace Putnam, "Their Program Needs a Push: This U.S. Women's Program Lacks Olympic Status, Not to Mention Funds," *Sports Illustrated*, December

26, 1994, https://vault.si.com/vault/1994/12/26/their-program-needs-a-push -this-us-womens-team-lacks-olympic-status-not-to-mention-funds.

CHAPTER TWELVE

1. Yael Latzer, Zohar Spivak-Lavi, and Ruth Katz, "Disordered Eating and Media Exposure among Adolescent Girls: The Role of Parental Involvement and Sense of Empowerment," *International Journal of Adolescence and Youth* 20, no. 3 (2015): 375–91.

2. William Joy, "Dallas Social Media Influencer Sued by Texas Attorney General," WFFA, ABC News, February 7, 2022, https://www.wfaa.com/article /news/local/texas-attorney-general-sues-social-media-influencer-brittany -dawn-davis-scamming-clients/287-ff5a7cb9-6355-452a-bddf-4064db766a8a.

3. Rangsima Kutthakaphan and Wahloonluck Chokesamritpol, "The Use of Celebrity Endorsement with the Help of Electronic Communication Channel (Instagram)" (master's thesis, Malardalen University School of Business, Society and Engineering, 2013).

4. "Kim Kardashian Called 'Toxic' for Advertising Diet Lollipop," BBC, May 16, 2018, https://www.bbc.com/news/newsbeat-44137700.

5. Dena Barsoum, "Kim Kardashian's Waist Trainers Are a Hit, but Doctors Warn of Side Effects," HHS Newsroom, October 2, 2019, https://news.hss.edu /dr-barsoum-waist-trainers-are-a-hit-but-doctors-warn-of-harmful-side-effects/.

6. Llewellyn Boggs and Robert T. Muller, "Social Media Affects Influencer's Health," *Psychology Today*, October 6, 2021, https://www.psychologytoday.com /us/blog/talking-about-trauma/202110/social-media-affects-influencers-men tal-health.

7. Mary Cain, "I Was the Fastest Girl in America, Until I Joined Nike," *New York Times*, November 7, 2019, https://www.nytimes.com/2019/11/07/opinion /nike-running-mary-cain.html.

8. Cain, "I Was the Fastest Girl in America, Until I Joined Nike."

9. Cain, "I Was the Fastest Girl in America, Until I Joined Nike."

10. "Relative Energy Deficiency in Sport (RED-S)," BWell Health Promotion, Brown University.

11. Meredith Lovelace and Geri Hewitt, "Female Athlete Triad," American College of Obstetricians and Gynecologists, June 2017, Committee Opinion no. 702.

12. Cain, "I Was the Fastest Girl in America, Until I Joined Nike."

13. "360 YOU: Building Your Village with Team Atalanta," *Women's Running*, January 18, 2022.

14. Jelena Damjankovic, "Female Athletes in Team Sports Need 50 Percent More Protein Than Non-active Males," University of Toronto, November 30, 2017, https://www.utoronto.ca/news/female-athletes-team-sports-need-50-cent -more-protein-non-active-males-u-t-study.

15. Carrie DeVries, "Why Are Women at Greater Risk for ACL Injuries?" *Sports-Health* blog, May 7, 2015, https://www.sports-health.com/blog/why-are -women-greater-risk-acl-injuries.

16. Marcus Vinicius Santos do Nascimento, "Nutrient and Food Inadequacies among Athletes: Gender Comparisons," *Journal of Physical Education* 27 (September 2016).

17. P. Kong and L. M. Harris, "The Sporting Body: Body Image and Eating Disorder Symptomatology among Female Athletes from Leanness Focused and Non-leanness Focused Sports," *Journal of Psychology* 149, no. 1–2 (January–April 2015): 141–60.

18. Diego Villacis, Anthony Yi, Ryan Jahn, Curtis J. Kephart, Timothy Charlton, Seth C. Gamradt, Russ Romano, James E. Tibone, and George F. Rick Hatch 3rd, "Prevalence of Abnormal Vitamin D Levels among Division I NCAA Athletes," *Sports Health* 6, no. 4 (2014): 340–47.

19. Eric W. Owens, Richard J. Behun, Jill C. Manning, and Rory C. Reid, "The Impact of Internet Pornography on Adolescents: A Review of the Research," *Sexual Addiction and Compulsivity* 19, nos. 1–2 (2012): 99–122.

20. Hattie Crisell, "What Female Gamers Want You to Know about Being Abused Online," BuzzFeed, February 17, 2016, https://www.buzzfeed.com/hattiecrisell/what-female-gamers-want-you-to-know-about-online-abuse.

21. Not in the Kitchen Anymore, http://www.notinthekitchenanymore.com.

22. Jonathan Israel, "It's Groundhog Day: Esports Confronts Another #MeToo Moment," *National Law Review*, July 20, 2020.

23. Kayleigh Connor, "The Male Domain: Exclusion of Women in Video Games," *Digital America*, no. 1 (October 21, 2013), https://www.digitalamerica.org/the-male-domain-exclusion-of-women-in-video-games-kayleigh-connor/.

24. C. P. Barlett and R. J. Harris, "The Impact of Body Emphasizing Video Games on Body Image Concerns in Men and Women," *Sex Roles* 59, nos. 7–8 (2008): 586–60.

25. Noelle Haslam, "Miss-Leading Characters: The Hyper-sexualization of Females in Video Games," Global Critical Media Literacy Project, April 1, 2019, https://gcml.org/miss-leading-characters-the-hyper-sexualization-of-females-in-video-games/.

26. Suzanne Scott, "Fangirls in Refrigerators: The Politics of (In)visibility in Comic Book Culture," in "Appropriating, Interpreting, and Transforming Comic Books," ed. Matthew J. Costello, special issue, *Transformative Works and Cultures* 13 (2013).

27. Kylie Mathis, "Sexual Violence and D.C. Comics," *Proceedings of GREAT Day 2018*, no. 19 (2019), https://knightscholar.geneseo.edu/proceedings-of-great-day/vol2018/iss1/19.

28. Jon Simpson, "Finding Brand Success in a Digital World," *Forbes*, August 25, 2017, https://www.forbes.com/sites/forbesagencycouncil/2017/08/25/finding-brand-success-in-the-digital-world/?sh=51b82822626e.

29. Rachel Gee, "The Representation of Women in Advertising Hasn't Improved Much in a Decade," Marketing Week, June 21, 2017, https://www.marketingweek.com/representation-women-ads/.

30. Amy Roeder, "Advertising's Toxic Effect on Eating and Body Image," Harvard School of Public Health, May 18, 2015, https://www.hsph.harvard.edu/news/features/advertisings-toxic-effect-on-eating-and-body-image/.

31. *Merriam-Webster*, s.v. "body-shaming," https://www.merriam-webster.com/dictionary/body-shaming#h1.

32. Christi Carras, "Alicia Silverstone Calls Out 'Hurtful' Body-Shaming She Suffered for 'Batman and Robin,'" *Los Angeles Times*, April 20, 2020, https://www.latimes.com/entertainment-arts/movies/story/2020-04-20/alicia-silverstone-batgirl-batman-and-robin-body-shaming.

33. Izabella Zaydenberg, "10 Times Olympians Were Body Shamed While Competing," Revelist, January 25, 2018, https://cafemom.com/entertainment/olympics-body-shaming.

34. Morty Ain, "Amanda Bingson: 'Athletes Come in All Shapes and Sizes,'" ESPN, July 6, 2015, https://www.espn.com/olympics/story/_/page/body amandabingson/hammer-thrower-amanda-bingson-says-athletes-come-all-shapes-sizes-espn-magazine-body-issue.

35. Ain, "Amanda Bingson."

36. Helene Elliott, "Mary Lou Was 4 Feet, 9 Inches of Muscle and Grit, Claiming the '84 Games as Her Own," *Los Angeles Times*, March 9, 2020, https://www.latimes.com/sports/story/2020-03-09/mary-lou-retton-gymnastics-olympics.

37. Allyson Chiu, "A '10' Isn't Enough: UCLA Gymnast Katelyn Ohashi's Flawless Floor Routine Breaks the Internet," *Washington Post/Denver Post*, January 14, 2019, https://www.denverpost.com/2019/01/14/katelyn-ohashi-ucla-gymnast-flawless-floor-routine/.

38. Becky Grey, "'I Was Told I Looked Like a Pig'—Viral Gymnast Star Katelyn Ohashi's Battles with Body Image," BBC Sport, May 23, 2019, https://www.bbc.com/sport/48340080.

39. UCLA Athletics, "Katelyn Ohashi—10.0 Floor (1-12-19)," YouTube video, 1:58, posted January 13, 2019, https://www.youtube.com/watch?v=4ic7RNS4Dfo.

40. Grey, "'I Was Told I Looked Like a Pig.'"

41. Grey, "'I Was Told I Looked Like a Pig.'"

42. Laura Ruhala, Richard Ruhala, Emerald Alexis, and E. Scott Martin, "Analyzing Hair Pulling in Athletics," *Sport Journal* 20, no. 1 (January 2017), https://thesportjournal.org/article/analyzing-hair-pulling-in-athletics/.

43. Andy Clayton, "Elizabeth Lambert, the Hair-Pulling College Soccer Player, Is Back after Serving Two-Game Suspension," *Daily News Sports*, August 28, 2010, https://www.nydailynews.com/sports/college/elizabeth-lambert-hair-pulling-college-soccer-player-back-serving-two-game-suspension-article-1.206471.

44. Brian Lowe, "Girls Three Times More Likely to Be Victims of Cyberbullying," *Global Times*, October 10, 2019, https://www.globaltimes.cn/page/201910/1166555.shtml.

45. Mario Palmer, "5 Facts about Body Image," Amplify, http://amplifyyourvoice.org/u/marioapalmer/2013/05/21/byob-be-your-own-beautiful.

46. Lori O. Favela, "Female Cyberbullying: Causes and Prevention Strategies," *Inquiries Journal/Student Pulse* 2, no. 11 (2010).

CHAPTER THIRTEEN

1. Sonia S. Anand, "Differences in the Management and Prognosis of Women and Men Who Suffer from Acute Coronary Syndromes," CURE Investigators, *Journal of the American College of Cardiology* 46, no. 10 (November 2005): 1845–51.

2. Bernadine Healy, "The Yentl Syndrome," *New England Journal of Medicine* 325, no. 4 (July 1991): 274–76.

3. L. Mosca, "Summary of the American Heart Association's Evidence-Based Guidelines for Cardiovascular Disease Prevention in Women," *Arteriosclerosis, Thrombosis, and Vascular Biology* 24, no. 3 (March 2004): 394–96.

4. M. Gershoni and S. Pietrokovski, "The Landscape of Sex-Differential Transcriptome and Its Consequent Selection in Human Adults," *BMC Biology* 15, no. 7 (2017).

5. "In Sickness and In Health: Differences in Male vs. Female Gene Expression Drive Infertility," Weizmann Compass, May 9, 2017, http://www.weizmann.ac.il/WeizmannCompass/sections/briefs/in-sickness-and-in-health.

6. Stacey Rosen, "When the Standard of Care Is Treating Women Like Little Men," Katz Institute for Women's Health, https://www.northwell.edu/katz-institute-for-womens-health/articles/standard-of-care-treating-women-like-little-men.

7. Cassidy R. Sugimoto, Yong-Yeol Ahn, Elise Smith, Benoit Macaluso, and Vincent Lariviere, "Factors Affecting Sex-Related Reporting in Medical Research: A Cross-Disciplinary Bibliometric Analysis," *Lancet*, February 9, 2019, https://doi.org/10.1016/S0140-6736(18)32995-7.

8. "About Us," Laura W. Bush Institute for Women's Health, https://www.laurabushinstitute.org/about-us/.

9. "Cultural Competence Education," Association of American Medical Colleges, 2005, p. 1, https://www.aamc.org/media/20856/download.

10. "Dr. Jan Werbinski's Work Has Made Her a National Advocate and Voice for Sex and Gender Based Medicine," Western Michigan University, Homer Stryker M.D. School of Medicine, February 27, 2020, https://med.wmich.edu/node/2269.

11. "Dr. Jan Werbinski's Work."

12. Esther H. Chen, Frances S. Shofer, Anthony J. Dean, Judd E. Hollander, William G. Baxt, Jennifer L. Robey, Keara L. Sease, and Angela M. Mills, "Gender Disparity in Analgesic Treatment of Emergency Department Patients with Acute Abdominal Pain," *Academic Emergency Medicine* 15, no. 5 (May 2008): 414–18.

13. Chetan P. Huded et al., "4-Step Protocol for Disparities in STEMI Care and Outcomes in Women," *Journal of the American College of Cardiology* 71, no. 19 (May 15, 2018): 2122–32.

14. Bonnie J. Floyd, "Problems in Accurate Medical Diagnosis of Depression in Female Patients," *Social Science & Medicine* 44, no. 3 (February 1997): 403–12.

15. G. Lyratzopoulos, G. A. Abel, S. McPhail, et al., "Gender Inequalities in the Promptness of Diagnosis of Bladder and Renal Cancer after Symptomatic Presentation: Evidence from Secondary Analysis of an English Primary Care Audit Survey," BMJ Open, 2013, doi: 10.1136/bmjopen-2013-002861.

16. Michelle Akers's website, https://www.michelleakers.org/michelle-akers-uswnt-career.

17. "Akers, the American Pioneer," FIFA.com, December 24, 2016, https://www.fifa.com/tournaments/womens/womensworldcup/chinapr1991/news/akers-the-american-pioneer-2861903.

18. "Akers, the American Pioneer."

19. "Michelle Akers, Center Midfields for the U.S. Women's National Soccer Team," JumpStart, WebMD, 2000.

20. Alyssa Roenigk, "Akers, Chastain Take Part in New CTE Study," ESPN, July 29, 2019, https://www.espn.com/soccer/fifa-womens-world-cup/story/3887627/akerschastain-to-take-part-in-new-cte-study.

21. Tatyana Mollayeva and Angela Colantonio, "Sex, Gender and Traumatic Brain Injury: Implications for Better Science and Practice," Brain Injury Association of America, 2018, https://www.biausa.org/public-affairs/media/sex-gender-and-traumatic-brain-injury-implications-for-better-science-and-practice.

22. BriScurry.com, https://www.briscurry.com/advocacy.

23. "BBC Elite British Sportswomen's Survey," BBC Sport, August 9, 2020, https://www.bbc.com/sport/53593459.

24. Patrick Hruby, "What Happens When an Athlete Takes 'The Pill'?" Global Sports Matters, February 8, 2022, https://hrealsports.substack.com/p/what-happens-when-an-athlete-takes.

25. Hruby, "What Happens When an Athlete Takes 'The Pill'?"

26. Chelsea Little, "It Shouldn't Be All That Surprising: A Link between Birth Control and Performance?" FasterSkier, August 17, 2011, https://fasterskier.com/2011/08/it-shouldnt-be-at-all-surprising-a-link-between-birth-control-and-performance/.

27. Abbey Anderson, "Hormonal Changes Affect Female Athletic Performance. Period," Penn Medicine, May 3, 2017, https://www.pennmedicine.org/news/news-blog/2017/may/hormonal-changes-affect-female-athletic-performance-period.

28. Kirsty J. Elliott-Sale, Kelly L. McNulty, Paul Ansdell, Stuart Goodall, Kirsty M. Hicks, Kevin Thomas, Paul A. Swinton, and Eimear Dolan, "The Effects of Oral Contraceptives on Exercise Performance in Women: A Systematic Review and Meta-analysis," *Sports Medicine* 50, no. 10 (October 2020): 1785–1812, https://doi.org/10.1007/s40279-020-01317-5.

29. "Blood Clots and Birth Control with Estrogen," Women and Blood Clots, https://womenandbloodclots.org/birth-control/.

30. C. Bushnell, L. D. McCullough, et al., American Heart Association Stroke Council; Council on Cardiovascular and Stroke Nursing; Council on Clinical Cardiology; Council on Epidemiology and Prevention; Council for High Blood Pressure Research, "Guidelines for the Prevention of Stroke in Women: A Statement for Healthcare Professionals from the American Heart Association/American Stroke Association," *Stroke* 45, no. 5 (2014): 1545–88.

31. Doodipala Samba Reddy, "Do Oral Contraceptives Increase Epileptic Seizures?" *Expert Review of Neurotherapeutics* 17, no. 2 (2017): 129–34.

32. Chloe Williams, "'The Pill' Might Shrink Certain Brain Regions among Women Taking It," Live Science, December 4, 2019, https://www.livescience.com/birth-control-brain-hypothalamus.html.

33. Mary Pflum, "Safe Medicine? More, Younger Girls Starting on the Pill," ABC News, July 20, 2011, https://abcnews.go.com/US/safe-medicine-younger-girls-starting-birth-control/story?id=14116032.

34. Tera Roberson, "After Daughter's Death, Family Works to Bring Awareness to Dangers of Birth Control Pills," NBC/Houston, October 15, 2019, https://www.click2houston.com/news/2019/10/16/after-daughters-death-family-works-to-bring-awareness-to-danger-of-birth-control-pills/.

35. Anne Branigin, "Women Are Comparing the Potential Risk of Blood Clots from Vaccines to Birth Control. It's More Complicated Than That, Experts Say," The Lily, April 13, 2021, https://www.thelily.com/women-are-comparing-the-risk-of-blood-clots-from-vaccines-to-birth-control-its-more-complicated-than-that-experts-say/.

36. Shankar Vedantam, "Money May Be Motivating Doctors to Do More C-Sections," NPR, *Morning Edition*, August 30, 2013; Erin Johnson and M. Marit Rehavi, "Physicians Treating Physicians: Information and Incentives in Childbirth," July 2013, NBER Working Paper No. w19242.

37. Evan Barlett, "Sanya Richards-Ross: 'Every Female Athlete I Know Has Had an Abortion,'" *Independent*, June 13, 2017, https://www.independent.co.uk/sport/general/athletics/sanya-richardsross-abortions-female-athletes-olympic-champion-track-field-a7787546.html.

38. Peta Bee, "Sportswomen Benefit from Pregnancy," *Times*, September 14, 2009, https://www.thetimes.co.uk/article/sportswomen-benefit-from-pregnancy-d02p9lgdkhs.

39. Elizabeth A. Sorensen, "Debunking the Myth of Pregnancy Doping," *Journal of Intercollegiate Sport* 2, no. 2 (December 2009): 269–85.

40. Seyda Belfin Aydin, "A Review on Abortion Doping Discussion in Athletes: Is It a Truth or a Myth?" *Perceptions in Reproductive Medicine* 4, no. 5 (2021).

41. "Abortion Is a Common Experience for U.S. Women, Despite Dramatic Declines in Rates," Guttmacher Institute News Release, October 19, 2017, https://www.guttmacher.org/news-release/2017/abortion-common-experience-us-women-despite-dramatic-declines-rates.

42. Carla Spivack, "To 'Bring Down the Flowers': The Cultural Context of Abortion Law in Early Modern England," *William and Mary Journal of Race, Gender and Social Justice* 14, no. 1 (2007): 133–35.

43. John M. Riddle and J. Worth Estes, "Oral Contraceptives in Ancient and Medieval Times," *American Scientist* 80, no. 3 (1992): 226–33.

44. H. Yarmohammadi, A. Zargaran, A. Vatanpour, E. Abedini, and S. Adhami, "An Investigation into the Ancient Abortion Laws: Comparing Ancient Persia with Ancient Greece and Rome," *Acta Medico-Historica Adriatica* 11, no. 2 (2013): 291–98.

45. Lisa Cannon Green, "Survey: Women Go Silently from Church to Abortion Clinic," Focus on the Family, June 21, 2018, https://www.focusonthefamily.com/pro-life/abortion/survey-women-go-silently-from-church-to-abortion-clinic/.

46. Sean Murphy, "Oklahoma Abortion Providers See Huge Influx of Texas Women," ABC News, February 15, 2022, https://abcnews.go.com/Health/wire Story/oklahoma-abortion-providers-inundated-texas-women-82909200.

47. Gabriella Borter, "Oklahoma Passes Ban on Abortions after Six Weeks," Reuters, April 28, 2022, https://www.reuters.com/world/us/oklahoma-house -passes-ban-abortions-after-six-weeks-2022-04-28/.

48. "Understanding Pregnancy Resulting from Rape in the U.S.," CDC.gov, June 1, 2020, https://www.cdc.gov/violenceprevention/sexualviolence/under standing-RRP-inUS.html.

49. Havelock Ellis, *Man and Woman: A Study of Human Secondary Sexual Characters* (New York: Scribner, 1894).

50. Lecia Bushak, "A Brief History of the Menstrual Cycle Period: How Women Dealt with Their Cycles throughout the Ages," Medical Daily, May 23, 2016, https://www.medicaldaily.com/menstrual-period-time-month-history-387252.

51. Anita Diamant, "It's Time to Free All Women from the Menstrual Tent," WBUR.org, February 8, 2019, https://www.wbur.org/cognoscenti/2019/02/08 /chhaupadi-menstruation-tents-anita-diamant.

52. Yingzhi Yang, "China Made 85 Billion Sanitary Pads Last Year, but Not One Tampon. Here's Why," *Los Angeles Times,* March 18, 2016, https://www.latimes .com/world/asia/la-fg-china-tampons-20160318-story.html.

53. M. J. De Souza and A. Nattiv, "Female Athlete Triad Coalition Consensus Statement on Treatment and Return to Play of the Female Athlete Triad, San Francisco (2012), Indianapolis (2013)," *British Journal of Sports Medicine* 48, no. 4 (2014): 289–99.

54. T. Oosthuyse and A. N. Bosch, "The Effect of the Menstrual Cycle on Exercise Metabolism," *Sports Medicine* 40, no. 3 (2010): 207–27.

55. Debra Fulghum Bruce, "Normal Testosterone and Estrogen Levels in Women," WebMD.com, May 4, 2022, https://www.webmd.com/women/guide /normal-testosterone-and-estrogen-levels-in-women#1.

56. Yi-Xin Wang and Mariel Arvizu, "Menstrual Cycle Regularity and Length across the Reproductive Lifespan and Risk of Premature Mortality: Prospective Cohort Study," *British Medical Journal* (September 20, 2020): 371.

57. Muhammad Ikhsan and Muhammad Fidel Ganis Siregar, "The Relationship between Ramadan Fasting with Menstrual Cycle Pattern Changes in Teenagers," *Middle East Fertility Society Journal* 22, no. 1 (March 2017): 43–47.

58. Malaka Gharib, "A Swimmers 'Period' Comment Breaks Taboo in Sports—And in China," NPR, August 17, 2016, https://www.npr.org/sections/goatsand soda/2016/08/17/490121285/a-swimmers-period-comment-breaks-taboos-in -sports-and-in-china.

59. Ben Morse, "Surprising Reporter with Surprising Answer," CNN, May 3, 2022, https://www.cnn.com/2022/05/03/golf/lydia-ko-period-pain-lpga-spt -intl/index.html.

60. Danielle Symons Downs et al., "Physical Activity and Pregnancy: Past and Present Evidence and Future Recommendations," *Research Quarterly for Exercise and Sport* 83, no. 4 (2012): 485–502.

61. James Clapp III, "How Pregnant Athletes Train . . . Safely," *The Athletic Woman, Clinic in Sports Medicine* 13, no. 2 (April 1994).

62. Alexandra Allred, author interview, 1999.

63. Alexandra Allred, *Entering the Mother Zone: Balancing Self, Health, and Family* (Terre Haute, IN: Wish Publishing, 2000).

64. "History of the Male and Female Genitalia," Stanford University, https://web.stanford.edu/class/history13/earlysciencelab/body/femalebodypages/genitalia.html.

65. Regina Morantz-Sanchez, "Feminist Theory and Historical Practice: Re-reading Elizabeth Blackwell," *History and Theory* 31, no. 4 (December 1992): 51–69.

66. Debra Michals, "Elizabeth Blackwell," National Women's History Museum, 2015, https://www.womenshistory.org/education-resources/biographies/elizabeth-blackwell.

67. Marjorie R. Jenkins, Alyssa Herrmann, Amanda Tashjian, Tina Ramineni, Rithika Ramakrishnan, Donna Raef, Tracy Rokas, and John Shatzer, "Sex and Gender in Medical Education: A National Student Survey," *Biology of Sex Differences* 7, no. 45, Supplement 1 (2016).

CHAPTER FOURTEEN

1. Harrison Smith, "Rene Portland, Penn State Basketball Coach Accused of Anti-gay Discrimination, Dies at 65," *Washington Post*, July 23, 2018, https://www.washingtonpost.com/local/obituaries/rene-portland-penn-state-basketball-coach-accused-of-anti-gay-discrimination-dies-at-65/2018/07/23/625993d4-8e81-11e8-8322-b5482bf5e0f5_story.html.

2. Steve Tignor, "The 50 Greatest Players in the Open Era: No. 3, Martina Navratilova," *Tennis*, February 28, 2018, https://www.tennis.com/news/articles/the-50-greatest-players-of-the-open-era-no-3-martina-navratilova.

3. Steve Tignor, "Martina's Moment," *Tennis*, April 29, 2013, https://www.tennis.com/news/articles/martina-s-moment.

4. "Mission & Vision," Federation of Gay Games, https://gaygames.org/Mission-&-Vision.

5. Cyd Ziegler, "Canadian Volleyball Coach Betty Baxter Fired amidst Rumors She Is a Lesbian," Outsports, August 30, 2011, https://www.outsports.com/2011/8/30/4051752/moment-34-canadian-volleyball-coach-betty-baxter-fired-amidst-rumors.

6. Dalton James Dover, *Greek Homosexuality* (Cambridge, MA: Harvard University Press, 1978).

7. Catherine Craft-Fairchild, "Sexual and Textual Indeterminacy: Eighteenth-Century English and Representations of Sapphism," *Journal of the History of Sexuality* 15, no. 3 (2006): 408–31.

8. Merlisa Lawrence Corbett, "Anna Kournikova Is the Best and Worst Thing to Ever Happen to Women's Tennis," *Bleacher Report*, June 16, 2013, https://bleacherreport.com/articles/1671532-anna-kournikova-is-the-best-and-worst-thing-to-ever-happen-to-womens-tennis.

9. Malcolm Folley, "Mandlikova to Raise Family with Another Woman," *Daily Mail UK*, May 6, 2001, https://www.dailymail.co.uk/news/article-43868/Mandlikova-raise-family-woman.html.

10. Arthur A. Raney and Jennings Bryant, eds., *The Handbook of Sports and Media* (New York: Lawrence Erlbaum, 2006).

11. Wayne Drehs, "A Coming-Out Party for Professional Sports," ESPN, 2001, www.espn.com/page2/s/drehs/010524.html.

12. Mary G. McDonald, "Rethinking Resistance: The Queer Play of the Women's National Basketball Association, Visibility Politics and Late Capitalism," *Leisure Studies* 27, no. 1 (2008): 77–93.

13. Juliet Macur, "Coast Cleared by Others, WNBA Finally Finds Its Gay Pride," *New York Times,* June 10, 2014, https://www.nytimes.com/2014/06/11/sports/wnba-finally-advertises-its-gay-pride.html.

14. Doug Feinberg, "Coming Out as Lesbians No Longer Generating the Kind of Controversy from Years Past for WNBA Stars," *Globe and Mail,* July 26, 2018, https://www.theglobeandmail.com/sports/article-coming-out-as-lesbians-no-longer-generating-the-kind-of-controversy/.

15. Christopher Clarey, "Homosexuality 'Is Part of My Life,' She Says: A Tranquil Mauresmo Is Hoping for Respect," *New York Times,* February 1, 1999, https://www.nytimes.com/1999/02/01/sports/IHT-homosexuality-is-part-of-my-life-she-says-a-tranquil-mauresmo-is.html.

16. T. Weir, "WNBA Sells Diversity," *USA Today,* July 24, 2001, 1C.

17. Sally Ann Drucker, "Betty Friedan: The Three Waves of Feminism," April 27, 2018, Ohio Humanities, http://www.ohiohumanities.org/betty-friedan-the-three-waves-of-feminism/.

18. Julia Carmel, "Phyllis Lyon, Lesbian Activist and Gay Marriage Trailblazer," *New York Times,* April 10, 2020, https://www.nytimes.com/2020/04/10/obituaries/phyllis-lyon-dead.html.

19. Anne M. Valk, "Lesbian Feminism," *Britannica,* https://www.britannica.com/topic/lesbian-feminism.

20. Liz Stanley, "'Male Needs': The Problem and Problems of Working with Gay Men," in *On the Problem of Men,* ed. Scarlet Friedman and Elizabeth Sarah (London: Women's Press, 1982), 191–98.

21. Rosemary Auchmuty, Sheila Jeffreys, and Elaine Miller, "Lesbian History and Gay Studies: Keeping a Feminist Perspective," *Women's History Review* 1, no. 1 (1992): 89–108.

22. Lisa M. Diamond, *Sexual Fluidity: Understanding Women's Love and Desire* (Cambridge, MA: Harvard University Press, 2009), https://www.hup.harvard.edu/catalog.php?isbn=9780674032262&content=reviews.

23. "Big Thinker: Simone de Beauvoir," Ethics Centre, May 18, 2017, https://ethics.org.au/big-thinker-simone-de-beauvoir/.

24. Michael A. Garcia and Debra Umberson, "Marital Strain and Psychological Stress in Same-Sex and Different-Sex Couples," *Journal of Marriage and Family* 81, no. 5 (October 2019): 1253–68, https://doi.org/10.1111/jomf.12582.

25. Maaike van der Vleuten, "Same-Sex Couples' Division of Labor from a Cross-National Perspective," *Journal of GLBT Family Studies* 17, no. 2 (2021): 150–67, https://orcid.org/0000-0003-1108-2446.

26. Gerrit Bauer, "Gender Roles, Comparative Advantages and the Life Course: The Division of Domestic Labor in Same-Sex and Different-Sex Cou-

ples," *European Journal of Population* 32, no. 1 (January 2016): 99–128, https://doi.org/10.1007/s10680-015-9363-z.

CHAPTER FIFTEEN

1. Susan K. Cahn, *Coming on Strong: Gender and Sexuality in Twentieth-Century Women's Sports* (Cambridge, MA: Harvard University Press, 1994).
2. Bonnie S. Fischer, Francis T. Cullen, and Michael G. Turner, *Sexual Victimization of College Women*, U.S. Department of Justice, Office of Justice Programs, December 2020, https://www.ojp.gov/ncjrs/virtual-library/abstracts/sexual-victimization-college-women.
3. Monica Seles, *Getting a Grip: On My Body, My Mind, My Self* (New York: Penguin, 2009).
4. Christine Yu, "This Must Stop," *Runner's World*, no. 6 (2019): 44–45.
5. TS Staff, "15 Female Athletes You Didn't Know Were Stalked by Creeps," *Sportster*, November 27, 2017, https://www.thesportster.com/entertainment/15-female-athletes-you-didnt-know-were-stalked-by-creeps/.
6. Gloria Steinem, *Moving beyond Words* (New York: Simon & Schuster, 1994).
7. "Timeline: A Short History of Breast Implants," Reuters, January 26, 2012, https://www.reuters.com/article/us-france-implants-pip/timeline-a-short-history-of-breast-implants-idUSTRE80P12V20120126.
8. Heidi J. Hennink-Kaminski, "The Content of Cosmetic Surgery Magazine Advertisements and Consumer Use and Interpretations of Cosmetic Surgery Advertising" (PhD diss., University of Georgia, 2006), 9–10, https://getd.libs.uga.edu/pdfs/hennink-kaminski_heidi_j_200612_phd.pdf.
9. Jean-François Rosnoblet, "French Breast Implant Boss Arrested," Reuters, January 26, 2012, https://www.reuters.com/article/us-france-implants/french-breast-implant-boss-arrested-idUKTRE80P0AZ20120126.
10. Mark W. Clemens, "Largest-Study Ever Shows Silicone Breast Implants Associated with Rare Diseases," University of Texas MD Anderson Cancer Center, September 13, 2018, https://www.mdanderson.org/newsroom/largest-ever-study-shows-silicone-breast-implants-associated-with-rare-diseases.h00-159227301.html.
11. Corinne E. Wee, "Understanding Breast Implant Illness, before and after Explantation," *Annals of Plastic Surgery* 85, no. S1 (July 2020): S82–S86.
12. Diane Spector, "How the *Sports Illustrated* Swimsuit Issue Became Bigger Than the Magazine Itself," *Business Insider*, February 14, 2012, https://www.businessinsider.com/sports-illustrated-swimsuit-issue-history-2012-2.
13. Amy Tikkanen, "Mia Hamm," *Encyclopedia Britannica*, March 13, 2020, https://www.britannica.com/biography/Mia-Hamm.
14. Lisette Hilton, "No Me in Mia," ESPN Classic, https://www.espn.com/classic/biography/s/Hamm_Mia.html.
15. Emma Bowman, "Basketball Star Sue Bird Says WNBA Players' Activism Is 'Non-negotiable,'" NPR, October 25, 2020, https://www.npr.org/2020/10/25/927492785/basketball-star-sue-bird-says-wnba-players-activism-is-nonnegotiable.

16. Brenda Alexander, "Destiny's Child's 'Bootylicious' Was Inspired by Beyonce's Weight Gain," CheatSheet.com, June 28, 2020, https://www.cheat sheet.com/entertainment/destinys-childs-bootylicious-was-inspired-by-be yonces-weight-gain.html/.

17. Alexander, "Destiny's Child's 'Bootylicious' Was Inspired by Beyonce's Weight Gain."

18. Laura Beck, "Is This What a Plus-Size Model Should Look Like?" *Cosmopolitan*, January 11, 2014, https://www.cosmopolitan.com/entertainment/celebs/news/a18375/plus-sized-models/.

19. Lauren Langford, "Alaska's Swimsuit Scandal Unfairly Polices Young Girls' Bodies," Medium, September 7, 2019, https://gen.medium.com/alaska-high-school-swimming-divings-inexcusable-swimsuit-scandal-33cc10f180b9.

20. Jason Duaine Hahn, "Serena Williams Speaks Out on Sexism in Sports," *People*, September 7, 2017, https://people.com/human-interest/serena-williams-speaks-out-on-sexism-in-sports-it-isnt-easy-to-have-someone-make-a-comment-about-your-body/.

21. Christopher Ingraham, "The Absurdity of Women's Clothing Size, in One Chart," *Washington Post*, August 11, 2015, https://www.washingtonpost.com/news/wonk/wp/2015/08/11/the-absurdity-of-womens-clothing-sizes-in-one-chart/.

22. "Mission Statement," American Society of Testing and Materials, https://www.astm.org/search/fullsite-search.html?query=Mission%20statement.

23. Julia Felsenthal, "A Size 2 Is a Size 2 Is a Size 8: Why Clothing Sizes Make No Sense," Slate, January 25, 2012, https://slate.com/culture/2012/01/clothing-sizes-getting-bigger-why-our-sizing-system-makes-no-sense.html.

24. Caroline Criado Perez, *Invisible Women: Exposing Data Bias in a World Designed for Men* (New York: Abrams, 2019).

25. Claire Bond Potter, "Queer Hoover: Sex, Lies, and Political History," *Journal of the History of Sexuality* 1, no. 13 (September 2006): 355–81.

26. Jocelyn Sears, "Why Women Couldn't Wear Pants on the Senate Floor until 1993," Mental Floss, March 22, 2017, https://www.mentalfloss.com/article/93384/why-women-couldnt-wear-pants-senate-floor-until-1993.

27. "FBI Files on Eleanor Roosevelt," PBS, https://www.pbs.org/wgbh/americanexperience/features/eleanor-fbi/.

28. Juliet Linderman, "A Look at Women's Advances over the Years in Congress," PBS, November 4, 2017, https://www.pbs.org/newshour/politics/a-look-at-womens-advances-over-the-years-in-congress.

29. Carl Anthony, "First Ladies Wearing Pants," National First Lady's Library, October 29, 2015, http://www.firstladies.org/blog/first-ladies-wearing-pants/.

30. Betty K. Koed, *Women of the Senate Oral History Project: Carol Moseley Braun* (Washington, DC: Senate Historical Office, September 22, 2017), 6, https://www.senate.gov/about/resources/pdf/moseley-braun-carol-9-22-2017.pdf.

31. Sears, "Why Women Couldn't Wear Pants on the Senate Floor until 1993."

32. Kerri Lee Alexander, "Mary Edwards Walker," National Women's History Museum, 2019, https://www.womenshistory.org/education-resources/biographies/mary-edwards-walker.

33. "Constance M. K. Applebee," *Encyclopedia Britannica*, January 22, 2021, https://www.britannica.com/biography/Constance-M-K-Applebee.

34. Janet S. Fink and Linda Jean Kensicki, "An Imperceptible Difference: Visual and Textual Constructions of Femininity in *Sports Illustrated* and *Sports Illustrated for Women*," *Mass Communication and Society* 5, no. 3 (2002): 317–39.

35. Gwen Moran, "Do Female Athletes Get Stiffed by the Sports Industry?" *Fast Company* magazine, August 19, 2016, https://www.fastcompany.com/3062979/when-it-comes-to-women-athletes-is-the-game-rigged.

36. Jennifer L. Knight and Traci A. Giuliano, "Blood, Sweat, and Jeers: The Impact of the Media's Heterosexist Portrayals on Perceptions of Male and Female Athletes," *Journal of Sport Behavior* 26, no. 3 (2003): 272.

37. Jennifer Calfas, "How Olympic Star Lindsey Vonn Makes and Spends Her Money," *Business Insider*, February 6, 2018, https://www.businessinsider.com/how-olympic-gold-medalist-skier-lindsey-vonn-makes-her-money-2018-2?jwsource=cl.

38. V. Carty, "Textual Portrayals of Female Athletes," *Frontiers: A Journal of Women Studies* 26 (2005): 138.

39. J. Schröder, S. Nick S, H. Richter-Appelt, and P. Briken, "Psychiatric Impact of Organized and Ritual Child Sexual Abuse: Cross-Sectional Findings from Individuals Who Report Being Victimized," *Int J Environ Res Public Health* 15, no. 11 (2018): 2417, doi: 10.3390/ijerph15112417.

CHAPTER SIXTEEN

1. Louise Radnofsky, "Star Gymnasts Give Senators an Unsparing Account of FBI's Failures in Nassar Investigation," *Wall Street Journal*, September 15, 2021, https://www.wsj.com/articles/simone-biles-mckayla-maroney-aly-raisman-senate-fbi-investigation-11631723958.

2. David Eggert and Ed White, "Michigan State Reaches $500 Million Settlement for 332 Victims of Larry Nassar," *Chicago Tribune*, May 16, 2018, https://www.chicagotribune.com/sports/college/ct-spt-michigan-state-larry-nassar-settlement-20180516-story.html.

3. Bridget Read, "Aly Raisman and Jordyn Wieber Confront Larry Nassar and USA Gymnastics in Court," *Vogue*, January 19, 2018, https://www.vogue.com/article/aly-raisman-jordyn-wieber-larry-nassar-testimony-usa-gymnastics.

4. Beatrice Verhoeven, "'Athlete A': 9 Most Shocking Details from Larry Nassar Sexual Abuse Documentary," TheWrap.com, June 24, 2020, https://www.thewrap.com/athlete-a-shocking-details-larry-nassar-sexual-abuse-documentary/.

5. Marisa Kwiatkowski, "Maggie Nichols: Olympic Dreams, Larry Nassar and Falling Back in Love with Gymnastics," *Indy Star*, October 1, 2018, https://www.indystar.com/story/news/investigations/2018/10/18/usa-gymnastics-chief-steve-penny-approached-head-fbi-agent-job/1687527002/.

6. Jon LaPook, "Gymnast Breaks Silence: First Athlete to Accuse Team Doctor Goes Public," CBS, January 11, 2018, https://www.cbsnews.com/news

/former-team-usa-gymnasts-describe-doctors-alleged-sexual-abuse-60-min utes-2019-08-09/.

7. Sarah Fitzpatrick and Lisa Cavazuti, "More Than 120 Larry Nassar Victims Call for DOJ to Release Report on FBI's Handling of Case," NBC, June 17, 2020, https://www.nbcnews.com/news/sports/more-120-larry-nassar-victims-call -doj-release-report-fbi-n1231211.

8. Abigail Pesta, "An Early Survivor of Larry Nassar's Speaks Out for the First Time," *Time*, July 18, 2019, https://time.com/5629228/larry-nassar-victim -speaks-out/.

9. Pesta, "An Early Survivor of Larry Nassar's Speaks Out for the First Time."

10. Dan Murphy, "Days after USA Gymnastics' Suspension, Coach John Geddert Says He's Retiring," ESPN, January 23, 2018, https://www.espn.com /olympics/story/_/id/22190691/coach-john-geddert-suspended-usa-gymnas tics-says-plans-retire.

11. David Tarrant and Terri Langford, "On Karolyi Ranch, Gymnasts with Olympic Dreams Endure 'Perfect Environment for Abuse,'" *Dallas Morning News*, February 23, 2018, https://www.dallasnews.com/news/investigations/2018 /02/23/on-karolyi-ranch-gymnasts-with-olympic-dreams-endured-perfect-envi ronment-for-abuse/.

12. Mitch Weiss and Holbrook Mohr, "Crippling Climate: Former Karolyi Gymnasts Say Toxic 'Ranch' Environment Let Doctor Nassar Thrive," Associated Press/*Columbus Dispatch*, February 24, 2018.

13. Weiss and Mohr, "Crippling Climate."

14. Jasmine Garsd, "Gold Medalist Dominique Moceanu Warned Us 10 Years Ago about Abuse in USA Gymnastics," TheWorld.org, January 25, 2018, https:// theworld.org/stories/2018-01-25/gold-medalist-dominique-moceanu-warned -us-10-years-ago-about-abuse-usa-gymnastics.

15. Kerri Lee Alexander, "Tarana Burke," National Women's History Mu seum, 2020, https://www.womenshistory.org/education-resources/biographies /tarana-burke.

16. Greg Evans, "Harvey Weinstein Guilty in Rape Trial; Appeal Assured," *Deadline Hollywood*, February 24, 2020, https://deadline.com/2020/02/harvey -weinstein-guilty-rape-trial-new-york-appeal-assured-1202862551/.

17. "Full Transcript of Donald Trump's Obscene Videotape," BBC, October 9, 2016, https://www.bbc.com/news/election-us-2016-37595321.

18. Alyssa Rosenberg, "Defending Sexual Assault Is Never Worth It. Really," *Chicago Tribune*, November 14, 2017, https://www.chicagotribune.com/opinion /commentary/ct-perspec-roy-moore-sexual-assault-1114-story.html.

19. Haley Sweetland Edwards, "How Christine Blasey Ford's Testimony Changed America," *Time*, October 4, 2018, https://time.com/5415027/christine -blasey-ford-testimony/.

20. Emma Brown, "California Professor; Writer of Confidential Brett Kava naugh Letter, Speaks Out about Her Allegation of Sexual Assault," *Washington Post*, September 16, 2018, https://www.washingtonpost.com/investigations /california-professor-writer-of-confidential-brett-kavanaugh-letter-speaks-out -about-her-allegation-of-sexual-assault/2018/09/16/46982194-b846-11e8-94eb -3bd52dfe917b_story.html.

21. Beth Harris, "Women Sue USA Swimming over Alleged Sexual Abuse by Coaches," Associated Press, June 10, 2020, https://apnews.com/article/lawsuits-olympic-games-sexual-abuse-california-sports-general-939b316a002b1dbf90a2e01428b0519a.

CHAPTER SEVENTEEN

1. Fernando Alfonso III, "What Is the Fourth Wave of Feminism and What Does 4chan Have to Do with It?" DailyDot, January 12, 2014, May 31, 2021, https://www.dailydot.com/unclick/4chan-fourth-wave-feminism/.

2. Charlie Taylor, "Technology Helps Female Athletes Achieve 'Unthinkable' Results," *Irish Times*, November 2, 2021, https://www.irishtimes.com/business/technology/technology-helps-female-athletes-achieve-unthinkable-results-1.4717072.

3. Elizabeth Howell, "NASA's Real 'Hidden Figures,'" Space.com, February 24, 2020, https://www.space.com/35430-real-hidden-figures.html.

4. "Ada and Beyond," Software Policies for the Department of Defense, National Academy of Sciences, 1997.

5. S. S. Canetto, "Suicidal Behaviors among Muslim Women: Patterns, Pathways, Meanings, and Prevention," *Crisis* 36, no. 6 (2015): 447–58.

6. Kelly Angus, "Female Sports Fans: An Untapped Sports Marketing Demographic," Asking Smarter Questions, https://www.askingsmarterquestions.com/female-sports-fans-an-untapped-sports-marketing-demographic/.

7. Annelise McGough, "How This Former Field-Hockey Star Created the World's Biggest Sports Brand for Women," FastCompany, October 4, 2017, https://www.fastcompany.com/40476580/how-this-former-field-hockey-star-created-the-worlds-biggest-tv-sports-network-for-women.

8. "HeForShe," UN Women, https://unwomenusa.org/advocacy-3.

9. Juliana Menasce Horowitz and Ruth Igielnik, "A Century after Women Gained the Right to Vote, Majority of Americans See Work to Do on Gender Equality," Pew Research Center, July 7, 2020, https://www.pewresearch.org/social-trends/2020/07/07/a-century-after-women-gained-the-right-to-vote-majority-of-americans-see-work-to-do-on-gender-equality/.

10. Victoria Magrath (Inthefrow), "I Had to Disable Comments," YouTube video, 27:53, posted March 15, 2018, https://www.youtube.com/watch?v=AdSHex1C2sE.

11. Alex DiBranco, "Male Supremacist Terrorism as a Rising Threat," International Centre for Counterterrorism, February 10, 2020, https://icct.nl/publication/male-supremacist-terrorism-as-a-rising-threat/.

12. Tammy Waitt, "Violent Actors in the Violent Periphery of the Incel Movement," American Security Today, October 31, 2019, https://americansecuritytoday.com/violent-actors-in-the-periphery-of-the-incel-movement-multi-video/.

13. Greg Iacurci, "Women Are Still Paid 83 Cents for Every Dollar Men Earn. Here's Why," CNBC, May 19, 2022, https://www.cnbc.com/2022/05/19/women-are-still-paid-83-cents-for-every-dollar-men-earn-heres-why.html.

14. Gary Meenaghan, "Rio Olympics' Middle Eastern A to Z: From Abughaush to Zenoorin," Al Arabiya, August 24, 2016, https://english.alarabiya.net/sports/2016/08/24/The-Rio-Olympics-Arab-A-Z.

15. Mike Wise, "Afghan Sprinter Tahmina Kohistani Shows What's Possible for Muslim Women," *Washington Post*, August 3, 2012, https://www.washington post.com/sports/olympics/afghan-sprinter-tahima-kohistani-shows-whats-pos sible-for-muslim-women/2012/08/03/aa7414f6-dda6-11e1-9ff9-1dcd8858ad02 _story.html.

16. Agnieszka Flak and Hassib Sadat, "Afghan Girls Throw Punches, Aim for Olympic Gold," Reuters, January 2, 2012, https://www.reuters.com/article/uk-afghanistan-boxing/afghan-girls-throw-punches-aim-for-olympic-gold -idUKTRE80104C20120102.

17. Eleonora Giovio, "The Female Afghan Boxers Who Found Sanctuary in Spain," El País, November 5, 2019, https://english.elpais.com/elpais/2019/11/04/inenglish/1572866890_870963.html.

18. Bill Simmons, "This Is Who I Am," ESPN, https://www.espn.com/espn/page2/story?page=simmons/050901.

19. Martha Bevan, "The Way We Watch: Sports, Women and the Male Gaze," Varsity, June 12, 2020, https://www.varsity.co.uk/sport/19410.

20. Kirsten Rasmussen et al., "Gender Marginalization in Sports Participation through Advertising: The Case of Nike," *International Journal of Environmental Research and Public Health* 18, no. 15 (July 2021): 7759.

21. S. L. Grau and Y. C. Zotos, "Gender Stereotypes in Advertising: A Review of Current Research," *International Journal of Advertising* 35, no. 5 (2016): 761–70, https://doi.org/10.1080/02650487.2016.1203556; L. J. Meân and J. W. Kassing, "'I Would Just Like to Be Known as an Athlete': Managing Hegemony, Femininity, and Heterosexuality in Female Sport," *Western Journal of Communication* 72, no. 2 (2008): 126–44, https://doi.org/10.1080/10570310802038564.

22. A. Jones and J. Greer, "You Don't Look Like an Athlete: The Effects of Feminine Appearance on Audience Perceptions of Female Athletes and Women's Sports," *Journal of Sport Behavior* 34, no. 4 (2011): 358–77.

23. Erin Valois, "The Rise and Struggle of Women in Sports in the 1990s," The Score, July 16, 2014, https://www.thescore.com/worldcup/news/538378.

24. Zach Diriam, "Florida's Mary Wise Earns AVCA National Coach of the Year Honors," NCAA.com, December 14, 2017, https://www.ncaa.com/news/volleyball-women/article/2017-12-14/ncaa-womens-volleyball-floridas-mary -wise-earns-avca.

25. Ryan Fagan, "Sporting News Ranks the 50 Greatest Coaches of All Time," *Sporting News*, June 29, 2016, https://www.sportingnews.com/us/other-sports/list/greatest-coaches-wooden-lombardi-jackson-bryant-krzyzewski-pat-summit t/5la0zndczflw1nj2z2m4vckas.

26. Dayna Evans, "Six Moments That Made Pat Summit a Legend," The Cut, June 28, 2016, https://www.thecut.com/2016/06/pat-summitt-legend.html.

27. Lindsay Gibbs, "Muffet McGraw Is Done Hiring Men," Think Progress, March 30, 2019, https://archive.thinkprogress.org/this-top-womens-college -basketball-coach-is-done-hiring-men-5f3b6d06609b/.

28. Mitchell Northam, "Mo'ne Davis, Former Little League World Series Star, Makes Her College Softball Debut for Hampton," NCAA.com, February 9, 2020, https://www.ncaa.com/news/softball/article/2020-02-07/mone-davis-former-little-league-world-series-star-makes-her.

29. Tim Nudd, "The 5 Best Ads of Super Bowl XLIX," Adweek, February 2, 2015, https://www.adweek.com/brand-marketing/5-best-ads-super-bowl-xlix-162716/.

30. Nat Ives, "Not Just Views but Real Engagement: Always' #Likeagirl Is a Super Bowl Winner," AdAge, February 2, 2015.

31. "DGA Nominations for Outstanding Directorial Achievement in Commercials in the Year 2014," Directors Guild of America, https://www.dga.org/Awards/Annual.aspx.

32. Dimitra Karali, "Always #LikeaGirl," Medium.com, March 11, 2018, https://medium.com/ad-discovery-and-creativity-lab/always-likeagirl-5d4c2b1472c3.

33. Editorial, "Insight & Strategy: #LikeAGirl," *Contagious*, May 21, 2015, 1.

34. "Backlash as Empowering 'Like a Girl' Super Bowl Commercial Sparks #likeaboy Hashtag on Twitter," *Daily Mail*, February 2, 2015, https://www.dailymail.co.uk/news/article-2936819/Backlash-empowering-Like-Girl-Super-Bowl-commercial-sparks-likeaboy-hashtag-Twitter.html.

35. "Backlash as Empowering 'Like a Girl' Super Bowl Commercial Sparks #likeaboy Hashtag on Twitter."

CHAPTER EIGHTEEN

1. W. Roscoe, "Priests of the Goddess: Gender Transgression in Ancient Religion," *History of Religions* 35, no. 3 (1996): 195–230.

2. Arshad Zargar, "LGBTQ+ Advocates Call First Islamic School for Transgender Students a 'Positive Step,'" CBS News, November 17, 2020, https://www.cbsnews.com/news/transgender-madrassa-bangladesh-lgbtq-advocates-say-positive-step-but-not-enough/.

3. Chloe Hadjimatheou, "Christine Jorgensen: 60 Years of Sex Change Ops," BBC, November 30, 2012, https://www.bbc.com/news/magazine-20544095.

4. Manny Millan, "She's a Transgender Pioneer but Renee Richards Prefers to Stay Out of the Spotlight," *Sports Illustrated*, June 29, 2019, https://www.si.com/tennis/2019/06/28/renee-richards-gender-identity-politics-transgender-where-are-they-now.

5. C. Matson, M. Murphy, A. Sarver, et al., "DMRT1 Prevents Female Reprogramming in the Postnatal Mammalian Testis," *Nature* 476 (2011): 101–4.

6. N. Henriette Uhlenhaut, "Somatic Sex Reprogramming of Adult Ovaries to Testes by FOXL2 Ablation," *Cell* 139 (December 11, 2009): 1130–42.

7. G. Spizzirri, F. L. S. Duran, T. M. Chaim-Avancini, et al., "Grey and White Matter Volumes Either in Treatment-Naïve or Hormone-Treated Transgender Women: A Voxel-Based Morphometry Study," *Scientific Reports* 8 (2018): 736.

8. Ernie Hood, "Are EDCs Blurring Issues of Gender?" *Environmental Health Perspectives* 113, no. 10 (2005): A670–67.

9. Kathleen Megan, "Transgender Sports Debate Polarizes Women's Advocates," *Connecticut Mirror*, July 22, 2019, https://ctmirror.org/2019/07/22/trans gender-issues-polarizes-womens-advocates-a-conundrum/.

10. "Caitlyn Jenner Opposes Trans Girls in Women's Sports as Unfair," BBC News, May 2, 2021, https://www.bbc.com/news/world-us-canada-56960011.

11. Catherine Thorbeck, "Transgender Athletes Speak Out as Parents Petition to Change Policy That Allows Them to Compete as Girls," ABC News, June 22, 2018, https://abcnews.go.com/GMA/News/transgender-athletes-speak-par ents-petition-change-policy-compete/story?id=56071191.

12. "Medicine Alone Does Not Completely Suppress Testosterone Levels among Transgender Women," Boston University School of Medicine, February 20, 2018, https://www.bumc.bu.edu/busm/2018/02/20/medicine-alone-does -not-completely-suppress-testosterone-levels-among-transgender-women/.

13. Becky McCall, "75% of Transgender Women Fail to Suppress Testosterone," MedScape, March 1, 2018, https://www.medscape.com/viewarticle/893280.

14. Gillian Brassil, "Who Should Compete in Women's Sports: There Are 'Two Almost Irreconcilable Positions,'" *New York Times*, August 3, 2021, https://www .nytimes.com/2020/08/18/sports/transgender-athletes-womens-sports-idaho .html.

15. Gillian Brassil and Jere Longman, "World Rugby Bans Transgender Women, Baffling Players," *New York Times*, October 31, 2020, https://www .nytimes.com/2020/10/26/sports/olympics/world-rugby-transgender-women .html.

16. "Eligibility Rule Keeps Transgender Runner Out of Trials," Associated Press, June 24, 2021, https://apnews.com/article/or-state-wire-nh-state-wire -2020-tokyo-olympics-olympic-games-sports-70f8cdf7ce15f18632ced45bb1f4af38.

17. James Sutherland, "Penn's Lia Thomas Opens Up on a Journey," Swim-Swam, December 9, 2021.

18. Robert Sanchez, "I Am Lia: The Trans Swimmer Dividing America Tells Her Story," *Sports Illustrated*, March 3, 2022, https://www.si.com/college/2022 /03/03/lia-thomas-penn-swimmer-transgender-woman-daily-cover.

19. *National Survey on LGBTQ Youth Mental Health*, The Trevor Project, 2019, https://www.thetrevorproject.org/wp-content/uploads/2019/06/The-Trevor -Project-National-Survey-Results-2019.pdf.

20. S. Zwickl, A. F. Q. Wong, E. Dowers, et al., "Factors Associated with Suicide Attempts among Australian Transgender Adults," *BMC Psychiatry* 21, no. 81 (2021), https://doi.org/10.1186/s12888-021-03084-7.

21. Dean Connolly and Gail Gilchrist, "Prevalence and Correlates of Substance Abuse among Transgender Adults: A Systemic Review," *Addictive Behaviors* 111 (December 2020), https://doi.org/10.1016/j.addbeh.2020.106544.

22. L. Puce, L. Marinelli, N. G. Girtler, et al., "Self-Perceived Psychophysical Well-Being of Young Competitive Swimmers with Physical or Intellectual Impairment," *Perceptual and Motor Skills* 126, no. 5 (2019): 862–85, https://doi .org/10.1177/0031512519865849.

23. Jonathan Avila et al., "Eating Disorder Screening in Gender Minority Adolescents and Young Adults," *Adolescent Health* 64, no. 2 (February 1, 2019), https://doi.org/10.1016/j.jadohealth.2018.10.218.

24. Marla E. Eisenberg et al., "Risk and Protective Factors in the Lives of Transgender/Gender Non-conforming Adolescents," *Journal of Adolescent Health* 61, no. 4 (2017): 521–26; Ilan H. Meyer et al., "Sexual Orientation Enumeration in State Antibullying Statutes in the United States: Associations with Bullying, Suicidal Ideation, and Suicide Attempts among Youth," *LGBT Health* 6, no. 1 (2019): 9–14.

25. Brad Hunter, "Swimmer Lia Thomas 'Bad Publicity' for Trans Community, Caitlyn Jenner Says," *Toronto Sun*, April 29, 2022, https://torontosun.com/entertainment/celebrity/swimmer-lia-thomas-bad-publicity-for-trans-commu nity-caitlyn-jenner-says.

26. Outer House, Court of Session Petition by Fair Play for Women, https://www.scotcourts.gov.uk/docs/default-source/cos-general-docs/pdf-docs-for-opinions/2022csoh20.pdf?sfvrsn=9a4944d9_1.

27. Jody L. Herman et al., *Age of Individuals Who Identify as Transgender in the United States* (Los Angeles: Williams Institute at UCLA School of Law, 2017), https://williamsinstitute.law.ucla.edu/wp-content/uploads/Age-Trans-Indi viduals-Jan-2017.pdf.

28. Matt Lavietes, "International Olympic Committee Issues New Guidelines on Transgender Athletes," NBC News, November 16, 2021, https://www.nbc news.com/nbc-out/out-news/international-olympic-committee-issues-new-guidelines-transgender-athl-rcna5775.

29. Alexandra Allred, "Name Withheld: Elite Female Athletes Weigh In," interviews, 2021–2022.

30. Melissa Tanji, "Complaint Filed over Transgender MIL Track Athlete," *Maui News*, February 29, 2020, https://www.mauinews.com/news/local-news/2020/02/complaint-filed-over-transgender-mil%E2%80%88track-athlete/.

31. Azeen Ghorayshi, "Trans Swimmer Revives an Old Debate in Elite Sports: What Defines a Woman?" *New York Times*, February 18, 2022, https://www.ny times.com/2022/02/16/science/lia-thomas-testosterone-womens-sports.html.

32. Issy Ronald, "Olympic Medalist Dina Asher-Smith Calls for More Research into How Periods Affect Athletic Performance," CNN, August 19, 2022, https://www.cnn.com/2022/08/19/sport/dina-asher-smith-periods-performance-research-spt-intl/.

33. Sean Ingle, "Caster Semenya Accuses IAAF of Using Her as a 'Guinea Pig Experiment,'" *Guardian*, June 18, 2019, https://www.theguardian.com/sport/2019/jun/18/caster-semenya-iaaf-athletics-guinea-pig.

34. Catherine Thorbecke, "Transgender Athletes Speak Out as Critics Allege Unfair Advantage," ABC News, June 22, 2018, https://abcnews.go.com/GMA/News/transgender-athletes-speak-parents-petition-change-policy-compete/story?id=56071191.

35. Tricia Ward, "Do Trans Women Athletes Have Advantages?" WebMD, July 15, 2021, https://www.webmd.com/fitness-exercise/news/20210715/do-trans-women-athletes-have-advantages.

36. Julie Kliegman, "Idaho Banned Transgender Athletes from Women's Sports," *Sports Illustrated*, June 30, 2020, https://www.si.com/sports-illustrated/2020/06/30/idaho-transgender-ban-fighting-back.

37. Daniel Villarreal, "Inside the Dispute between USA Powerlifting and a Minnesota Trans Woman Athlete," Outsports, October 31, 2019, https://www

.outsports.com/2019/10/31/20939582/usa-powerlifting-transgender-ban-min
nesota-jaycee-cooper-larry-maile-joanna-harper.

38. Sakshi Venkatraman, "Transgender Athlete Sues USA Powerlifting over
Competition Ban," NBC News, January 13, 2021, https://www.nbcnews.com
/feature/nbc-out/transgender-athlete-sues-usa-powerlifting-over-competition
-ban-n1253960.

39. "Female Athletes Told to 'Be Quiet' on Transgender Issue, Ex-lifter," Reuters, May 7, 2021, https://www.reuters.com/lifestyle/sports/females-told-be
-quiet-transgender-issue-ex-weightlifter-2021-05-07/.

40. Bernard Lane, "Female Pushback over Trans Sport Rules," *Weekend Australian*, October 10, 2020, https://www.theaustralian.com.au/subscribe/news
/1/?sourceCode=TAWEB_WRE170_a_GGL&dest=https%3A%2F%2Fwww
.theaustralian.com.au%2Fnation%2Ffemale-pushback-over-trans-sport-rules.

41. Lane, "Female Pushback over Trans Sport Rules."

42. Anna Brown, "Deep Partisan Divide on Whether Greater Acceptance of
Transgender People Is Good for Society," Pew Research Center, February 11,
2022, https://www.pewresearch.org/fact-tank/2022/02/11/deep-partisan-di
vide-on-whether-greater-acceptance-of-transgender-people-is-good-for-society/.

43. Justin McCarthy, "Mixed Views among Americans on Transgender Issues,"
Gallup Poll News, May 26, 2021, https://news.gallup.com/poll/350174/mixed
-views-among-americans-transgender-issues.aspx.

44. Jeffrey Jones, "LGBT Identification Rises to 5.6% in Latest U.S. Estimate,"
Gallup, February 24, 2021, https://news.gallup.com/poll/329708/lgbt-identifi
cation-rises-latest-estimate.aspx.

45. Kailyn Brown, "Martina Navratilova Says, 'Put an Asterisk' Next to Transgender Swimmer Lia Thomas," *Los Angeles Magazine*, March 18, 2022, https://
www.lamag.com/citythinkblog/martina-navratilova-on-trasgender-swinner-lia
-thomas/.

CHAPTER NINETEEN

1. "Where Are the Women?" NCAA.org, *Champion* magazine, Winter 2017,
https://www.ncaa.org/sports/2017/1/13/where-are-the-women.aspx.

2. Chuck Stewart, "Influential Washington State University Administrator Joanne Washburn Dies at Age 83," *Spokesman-Review*, September 16, 2020,
https://www.spokesman.com/stories/2020/sep/16/influential-washington
-state-university-administra/.

3. Stewart, "Influential Washington State University Administrator Joanne
Washburn Dies at Age 83."

4. Hannelore Sudermann, "History Was Made . . . The Fight for Equality
for Women's Athletics in Washington," *Washington State* magazine, July 6, 2009,
https://magazine.wsu.edu/2009/07/06/history-was-made-the-fight-for-equity
-for-womens-athletics-in-washington/.

5. "Debunking the Myths about Title IX and Athletics," National Women's
Law Center, November 2010, https://www.nwlc.org/sites/default/files/pdfs
/debunking_myths_november_2010.pdf.

6. "Debunking the Myths about Title IX and Athletics."

7. Caleb Diehl, "Foul Play," Oregon Business, March 25, 2019, https://www.oregonbusiness.com/article/education/item/18707-college-sports.

8. "NCAA Football Coach Salaries in Real-Time," EdSmart, https://www.edsmart.org/ncaa-football-coach-salaries/#content-anchor.

9. "Women's College Basketball Coach Salary," ZipRecruiter.com, https://www.ziprecruiter.com/Salaries/Womens-College-Basketball-Coach-Salary.

10. Vanessa Longoria, "Social Injustices of Women's Sports," Tarleton State University, Department of Kinesiology, March 2021; M. Hensley-Clancy, "College Softball Coaches Decry Treatment by NCAA: 'What's Lower Than an Afterthought?'" Washington Post, April 26, 2021, https://www.washingtonpost.com/sports/2021/04/23/ncaa-softball-college-world-series-disparities/.

11. Beth Brooke-Marciniak and Donna de Varona, "Amazing Things Happen When You Give Female Athletes the Same Funding as Men," World Economic Forum, August 25, 2016, https://medium.com/world-economic-forum/amazing-things-happen-when-you-give-female-athletes-the-same-funding-as-men-3f5e355fa90b.

12. Celene Reynolds, "The Mobilization of Title IX across U.S. Colleges and Universities, 1994–2014," Social Problems 66, no. 2 (May 2019): 245–73.

13. Jake New, "You Called Me a Liar," Inside Higher Ed, September 9, 2016, https://www.insidehighered.com/news/2016/09/09/student-writes-online-essay-accusing-u-richmond-mishandling-her-sexual-assault.

14. Michael Stratford, "'Wake-Up Call' on Sex Assault," Inside Higher Ed, July 10, 2014, https://www.insidehighered.com/news/2014/07/10/mccaskill-says-her-survey-shows-colleges-falling-short-dealing-sex-assaults.

15. Jake New, "Consequences at Baylor," Inside Higher Ed, May 27, 2016, https://www.insidehighered.com/news/2016/05/27/baylor-university-regents-fire-head-football-coach-ken-starr-steps-aside.

16. Jake New, "The Black Hole of College Sports," Inside Higher Ed, February 9, 2017, https://www.insidehighered.com/news/2017/02/09/baylor-not-alone-shielding-athletes-accused-misconduct-punishment.

17. Nick Anderson, "Survey Shows Colleges with the Most Reports of Sexual Assault," Chicago Tribune, June 9, 2016, https://www.chicagotribune.com/nation-world/ct-college-sex-assault-survey-20160609-story.html.

18. Sarah Brown, "It's Been 2 Years since Scandal Erupted at Baylor. Yet the Allegations Continue," Chronicle of Higher Education, October 2, 2018, https://www.chronicle.com/article/its-been-2-years-since-scandal-erupted-at-baylor-yet-the-allegations-continue/.

19. Brown, "It's Been 2 Years since Scandal Erupted at Baylor."

20. Zac Ellis, "A Timeline of the Baylor Sexual Assault Scandal," Sports Illustrated, May 26, 2016, https://www.si.com/college/2016/05/26/baylor-art-briles-sexual-assault-ken-starr.

21. Ellen J. Staurowsky and Erianne Weight, "Title IX Literacy: What Coaches Don't Know and Need to Find Out," Journal of Intercollegiate Sport 4 (2011): 190–209.

22. Elizabeth A. Daniels and Heidi Wartena, "Athlete or Sex Symbol: What Boys Think of Media Representations of Female Athlete," *Sex Roles: A Journal of Research* 65, nos. 7–8 (October 2011): 566–68.

23. Michael Messner, Margaret Carlisle Duncan, and Kerry Jensen, "Separating the Men from the Girls: The Gendered Language of Televised Sports." *Gender and Society* 7, no. 1 (1993): 129, 133.

24. Andrew Zimbalist, "Female Athletes Are Undervalued, in Both Money and Media Terms," SportsMoney, April 10, 2019, https://www.forbes.com/sites/andrewzimbalist/2019/04/10/female-athletes-are-undervalued-in-both-money-and-media-terms/?sh=5e5017fb13ed.

25. Michel Martin, "The Veteran and NFL Player Who Advised Kaepernick to Take a Knee," NPR, September 9, 2018, https://www.wbur.org/npr/646115651/the-veteran-and-nfl-player-who-advised-kaepernick-to-take-a-knee.

26. Mattie Kahn, "Women Athletes Have Been Protesting for Over a Year," *Elle*, October 2, 2017, https://www.elle.com/culture/a12656426/women-athletes-protest-take-a-knee-trump-wnba/.

27. Dan Cancian, "Colin Kaepernick Net Worth: How Much Will Nike Deal Pay?" *Newsweek*, September 4, 2018, https://www.newsweek.com/colin-kaepernick-net-worth-how-much-will-nike-deal-pay-1103437.

28. Meshelle Voepel, "Sparks Agree on 'Unity and Solidarity,' Stay in Locker Room for Game 1s National Anthem," ESPN, September 24, 2017, https://www.espn.com/wnba/story/_/id/20805331/los-angeles-sparks-stay-their-locker-room-national-anthem-game-1-wnba-finals.

29. Kahn, "Women Athletes Have Been Protesting for Over a Year."

30. Amira Rose Davis, "Black Cheerleaders and a Long History of Protest," African American Intellectual History Society, Black Perspectives, January 3, 2019.

31. Davis, "Black Cheerleaders and a Long History of Protest."

32. Victoria Wolcott, *Race, Riots and Roller Coasters: The Struggle over Segregated Recreation in America* (Philadelphia: University of Pennsylvania Press, 2012).

CHAPTER TWENTY

1. Kinga Philipps, "Meet a Real-Life Lara Croft," Inside Hook, September 10, 2018, https://www.insidehook.com/article/action/meet-real-life-lara-croft-lauren-mcgough-anthropologist-skydiver-falconer.

2. "Kazakhstan's Lone Female Eagle Hunter: Makpal Abdrazakova," Reuters, March 12, 2012, https://www.reuters.com/article/idUS114113938320120306.

3. Adrienne Mayor, "The Eagle Huntress: Ancient Traditions, and Evidence of Women as Eagle Hunters, Part I," Ancient Origins, April 5, 2016, https://www.ancient-origins.net/news-history-archaeology/eagle-huntress-ancient-traditions-and-evidence-women-eagle-hunters-part-i-020797.

4. Burkhart Ford, "Frances Hamerstrom, Author and Biologist, Is Dead at 90," *New York Times*, September 7, 1998, https://www.nytimes.com/1998/09/07/us/frances-hamerstrom-author-and-biologist-is-dead-at-90.html.

5. D. S. Eitzen and G. H. Sage, *Sociology of North American Sport* (Boulder, CO: Paradigm, 2009).

6. Jay Atkinson, "How Parents Are Ruining Youth Sports," *Boston Globe*, May 4, 2014, https://www.bostonglobe.com/magazine/2014/05/03/how-parents-are-ruining-youth-sports/vbRln8qYXkrrNFJcsuvNyM/story.html.

7. "Women's Wrestling Facts and Resources," NWCAOnline.com, http://www.nwcaonline.com/growing-wrestling/growing-womens-wrestling/womens-wrestling-facts-resources/.

8. "Michaela Hutchison Beats the Boys," Alaska Sports Hall of Fame, https://alaskasportshall.org/inductee/michaela-hutchison-beats-the-boys/.

9. John Cobbcorn, "The Most Influential Women's Wrestler of All Time," *Bleacher Report*, October 29, 2011, https://bleacherreport.com/articles/916045-the-most-influential-womens-wrestler-of-all-time.

10. Cody Goodwin, "Once a Trailblazer for Girls' Wrestling in Iowa, Cassy Herkelman Now Coaches the Girls' Team," *Des Moines Register*, January 23, 2020.

11. "Girls Football," *Toledo Blade*, September 5, 1978.

12. Adrienne Smith, "History of Women's Professional Football," Gridiron Queendom, April 1, 2014.

13. "Is Lingerie Football League Sexist?" Morning Call, February 9, 2011, https://www.mcall.com/opinion/mc-xpm-2011-02-09-mc-chatter-sounding-board-0210-20110209-story.html.

14. Sheinelle Jones, "Female Football Team Winning Big," *Today Show*, October 4, 2021, https://www.bostonrenegadesfootball.org/female-football-team-winning-big-today/.

15. Pat Borzi, "Women GMs Mean Business in Minors," ESPN, May 12, 2012, https://www.espn.com/espnw/news-commentary/story/_/id/7946245/women-gms-mean-business-minor-league-baseball.

16. Carrie N. Baker, "Working Harder, Earning Less: Inside the Women's Soccer Team Lawsuit for Equal Pay," *Ms.*, August 8, 2019, https://msmagazine.com/2019/07/08/working-harder-earning-less-inside-the-womens-soccer-team-lawsuit-for-equal-pay/.

17. Doug Feinberg, "Becky Hammon: It Was an Easy Decision to Leave the NBA, Return to WNBA," NBA.com, January 18, 2022, https://www.nba.com/news/becky-hammon-it-was-easy-decision-to-leave-nba-return-to-wnba.

18. Judy Battista, "Sarah Thomas Blazes Trail as NFL First Full-Time Official," NFL.com, April 8, 2015, https://www.nfl.com/news/sarah-thomas-blazes-trail-as-nfl-s-first-full-time-female-offic-0ap3000000484343.

19. Analisa Novak, "Sarah Thomas on 'Falling in Love' with Officiating Football and Being the First Woman to Referee the Super Bowl," CBS News, February 10, 2021.

20. Jesse Rogers, "Miami Marlins Hire Kim Ng as MLB's First Female General Manager," ESPN, November 13, 2020, https://www.espn.com/mlb/story/_/id/30310018/miami-marlins-hire-kim-ng-mlb-first-female-general-manager.

21. Allyson Felix, "My Own Nike Pregnancy Story," *New York Times*, May 22, 2019, https://www.nytimes.com/2019/05/22/opinion/allyson-felix-pregnancy-nike.html.

22. Abu Murbarik, "'I Was Told to Know My Place': Olympian Shares Why She Left Nike to Launch Her Own Shoe Brand," Face2Face Africa, July 27, 2021,

https://face2faceafrica.com/article/i-was-told-to-know-my-place-olympian
-shares-why-she-left-nike-to-launch-her-own-shoe-brand.

23. "Modern Family Index," Bright Horizons, 2018, https://www.bright
horizons.com/-/media/BH-New/Newsroom/Media-Kit/MFI_2018_Report
_FINAL.ashx.

24. Gina Lucrezi, "About Trail Sisters," Trail Sisters, https://trailsisters.net
/about/.

25. National Congress of American Indians, "Violence against AI/AN
Women," NCAI Policy Research Center, February 2018, https://www.ncai.org
/policy-research-center/research-data/prc-publications/VAWA_Data_Brief
__FINAL_2_1_2018.pdf.

26. Dave Trimmer, "'When I Run about It, People Will Notice': Rosalie Fish
Runs for Missing and Murdered Indigenous Women," *Seattle Times*, June 1, 2019,
https://www.seattletimes.com/sports/high-school/but-when-i-run-about-it
-people-will-notice-muckleshoot-tribals-rosalie-fish-runs-for-missing-and-mur
dered-indigenous-women/.

27. Ellis O'Neill, "Indigenous Runners Rosalie Fish and Jordan Marie Daniel
Run for Their People," WBUR.org, January 3, 2020.

28. O'Neill, "Indigenous Runners Rosalie Fish and Jordan Marie Daniel Run
for Their People."

29. Mark Stelzer, "Measuring Bias against Female Political Leadership," *Politics
& Gender* 15, no. 4 (December 2019): 695–721.

30. Susan R. Madsen and Maureen S. Andrade, "Unconscious Gender Bias:
Implications for Women's Leadership Development," *Journal of Leadership Studies*
12, no. 1 (Spring 2018): 62–67.

31. *"The Double-Bind Dilemma for Women in Leadership,"* Catalyst.org, August 2, 2018, https://www.catalyst.org/research/infographic-the-double-bind
-dilemma-for-women-in-leadership/.

32. S. Mukkamala and K. L. Suyemoto, "Racialized Sexism/Sexualized Racism:
A Multimethod Study of Intersectional Experiences of Discrimination for Asian
American Women," *Asian American Journal of Psychology* 9, no. 1 (2018): 32–46.

33. Michelle Harrison, Silvana Koch-Mehrin, and Hanna Birna Kristjánsdóttir,
"The Reykjavik Index for Leadership: Measuring Perceptions of Equality for Men
and Women in Leadership," *Kantar* (2020–2021): 5–12.

CHAPTER TWENTY-ONE

1. Tom Rosentiel, "Michelle Obama's Strong Personal Image," Pew Research
Center, January 21, 2010, https://www.pewresearch.org/2010/01/21/michelle
-obamas-strong-personal-image/.

2. Deutsche Presse-Agentur, "Survey: Barack and Michelle Obama Are World's
Most Admired People," dpa-international, September 25, 2020.

3. Terre Ryan, "'Changing the Conversation': Contexts for Reading Michelle
Obama's *American Grown: The Story of the White House Kitchen Garden and Gardens
across America,*" *Frontiers: A Journal of Women Studies* 37, no. 2 (2016): 75–108.

4. Allison Aubrey, "First Lady: Let's Move Fruits and Vegetables to 'Food Deserts,'" NPR, July 20, 2011, https://www.npr.org/sections/health-shots/2011/07/20/138544907/first-lady-lets-move-fruits-and-veggies-to-food-deserts.

5. Aura Lewis, *The Illustrated Feminist: 100 Years of Suffrage, Strength, and Sisterhood in America* (New York: Abrams Image, 2020).

6. Simone Manuel, "Simone Manuel: A Letter to My Younger Self," The Undefeated/AndScape, July 24, 2018, https://andscape.com/features/simone-manuel-no-ceilings-a-letter-to-my-younger-self/.

7. "German Gymnasts' Outfits Take on Sexualisation in Sport," BBC, April 23, 2021, https://www.bbc.com/news/world-europe-56858863.

8. Alise Zvigule, "Stop the Sexualization of Female Climbers," Climbing, August 21, 2021, https://www.climbing.com/news/stop-the-sexualization-of-female-climbers/.

9. Mariana Alfaro, "Michigan GOP Candidate Says He Tells His Daughters to 'Lie Back and Enjoy It' If Rape Is Inevitable," *Washington Post*, March 8, 2022, https://www.washingtonpost.com/politics/2022/03/08/gop-candidate-rape-2020-election/.

10. Laura Stampler, "Ford Apologizes for Offensive Car Ad We Were Never Supposed to See," *Business Insider*, March 22, 2013, https://www.businessinsider.in/advertising/ford-apologizes-for-offensive-car-ad-we-were-never-supposed-to-see/articleshow/21232857.cms.

11. "Italy's 'Stifling' Treatment of Women: By the Numbers," The Week, January 8, 2015, https://theweek.com/articles/489291/italys-stifling-treatment-women-by-numbers.

12. Nicole Winfield, "Italy Outraged as Court Finds Victim Too Ugly to Be Raped," Associated Press, March 13, 2019, https://apnews.com/article/international-news-europe-italy-ap-top-news-6361b8de2200469d8f423b8fecdee771.

13. David Gritten, "Elnaz Rekabi: Crowd Greet Iranian Climber Who Broke Hijab Rule on Return," BBC News, October 19, 2022, https://www.bbc.com/news/world-middle-east-63309101.

14. Antonia Kirkland, "When It Comes to Constitutional Equality, the U.S. Lags behind the Rest of the World," *Ms.*, August 26, 2020, https://msmagazine.com/2020/08/26/when-it-comes-to-constitutional-equality-the-u-s-lags-behind-the-rest-of-the-world/.

15. "Statement from President Biden on the Equal Rights Amendment," White House, January 27, 2022, https://www.whitehouse.gov/briefing-room/statements-releases/2022/01/27/statement-from-president-biden-on-the-equal-rights-amendment/.

16. Stacy Sims, "Women Are Not Small Men: A Paradigm Shift in the Science of Nutrition," TEDxTauranga, YouTube video, 13:45, posted September 23, 2019, https://www.youtube.com/watch?v=e5LYGzKUPlE.

17. Sims, "Women Are Not Small Men."

18. Sims, "Women Are Not Small Men."

19. Sims, "Women Are Not Small Men."

20. Sims, "Women Are Not Small Men."

21. "Female Athlete Program," Boston Children's Hospital, https://www.childrenshospital.org/centers-and-services/programs/f-_-n/female-athlete-program.

22. Mirel Zaman, "Kathryn Ackerman Is Going to Get Female Athletes in the Spotlight Once and for All," *Shape* magazine, August 16, 2019, https://www.shape.com/celebrities/interviews/dr-kathryn-ackerman-female-sports-advocate.

23. https://www.fitrwoman.com/.

24. Ann Richards, *Straight from the Heart: My Life in Politics & Other Places* (New York: Simon & Schuster, 19).

25. Ginger Rogers, *Ginger: My Story* (New York: HarperCollins, 1991).

26. "Misquotation: Backwards and in High Heels," Oxford Academic, Tumblr, January 23, 2014, https://oupacademic.tumblr.com/post/74326381160/misquotation-ginger-rogers.

POSTSCRIPT

1. Julie Moreau, "Students Rallied to Get Lacrosse Coach Rehired after She Listed Her Wife as an Emergency Contact," NBC News, September 23, 2021, https://www.nbcnews.com/nbc-out/out-news/backlash-illinois-catholic-school-reverses-course-hires-lesbian-coach-rcna2177.

Acknowledgments

Without question, I have to thank my family. Well before the internet or the term "foodie," my grandmother, Violet Watkins (1915–2000), was a social influencer in the 1940s and 1950s with her own newspaper column on, of all things, recipes and how to be the perfect hostess. She also fed the rumor mills, as she insisted on riding the notoriously aggressive horse, Widow Maker, among country club members, wore pants, and engaged in many "unladylike" activities. Following in her mother's footsteps, my mother, Karen Watkins Powe (1941–2017), became a devout civil rights activist in the 1960s and rarely walked away from an argument.

It stood to reason, then, that my sister and I would later become members of the first-ever U.S. women's bobsled team. That we had never been in a bobsled prior to tryouts did not matter. What mattered was that someone had previously said that women could not bobsled, and so we stood.

Dr. Kayla Peak, dean of Tarleton State University's kinesiology department, is another such pioneer who has stood for women in sport, and it was she who set me on this path to discover and honor all those incredible women in history who dared to change the world in pursuit of education, sports, and equality.

Christen Karniski, senior acquisitions editor at Rowman & Littlefield, gave new voice to the trailblazers of *When Women Stood* when she sent an email in late fall of 2021 to express her interest in women's studies and that the editorial board had called this a "timely and important work." The publishing industry, once believed to be too taxing and stressful for women, now has such leaders as Nicole Carty, Samantha Delwarte, Erinn Slanina, and Suzanne Staszak-Silva—all part of Team *When Women Stood*.

Harvard professor Laurel Thatcher Ulrich (1938–) coined the phrase "Well-behaved women seldom make history" in the 1970s, and she was right. Women were erased from history—as you will read—throughout time, as their achievements and actions were never thought to be noteworthy. But for every roadblock placed before them, they found new routes.

My greatest thanks go to the incredible women of this book, many of whom sent me on hours- and day-long research hunts only to have a single sentence or paragraph identify them (for page-count purposes). They ultimately changed my life. I may never again see a tennis racquet, MMA or soccer match, or WNBA game in the same light, for my sisters in time have shown me so much. It is my hope to honor what they have given all of us. Those women who *misbehaved* did not *make* history; rather, they *are* history.

Index

#Awareness, 139
#BelieveWomen, 202
#BikiniBridge, 205
#BlackLivesMatter, 247
#BoycottNFL, 247
#FixGirlsSports, 139
#GirlPower, 258
#HeForShe, 209
#LikeABoy, 218
#LikeAGirl, 218
#MenstruationMatters, 165
#MeToo, 200, 202
#NoDAPL, 50
#NotOkay, 202
#RepealtheNineteenth, 209
#StandFortheFlag, 247
#TakeAKnee4Me, 246
#TakeTheKnee, 246
#ThrowLikeAGirl, 216–18
#TimesUp, 193
#VisibilityMatters, 108
#WaterIsLife, 50
#WhyIDidntReport, 202
#WomenEmpowerment, 139
#YesAllWomen, 202

Abbott, Greg (politician), 162
Abbott, Margaret (golfer), 22
Abbott, Mary (golfer), 22
Abbott, Senda Berenson ("Mother of
    Women's Basketball"), 25
Abdrazakova, Makpal (ancient eagle
    huntress), 250
abolitionist(s), 39–42

abortion: doping, 160; history of,
    160–62
Abuljadayel, Kariman (track and field
    athlete), 211–12
Ackerman, Kathryn (sports medicine),
    277. See also Female Athlete Program
"Ada," or Ada Lovelace, 206
Adams, Katrina, 110. See also United
    States Tennis Association (USTA)
Adams, Sharon Sites (sailor), 110
Adelita, 58. See also escaramuza charro
Agesilaus, King, 2
Akers, Michelle, 154–56. See also
    concussion; traumatic brain injury
    (TBI)
Alaskan Native (AN), 26
Alaska's Aviation Grocery Girl, 70. See
    also Crosson, Marvel
Al-Atrash, Mary (swimmer), 211
Alfonso, Fernando, 205
All-American Girls Professional
    Baseball League (AAGPBL), 77–80
Allard, LaDonna Tamakawastewin
    Brave Bull, 50–51. See also Dakota
    Access Pipeline (DAPL)
all-women's spacewalk, 188–89. See
    also National Aeronautics and
    Space Administration (NASA)
Alpern, Stanley (historian), 288
Always. See sanitary pads
Amateur Athletic Union (AAU), 20,
    29, 32, 87, 133, 179
Amazon, ix, 4–8, 23, 48, 57, 90–92,
    172–73, 177–78, 248–50, 258–59

American Basketball League (ABA), 192, 252, 281

American Board of Medical Specialists (ABMS), 183

American Civil Liberties Union (ACLU), 223

American College of Obstetrics and Gynecology, 159, 166

American Equal Rights Association (AERA), 39

American Football Verband Deutschland (American Football Association of Germany, AFVD), 252

American Gladiators, 117–18

American Indian (AI), 263

American League (AL), 80

American Medical Association, 153, 223

American Medical Colleges, 153, 223

American Medical Women's Association (AMWA), 153

American Ninja Warriors, 258, 285

American Society of Testing and Materials (ASTM), 188

American University, 13

American Woman Suffrage Association (AWSA), 29, 40, 49

Amherst College, 229

Amini, Mahsa (activist), 273

Anani, Sumya ("the Island Girl," boxer), 132, 281

anemia. *See* female triad; iron deficiency

Annette Kellerman Collection, 24

Anthony, Susan B., 17, 29–30, 39–40. *See also* Anthony Amendment

"Anthony Amendment," 43

antifeminist, 205–6, 209–10, 271

Applebee, Constance M. K. (field hockey player), 191–92

Aquilina, Rosemarie (judge), 201–2

archery, 11, 21–23

Archidamus II, King, 2

Ardhanarishvara (half man/half woman), 219

Aristotle, 3, 9, 161, 168

Asher-Smith, Dina (British sprinter), 229

Ashford, Evelyn (sprinter), 123, 167

Astraea, goddess for justice, 56. *See* Juarez, Jovita Idar

Atlanta Baptist Female Seminary (now Spelman College), 40–41

Auburn University, 240

Austin Rage, 252–56. *See also* Women's Professional Football League (WPFL)

autoimmune disease, 151, 154, 184

Ave Negra. *See* Juarez, Jovita Idar

Avon, 172

Baiul, Oksana (ice skater), 123

Bakken, Jill (Jill Bakken Linder), 134–35

Barnes, Florence "Pancho" (aviator/pilot), 69

Barnes, Paulette, 119. *See also* Title VII

baseball, x, 20–21, 31–32, 58, 77–81, 147, 179, 240, 255, 257

basketball, 25, 32, 37, 45, 54–55, 126–27, 173–74, 192, 214–15, 239–44, 247–48, 252, 256

Batgirl, 145–16

bathing suit, 24–25; history, 152–53, 185–87. *See also* "Annette Kellerman Collection"

battle of the sexes, 93, 95, 101–3. *See also* King, Billie Jean

Baxter, Betty (coach), 172. *See also* Gay Games

Bayh, Birch, U.S. Senator, 101

Baylor University, 241–43

Beardsley, Marion "Mimi" (presidential intern), 201

beauty contests, 115, 179, 200–201

de Beauvoir, Simone (author), 177–78

Bell, Judy, 112. *See also* U.S. Golf Association (USGA)

Berlin Games, 33, 85

Berman, Jessica (NHL and NLL), 258

Bethune, Mary McLeod, 40

biathletes, 157

bicycle, ix, 15–17, 23, 247, 274. *See also* bicycle face; cycling
bicycle face, 16, 25
Biden, Joseph, 274
bikini medicine, 152–54
Biles, Simone (gymnast), 147, 195–98
Bingson, Amanda (hammer thrower), 146–47
biological females and males, medical markers, 140–41, 146–47, 152–57, 160, 165–66, 219–29, 230–33, 277
bipotential primordium, 220–21
Bird, Sue (basketball player), 186
birth control pills, effects of, 107, 139, 157–60, 161
bisexual, 171–74, 221
Bissell, Kim (professor), 273–74
Black cheerleaders, 247–48
Black Lives Matter, 247
Black Panther, 7
Blackwell, Elizabeth (physician), 168–69
Blackwell, Emily (professor), 169
Blankers-Koen, Fanny ("The Flying Housewife," Danish track athlete), 84–89, 92, 166
Blatt, Josephine "Minerva" (bodybuilder), 105
Bliss, Mildred (aka Mildred Burke, pro wrestler), 251–52
blood clots, 158–59. *See also* birth control pills, effects of
Bloomer, Amelia, 16. *See also* bloomers
bloomers, ix, 5, 16, 31, 85
bobsled, 132–35, 329
Bocharova, Nina Antonovna (gymnast), 91
bodybuilding, 105, 113–18. *See also* weightlifting
body dysmorphia, 227
body fat, 139–41, 146, 224–25, 274–77. *See also* female triad
body measurements, 13, 145, 152, 188
body shaming, 90, 139, 145–50, 185–89, 199, 205, 259
Bolden, Blake (hockey player), 258
Bolshevik Revolution, 90
Bonaly, Surya (figure skater), 270–71

bootylicious, 185–87
Boston Marathon, 97–99, 263–64
"Boston marriages," 173. *See also* lesbian
Boston Renegades, 254. *See also* Women's Football Alliance
Boston University School of Medicine, 223–24. *See also* transgender
Boubakri, Ines (fencing), 211
Boudreau, Carrie Lynn (weightlifting), 117
Boyer, Lisa (NBA assistant coach), 255
Boyer, Nate (military), 247. *See also* Kaepernick
brain injury, 154–57. *See also* concussion
breast, 4, 113, 115–16, 188; augmentation, 115–16, 182–85; breast implant illness (BII), 184; cancer, 158–59; implants, 115–16, 182–85
Briles, Art (disgraced football coach), 241–43
British Columbia Supreme Court, 133
British Ladies Amateur, 82
British Olympic Council, 22
British Royal Air Force, 69
Brown, Hallie Quinn, 44
Brown University, 239, 248
Brunei, 211
"brunettes versus blondes," 20–21. *See also* Vassar College
Bucha-Kerscher, Sandra (swimmer), 228
Budanova, Yekaterina (aviator/pilot), 66
Budd, Zola (track and field athlete), 121–22. *See also* Decker, Mary
Bueno, Maria Esther, 59
Bundchen, Gisele (model), 192
Bureau of Justice Statistics, 180, 182
Burke, Mildred (Mildred Bliss), 251–52
Burke, Tarana (activist), 200
Burns, Lucy (suffragist), 43
Bush, Barbara (First Lady), 190
Byrd, Alma English (basketball player), 145

Cahill, Allison (female quarterback), 254

Cahn, Susan K. (author), 54

Cain, Mary, 138–39, 187, 276–77. *See also* Nike's Oregon Project

Cambridge University, 33

Canadian Association for the Advancement of Women in Sport, 172

cancer, 158–59, 164, 184

Carlos, John (Olympian), 247

Carter, Rosalynn (First Lady), 190

Cary, Mary Ann Shadd, 41

Casey, Ellen (doctor), 158. *See also* Penn Center for the Female Athlete

Cellucotton, 36–37. *See also* Kotex

Center for Critical Sports Studies, 245

Center on Gender Equality and Health, 182

Cevallos, Manolo (sports radio commentator), 60

Chambers, Marcia (golfer), 112

Channels, Isadore "Izzy," 54–55. *See also* Roamer Girls

Chapman, Doris Neale, 32

chariot races, 2

Charlie's Angels, 278

Chastain, Brandi (soccer player), 80, 186, 193, 245

cheerleading, 156, 197, 244, 247–48. *See also* Black cheerleaders

Chinese citizenship, 47

Chloris (mythical great granddaughter of Zeus), 3

chronic fatigue and immune dysfunction syndrome (CFIDS), 155. *See also* autoimmune disease

chronic traumatic encephalopathy (CTE), 155

Church (views), 3, 9, 40, 54, 56, 107, 161–63, 201. *See also* religious practices

cisgender, 177, 221–35

Citizenship for Native Americans, 46–47

Civil Air Patrol, 68–69. *See also* Nichols, Ruth Rowland

Civil Rights Act of 1964, 28, 95–103, 273. *See also* Title VII

Clapp, James, III., 166–68

Clemens, Mark W., 184. *See also* University of Texas MD Anderson Cancer Center

clinic trials, 151–54, 223, 276. *See also* bikini medicine

Clinton, Bill "William," 180, 201

Clinton, Hillary, 190, 207–8, 216

Coachman, Alice (track athlete), 85, 87, 92

Cold War, 89–92

Coleman, Bessie (aviator), 164–65

Coleman, Robin (American Gladiator), 117–18

Collins, Dottie (baseball player), 79

Collins, Luci (gymnast), 87–88

Colvin, Claudette (activist), 96. *See also* Civil Rights Act of 1964

Comaneci, Nadia (gymnast), 91, 112

concussion, 154–56. *See also* traumatic brain injury (TBI)

Confederate Army, 41, 44

Connecticut Interscholastic Athletic Conference, 222–23

Connor, Kaleigh, 142–43. *See also* gamer

Conte, Victor, 124–25

Controllers of Women, 17–18, 193, 273

Cook, Joan (PhD, professor of psychiatry), 182

Cooper, Charlotte (tennis player), 22

Cooper, JayCee (powerlifter), 232. *See also* transgender female athletes

Copeland, Misty (ballet dancer), 270–71

Coronavirus, 159. *See also* oral contraceptives

corsets, 13–15, 138, 271

Cosby, Bill (rapist), 200–201

De Coubertin, Baron Pierre, 23, 33–34

Couch, Jane (British boxer), 131

Coulter, Jeannie (stuntwoman), 278

Council of Matrons, 49–50

Court, Margaret (tennis player), 102

Court of Arbitration for Sport (CAS), 230. *See also* intersex
Crawford, Patty (Title IX coordinator), 242–43
cricket, 24, 33
croquet, 11, 22
CrossFit, 117
Crosson, Marvel, 70
Croteau, Julie (NCAA men's baseball player), 255
Crouch, Sarah (professional distance runner), 157–58
Crump, Diane (jockey), 108–9
C-section/Cesarean delivery, 159–60
Cure, Dorothy (high jumper), 54
Curse of Eve, 164, 166. *See also* menstrual cycle
cyberbullies, 141–43, 149–50, 180–82, 210; cyber-stalking, 143; mean girls, 149–50
cycling, ix, 15–17, 23, 32–33, 53, 233, 247, 274
Cyniska, 2. *See* Kyniska
Czerny, Vincenz ("Father of Plastic Surgery"), 183

Dahomey warriors, 1–2, 7–8. *See also* Kingdom of Dahomey
Dakota Access Pipeline (DAPL), 50
Daley, Arthur, 90–91
Daniel, Jordan Marie Brings Three White Horses (runner/activist), 263–64
Daniels, Elizabeth. *See also* Center for Critical Sports Studies
Dantzscher, Jamie (gymnast), 196–97
Dartmouth, 248, 254
Daughters of Bilitis (DOB), 176
David, "Pepper" Paire Davis, 79. *See also* All-American Girls Professional Baseball League (AAGPBL)
Davis, Amira Rose (professor of women's studies), 45
Davis, Kim (NHL executive), 257–58
Davis, Laura (golfer), 180
Davis, Mo'ne (Little League World Series player), 216–17

Davis, Pauline (sprinter), 164–65
Davis-Kimball, Jeannine (archeologist), 5–6
Dawes, Dominique (gymnast), 87–88
Dawes Act, 46–47
Dawn, Brittany (social influencer), 137–38
DC Comics, 143–44
Decker, Mary (track athlete), 121–22
Denhollander, Rachael (gymnast, survivor), 196–98
depression, 15–16, 69, 151, 154, 159, 226
Deves, Katherine, 233–34. *See also* Save Women's Sports
Dewey, Katharine (bobsledder), 133
Diamond, Lisa (author), 177
distance running, 30, 179, 260–62
diving, 23–24, 31–32, 59, 88, 113, 197
doping, 124. *See also* performance-enhancing drugs (PEDs)
Dora Milaje, 7. *See also* Dahomey warriors
Douglas, Gabrielle (gymnast), 88, 197
Douglass, Frederick, 29–30, 39–40, 42
Doyle, Geraldine Hoff, 73. *See also* Rosie the Riveter
Draves, Vicki Manalo (diver), 88
Driscoll, Patty (bobsledder), 134–35
Duke University, 202, 207
Dunlap, Carla (bodybuilder), 115
Durham, Dianne (gymnast), 88
Durrant, Sue (Title IX), 237–38
Duy, Tim (economist), 239–40. *See also* University of Oregon

Earhart, Amelia (aviator), 65–70, 81
Easton, Shannon (football line judge), 257
eating disorders, 137–41, 145. *See also* female triad
Ebers, Papyrus, 161
Ederle, Gertrude, 37–38, 91–92
Edmonton Grads (basketball team), 32
Edwards, Harry (Olympic Project for Human Rights), 248–49
Eisenhower, Dwight D., 91

Elder, Ruth (aviator), 69
Elghobashy, Doaa (volleyball player), 211–12
Ellenburg Normal School basketball, 25
Ellis, Sarah Kate, 174–75. *See also* Gay and Lesbian Alliance Against Defamation (GLAAD)
Empowering Women and Girls Through Sport, 207–9
energy availability (EA)/residual energy, 139–40
English Channel, 30, 37, 64
Epstein-Barr, 155
Equal Employment Opportunities Commission (EEOC), 120
Equal Rights Amendment (ERA), 101, 274
equestrian, 3, 22
Ernst, Chris (rower, Yale protest), 106
escaramuza charro, 58
ESPN, 146, 148, 207, 214, 281
espnW, 207–9
esports, 141–43. *See also* gaming/gamers
essential women/nonessential women, 10–11
estrogen, 156, 158, 163–64, 221, 276
eugenics, 168, 219
Eunuchs, 168, 219
Evans, Richard (sports historian), 181
Eve/Eve's original sin, 163–64
Everson, Corinna "Cory," 117–18. *See also* Ms. Olympia
explicit bias, 271–74. *See also* implicit bias

Fahy, Claire Mae (aviator), 70
fainting couch, 13–15
Fair Play for Women, 228
Falconer, 249–50, 285. *See also* McGough, Lauren
Fawcett, Joy (soccer player), 186
Federal Bureau of Investigation (FBI), 189, 195, 198–99, 201
Fédération Aéronautique Internationale, 64

Federation of Gay Games, 172
La Fédération Sportive Féminine Internationale (FSFI). *See also* Milliat, Alice
Felix, Allyson (track and field Olympian), 259–60
Female Athlete Program, 277
Female Coaching Network, 216
female spacesuit, 188–89. *See also* spacewalk
Female Sports Association, 23
female triad, 139–41, 158, 199, 222
feminine hygiene, 37, 163, 168–69, 216–17
feminine ideal. *See* hegemonic feminine ideal
Feminine Mystique, 107. *See also* Friedan, Betty
feminism, 41, 102–3, 132–33, 175–76, 218; first wave, 102–3; fourth wave, 193, 205–7, 210–11; second wave, 105–10, 175–76; third wave, 117–21, 205. *See* suffragist
feminist, 41, 58–59, 74, 100, 118, 120, 132, 142, 174, 176–77, 209–11, 271
fencing, 30, 211
Fernandez, Lisa (softball player), x
fibromyalgia, 153. *See also* autoimmune disease
field hockey, 30, 32–33, 46, 191–92, 207, 285. *See also* skirts
Fifteenth Amendment, 40
figure skating, 17, 22–23, 122–23, 147, 197, 270–71
Finch, Rachael (actress), 184
First Ladies, 70, 189–90, 267–70
First Mexican Congress (El Primer Congreso Mexicanista), 56–57
Fish, Rosalie (runner/activist), 261, 263–64
Five Nation Iroquois Confederacy, 48
flapper, *35–37*, 179
Fleming, Peggy (ice skater), 281
Fletcher, Alice (anthropologist and suffragist), 47–48
Florida State University, 128

fluctuating hormones, 160, 224, 261, 276–77. *See also* menstrual cycle

Fly Girls, 71

Folz, Edith, 69. *See also* British Royal Air Force

football (American), 30, 36, 82, 92, 99, 129, 148–49, 238–42, 252–57

foot binding, 14–15

Ford, Betty (First Lady), 190

Ford, Christine Blasey (professor of psychology), 201

Ford, Krista (bobsledder and powerlifter), 117

Ford Motor Company, 273

Foudy, Julie (soccer player), 180, 186

Fourteenth Amendment, 46

Fox, Fallon (MMA fighter), 228. *See also* transgender female athletes

Fraley, Naomi Parker, 74. *See also* Rosie the Riveter

Francis, Bev, 113–14, 254. *See also Pumping Iron II*

Franklin, Missy (swimmer), 225

Freedom Summer, 45. *See also* Civil Rights Act of 1964

free-floating organ, 14–15. *See also* uterus

French Academy of Sports, 30

Freud, Sigmund, 13–15

Friedan, Betty, 106–7, 176

Friedman, Elizabeth Smith (codebreaker), 206

Fugitive Slave Law of 1850, 41

Fuhrman, Diane (weightlifting), 117

Gage, Matilda Joslyn, 43, 49–50

Galen (philosopher and physician), 15

Gallica, Paul (reporter), 182

Galton, Francis (creator of eugenics theory), 54

gaming/gamers, 141–43

gang rape, 99, 241–42, 273. *See also* Sandler, Bernice

Gay and Lesbian Alliance Against Defamation (GLAAD), 174–75

Gay Games, 172

Geddert, John (coach and rapist), 198–99

gender-blind medicine, 152–53. *See also* one-sex medicine

gender-fluidity female, 220

gender roles, 82, 178, 192, 214

gender specific (or gender-based), 165

gender stereotypes, 61, 214, 265. *See also* patriarchal system

Gentile, Laura, 207–9, 211. *See also* espnW

Ghribi, Habiba (steeplechase athlete), 211

Gibb, Roberta "Bobby" Bingay (marathon runner), 97

Gibson, Althea (tennis player), 91, 110–12

Gibson Girls, 34–35

Gilbert, Olive, 40. *See also The Narrative of Sojourner Truth*

Gilder, Virginia "Ginny" (rower, WNBA owner), 106

Gilooly, Jeff, 122. *See also* Harding, Tonya

Glanville, Ann (regattas, rower), 12–13

Glenn, John (astronaut), 206

Glenney, Judy (weightlifter), 117

Global Sports Mentoring Program, 216. *See also* espnW

Gloster, Ernestine (track medalist), 55

Gmitroski, Wynn (soccer coach), 157. *See also* birth control pills, effects of

goddess, 2–3, 56, 142, 219

Godmother of Title IX, 99

Gogarty, Deirdre (boxer), 132

goggles, invention of, 37, 46

golf, 11, 19, 21–22, 30, 58, 81–82, 110–12, 174

gonzo journalism, 107

Gorokhovskaya, Maria (gymnast), 91

goths, 6–7

Goucher, Kara (track and field Olympian), 259, 278–79

Graf, Steffi (tennis player), 181

Graff, Jessie (American Ninja Warrior and stuntwoman), 258, 278

Grant, Linda (historian), ix

Green, Edith (U.S. Representative), 100

Greenfield, Lauren (filmmaker), 217

Griffin, Pat (coach), 174

Griner, Brittney (WNBA player), 174, 214–15

Grodensky, Debra (swimmer), 203

Guinness Book of World Records, 117

Guthrie, Janet, 109

gymnastics, 22–23, 32, 87–88, 91–92, 112, 146–47, 195–203, 214, 238, 271–72

Haizlip, Mary (aviator), 69

Hall, Cynthia Holcomb (judge, Title IX), 243–44, 274

Hall, Edith (historian of Ancient Greece), 3

Hallback, Chevelle "Fist of Steel" (boxer), 132

Halmich, Regina (boxer), 132

Hamerstrom, Frances "Fran" (naturalist, author, and pioneer), 250

Hamm, Mia (soccer player), 180, 186

hammer thrower, 146

Hammon, Becky (NBA and WNBA coach), 257

Hantze, Karen (tennis player), 102

Haberton, Lady Florence (Rational Dress), 16

Harding, Florence (First Lady), 190

Harding, Tonya (ice skater), 122–23, 129

Harlem "Bloomer Girls," 31

Harper, Ida Husted, 43

Harper, Joanna (athlete/researcher), 231. See also transgender female athletes

Harris, Lucy (NBA player), 110

Harvard, 106, 191, 277

Hayes, Lucy (First Lady), 189–90

Healy, Bernadine (NIH director), 151

heart attack, 151, 154

heart disease, 151, 164

heart rate, and pregnancy, 166–68

hegemonic feminine ideal, 9, 45, 56, 83, 112, 127, 146–47, 149–50, 173, 185–89, 192, 214–15, 249, 267–69, 272–73, 278–79

Helsinki Games, 89–92

Hemmen, Lucie, 137–38. See also thigh gap

Henwood, Kate (lacrosse coach), 282

Hera (goddess), 2–3

Heraean Games, 2–3

Hercules, 4

Herkelman, Cassy (wrestler), 252

Hidatsa tribe, 49

Higher Education Act, 100–101

hijab, 211–12

Hill, Anita (activist), 120

Hill, Sarah (research psychologist and professor), 159

Hirschfeld, Dr. Magnus (transgender surgery), 220

hockey, 33, 130–31, 133, 238, 258

Hogshead-Maker, Nancy (swimmer, Title IX), 180, 202–3, 244

Holdsclaw, Chamique (WNBA player), 126

Holm, Holly (MMA fighter), ix

Homer, author of *Iliad*, 4–5

homophobia, 1, 174

Hood, Victoria (cyclist), 228–29

Hoover, J. Edgar, 189, 206

hormones: hormonal changes, 140, 158, 160, 163–64, 169, 206, 224–26, 261, 274–77

hormone therapy, 220–26, 231, 261

Hubbard, Laurel (powerlifter), 233. See also transgender female athletes

Hughes, Dorothy Pitman (publisher/activist), 107

Hulick, Helen, ix–x

human computers, 206

Huns, 6–7

Hutchins, Carole (softball coach), 215

Hutchinson, Michaela (wrestler), 251

Hyfield, Hannah (boxer), 12

hypermenorrhea (heavier, prolonged bleeding), 157

hypoandrogenism, 230. *See also* intersex

hyponatremic state, 275

hysterical: hysterical women, 13–15, 144, 155, 206, 265

Iliad, 4–5

Immaculata University, 110

implicit bias, 271–72. *See also* explicit bias

incels, 210–11

Independent Women's Football League (IWFL), 252, 254

Indiana Fever, 247

Indiana Pacers, 125

Indianapolis 500, 109, 165. *See also* St. James, Lyn

indigenous: communities, 46–48, 50, 53, 56, 59, 64–66; rights, 46–48, 263

Industrial Revolution, 10

infanticide, 161

inner-core temperature, 166–68. *See also* pregnancy

International Amateur Athletic Federation (IAAF). *See* World Athletics

International Association of Athletics Federations (IAAF). *See* World Athletics

International Centre for Counterterrorism (ICCT), 210

International Council of Women, 48

International Day of the Girl, 268

International Federation of Association Football (FIFA), 154

International Federation of Sport Climbing (IFSC), 273

International Ice Hockey Federation's (IIHF), 131

International Olympic Committee (IOC), x, 22–23, 31–32, 34, 90, 133–34, 139, 142, 168, 212, 219, 222–24, 227–31, 271–72

International Powerlifting Hall of Fame, 117

International Ski Federation, 192

International Society of Olympic Historians, 23

International Surfing Hall of Fame, 109

International Swimming Hall of Fame, 202, 209

International Women's Day, 210

International Women's Media Foundation, 107

intersex, 229–31

Interstate Stalking Act, 180

iron deficiency, 141

Ironman, 274–76

Iroquois, 48–50

ischemic strokes, 158–59

Jackson, Andrew (politician), 43

Jackson, Mary (human computer), 206

Jantzen Knitting Mills, 24–25

Jantzi, Sarah (gymnast coach), 197–98

Japanese citizenship, 47, 53

javelin, 3, 81, 114

Jenkins, Marjorie (cofounder, Laura Bush Institute), 153–54

Jenkins, Patty (producer), 258

Jenner, Bruce. *See* Jenner, Caitlyn

Jenner, Caitlyn (decathlete), 113, 222, 227, 234

Jennings, Kerri Walsh (volleyball), 128–29

Jerome, Jessica (ski jumper), 133

Jim Crow Laws, 29, 44

jockey, 13, 108–9

JogBra, 113. *See also* Lindahl, Lisa

John, Judy (#LikeAGirl creative officer), 217

Johnson, Daisy, 32

Johnson, Julie Ann (stuntwoman), 278

Johnson, Katherine (human computer), 206

Johnson, Lyndon B., 96

Jones, Marion (track and field athlete), 124. *See also* performance-enhancing drugs (PEDs)

Jordan, Michael (NBA player), 126, 128

Jorgensen, Christine, 220

Joyner, Al (track athlete), 124
Joyner, Florence Griffith "Flo Jo" (track and field athlete), 123–25, 180
Juan Crow, 56–57
Juarez, Jovita Idar, 56–57

Kaepernick, Colin (former NFL player, activist), 246–47
Kamenshek, Dorothy "Kammie" (AAGPBL), 77
Kammes, Amanda (lacrosse), 282–85
Karasyova, Olga (gymnast), 160
Karkazis, Katrina (anthropologist), 229
Karolyi, Bela, 197–200
Karolyi, Martha, 197–200
Katz Institute for Women's Health, 152
Kavanaugh, Brett, 201–2
Keck, Karla (ski jumper), 132–33
Kellerman (Kellermann), Annette (swimmer), 24–25
Kennamer, Dee (WPFL coach), 253–54
Kennedy, Jacqueline "Jackie" (First Lady), 190
Kennedy, John F., 90–91, 95, 201
Kentucky Derby, 109
Kerrigan, Nancy (ice skater), 122–23, 129, 180
Kersee, Bob (track coach), 123
Kersee, Jackie Joyner (track and field athlete), 123–24, 281
Khomiakova, Lt. Valeriia (Soviet pilot), 66
Kilbourne, Jean (filmmaker, activist), 145
Kimberly-Clark, 36
King, Billie Jean (tennis player), 101–3, 106, 108–10, 147, 171–72
King, Martin Luther, Jr., 95
King, Maxine Joyce "Micki" (diver), 109
Kingdom of Dahomey, 7
Klan. *See* Ku Klux Klan
Knowles, Beyoncé (singer), 186–88. *See also* bootylicious
Ko, Lydia (golfer), 166

Kohistani, Tahmina (track and field athlete), 212–13
Kokorina, Zinaida (Soviet aviator), 66
Kondras, Holly (sports publisher), 148–49
Korbut, Olga (gymnast), 91
Kotex, 36–37. *See also* Kimberly-Clark
Kournikova, Anna (tennis player), 173, 180
Kraus-Weber, 91
Ku Klux Klan (KKK), 53, 56, 83
Kunz, Opal (aviator), 69
Kwan, Michelle (ice skater), 122, 180
Kyniska, 2

labor and delivery, 15, 159–60, 168
labor pains, pain medication, 161
Labreck, Jesse "Flex" (American Ninja Warrior), 258
lacrosse, 24–25, 46, 141, 191–92, 258, 282–83, 285
Ladies Professional Golf Association (LPGA), 110, 112
Lamarr, Hedy (actress/inventor), 206. *See also* Secret Communication System
Lambert, Elizabeth (soccer player), 148
Lambrechs, Tracey (powerlifter), 233
Lane, Temryss Xeli'tia (soccer player, activist, Standing Rock), 50–51
Langford, Lauren (swim coach), 187
Larson, Mattie (gymnast), 199
Latina Rosa Parks. *See* Torres, Carmelita
Laura W. Bush Institute for Women's Health, 153–54. *See also* Texas Tech University Health Sciences Center
Law, Ruth (aviator), 63
League of Mexican Women, 56–57
League of Their Own, 77–81
Ledecky, Katie (swimmer), 225
Legends Football League (LFL), 253
Lenin, Vladimir, 90
Lenk, Maria (swimmer), 59

lesbian: lesbianism, 4, 171–78, 185, 232–33

Leslie, Lisa (WNBA player), 126, 192

Let's Move. *See* Obama, Michelle

Lewinski, Monica (presidential intern), 201, 241

Lewis, Tamsyn (track athlete, activist), 233

Lewis and Clark. *See* Sacagawea

Lieberman, Nancy (basketball player, coach), 256

Life magazine, 31, 110, 251

Like A Girl, 216–18

Lillehammer Games, 123, 129

Lilly, Kristine (soccer player), 186, 244–46, 258

Lindahl, Lisa, 113. *See also* sports bra

Lindsey, Timmie Jean (breast implant recipient), 183

Little League World Series, 216

Lobo, Rebecca (WNBA player), 126

London Games, 22, 84–85, 211–13

London School of Medicine for Women, 169

Lopiano, Donna (WSF director), 222

Los Angeles Games, 81–82, 120–21, 167

Los Angeles Sparks, 247

Loughborough University, 231

Lovelace, Ada, 206. *See also* U.S. Department of Defense

Lowe, Maria R. (author), 116

Lucrezi, Gina, 260–61, 281–82. *See also* Trail Sisters

Lummi Nation, 50

Lyon, Phyllis, 176

MacLean, Noella "Babe" Belanger (basketball player), 32

Magrath, Victoria (vlogger), 210

Major League Baseball (MLB), 77–79, 80, 256–57

male gaze, 214–15

male superiority culture, 3, 32, 60, 119, 144, 214

male supremacy, 210. *See also* incels

Mammy, "Mammy of the South," 44

Mandlikova, Hana (tennis player), 173

Manuel, Simone (swimmer), 270

marathon, 22, 92, 96–99, 263–64, 281

Maroney, McKayla (gymnast), 195–98

Marshall, Karyn (weightlifter), 105

Marshall, Penny (*A League of Their Own* director), 77, 80

Marta. *See* da Silva, Marta Vieira

Martin, Christy (boxer), 132, 171

Martin, Del (activist), 176

Martin, Meagan (American Ninja Warrior), 258–59

Marvingt, Marie (French athlete), 30

Mary, Queen of Scots, 19

Masters, Catherine (coach and women's football owner), 252–53

Mathis, Kylie (author), 143–44

Matters, Muriel (balloonist), 30

Mauresmo, Amelie (tennis player), 175

Mayor, Adrienne (author), 250

May-Treanor, Misty (beach volleyball player), 128–29

McAnena, Fiona, 228. *See also* Fair Play for Women

McCaskill, Claire (politician), 241

McGann, Michelle (golfer), 180

McGough, Lauren (anthologist, falconer), 249–50, 285

McGraw, Muffet (coach), 215–16

McKinnon, Rachel (transgender cyclist), 228–29

McLish, Rachel (bodybuilder), 113–15

Mean Girls, 149–50

Melinek, Dr. Judy, 166

Melpomene, 23. *See* Revithi, marathon

meninists, 217. *See* men's rights movement (MRM)

menopause, 158, 276

men's rights movement (MRM), 210–11, 217

menstrual abnormalities, 139–40, 156–59, 164–65, 275–77

menstrual cycle, 93, 131, 139–40, 156–59, 164–65, 206, 224, 261, 272, 275–77

menstruation huts, 163

metabolism, 164, 233

Mexican Revolution, 57–58
Meyers, Carol (biblical scholar and archeologist), 285
Michigan State University, 195–96, 199–200
micro-celebrities, 139
midwives, 49, 161
migraine, 151, 154–55
Mikulski, Barbarai (politician), 190
Milano, Alyssa (actress and activist), 200
military uniforms, 63, 67, 71–71, 75
Miller, Hinda Schreiber (inventor, JogBra), 113
Miller, Jessie (aviator), 70
Miller, Shannon (gymnast), 180
Miller, Terry (track and field trans athlete and activist), 231
Millett, Laurie (bobsledder), 135
Milliat, Alice, 33–34
Mink, Patsy Matsu Takemoto (politician), 100–101. *See also* Patsy T. Mink Opportunity in Education Act
Minnesota Lynx, 247
misdiagnosis (women in medicine), 154, 276. *See also* bikini medicine
misogynism, 31–32, 103, 141–42, 144, 206–7, 210, 243, 271, 273. *See also* patriarchal system
Missing and Murdered Indigenous Women (MMIW), 263
Miss Teen USA, 200
Miss Universe, 200
Mitchell, Virne Beatrice "Jackie" (baseball player), 77–78
Mixed Martial Arts (MMA), ix, 12, 228
Moceanu, Dominique (gymnast/ activist), 199–200
Monroe, Rose Will (Rosie the Riveter), 73–74
Montaño, Alysia (track and fielder), 259
Monteleone, Cynthia (track athlete and coach), 228–29
Montes, Margarita "La Maya" (boxing), 58

Montreal Games, 106, 112, 222, 227, 256
Moran, Suzette (swimmer), 203
Moreno, Alex (gymnast), 143
Mormon Women for Ethical Government, 201
"morning after" treatments, 161. *See also* oral contraceptives
Moseley-Braun, Carol (politician), 190
Moss, Lanny (minor leagues GM), 255
Mother of Boxing. *See* Wilkinson, Elizabeth
Mother of Golf. *See* Mary, Queen of Scots
Mother of Women's Basketball, 25
Mott, Kim (WPFL player), 253–54
Mott, Lucretia (suffragist), 39
mountain climbing, 30, 258, 273
Mowatt, Marilyn (activist, Washington State University), 237–38
Ms. Foundation for Women, 107
Ms. magazine, 107, 120, 182–83
Ms. Olympia, 114–16, 117
Muhammad, Ibtihaj (fencer), 211
Muldowney, Shirley "Cha Cha" ("First Lady of Drag Racing"), 109
Mulkey, Kim (basketball player, coach), 215
Munich Games, 88, 109
Murphy, Mary Elizabeth ("Queen of Baseball"), 78–79
Murray, Pam Sproule (boxer), 90–93
Muslim women, 164, 207, 209, 211–13. *See also* Ramadan
Musselburgh Golf Club, 19

Naismith, James (inventor of basketball), 32
Nakken, Alyssa (MLB coach), 257
The Narrative of Sojourner Truth, 40
Nassar, Larry (serial rapist), 195–203
National Aeronautics and Space Administration (NASA), 69, 188–89, 206
National Air Races, also National Women's Air Derby, 65–66

National American Woman Suffrage
Association (NAWSA), 29
National Association for the
Advancement of Colored People
(NAACP), 44, 248
National Association of Colored
Women (NACW), 44
National Association Oppressed to
Woman Suffrage (NAOWS), 34
National Basketball Association
(NBA), 110, 125, 173–74, 255–57
National College Women Sexual
Victimization study, 180
National Collegiate Athletic
Association (NCAA), 99, 109–10,
126, 141, 157, 172, 207, 215–16, 222,
225, 227, 239, 240–41, 244, 263, 270
National Football League (NFL), 148,
154–56, 208, 246–47, 252, 256–57,
269
National Hockey League (NHL),
130–31, 256–58
National Institutes of Health (NIH),
151–52
National Lacrosse League (NLL), 258
National March on Washington for
Lesbian, Gay and Bisexual Rights,
172
National Organization of Women
(NOW), 99, 107
National Sports Council, 59
National University of Ireland, 206
National Woman's Party, 65
National Woman's Rights Convention,
39–40, 43
National Woman Suffrage Association
(NWSA), 40
National Women's Air Derby, 65,
69–70
National Women's Football
Association (NWFA), 252–53
National Women's Football League
(NWFL), 252–53
National Women's Hall of Fame, 29
National Women's Law Center, 120
National Women's Political Caucus,
107

National Wrestling Alliance (NWA),
251
National Wrestling Coaches
Association, 251
Navratilova, Martina (tennis player,
activist), 171–74, 235
Nawi (Dahomey Amazon), 7–8
NCAA's Women in Sports Conference,
172
Negro League, 80
Nelson, Alice Dunbar, 40
Nelson, Donnie (Dallas Mavericks
creator), 256
Neville, Joy (rugby referee), 257
Newall, Queenie (gold medalist
Olympian, archery), 22
New York Female Giants, 31
New York Liberty, 247
New York Times, 13, 31, 70, 90, 106, 115,
139–40
Ng, Kim (Miami Marlins GM), 257–58
Nichols, Maggie (gymnast), 195–98
Nichols, Ruth Rowland (aviator/
pilot), 68–69
Nievas, Alhambra (referee), 257
Night Witches, 67–68
Nike, 126–28, 138–40, 174, 187, 214,
239, 247, 259
Nike's Oregon Project, 138–39
Nineteenth Amendment, 43, 175,
274
The Ninety-Nines, 65, 69, 70
Nixon, Patricia, "Pat" (First Lady),
190
Nixon, Richard M., 101
nonessential women. *See* essential
women/nonessential women
Northern Illinois University, 248
Northwestern University, 27, 158
Noyles, Blanche (aviator), 69

Obama, Barack, 216, 268
Obama, Michelle, 267–70
Oberg, Margo (surfer), 109
O'Donnell, Gladys ("The Flying
Housewife," aviator), 70
Ohashi, Katelyn (gymnast), 147–49

Olympic Project for Human Rights, 248–49
Omile, Phoebe (aviator), 70
one-sex medicine or gender-blind medicine, 154
oral contraceptives, 46, 58, 157–60, 161
Oregon State, 239
Ormsby, Sir Lambert H., 25. *See also* Royal College of Surgeons
Orreco, 206. *See also* National University of Ireland
oversexualized female, 143
Owens, Jesse, 85, 88

Palmero, Tracy (swimmer), 203
pants, also trousers, ix–x, 5, 16, 31, 75, 85, 137, 179, 189–91, 247, 250, 269, 285
Paris, Neva (aviator), 69
Paris Games, 33
Parks, Ernestine Gloster, 55
Parks, Rosa, 28, 57, 95–96
Parr-Smestad, Liz (bobsledder), 133
patriarchal system, ix, 1, 6, 9–10, 13–16, 34–36, 37, 41, 92–93, 107–8, 117, 137, 150, 171–73, 177–79, 189–93, 271–72
Patrick, Sandra Farmer (hurdler), 167
patrilocal residence, 1
Patsy T. Mink Opportunity in Education Act, 101
Paul, Alice, 29, 43
Peck, Annie Smith, 30
Penn Center for the Female Athlete, 158
Penn Medicine, 45, 158
Penn State, 171, 225, 232
Penny, Steve (USA Gymnastics CEO), 198
pentathlon, 3, 180
performance-enhancing drugs (PEDs), 24. *See also* steroids
periods, 79, 162–64, 166. *See also* menstrual cycle
Perry, Margaret (aviator), 69
Petrillo, Valentina (Paralympic transgender athlete), 231

Phoenix Mercury, 174
Pickett, Tidye (track athlete), 55, 83–87
Pierce Franklin University, 225. *See also* Telfer, CeCe
Pikes Peak Marathon, 97
the pill. *See* birth control pills, effects of
pink, color, 132, 189, 201
pink hats, 201
Plato, 161
Playboy magazine, 107, 131
Playtex, 113
Pliny (Roman philosopher), 163
Plus-sized models, 187–88
PMS. *See* premenstrual syndrome/PMS
Police Woman, 278
Polihronis, Rebecca (Indian Pacers intern), 125
Polk, James, 74
Pope, Martha (Senate sergeant at arms), 190
Popovich, Gregg (coach), 257
Portland, Rene (coach), 171
de Pourtalès, Hélène (sailor), 22
Powe, Michelle (bobsledder), 133
powerlifting, 113–18, 232
pregnancy, 79, 89, 158, 160–62, 166–68, 259–60, 276; steroidal effect, 158, 160; and training, 166–68, 259–60, 276
premenstrual syndrome/PMS, 131
Presidential Medal of Honor, 190, 216
President's Council on Physical Fitness, 91, 109
President's Council on Youth Fitness, 91
Prevention of Harassment and Abuse in Sports (PHAS), 142
Princeton University, 106, 268
progesterone, progestin, 156, 158, 163–64, 221
prostitutes or prostitution, 2, 79, 183
puberty, 3, 217, 221, 223–29, 276
Puică, Maricica (track and fielder), 121
Pumping Iron II, 117–18
Purdue University, 37, 275

Qatar, 211
Quant, Mary (coined "miniskirt"), 107–8
Queen Mary's Army Auxiliary Corp, 72
Queen of Scots, 19
Quimby, Harriet, 64

Racine, Jean (bobsledder), 134
Rahimi, Sadaf (boxer), 213
Rahimi, Shabnam (boxer), 213
Raisman, Aly (gymnast/activist), 195–98
Ramadan, 164
Rankin, Jeannette (politician), 189
rape, 4, 6–7, 99, 141–43, 161–62, 175, 180–82, 195–203, 241–43, 273–74
Rapinoe, Megan (soccer player), 185
Rasche, Thea (aviator), 70
Raskova, Marina (the "Soviet Amelia Earhart"), 66–68
Rational Dress League, 15–16
Rawlinson, Mabel (WASP, World War II), 71–72
Reagan, Nancy (First Lady), 190
Red Diving Girl, 24–25
RED-S syndrome, 139. *See also* relative energy deficiency (RED-S syndrome)
Reece, Gabrielle (volleyball, model), 127–29, 180
Regan, Robert "RJ" (politician), 273
Reid, Charlotte, T. (politician), 189
Rekabi, Elnaz (rock climber, activist), 273
relative energy deficiency (RED-S syndrome), 139. *See also* female triad
Relief Wings, 68–69
religious practices, 1, 5, 7, 34, 42, 47, 162–63, 213, 222, 242, 271, 285
reproductive organs, 9, 60, 99, 164, 221, 205
residual energy. *See* energy availability (EA)/residual energy
Retton, Mary Lou (gymnast), 146–47
Revithi, marathon, 22–23

Reykjavik Index for Leadership, 265
Rhéaume, Manon (hockey player), 131
Richards, Ann (politician), 278
Richards, Renee (transgender tennis player), 220
Richards-Ross, Sanya (sprinter), 160. *See also* abortion
Riggs, Bobby (Battle of the Sexes player), 101–3
right-wing extremist, 210–11. *See also* International Centre for Counterterrorism (ICCT)
Rihanna (singer), 192
Rijker, Lucia (boxer), 132
Rio Olympic Games, 146, 211, 270
Rising Hearts, 263
Roamer Girls, 54–55, 83
Robinson, Eroseanna "Rose" (track and fielder), 248
Robinson, Jackie, 80
Roebuck, Donna (WPFL coach), 253–54
Roe v. Wade, 162
Rogers, Ginger, 278
Rolle, Renate (archeologist), 5
roller derby, 108
Roman Catholic Church, 9, 56. *See also* Church
Roman Empire, 6–7
Roosevelt, Eleanor, 70, 189, 190, 269
Roosevelt, Theodore, 20
Rosen, Dr. Stacey (Katz Institute senior vice president), 152
Rosie the Riveter, 73–75
Ross, Araminta. *See* Tubman, Harriet
Rousey, Ronda (MMA fighter), ix, 228
Rowan, Alexandra, 159
rowing, 12, 32–33, 92, 106, 197, 275, 277
Royal College of Surgeons, 25
Rudolf, Wilma (track athlete), 87, 108, 147
rugby, 224, 257
running, the impact of, 33, 93, 98, 113, 157, 181–82, 260–62
Russell, Ivy (weightlifter and bodybuilder), 105

Rutgers University, 239
Ruth, Babe, 77–79

Sacagawea, 49–50
sailing, 22
salaries, 35, 247
saline. *See* silicone
Sampaio, Valentina (Sports Illustrated model), 185
San Antonio Spurs, 256–57. *See also* Hammon, Becky
Sanders, Summer (swimmer), 180
San Diego University, 238
Sandler, Bernice ("Godmother of Title IX"), 99–101
Sandwina, Catarina "Katie" Brumbach (bodybuilder), 105
sanitary pads, 36–37, 113, 163, 216–18, 261. *See also* tampons
Saudi Arabia, 211
Save Women's Sport, Australia, 233
Save Women's Sports, U.S., 234
Scarton, Dana (reporter), 122
Schaeffer, Rebecca (actress), 180. *See also* stalking
Schmitt, Allison (swimmer), 206
Schnall, Ida, 31–32
Scott, Blanche (aviator), 64
Scurry, Brianna (soccer), 154–57, 271. *See also* traumatic brain injury (TBI)
Scythians, 4–7, 177–78
Sears, Eleanora (sports pioneer), 30–31
Seattle Storm, 106
The Second Sex, 177
Secret Communication System, 206
seizures, 158. *See also* birth control pills, effects of
Seles, Monica (tennis player), 181. *See also* stalking
self-harm, 139–40, 149–50, 156, 202, 207, 210, 226–27
Semenya, Mokgadi Caster (intersex cisgender track athlete), 229–30
Seneca County Courier, 39
Seneca Falls, New York, 39, 107
Seoul Games, 124–25

Serrano, Laura (boxer), 132
sex characteristics, 221
sex reassignment, 220
sexual harassment, 27, 100, 119–20, 141–42, 180, 241, 255
sexual revolution, 107, 179–80
Shakespeare, William, 161
shaman, 48
Sharapova, Maria (tennis player), 182
Sharpe, Stephanie (NCAA and NFL coach), 258
Sherlock, Dot Johnson, 32
shoe endorsement, 113, 126–28, 154, 192, 215
Shoshone, 49
Shumway, Kassidy (soccer player), 148
Silent Sentinels, 43–44
silicone, 183–84
da Silva, Marta Vieira (soccer player), 60–61
Silverstone, Alicia, 145–46
Simone, Gail (Women in Refrigerators website creator), 144
Sims, Angel Martino (swimmer), 167
Sims, Dr. Stacy (exercise psychologist), 164, 275–77
Sioux Nation, 50
ski jumping, 30, 132–33
skirted-soldiers, 71–72
skirts (on and off field), ix, 13, 16–18, 25, 31–32, 35, 71, 79, 80, 107–8, 119, 175, 179–80, 189, 191–92, 271–72, 285
Smith, Amanda (gymnast), 198
Smith, Helen "Streamline," 54
Smith, Marshall (golfer), 110–11
Smith, Polly (inventor, JogBra), 113
Smith, Tommie, 247
Smith College, 25, 255
Snyder Act of 1924, 46
soccer, 37, 50–51, 59–61, 72, 92–93, 140, 148, 154–56, 180, 186, 214, 244–46, 257, 271
social influencers, 137–38
social media, 137–38, 147, 166, 205–6, 212, 244, 263–64, 283
softball, x, 81, 179, 197, 215, 240

Sorenstam, Annika (golfer), 180
Soviet Amelia Earhart, 66–67
Soviet Union, Soviets, 66–68, 89–92, 160
spacewalk, 188
Sparta, 2–5, 7, 17, 20, 92, 251, 270
Spelman College. *See* Atlanta Baptist Female Seminary
sports bra, 113
Sports Illustrated, 90, 102, 124, 130, 133, 185–86, 216, 225, 244
Squire, Belle (suffragist), 29
SRY, 220–21
Staley, Dawn (WNBA Hall of Fame player, coach), 126–27
Stalin, Joseph, 66–67
stalking, 143, 150, 180–82, 232
Standing Rock, protests, 50–51
Stanford, 25, 270
Stanton, Elizabeth Cady, 39–40
Starr, Kenneth, 241–43
Steinem, Gloria (activist), 107–8, 182
Stelzer, Beth (powerlifter), 232–34
steroids, 124, 203
Stine, Arlene Pieper Pikes Peak Marathon, 97
St. James, Lyn (auto racer), 165
St. Louis Expedition Games. *See* St. Louis World's Fair
St. Louis Olympic Games, 53–54
St. Louis World's Fair, 53–54
Stockett, Barclay (American Ninja Warrior), 258
Stockton, Abbye "Pudgy" (Queen of the Barbells), 105
Stokes, Louise (U.S. track athlete), 83–87
stola. *See* tunic
Stone, Lucy (suffragist), 40, 43–44
Stone, Marcenia Lyle "Toni" (baseball player), 80
Stop Street Harassment, 181–82
Street, Picabo (skier), 129–30
Stringer, C. Vivian (basketball coach), 215
Strongest Woman in the World, 114, 117

suffragist, 17, 29, 30, 33, 36, 41, 43–49, 176, 271
suicide, 69, 139, 156, 199, 202, 207, 210, 226–27
Sullivan, James Edward, 31–32, 108
Summit, Patricia "Pat" (basketball coach), 215–16
Sun-Higginson, Shannon (gamer), 241–42
surf, surfing, 109
Swanson, Becca (bodybuilder and powerlifter), 118
Swedish Amatuer Boxing Association, 131
swimming, 21, 23–24, 30–32, 37, 53, 59, 81, 109, 180, 202–3, 225, 229, 238, 270
swimsuits, swim wear, 23–24
Switzer, Kathrine (marathon runner), 95–99, 281
Swoopes, Sheryl, (WNBA player), 126–28, 174, 180, 281
Syers, Madge ("Mother of Figure Skating"), 17
Syracuse University, 96–97

Talbert, Mary Morris Burnett, 44
Tamini, Noël (Swiss writer and runner), 23
tampons, 163, 261. *See also* sanitary pads
Taormina, Sheila (track and fielder), 180–81. *See also* stalking
Tate, Sonja (ALA and WNBA player), 281
Taylor, Margaret Phelan (WASP, World War II), 71
Teigen, Chrissy (social influencer), 184
Telfer, CeCe (transgender athlete), 225
tennis, 11, 19, 21–23, 30, 32–33, 58–59, 82, 101–2, 110, 146, 171–75, 180–81, 220, 234–39, 269–70
Teristi, Sara (gymnast), 198
Terrell, Mary Church, 40
testosterone, effect of, 157–58, 160, 221–25, 227, 233, 261
tethrippon, chariot, 2

Texas Rangers, 56–57, 199
Texas Tech University Health Sciences
    Center, 153
Thaden, Louise (aviator), 70
thigh gap, 137
third gender (or sex), 83, 219–21
Thomas, Lia (transgender swimmer
    and athlete), 225–27, 234
Thomas, Sarah (NFL referee), 257
Tillman-Brooks, Chenell "SoHo"
    (WPFL Hall of Famer, coach),
    254–55
Tisdale, Ashley (actress), 184
Title IX, 31, 95–103, 105–6, 109, 113,
    117, 117, 171, 179, 198, 202, 207, 223,
    237–44, 250–51
Title VII, 95–96, 99, 119
Todd, Janice "Jan" (weightlifter), 117
Torrence, Gwen (sprinter), 125, 165
Torres, Carmelita (Bath Riots leader),
    57
Trail Sisters, 260–61, 281–82
transgender, 144, 169, 185, 219–35, 261,
    276
transgender female athletes, 144, 185,
    219–21, 225–26, 228, 231–33, 243–35
traumatic brain injury (TBI), 156
Troianello, Karen Blair (track athlete,
    activist), 237
trousers. *See* pants
Trout, Evelyn "Bobbi" (aviator), 70
Trump, Donald J., 200–201, 274
Truth, Sojourner, 39–40
Tubman, Harriet, 41–43, 96
Tucker, Ross (World Rugby head
    scientist), 224
tunic, 3, 5, 17–18
Tuskegee Institute, 87
Tyus, Wyomia (track athlete), 109–10

Under Armour, 192
Underground Railroad. *See* Tubman,
    Harriet
uniform, women's uniforms, 18, 141,
    180, 187, 214, 239–40, 247, 271–72,
    285

United Daughters of the Confederacy
    (UDC), 44
United Nations (UN), 207, 212
United States Bobsled & Skeleton
    Federation (USBSF), 133
United States Field Hockey
    Association, 191
United States Olympic Committee
    (USOC), 32, 122, 133–34, 195, 260,
    329
United States Powerlifting (USPL), 232
United States Tennis Association
    (USTA), 110
University of Alabama, 272
University of California, Berkeley, 25,
    248
University of California, Davis, 282
University of California, LA (UCLA),
    147
University of California, San Diego,
    182
University of Maryland, 100, 110
University of New Mexico, 148
University of Oregon, 239–40
University of Pennsylvania, 282
University of Tennessee Center for
    Sport, Peace, and Society, 209
University of Texas, 184
University of Texas MD Anderson
    Cancer Center, 184
University of Washington, 25, 264
UN Women, 209
USA Gymnastics, 195–200
U.S. Air Force, 68, 71–72, 109
U.S. Army Intelligence Hall of Fame,
    42
U.S. Department of Defense, Ada, 206
U.S. Department of State's Council
    to Empower Women and Girls
    Through Sport, 207, 216
U.S. Food and Drug Administration
    (FDA), 183
U.S. Golf Association (USGA), 111
U.S. Military Academy, 109
U.S. Senate Judiciary Committee, 41,
    120, 195

U.S.S.R. Sport Commission, 92–93
U.S. Women's Lacrosse Association, 191
uterus, 14–15, 163, 168

vaginal birth, 159–60, 166
Van, Lindsey (ski jumper), 133
Vancouver Games, 130, 133
Van Wageners, 39
VanDerveer, Tara (basketball coach), 215
vanity-sizing, 188
Vassar College, 20–21
Vaughan, Dorothy (human computer), 206
de Varona, Donna (swimmer), 109
Victoria, Queen Victoria, 12
Victorian Era, 10, 13–16, 138, 206, 271
Viking, 6–7
Virchow, Dr. Rudolf ("Father of Pathology"), 25
Virginia Slims Circuit, 102
von Mach, Mary (aviator), 69
Vonn, Lindsey (skier), 129–30, 192–93
Voss, Sarah (gymnast), 272
Voting Rights Act (1965), 47, 96

wage gap, 20, 211
Wagner-Assali, Jennifer (cyclist), 228–29
waist trainers, 13–15, 138, 271. *See also* corsets
Walker, Mary (abolitionist, doctor, prisoner of war), 190–91
Walker, Rebecca (journalist, activist), 120
Walker, Vera Dawn (aviator), 69
Walsh-Jennings, Kerry, 128–29
Wambach, Abby (soccer player), 186
Warner, Anne (rower), 106
Wartena, Dr. Heidi (Center for Critical Sports Studies), 245
Washburn, Joanne "Jo" (athletic director, pioneer), 237–38
Washington State University, 237–38
Watson, Emma (actress), 209
weightlifting, 105, 117

Weinstein, Harvey (former director and convicted rapist), 201
Wells, Ida B., 28–29, 40, 45
Welter, Jen (football player, NFL coach), 257
Werbinski, Dr. Jan (AMWA president-elect), 153
Westerman, Joyce Hill (AAGPBL player), 81
Whaley, Suzy (LPGA qualifier, PGA Board of Directors secretary), 112
Wheaties, 81, 186
White, Stephanie (WNBA coach), 247
Wicks, Sue (basketball player), 174
Wieber, Jordyn (gymnast/activist), 257
Wilkinson, Elizabeth (boxer), 11–12
Willard, Frances, 27–29
Williams, Miriam Kate (bodybuilder), 105
Williams, Dr. Nicola (research scientist in human biology), 231–34
Williams, Serena (tennis player), 146, 187, 270
Williams, Venus (tennis player), 270
Willis, Breckynn (swimmer), 187
Wise, Mary (volleyball coach), 215
Witt, Katerina (ice skater), 180
Wolfe, Ann (boxer), 132
Wolffe, Jabez, 37
Woman's Christian Temperance Union (WCTU), 27
Woman's College of Northwestern University, 27
Women, Men and Media, 106–7
Women Accepted for Voluntary Emergency Services (WAVES), 71, 75
Women in Refrigerators, DC Comics, 144
Women's Airforce Service Pilots (WASP), 71–72, 75
Women's American Basketball Association (WABA), 252
Women's Army Auxiliary Corps (WAAC), 72
Women's Army Corp (WAC), 71–73, 75

Women's Basketball Development Association (WBDA), 252
Women's Basketball Hall of Fame, 256
Women's Beach Volleyball League, 128
Women's College World Series, 240
Women's Collegiate Wrestling Association, 251
Women's Equity Action League, 100
Women's Football Alliance, 253
Women's Football League, 252
Women's Games, 33
Women's Gaming Summit, 142
Women's Health Initiative, 151
Women's Initiative, 207
Women's March, 29, 201
Women's National Basketball League (WNBA), 106, 126–27, 148–49, 173–77, 186, 192, 210, 214–15, 247, 252, 256–57, 281
Women's Olympic Games, 33
Women's Professional Football League (WPFL), 252–54
Women's Rights Convention, 39–43
Women's Royal Navy Service, 72
Women's Sports Foundation (WSF), 100, 109, 165, 202, 222
Wonder Woman, 128, 143–44, 248, 258, 274
Woodhull, Nancy, 106–7, 113
Woolworth's department store, 36

World Athletics, 85, 88–89, 121, 224–25, 230
World Figure Skating Championship (WFSC), 17
World Health Organization (WHO), 159, 226
World Rugby, 224
World War I, 32, 35–36, 71–72
World War II, 71, 74–75, 77, 80, 84–85, 89, 96, 183, 188
wrestling, 3, 32, 53, 197, 238, 250–52
Wright, Mary Kathryn "Mickey" (golfer), 110

Xena Warrior Princess, 278

Yale, 106, 182, 248
Yale School of Medicine, 182
Young Men's Christian Association (YMCA), 20–21, 54
Yuanhui, Fu (swimmer), 165
Yuen-ting, Chan (men's soccer coach), 257

Zaharias, Mildred Ella Didrikson "Babe," 85, 87, 91, 112
Zenker, Helen (baseball player), 31
Zeus, 1–3
Zmeskal, Kim, gymnast, 147
Zonouzi, Kimia Alizadeh (tae kwon do Olympian), 211–12

About the Author

Alexandra Allred made sports (and medical) history through activism and determination. When she learned that women were not allowed in bobsled, she lobbied for equal status and would ultimately win the U.S. Nationals in September 1994, making sports history as she was named to the first-ever U.S. women's bobsled team, coauthoring the first women's bylaws, and fought to get women into the Olympic Games. When the United States Olympic Committee named her Athlete of the Year for her sport, it made international news as Allred was also pregnant when she made the team.

At the time, there was very little data on elite pregnant athletes and powerlifting/plyometrics. While Allred became the "poster child" of the Case Western OB/GYN international study, Allred was, at nearly five months pregnant, squatting 375 pounds and clocking at twenty miles per hour while running. The results of this study changed how to measure the safety of baby in utero for competitive athletes. Both the United States and International Olympic Committee use Allred's training data as a safety guide for pregnant athletes, and she served as a fitness/nutrition expert for two decades. Upon retirement, *Sports Illustrated* asked her to try out for a women's professional football team and write about her experiences in the award-winning book *Atta Girl! A Celebration of Women in Sport*. Allred later became the first American (male or female) to test drive the Volvo Gravity car for *Volvo* magazine in North America.

Allred turned to activism, testified before the IOC at the London Games, served as an Air Ambassador, lobbied on Capitol Hill, and was nominated as a *White House Champion of Change for Public Health*. She is an award-winning documentary filmmaker/author and continues to freelance nationally and internationally, and is an adjunct professor of kinesiology at Tarleton State University.

CPSIA information can be obtained
at www.ICGtesting.com
Printed in the USA
LVHW112049180123
737428LV00001B/1